THE TWELVE PLAYS OF CHRISTMAS

THE TWELVE PLAYS OF CHRISTMAS

Traditional and Modern Plays for the Holidays

Edited with introduction by

LOWELL SWORTZELL

APPLAUSE

NEW YORK • LONDON

An Applause Original

The Twelve Plays of Christmas

Edited with an introduction by LOWELL SWORTZELL

Library of Congress Cataloging-in-Publication Data

Library of Congress Card Number: 99-068323

British Library Cataloging-in-Publication Data
A catalog record for this book is available from the British Library.

APPLAUSE BOOKS

1841 Broadway # 1100
New York, NY 10023
Phone (212) 765-7880
Fax: (212) 765-7875

Combined Book Services Ltd.
Units I/K Paddock Wood Distribution Centre
Paddock Wood, Tonbridge, Kent TN12 6UU
Phone: (44) 01892 837171
Fax (44) 01892 837272

CONTENTS

PART THREE: NON-RELIGIOUS PLAYS

INTRODUCTION

In a 1943 essay George Orwell claims that although Christmas is the most popular of British festivals it has produced "astonishing little literature." He acknowledges some medieval carols, a sprinkling of poems, and, to be sure, Charles Dickens' beloved holiday stories but little else. Dickens he sees as the exception to this meager historical output for among modern writers he is almost alone in creating "a convincing picture of happiness." Orwell nonetheless finds Tiny Tim disgusting and believes the Cratchits had better be happy this one day since tomorrow the wolf will be back at their door and the pawnshops and sweatshops once again in full swing. Inasmuch as Utopias don't exist, Orwell argues permanent happiness is doomed to failure and no author has convinced him otherwise.

This cynical philosophy and stern political stand (the essay is entitled "Can Socialists Be Happy?") might be reason enough to invent Christmas if it did not already exist. In pre-Christian times such celebrations came about largely as a means to offset the dark, cold hardships of winter. How better than a season of excessive eating and drinking, even when knowing that poverty rations and misery may follow? And so began the tradition of over indulgence: the five-to-ten holiday pounds gained annually only to be shed in the New Year (or so one no doubt hoped then as now). Accompanying these gastronomic pleasures, the desire to be entertained was satisfied in songs, dances and plays. When in the fourth century the pagan revels became Christianized the appeal of the wassail bowl and the boar's head remained as great as before but now they also became part of the feasts celebrating the birth of Jesus. Countless such fusions of secular and religious observances developed and many are still practiced today. When we top a pagan evergreen tree with the star of Bethlehem or when we dream of a "White Christmas" to honor an event that took place in a stable in the desert, we are making contradictions that are part of the sacred-and-profane fascination of Christmas. Even the plays in this book are arranged according to their religious and non-religious content. Christmas traditions in Western culture clearly are both.

Whether or not we can sustain happiness in Orwellian terms, we have managed in most places to stretch the holiday celebration to twelve days, and in the United States to extend it from the day after Thanksgiving to well into January. We likewise have produced a body of writing on every aspect of the season but particularly on our penchant for the past — yearnings for Christmases of long ago — that most critics recognize as literature. Thornton Wilder's *The Long Christmas Dinner*, Gian-Carlo Menotti's *Amahl and the Night Visitors* and Dylan Thomas' *A Child's Christmas in Wales* are modern classics worthy of Dickens' hope for readers of *A Christmas Carol* that it would "haunt their houses pleasantly." And, in the ever-expanding repertory of Christmas plays, our heads, hearts and senses of humor may well be haunted, too.

More plays, in fact, are seen in the English-speaking world during the holiday season than at any other time of the year. Churches, schools, and community centers along with professional theatres have made "the Christmas play" a modern tradition that for many youngsters marks their first theatrical experience, either as members of the audience or as members of the cast. Regional theatres often earn significant portions of their annual income through Yuletide performances, with productions running from four to six weeks of *A Christmas Carol* or *The Nutcracker*. Our dramatic literature (not to mention films such as *It's a Wonderful Life* and *Miracle on 34th Street*, among countless others) observes every aspect of the season: illustrating the scriptures, invoking the Mummers of the middle ages or reincarnating Mr. Pickwick being kissed under the mistletoe at Dingley Dell. Contemporary portraits of festive practices, too, are regularly added as in such recent plays as *Kringle's Window* and *Tiny Tim is Dead*. Christmas today takes stages of every kind from Radio City Music Hall's annual "Spectacular" and Madison Square Garden's extravaganza of *A Christmas Carol* to the local Sunday School's platform-pageant performed in homemade costumes with no two angels wearing the same style of wings and halos. Together the productions share a common purpose: to glorify concepts of Christmas by re-enacting and celebrating traditions, distant and modern, which as their continuing popularity proves, quite obviously, do make us happy.

The observant reader already will have discovered that there are more than twelve plays here. Call the extras Christmas bonuses or stocking stuffers and be grateful. Their inclusion demonstrates the wide range of works to be read, staged and enjoyed at this time of year. Plays as old as the 14th century, *The Second Shepherd's Play*, stand here along with the brand new: *The Match Girl's Gift*: *A Christmas Story* which is published in these pages for the first time. Classics appear such as *A Christmas Carol*, and those less well known, *The Shepherds of St. Francis*, followed by comic interludes, *A Partridge in a Pear Tree*, and a serious interpretation, *The Long Christmas Dinner*. A contemporary story, *Tiny Tim is Dead*, portrays an aborted effort among the homeless to cheer one another. Plays of particular interest to young readers and audiences (actually, with exception of *The Long Christmas Dinner* and *Tiny Tim is Dead*, they all should be), include *The Match Girl's Gift*, *A Visit from St. Nicholas*, *Kringle's Window* and *Amahl and the Night Visitors*. A list of some helpful resources of Yuletide traditions is found at the end of the book.

The collection begins with three traditional offerings: a Christmas pageant drawn from the gospels of Saint Luke and Saint Matthew; *The Second Shepherd's Play*, a vivid mixture of comedy and religious drama; and a medieval Mummer's play, adapted for modern performance.

A Christmas Pageant

The pageant presents the story of the Nativity in a series of tableaux, scenes frozen to illustrate the most telling moments of the action. Connecting these are carols from a variety of sources, to which casts may add their own favorites. The text is divided into five short scenes but the performance should be continuous with song and narration. The stage directions will be helpful to the director and choirmaster whether they choose to produce the text in the nave or chancel of a church, on the proscenium stage of an auditorium or outside in a town square or mall. They should invite everyone to join in the singing of the familiar carols so that the audience feels part of the performance.

The Second Shepherd's Play

The anonymous *The Second Shepherd's Play* belongs to the Townley or Wakefield cycle of short plays first produced in England near the end of the 1300s or at the beginning of the 1400s. A combination of the sacred and profane, the play is particularly appealing for its realistic portrait of Mak, the sheep stealer and his wife. Their attempt to hide a stolen lamb in a crib and to claim it as their newborn babe when the shepherds come to investigate is the stuff of genuine folk comedy, as funny now as it was then. The parallel of this false birth with the Advent of Christ announced at the end of the play bridges the two stories and results in the first major text about Christmas in the English language. The title, by the way, has nothing to do with the character of the second shepherd who is no more important than the other two but results from the fact that in the cycle there are two shepherd plays of which this is the second. Playwright Aurand Harris has modified the complex rhyming and some of the archaic language of the original script to make this version easily playable for audiences today.

Saint George and the Dragon at Christmas Tide

This Mummers' play was adapted by Marjorie Sigley for presentation by students and faculty of the HB Studio, a theatre school in New York City, as a holiday gift to their families and friends. Over the years since 1991 it has become an annual offering, appearing here in print for the first time.

Who were the Mummers and what is a Mummers' play? Well may you ask. They were Yuletide merrymakers who went about the British countryside in the 14th, 15th and 16th centuries wearing disguises and performing favorite stories in rhyme, music and dance. Their plays celebrated good triumphing over evil, and reminded spectators that after the discomforts of winter spring would restore the easy life. At their center, stood Saint George, the hero renowned for his bravery in slaying the dragon and saving the fair maiden, so popular a figure that he eventually was adopted as England's patron saint which he remains to this day. Accompanying George, the comic characters of the Doctor, the Fool and the Hobbyhorse embellished their clownish capers at every opportunity, no doubt greatly encouraged by the audience.

Integral to the Mummer's plays, Morris Men performed a dance first developed by the Moors in Spain during the 15th century. They stepped, hopped, circled left and right and crossed in patterns that later were incorporated into American square dancing. But the most impressive sections involved the interlacing and locking of their swords into geometric designs that configured symbols of bonding and teamsmanship. They accentuated their movements by wearing tiny jingling bells tied about their legs and by flourishing long white handkerchiefs in one hand while holding swords in the other. *Saint George* is welcome evidence that medieval village life was not all hardship and hunger (as *The Second Shepherd's Play* would have us believe) but could be warm and festive, especially at Christmastime.

Black Nativity

Billed as "Gospel on Broadway," *Black Nativity* opened in 1961 with a cast of notable singers including Marion Williams, Princess Stewart, and the Stars of Faith. It later made appearances at the International Jazz Festival in Washington, D.C. and at the Festival of Two Worlds at Spoleto, Italy, where a critic reported that "sophisticated Italian audiences greeted *Black Nativity* with enthusiasm, taking part in the singing and hand-clapping and insisting on curtain call after curtain call." This gospel song-play portrays the birth of Jesus in dialogue, dance and mime but most of all in the vigorous religious spirit with which the cast sings "Wasn't that a Mighty Day!," "Joy to the World," and "Oh, Come All Ye Faithful."

Langston Hughes, the poet-playwright whose rise through the Harlem Renaissance literary movement resulted in its most famous voice, arranged his favorite carols and songs in *Black Nativity* to make what he hoped would be a loud and joyful noise. And the text as it appears here invites readers and producers to add their favorite music, traditional and modern, that will do the same.

The Shepherds of Saint Francis

Legend has it that Saint Francis of Assisi staged the first Christmas pageant when in 1223 on a hillside outside the town of Greccio he reenacted the Nativity with a cast of villagers, accompanied by their cows, goats, and donkeys. It is also said, so many witnesses attended this production that the candles they carried brightened the night to look like day. Why would Francis decide to dramatize the scriptures rather than simply to read them from the pulpit as other priests did? What happened to inspire him to start a tradition that has become a part of Christmas celebrations throughout the world? A number of possible answers are the basis of the play included here — the story of the first Christmas pageant. Once more, Francis stages his play, and this time the audience is asked to be in it, playing one of the animals gathered in and around the stable, an acting opportunity few can resist.

Amahl and the Night Visitors

With words and music by Gian-Carlo Menotti, *Amahl and the Night Visitors*, the first opera commissioned especially for television, premiered on NBC-TV, on Christmas Eve, 1951, and at once became recognized as a major musical contribution to the season. Menotti said he had tried to recapture his youth in his work, a childhood spent in Italy where traditionally Christmas gifts were delivered not by Santa Claus but by the Three Kings. Each year he hoped to stay awake to see their arrival but never quite managed although once he thought he heard them outside in the snow. Still, when searching for a topic for his opera, he came upon the painting of the Adoration of the Kings by Hieronymous Bosch and before him appeared his old friends, the Royal Visitors, Kaspar, Melchoir and Balthazar. Immediately he knew they would be central to his opera; once again, they had brought him a gift, the inspiration for *Amahl*.

In the decades since its premiere, *Amahl* has become the most performed opera in English, seen in school, church, and professional performances throughout the world. What may come as a surprise to readers is the beauty of the libretto which without the music emerges as a lyrical landmark. Not many libretti, especially those in English, can make that claim.

The Nutcracker and the Mouse-King

While Hoffman's tale first appeared in 1816 the ballet derived from it was not staged until 1891 and then in a vastly changed form that ignored the story's deeper, darker meanings. The protagonist Marie no longer stood at the center but from the side-lines observed a marzipan world of confections, fairies and snowflakes. And her godfather Drosselmeier, the mysterious clock maker so essential to the magical proceedings of the original, became little more than an excuse for an aging dancer to perform briefly in mime. Yet we all know *The Nutcracker* is the mainstay of professional and amateur ballet companies throughout the world each holiday season and no one wants to deny its great appeal. This may give us some exciting dancing but it also results in keeping one of our best Christmas stories incomplete and unloved for itself. To overcome this loss, a few translators and illustrators have returned to Hoffman to publish the full text and in the instance of Maurice Sendak to give it a splendidly theatrical setting.

The scenario printed here also emphasizes the story's strong theatrical elements, but even so may be performed at home in the living room (which is the setting of the play), in a classroom or school auditorium or on a professional stage. The production likewise may be presented in simple, improvised costumes (hats, gloves, shawls to suggest the past) or in specifically designed outfits of the early 1800s. The less money spent on spectacle, however, the better the story's chances to charm and challenge the imaginations of the audience.

The key to bringing this scenario to life is to find the actions in each sentence and paragraph and to work out a means of communicating them through body language, large movements, facial expressions and, yes, when necessary, in words. But not necessarily in words memorized from the script but in those derived from experiencing each situation until it happens spontaneously again and again, each time feeling true to the character and the story. Then when Marie, her family and friends and even the seven-headed Mouse-King enact their adventures, the audience will join in to discover that there is more to *The Nutcracker* than they may have thought when seeing it danced.

A Christmas Carol: Scrooge and Marley

Even though Charles Dickens intended in *A Christmas Carol* (1843) "to seize upon the associations belonging to Christmas and to embody them in a more permanent form," many customs cherished today are altogether missing. The Christmas tree and card, for instance, did not become common until Queen Victoria's tree at Buckingham Palace was copied widely in British homes in the late 1840s and 50s and greeting cards began to be exchanged in the 1860s and 70s. The practice of having the day off was barely beginning and the custom of providing for the poor through seasonal charities was as yet unknown. Still, *A Christmas Carol* accomplished its author's intentions as London emerged the verbal picture of a bustling city filled with caroling well-wishers going about their shopping, decorating, dancing and feasting. And with Ebenezer Scrooge's redemption from miserliness and his awakening to the joyful meaning of family celebrations, Dickens' "little book," as he called it, has come to epitomize the holiday spirit to much of the modern world.

Actor Patrick Stewart proved the theatricality of the story simply by standing in a spotlight on a bare stage reciting *A Christmas Carol* page by page, playing all the roles, and successfully making audiences imagine the action. More common, of course, are the annual productions which delight in bringing Dickens to life with large casts in Victorian costumes inhabiting spectacular settings representing Christmas Past, Present and Future. Even though in recent years *A Christmas Carol* has become the most produced play in the United States, there is no single version but almost as many dramatizations as there are productions. The adaptation by Israel Horovitz included here is particularly rich in Dickensian detail and in making most of the theatricality imbedded in the story. "It is remarkable," Horovitz writes, "how little of Charles Dickens' small masterpiece has been altered in any way in the forming of this stage version. It seemed to me sheer folly to think of even changing the text, except in those areas essential to the transporting the story from prose fiction to stage drama." The major intention of this dramatization is to keep the presence of Jacob Marley throughout the play as its logical narrator.

Playwright Horovitz asks that no one produce this adaptation unless they "cherish" it and that every aspect of the performance — songs, dances, sounds and colors — are born of Dickens' imagination for he believes, "There is still much to be learned from the Master."

A Visit from St. Nicholas

Legends abound over the origins of St. Nicholas, the familiar figure who has come to personify the practice of Christmas gift-giving among families and friends. A Bishop of the Fourth Century A.D., the actual Saint Nicholas traditionally was remembered on December 6, his saint's day, as a benefactor both of sailors whose lives he saved in storms at sea and of impoverished young ladies whose lives he changed by giving them large sums of money to attract husbands. Since he also was associated with kindness to children, he became the basis for Father Christmas who as his myth developed gained the ability to fly. Whether called Saint Nick, Kriss Kringle or Santa Claus, his visual form became fixed once Clement Clarke Moore had described his dimples, little round belly and other enduring features in the now classic poem of 1823 "The Visit of St. Nicholas, or The Night Before Christmas." It is this figure we see imitated annually by department store Santas around the world. The lively events of the particular night Moore first spoke "not a creature was stirring" are dramatized in Lowell Swortzell's comedy, which tells how close we came to never hearing those famous lines. According to scholar and folklorist William Samson, Moore's poem, along with Dickens' *A Christmas Carol*, have influenced our modern concept of the celebration of Christmas more than any other works.

The Long Christmas Dinner

In his one-act plays Thornton Wilder experimented with the theatrical means to depict one of his favorite themes, the passage of life as a series of commonplace, yet wonderful events. In *The Happy Journey to Trenton and Camden*, an automobile ride signifies our lives from birth to death, and in Pullman Car Hiawatha, a train journey from the West to East Coasts telescopes a similar lifelong journey. And, of course, in *The Long Christmas Dinner*, the continuity of the annual family gathering symbolizes both the sameness in our lives and the realization that it is constantly changing. The dinner covers some ninety years as time determines how long each guest remains at the table. Wilder makes the inevitability of these arrivals and departures natural and even peaceful by placing two doorways right and left, the portals of life and death through which the characters pass.

John Gassner called *The Long Christmas Dinner* "the most beautiful one-act play in English prose" and praised its mixture of simple and sophisticated uses of both drama and theatre. Critic Mel Gussow reporting in *The New York Times* a 1997 symposium on Wilder's legacy concluded, ". . .in his work, he stripped art to essentials, emotionally as well as scenically, as part of his quest to live — and to articulate — a full life of the mind and heart."

After reading this play, it is difficult not to be reminded of the passing parade of loved ones at our own holiday dinners.

A Child's Christmas in Wales

Perhaps no writer in one work has encapsulated so many festive images of one day, December 25 from morning to night, as Dylan Thomas does in *A Child's Christmas in Wales*. Mince pies, tobogganing, snowballs, oranges, tin whistles, holly, glass bells on the tree, teddy bears and blindman's bluff are just a few memories from only one page of what he says is a day he will never forget at the end of a year he can't remember.

The play like the story simply follows the day itself taking the audience through the impressions of a young boy, surely Dylan himself: "I can never remember whether it snowed for six days and six nights when I was twelve or twelve days and twelve nights when I was six." As all of Thomas' writing cries out to be read aloud (he wrote *Under Milkwood* to be staged as a play for voices), so does this adaptation by Jeremy Brooks and Adrian Mitchell which premiered at the Great Lakes Shakespeare Festival and has since been seen at many other theatres as well. However far from Wales our own childhood Christmases may have been, they come thrillingly back to life as we hear Dylan Thomas relive his.

Kringle's Window

First written as a screenplay, *Kringle's Window* later was adapted for the stage by its author Mark Medoff and premiered by The Louisville (Kentucky) Children's Theatre in 1991. It was one of a dozen plays commissioned from established dramatists to write expressly for young audiences. Medoff, of course, was well known for his award-winning play and film, for which he was nominated for an Academy Award, *Children of a Lesser God*, along with other plays such as *When You Comin' Back, Red Ryder?* and *The Wager*.

This contemporary comedy, *Kringle's Window* focuses on two sisters, one, aged eight, who believes in Santa Claus and one, aged twelve, who doesn't. Their father's attempt to play Santa will amuse anyone who has ever undertaken this task and serve as a warning to those who plan to do so in the future. The mysterious Mrs. Rosen who lives in a tree and wears trinkets from throughout the world demonstrates the universality of the Christmas spirit. This may well be the first Yuletide play in which a computer is essential to the action: Becka hopes to open Santa's or Kringle's window "and look into his world." In this light-hearted and well-meaning story, Christmas is on line. On critic compared it to a fruitcake for the rich ingredients that are "likely to become a holiday tradition."

Tiny Tim is Dead

This examination of six street people making their uncertain way through Christmas Eve and the next morning in a cardboard shelter was developed by playwright Barbara Lebow with the cooperation of the Atlanta Day Shelter for Women, St. Luke's Community Kitchen and many "people of the brick" who shared their memories and opinions. The resulting characters register indelibly upon our consciences. Verna is seven months pregnant and accompanied by her thin, mute son who tries to protect her; Charlie is a drug addict weighed down by guilt of lost opportunities; Otis is a cynic and self-appointed head of the group; Azalee is unable to leave because she wants to help the others; Filomeno is a recent arrival from Central America whose limited English makes him identify with the silent little boy. When they discover amidst the trash a worn-out copy of *A Christmas Carol*, they begin to perform key moments, with Verna eager to play Tiny Tim. Filo, not understanding the story, turns Marley's ghost into a dancing reggae figure, which causes Pope to halt the dramatization and to destroy their hopes. They then give way to their addictions to drugs and violence and abandon each other, leaving only the boy to hear Pope's departing words, "Christmas only an excuse to hope for something, to make a promise. But all days is the same. And every day break the promise of the day what came before."

Tiny Tim is Dead, in its brutal but honest portraits of this lost "family" of outcasts, will strike some readers as a sadly inappropriate work with which to celebrate a joyous holiday. But it is a powerful reminder that for many among us their futures offer little or no promise — indeed they have all been broken —and, if not at Christmas, when do we remember them?

The Match Girl's Gift: A Christmas Story

Hans Christian Andersen centered two of his tales, *The Fir Tree* and *The Little Match Girl*, around the spirit of Christmas. A great admirer of Dickens, he also portrayed the effects of poverty upon children but in doing so often sentimentalized their plight; his match girl freezes to death almost inch by inch in the snow. Determined to avoid this tearjerking pitfall, Laurie Brooks Gollobin retells Andersen's story: her heroine Lizzie refuses to surrender her courage or hope and so survives. Set in New York City's Washington Square in the early 1900's, the play contrasts two worlds, that of the hungry homeless and that of the dysfunctional rich which come together when Lizzie is carried almost lifeless into a Fifth Avenue mansion. How her presence brings about an understanding of their respect and responsibility for one another is the substance of the action.

Commissioned by the Nashville Children's Theatre in 1998, *The Little Match Girl's Gift* was directed by Scot Copeland who defined the purpose of his production, "You can see this as a Turn-of-the-Century melodrama, but the truth is, these two children, in absolute historical accuracy, are fighting for bare survival. They could die on the street that night. It was true of that time and place, and it's true of our own. Christmas is the best time to look at the larger social picture." One critic said that this new twist on an old story provides "an absorbing hour —- a holiday entertainment that trembles with the true, radiant spirit of Christmas giving."

Author Gollobin has emerged in the 1990s as a major voice in theatre for young audiences with her award-winning *Selkie* and *The Wrestling Season*, both first seen at the New Visions/New Voices symposium sponsored by the Kennedy Center in Washington, D.C.

A Partridge in a Pear Tree

If one literally turned this old carol into a play, it would require a cast of twelve ladies dancing, eleven lords a-leaping, ten drummers drumming, nine pipers piping, eight maids a-milking, and so on, more that most stages can accommodate or production budgets can afford to costume. So, thankfully, in the one-act play included here, these and the other gifts of the twelve days are mimed, no less present, but seen only in our imaginations. Likewise the setting of a country town consists of three wooden benches on a bare stage. Using the popular medieval comic device of the trickster being tricked, the plot shows how a birdcatcher is almost caught in an unwanted marriage. When the tables turn, however, Simon discovers he really loves Tib and everyone celebrates their happiness. And, of course, the singing of the carol at every stage of the story holds the play together, making it a mini-musical with one song, but certainly one of the season's favorites.

With its lack of any religious connotations or references, the play has become popular in public school presentations, as well as with community groups looking for holiday entertainment for a wide audience. It is short enough to be incorporated into Christmas assemblies and concerts and once was a part of a program presented by the Saint Louis

Symphony. Whether with symphony or piano, the audience should be invited to join in the singing of the carol at least once.

Read for pleasure or in search of texts for forthcoming productions, these plays invite us to re-live Christmases from the earliest times to the present and to be reminded of the happiness the holiday has brought for two thousand years. Their meaning shines through the darkness of winter and warms us when we come together to enjoy their great variety of action, music, and color. They even may lead us to that epiphany Scrooge experiences near the end of *A Christmas Carol* when: "Running to the window, he opened it and put out his hand. No fog, no mist; clear, bright, jovial, stirring, cold, piping for the blood to dance to; Golden sunlight; Heavenly sky; sweet fresh air; merry bells. Oh, glorious! Glorious! Christmas Day!"

To which we add, "Oh, glorious! Glorious! Christmas plays!"

Part One:

TRADITIONAL PLAYS

A CHRISTMAS PAGEANT

Anonymous, drawn from the Scriptures

A CHRISTMAS PAGEANT

CHARACTERS

READER
MARY
JOSEPH
ANGEL GABRIEL
FIRST SHEPHERD
SECOND SHEPHERD
THIRD SHEPHERD
FIRST WISE MAN
SECOND WISE MAN
THIRD WISE MAN
A MULTITUDE OF ANGLES
OTHER SHEPHERDS

MUSIC FOR THE CHOIR

SCENE 1. *"Once in Royal David's City" by Henry J. Gauntlett or "O Come, Emmanuel," a plainsong tune adapted by Thomas Helmore*

   "Gabriel's Message," a Basque carol

SCENE 2. *"What Child Is This?" to the old English tune "Greensleeves"*

SCENE 3. *"The Snow Lay on the Ground," a traditional carol*

SCENE 4. *"Angels We Have Heard on High," a traditional French carol*

SCENE 5. *"We Three Kings" by John Henry Hopkins*

   "Silent Night" by Franz Grueber

   "O Little Town of Bethlehem" by Lewis H. Redner or

   "Forest Green," a traditional tune

[Other favorite Christmas songs may be used.]

Opening music: "Once in Royal David's City" or "O Come, Emmanuel."

SCENE 1. *The Annunciation.*

Luke I:26-27

READER: [*Enters and stands at side.*] And it came to pass that in the sixth month the Angel Gabriel [*Gabriel enters R, crosses to C.*]—was sent from God unto a city of Galilee, named Nazareth. To a virgin—[*Mary enters at L, crosses to C.*]—espoused to a man, whose name was Joseph, of the house of David, and the virgin's name was Mary.

GABRIEL: Hail, Mary, Thou are highly favored. The Lord is with thee; blessed art thou among women. [*Mary reacts.*] Fear not, Mary: for thou has found favor with God. And behold, thou shalt bring forth a son, and shalt call his name Jesus.

MARY: Behold the handmaid of the Lord; be it unto me according to thy word. My soul doth magnify the Lord. [*Tableau: Gabriel blessing Mary. Choir sings "Gabriel's Message." Gabriel exits at the end of the song. Mary sits on the stool by the cradle.*]

SCENE 2. *The Nativity*

Luke II:1-7

READER: In those days there went out a decree from Caesar Augustus that all the world should be taxed. And all went to be taxed, everyone into his own city. And Joseph—[*Joseph enters at L, and walks to Mary.*]—also went up from Galilee unto Bethlehem, with Mary, his espoused wife, being great with child. [*Joseph stands behind Mary.*] And so it was while they were there, the days were accomplished that she should be delivered. And she brought forth her first born son, and wrapped him in swaddling clothes and laid him in a manger, because there was no room at the inn.

[*Light goes on inside the cradle. Tableau: Mary rocks cradle while Joseph stands watching. Choir sings "What Child Is This?"*]

SCENE 3. *Shepherds Watch by Night.*

Luke II:16-19

READER: And there were in the same country shepherds—[*Three, or more shepherds, enter at R, cross to C, frightened and looking at the sky.*]—abiding in the field, keeping watch over their flocks by night. And, lo, the angel of the Lord came upon them, and the glory of the Lord shone round about them; and they were sore afraid.

FIRST SHEPHERD: [*Shepherds stand at C, masking Mary and the cradle.*] 'Tis a strange night.

SECOND SHEPHERD: Thou speakest truly. Even the sheep do not lie still.

THIRD SHEPHERD: On such a night, wonders are said to happen. [*Gabriel enters at R.*]

SECOND SHEPHERD: Look, look! See the strange person! [*Shepherds huddle together.*]

GABRIEL: Fear not; for behold, I bring you glad tidings of great joy, which shall be for all people. For unto you is born this day in the city of David, a Saviour, which is Christ the Lord. And this shall be a sign unto you: Ye shall find the babe wrapped in swaddling clothes, lying in a manger.

[*Tableau: Gabriel stands, arms lifted. Shepherds kneel, backs to audience. Choir sings "The Snow Lay on the Ground." During the song many Angels enter singing, stand in a pictorial grouping, and then exit at the end of the song. Gabriel leaves last.*]

SCENE 4. Adoration by the Shepherds.

Luke II:16-19

FIRST SHEPHERD: [*Shepherds rise.*] Let us go now even unto Bethlehem, the city of David.

SECOND SHEPHERD: Yes, let us hasten to see this thing which has come to pass.

THIRD SHEPHERD: This is the thing which was foretold by the prophets of old. [*Shepherds exit at R.*]

READER: And the shepherds came with haste, and found Mary and Joseph and the Babe lying in a manger. And when they had seen it, they made known abroad the saying, which was told them concerning the child. And they that heard it wondered at those things which were told them by the shepherds. But Mary kept all these things and pondered them in her heart.

THIRD SHEPHERD: [*Shepherds enter at R.*] Did not the Holy One say we should find the Babe lying in a manger?

FIRST SHEPHERD: That is so.

SECOND SHEPHERD: [*Points to cradle at C.*] Look. Look! There is a manger over there.

THIRD SHEPHERD: [*Calls.*] Ho, stranger! Where shall we find the infant Saviour?

JOSEPH: The Babe is here, lying in a manger, beside Mary, his mother. [*Tableau: Shepherds kneel at R of cradle. Choir sings, "Angels We Have Heard on High."*]

SCENE 5. *Adoration by the Magi.*

Matthew II:9-11.

READER: Now when Jesus was born in Bethlehem in the days of Herod the King, behold there came wise man from the East to Jerusalem, led by the star which they saw in the East, and which went before them till it came and stood over where the young child was. When they saw the star they rejoiced with exceeding great joy. And when they were come into the house, they saw the young child with Mary, and fell down and worshipped him, and they had opened their treasures, they presented unto him gifts: gold, frankincense, and myrrh.

[*Choir sings "We Three Kings." On the second, third, and fourth verses the First Wise Man, the Second Wise Man, and the Third Wise Man enter from L, each carrying a gift. Each lays his gift in front of the cradle, and then kneels at L. Tableau: Choir sings, "Silent Night." Gabriel enters and stands behind Mary and Joseph, blessing them. The other Angels enter and form a background, with arms lifted. Shepherds remain kneeling at R. Wise Men remain kneeling at L. The Pageant ends with the end of the song. The curtains close, or all exit. After music: "O Little Town of Bethlehem" or "Forest Green."*]

CURTAIN

THE SECOND SHEPHERD'S PLAY

Adapted for modern performance by Aurand Harris

THE SECOND SHEPHERD'S PLAY

CAST

FIRST SHEPHERD	Coll
SECOND SHEPHERD	Gib
THIRD SHEPHERD	Daw
MAK	a sheep-stealer
GILL	his wife
ANGEL	
MARY	

[*A field.* FIRST SHEPHERD *enters.*]

FIRST SHEPHERD: Lord, but these weathers are cold; And I am ill
wrapped.
    I am near numb, so long have I napped;
    My legs they fold, my fingers are chapped.
    The rich land-owners on us they thrive.
    It were a great wonder that we stay alive.
    It does me good, as I walk thus by mine own,
    Of this world for to talk in manner of moan.
    To my sheep will I stalk, and sit on a stone
    For I trust, full soon,
    We get more company ere it be noon.

SECOND SHEPHERD: [*Enters. He does not see* FIRST SHEPHERD.]
    Blessings upon us, such days I seldom have seen.
    Lord, these weathers are spiteous, and the winds full keen.
    And the frost so hideous they water mine eyes.
    It is not all easy. I speak no lies.
    But as far as I've been, or yet as I go,
    We men who are wed suffer a great woe.
    Some men will have two wives,
    And some men three.
    Some are grieved that have any.
    Woe to him that has many.
    But, know what you wrought young men of wooing,
    Be well ware of wedding, and think what you're doing.

"Had I known" is a thing that serves nought.
Much grief and mourning has wedding home brought.
Alas, for I have one for my wife,
Rough as a burr; tongue sharp as a knife.
She's great as a whale, full of gall that does foster.
I would I had run till I had lost her.

FIRST SHEPHERD: Look about. Full deafly ye stand there. Saw thou young Daw?

SECOND SHEPHERD: He comes.

FIRST SHEPHERD: Where?

SECOND SHEPHERD: He will tell us a lie. Best we beware.

THIRD SHEPHERD: [*Enters. He is a boy. He does not see the other shepherds.*]
Was never since Noah's flood such floods seen,
Winds and rains so rude and storms so keen—
We that walk in the nights, our cattle to keep,
We see sudden sights when other men sleep.

[FIRST *and* SECOND SHEPHERD *move. He is frightened.*]

Yet—methinks—two giants!—my heart skips a beat!
Two rogues—two giants!—I meet.
Back to my sheep I will slip and go,

[*Tip-toes away.*]

And pray I do not trip my toe.

FIRST SHEPHERD: Daw! Why and whence trot ye?

THIRD SHEPHERD: Tis my master! I knew not ye.

SECOND SHEPHERD: Where are our sheep? Blow ye the horn.

THIRD SHEPHERD: Safe they are left in the corn.
They have pasture good, they can not go wrong.

FIRST SHEPHERD: That is right. By the rood, these nights are long!
Ere we went, how I would that one gave me a song.

SECOND SHEPHERD: Let me pitch the tenory.

FIRST SHEPHERD: And the treble I bring.

THIRD SHEPHERD: Then the mean falls to me.

FIRST SHEPHERD: Together we sing.

[*They sing.* MAK *enters, wearing a cape.*]

MAK: Oh, Lord, maker of the stars and all,

> And of more than I can recall,
> Were I in heaven where no children stirred,
> Nor ranting of a wife was heard!

FIRST SHEPHERD: Who is that who pipes off tone?

MAK: A man who has no life of his own.

SECOND SHEPHERD: Mak, where hast thou gone? What tidings bring?

THIRD SHEPHERD: Mak? Then each one take heed to his thing!

FIRST SHEPHERD: What means this so late thou goes,
> A rogue in the night, taking a peep,
> Men will suppose thou has a good nose.
> For stealing a sheep.

MAK: I am true as steel, all men wet;
> But a sickness I feel, that holds me full hot;
> My belly fares not well; it is out of estate.

THIRD SHEPHERD: Seldom lies the devil dead by the gate.

MAK: I am ill, fullsore;
> May I stand stone-still,
> If I have eat meat
> This month or more.

FIRST SHEPHERD: How fares thy wife? By the hood, how fares she?

MAK: Lies lolling a-bed, calling for brew
> Each year a baby she brings anew,
> And some years bringeth two.

SECOND SHEPHERD: I am weary of watching sheep in the night.

THIRD SHEPHERD: I am cold. I would be near a fire burning bright.

FIRST SHEPHERD: I am tired and would sleep. Stay awake thou?

SECOND SHEPHERD: Nay, I be with you and sleep now.

> [*They lie down.*]

THIRD SHEPHERD: As good a man's son am I as any of you.
> But, Mak, come hither. Rest between us two.

> [*Lies down.*]

MAK: I'll hear secrets ye whisper, but I'll do.

> [*Sits between them.*]

> A prayer I say, on bended knee.
> From my top to my toe,

Manus tuas commendo,   ("Into thy hands I commend,
Poncio Pilato;   Pontius Pilate.")
May Christ's cross cover me.

[*He lies down.* THREE SHEPHERDS *snore.* MAK *rises.*]

Now's the time for a man that lacks what he would
To privily take from the fold what he could.

[*Makes a magic spell around* SHEPHERDS.]

Here about you a circle I make, as round as a moon,
Till I have done what I will; sleep ye till noon.
May ye lie stone-still till I be done.

[*Waves hand over their heads.*]

Over your heads, my hand I run.
Out go your light. Fordo your sight!

[SHEPHERDS *snore louder.*]

Lord, how they sleep hard, and buzz like a fly.
Was I never a shepherd, but now will I try.
Though the flock be scattered, I'll catch one.

[*Cautiously catches a stuffed sheep.*]

Nab—grab—a prize I've won!
A fat sheep, I dare say,
A good fleece, dare I lay,
Repay when I may,
So ends my sorrow,
For this will I borrow.

[*He takes sheep, hidden under his cape; to his house.*]

How, Gill, art thou in? Get us some light

GILL: Who makes such a din this time of night?

MAK: Good wife, open. I bring meat to eat.

GILL: [*Opens door.*] Ah, come, my husband, my sweet.

MAK: See. In a pinch—and in my way—
    I get more than they that sweat all day. [*Shows sheep.*]
    I would it were slain; I would well eat.
    This twelvemonth I taste not one sheep-meat.

GILL: Come they before it be slain, and hear the sheep fret—

MAK: Then might I be taken. That were a cold sweat!

GILL: A good trick have I spied, since thou can none;
　　　Here shall we him hide till they be done—
　　　In the cradle abide. Let me alone.
　　　And I shall beside the sheep lie, and groan.

MAK: And I shall say thou was light
　　　Of a male-child this night.

GILL: This is a good guise and a fair cast;
　　　A woman's advice helps at the last.
　　　But I fear they awake; return, go thou fast.

MAK: I'll go ere they rise, or they'll blow a cold blast.

[MAK *returns to* SHEPHERDS.]

　　　Yet still sleep, these three.
　　　In I shall creep, and be
　　　As though I had not been he
　　　Who stole their sheep.

[MAK *lies down in place.* FIRST SHEPHERD *and* SECOND SHEPHERD *awake.*]

FIRST SHEPHERD:

Resurrex a mortunus.	("Resurrection from the dead)
Have hold my hand.	
Judas carnas dominus!	("Judas, lord of the flesh.")
I can not well stand.	

SECOND SHEPHERD: Lord, what I have slept well!
　　　And thus I feel
　　　As fresh as an eel;
　　　As light, ah, ye,
　　　As a leaf on a tree.

THIRD SHEPHERD: [*Awakes.*]
　　　Blessing be herein! My body does quake;
　　　My heart out of skin, thus does shake.
　　　See you ought of Mak now?

FIRST SHEPHERD: We were up ere thou.

SECOND SHEPHERD: Man, I give God a vow
　　　That he did not stir.
　　　He sleeps as a kitten doth purr.

THIRD SHEPHERD: Methought, when we napped, he, in a wolf-skin
　　　trapped a fat sheep, but made no din.

SECOND SHEPHERD: Be still! Thy dream makes thee mad.
    It is but a phantom, my lad.

[*They awaken* MAK.]

    Rise, Mak, for shame! Thou liest right long.

MAK: What is this? Ah, my neck has lain wrong.
    I trust I be the same.
    Alack! My leg is lame.

[*Others help him.*]

    Many thanks since yester-even,
    Now by Saint Steven,
    A bad dream did my head fill
    That did stop my heart still!
    I thought my wife, Gill, croaked full sad,
    And gave birth to another child lad!
    Too many ere before she has had,
    Now another she doth add!
    Oh, my head!
    Woe for him what numbers grow,
    And there be little bread!
    I must home, by your leave, to Gill, as I thought.
    I pray look in my sleeve, that I steal nought.
    I am loath you to grieve, or from you take ought.

[*He leaves.*]

THIRD SHEPHERD: Go forth. Best we sought
    If a sheep be naught.

FIRST SHEPHERD: We'll meet before the morn.

SECOND SHEPHERD: Where?

THIRD SHEPHERD: At the crooked thorn.

[*They depart.*]

MAK: [*At his door.*]
    Undo the door! How long shall I stand?

GILL: Who is there?

MAK: I, Mak, your husband.

GILL: Ah, Sir Guile! Let him cool his toes.
    Let him attend, so he knows
    Who brews, who bakes, who makes us our hose?

MAK: [*Aside.*] Day and dark thus her mouth goes.

GILL: Full woeful is a man's life
    What lacks a helpful wife.

[*Opens door.*]

    What end has thou made with the shepherds, Mak?

MAK: The last word they said when I turned my back
    They would look that they had their sheep, all the pack.
    I think there will be trouble when they their sheep lack.
    Here they will hie and peep.
    "Thief!" they'll cry. "Where be the sheep?"
    Quick! Thou must do as thou said.

GILL: I shall swaddle the sheep in the cradle bed.

[*Gill puts sheep in cradle.*]

    Twere better, if I helped still.
    I will lie down. Come wrap me.

MAK: I will. [*Covers her.*]

GILL: Behind! Watch. Give a sign full straight
    When Coll comes and his mate.
    Harken well. Thou sing alone.
    Thou sing "lullay" for I must groan.

[*Practices crying loudly.*]

[THREE SHEPHERDS *meet.*]

THIRD SHEPHERD: Ah, Cell, why lookest thou so bobbed?

FIRST SHEPHERD: Alas, of one sheep we have been robbed!

SECOND SHEPHERD: The devil you say!

THIRD SHEPHERD: A sheep astray!

SECOND SHEPHERD: Who should do us this foul play?

FIRST SHEPHERD: I have sought with my dogs
    All Horbury bogs,
    Of the fifteen we keep
    Found all but one sheep.

THIRD SHEPHERD: Now believe me, if you will, iwis,
    Either Mak or Gill hath done this.

FIRST SHEPHERD: Peace man, be still.
    I saw when he went.

Thou slanderest him ill;
Thou ought to repent.

SECOND SHEPHERD: I will stake my life if need,
It were he, what did the deed.

THIRD SHEPHERD: Go we thither. Search about.
I shall never eat bread, till the truth is out.

SECOND SHEPHERD: Brother. Let us swear in our plight,
Until we see him in sight,
Shall we never sleep one night
Where we do another.

[SHEPHERDS *approach Mak's house.* GILL *begins to groan.* MAK *sings loudly.*]

THIRD SHEPHERD: Will ye hear how they hack? Our sire can croon.

FIRST SHEPHERD: Heard I never none sing so clear out of tune. Call on him.

SECOND SHEPHERD: Mak, undo your door soon!

MAK: Who is that spake, as it were noon?

THIRD SHEPHERD: Good fellows what ye know and see oft.

[SHEPHERDS *enter the house.*]

MAK: I beg, sirs, speak soft.
A sick woman, in bed, lies distressed.
I had rather be dead than give her unrest.

GILL: Come not by my bed! My breath wheezes.
Each step that ye tread, my nose sneezes.

MAK: Ye have run in the mire, and are wet yet!
I shall make you a fire, if ye will sit.
I have sons, if ye knew,
Well more than a few!
Yet another is born to add to the brood.

[*Points to cradle.*]

Ere ye go ye must take drink and some food.

SECOND SHEPHERD: Nay, meat nor drink mends not our mood.

MAK: Why, sir, tell me, is ought not good?

THIRD SHEPHERD: Our sheep were stolen as they stood.

MAK: Sirs, drink! Had I been near
Some should have felt it full dear!

FIRST SHEPHERD: Some men hold that ye were there.
    And so think I, I swear.

SECOND SHEPHERD: Mak, some men propose that it were ye.

THIRD SHEPHERD: Either ye or your spouse, so say we.

MAK: If ye suppose it of Gill or of me—
    Search our house, and ye will see
    If I have a sheep or half,
    Or if I have a cow or a calf.
    And Gill, my wife, less live than dead,
    Rose not, from her child-bearing bed.
    I swear tis true what I say,
    Or this be the first meal I eat today.

    [*Points to cradle.*]

    [SHEPHERDS *begin to search.*]

GILL: Out thieves, away from me go!
    Ye come to rob us, that I know.

MAK: Hear ye not how she groans?

GILL: I swelt!

MAK: Hark! Do ye hearts not melt?

GILL: Off, thieves. Away from the son I bore!

MAK: Ah, the pain she is in, be ye hearts not sore?

GILL: Oh, my middle! I pray to God so mild,
    If ever I you beguiled.
    That I will eat this child!

MAK: Please, woman, for God's pain, cry not so.
    Thou spill your brain, and make me great woe.

SECOND SHEPHERD: What find ye two? I think our sheep be slain.

THIRD SHEPHERD: We may as well go. No sheep is here, tis plain.

FIRST SHEPHERD: As the wind blows, I know by my nose.
    Of all animals, boy or beast that dwells,

    [*Points to cradle.*]

    None do as loud as he smells!

GILL: Nay, to a mother tis a sweet smelling child.

FIRST SHEPHERD: We have marked amiss; I hold us beguiled.
    [*To Mak.*] Friends we be for we are one.

MAK: Nay. No one helps me.

SECOND SHEPHERD: We are done.

MAK: [*Aside.*] Go then and be about.
    Farewell all three.

THIRD SHEPHERD: Fair words they be, but love is left out.

[SHEPHERDS *leave the house.*]

FIRST SHEPHERD: Gave ye the child anything?

SECOND SHEPHERD: I swear not one farthing.

THIRD SHEPHERD: Fast again will I run.
    Abide here.

[*Runs to house.*]

    I bring, Mak, a gift for your son.

MAK: Nay, to me foul hast thou done!

THIRD SHEPHERD: By your leave, let me give him but sixpence.

MAK: Nay, I pray you go hence. He sleeps.

[*Other* SHEPHERDS *enter. Sheep "Baa's."*]

THIRD SHEPHERD: Methinks he peeps.

MAK: When he wakens he weeps.

THIRD SHEPHERD: Give me leave him to kiss, and lift up the clout.

[*Lifts cover.*]

    What the devil is this? He has a long snout!

[*Others look.*]

FIRST SHEPHERD: He is marked amiss. We wait not about.

SECOND SHEPHERD: Look! He is like to our sheep!

THIRD SHEPHERD: How, Gib, may I peep?

SECOND SHEPHERD: This is a prank, a trick, a false riddle!

THIRD SHEPHERD: See how the four feet they tied in the middle.
    Two horns saw I on many a cow,
    But never two horns on a boy ere now!

MAK: Peace bid I! Leave off your care.
    I be the father, yond woman him bear.

GILL: A pretty child as ere a mother had.
    A dillydown, sweet little baby lad.

THIRD SHEPHERD: Tis our sheep! His ear-mark proves a good token.

MAK: I tell you sire. His nose was broken.
> Twas told he was bewitched one night.

FIRST SHEPHERD: This is false work. We will make it a-right!
> Get weapons!

GILL: He was taken with an elf.
> At the stroke of midnight. I saw it myself.

SECOND SHEPHERD: Ye two are clever, but we are not misled.

FIRST SHEPHERD: They repent not their stealing. Let's see them both dead.

MAK: If again I trespass, cut off my head.
> Give mercy, I beg you.

FIRST SHEPHERD: Listen and dread.
> We will neither curse nor fight,
> Chide nor smite,
> Hang nor beat,
> But cast him in a sheet.

[*They toss* MAK *in a sheet. Then they return to the field.*]

FIRST SHEPHERD: Lord, what I am sore. My strength put to a test.
> Faith, I may do no more; therefore will I rest.

SECOND SHEPHERD: I vow, Mak weighed more than seven score.
> For to sleep anywhere me think that I best.

THIRD SHEPHERD: Now I pray you lie on the grass yonder.

FIRST SHEPHERD: On these thieves I still ponder.

SECOND SHEPHERD: Peace. Silent keep and sleep.

[SHEPHERDS *lie down and sleep.*]

ANGEL: [*Enters and sings "Gloria in excelsis."*]
> Rise herdsmen kind, for now he is born,
> The Savior who can the devil destroy.
> God is made your friend now at this morn.
> He requests, to Bethlehem go ye and see the boy.
> In a rude crib he lies, waxen and wealed.
> Ye will find him there betwixed two beasts of the field.

[ANGEL *withdraws.* SHEPHERDS *rise.*]

FIRST SHEPHERD: This was a sweet voice that ever yet I heard.
> It is a marvel to hear, thus to be stirred.

SECOND SHEPHERD: As I woke, of God's son of heaven he spoke.
　　Like a wonderous light, methought the sky be bright.

THIRD SHEPHERD: In Bethlehem born,
　　He spoke of a child fair.

FIRST SHEPHERD: That betokens yon star. [*Points.*]
　　Let us seek him there.

SECOND SHEPHERD: Say, what was his song? Heard ye not
　　How fine he split a note?

THIRD SHEPHERD: Yea, marry, twas a sweet trill, I wot.

FIRST SHEPHERD: I'll try the song among us, by rote.

SECOND SHEPHERD: Let see how ye croon.
　　Can ye bark at the moon?

FIRST SHEPHERD: Hold your tongue. Be ye still—and I will.

　　[*He sings.*]

SECOND SHEPHERD: To Bethlehem he bade that we be gone;
　　I am full 'fraid that we tarry too long.

FIRST SHEPHERD: Hie we thither therefore,
　　Though we be weary with woe.
　　To that child and that lady;
　　We have it in haste to go.

THIRD SHEPHERD: The angel said of that child
　　In a crib he lay meek and mild.

FIRST SHEPHERD: We shall see him this morn, I feel.
　　And know it be true as steel
　　All that the prophets spoke clear,
　　To so poor as we he would appear.

SECOND SHEPHERD: Go we now. The place is near.

THIRD SHEPHERD: I am ready and with you; go we with cheer.
　　Lord, if they will it be—
　　We are humble all three—
　　Now grant us the joy
　　To comfort thy boy.

　　[*The stable is revealed.*]

FIRST SHEPHERD: [*Kneels.*]
　　Hail, comely and clean! Hail, young child!
　　Hail, maker, as I mean, of a maiden so mild.
　　Thou has beaten, I ween, the devil so wild.

Lo, he laughs, my sweeting!
A welcome meeting.
I here have a gift and do—
Give a bob of cherries—to you.

SECOND SHEPHERD: [*Kneels.*]
Hail, sovereign savior, for thou have we sought!
Hail, noble child, that all things has wrought.
Hail! I kneel. A bird have I brought
To you from afar. Hail, a little day-star.

THIRD SHEPHERD: [*Kneels.*]
Hail, darling dear. Hail, sweet is thy cheer.
I pray thee be near when I have need.
Wrapped thee so poor, makes my heart bleed.
Pray put forth thy tiny fist,
That I may in it put, I wist,
The gift from me I bring to thee.
Tis all I have—and it be small,
I bring thee but a ball.

MARY: The Father of Heaven, God Omnipotent,
That made all things, his son has he sent.
I fulfilled God's intention, as he meant;
And now is he born.
He keep you from woe.
I shall pray him so.
Tell forth as ye go,
And remember ye this morn.

FIRST SHEPHERD: Farewell, lady, so fair to behold,
With child on thy knee.

SECOND SHEPHERD: But he lies full cold.
Lord, well is me. Now we go, thus behold.

THIRD SHEPHERD: Forsooth, full oft this night will be told.

FIRST SHEPHERD: What grace we have found.

SECOND SHEPHERD: Come forth. Glad tidings we sound.

THIRD SHEPHERD: Let voices abound!
Cries of joy let ring!
Lift ye aloft your voice and sing!

[*They sing, and go out.*]

END

SAINT GEORGE AND THE DRAGON AT CHRISTMAS TIDE

A Medieval Mummer's Play for Performance Today

Adapted by Marjorie Sigley

Characters:

ADAM OLIPHANT/OLD FATHER CHRISTMAS

TIMOTHY POTTLE/BOY

WALTER CRADDOCK/SAINT GEORGE

GREGORY CARTWRIGHT/THE DRAGON

JEREMIAH BOTTLE/BEELZEBUB

MATTHEW SHOESMITH/BLUNDERBORE

SOLOMON SLEEMAN/DOCTOR BALL

FRANCIS CATCHPOLE/FOOL

JASPER MUDDIMAN/HOBBY HORSE

KING ALFRED

ALFRED'S QUEEN

KING WILLIAM

WILLIAM'S QUEEN

KING CHARLES

KING COLE

COLE'S QUEEN

PAGE

MORRIS DANCERS

OGRES and DEVILS

THE PROLOGUE

Place: A medieval village hall or meeting place. Enter JEREMIAH BOTTLE, *the local taverner followed by his "pot" boy,* TIMOTHY POTTLE. BOTTLE *is carrying a large stone flagon of ale,* POTTLE *a wickerbasket with metal tankards in it. These are placed on a small wooden table. Two long wooden benches are arranged on either side, at an angle, opening out into a wide inverted V.*

JEREMIAH B.: Master Town Clerk may well ask us to bring forth the ale, but who is to pay?

TIMOTHY P.: Why, those that drink it.

JEREMIAH B.: Midsummer's day could turn into Christmas afore some that come would part with a farthing.

TIMOTHY P.: 'Tis true.

JEREMIAH B.: And count the tankards—for fear of losing them.

TIMOTHY P.: Aye, sir.

JEREMIAH B.: And dust the benches.

[POTTLE *obliges, but seeing a dangling rope, pulls it and is startled by the bell that rings out loudly.*]

JEREMIAH B.: Pottle—attend to your business. [*He holds up a slate*]

[*Enter a number of* VILLAGERS *who, commenting on the cold weather, the gathering and the absence of the* TOWN CLERK, *make for the ale before signing in on the slate held by the* POT BOY. *Suddenly there is a flurry of activity off stage. Enter* ADAM OLIPHANT, TOWN CLERK *and instigator of the "drama," followed by a number of* YOUNG VILLAGERS *who are told to sit in the back of the benches, which they do with some fuss*]

WALTER C.: [*VOS*] Master Oliphant! Master Oliphant!

[ADAM O *looks up, takes no notice of them, looks for the* POT BOY *who is quite confused by those that have made their mark and those that haven't. Enter Walter Craddock,* THE MILLER, *noted by some of the villagers, with derision. He is the wealthiest man in the village and many owe him money*]

ADAM O.: Are we all met?

POT B.: I don't know, sir.

WALTER C.: How many, Master Oliphant, did you call?

ADAM O.: Why, generally any and all that should care to take part in our play. Some I did speak to directly.

WALTER C.: How so?

ADAM O.: There are parts in this play that need particular undertaking. Particular skills and accomplishments are required. Certain . . . talents, certain . . . .

[*The* MILLER *prances around him.*]

WALTER C.: Pray, sir, say what they be.

ADAM O.: Stay, Master Craddock. First we must see what company hath assembled. Timothy Pottle, have you the list?

[POT BOY *comes forward.*]

TIMOTHY P.: Master Oliphant, there are some that made a dirty mark. [ADAM O. *cuffs his ear*] Ouch! 'Twas not I.

ADAM O.: Good masters, answer to your name and be seated.

[*They all look at each other; they are already seated so they stand up in unison.*]

Gregory Cartwright—joiner.

GREGORY C.: Here, Master Oliphant.

ADAM O.: Jeremiah Bottle. Innkeeper.

JEREMIAH B.: Here, Master Oliphant.

ADAM O.: Matthew Shoesmith, Blacksmith.

TIMOTHY P.: See, Sir, the smudge. [BLACKSMITH *cuffs him*]

MATTHEW S.: [*An enormous man of great girth*] Present, your worship.

ADAM O.: Solomon Sleeman, Apothecary.

SOLOMON S.: [*Anxiously*] Here, Master Oliphant. I cannot stay too long for I am in the midst of my winter brew for the influenza.

GREGORY C.: An evil potion—

MATTHEW S.: Which remedies all ills—

JEREMIAH B.: Or kills! My wife's sister's husband lies yonder in the churchyard . . . . .

ADAM O.: Francis Catchpole, Tax Collector.

[*General mumblings of discontent at his presence.*]

FRANCIS C.: Master Oliphant, I did make it clear when first you requested my company that I have my books to attend to primarily and before all else.

ADAM O.: Why then, here is a marvelous opportunity for you to make merry and forget the aggravation of figures that will not multiply to the divided amount.

FRANCIS C.: [*Mystified by this statement, in his ear*] I am somewhat afeared of making an exhibition of myself in front of [*whispers and points to people on the benches*] them.

ADAM O.: Come, Master Catchpole, let not your occupation come betwixt you and a merry part in our mummers play. Pray be seated. Jasper Muddiman, Ploughboy.

[JASPER MUDDIMAN *is a poor ploughboy who has been given a hat for the occasion. It is too small and continually falls off, to his great embarrassment.*]

JASPER M.: Yea. [*Stands up*] Nay. [*Sits dwn*] Here. [*Stands up*] Oh, Lord, I would I'd never come. [MATTHEW SHOESMITH *pulls him down on to the bench*]

ADAM O.: You, Masters, I have set down for named parts. [*He goes upstage and speaks to the younger villagers*] For the rest, I will apportion some action in due course.

YOUNG MAN: [*Angrily*] You promised me a part! Our barn is to be your meeting place in agreement of which you promised my father I should be given preference.

ALL: Preference? What preference? That's bold.

ADAM O.: [*Flustered*] So he it! In due course! I will attend to it! You all do talk at once and so confuse me.

WALTER C.: How now, Master Town Clerk, what about me? You have not called forth my name. Am I left out?

[ADAM OLIPHANT *beckons the boy to bring the list and cuffs his ear.* POTTLE *is always caught out*]

ADAM O.: [*Scrutinizes the list*] You did not sign?

WALTER C.: I was not asked. [*Cuffs* BOY, *grabs paper and signs*]

ADAM O.: [*Sighing*] Good Master Craddock, you are most welcome.

WALTER C.: Then let us proceed. Say what the play is about and name us the parts.

[*He sits down next to* GERGORY CARTWRIGHT *who edges away*]

ADAM O.: Our drama is the fearsome tale, yet merry play of St George and the Dragon at Christmas Tide . . . .

WALTER C.: [*Interrupting*] An excellent piece, I assure you.

ADAM O.: [*Cont.*] ...that hath been told for many a year afore us and will be forever after.

POT B.: [*Standing behind* CRADDOCK] I've never seen it.

[CRADDOCK *cuffs him and he falls on* GREGORY]

JASPER M.: [*To* M. SHOESMITH] Pray, what is the play about?

[ADAM O. *overhears*]

ADAM O.: Why 'tis the true story of the triumph of goodness over evil.

JASPER M.: [*Rising*] Then 'tis too clever for me. [*Starts to go*]

ADAM O.: Stay! 'Tis told in a simple way. Goodness in the form of St George is called forth to rescue a land from the wicked deeds of three malefactions.

CATCHPOLE: Don't you mean malefactors?

GREGORY C.: [*Leaping to his feet*] St George. Our patron saint, our knight in shining armor. Pray, Master Oliphant, let me play St George, I have great sympathy with the saint. [CRADDOCK *leaps up and grabs* GREGORY'*s hat which he tosses in the air*]

WALTER C.: You are some 6 inches short of saint! This part requireth a tall man, a fine man, an heroic man, a handsome, fearless man, a . . . .

ADAM O.: Master Craddock, I will decide who is most fit for each and every part. You, Gregory Cartwright, are set down for the Dragon.

GREGORY C.: [*Dumbfounded*] The Dragon? Pray, Master Oliphant, let me not play a dragon. I am a mild man, I cannot roar . . . . I am most undragonly.

ADAM O.: Then you must practice.

[ADAM O. *lifts his hands as paws and meows like a kitten.* GREGORY *copies him*]

MATTHEW S.: [*Roars, makes everyone jump*] A dragon, you say? A monstrous creature that rolls its bloodshot eyes, spits fire and tears flesh, [*demonstrates*] let me play the dragon.

ADAM O.: You, Matthew Shoesmith, are set down for the giant.

ALL: Giant? [*Sniggers*]

MATTHEW S.: What giant? [*Threatening them with his eyes*]

ADAM O.: The fearsome, mighty Blunderbore.

WALTER C.: Mighty you say?

ADAM O.: Aye! Tall as a mountain, and wide as a valley.

WALTER C.: [*Jumps up*] Let me play the giant. I am the taller man here. I can grow into a monstrous Ercules, a terrible tyrant.

[*Moves into the center and clears it with the actions he makes*]

WALTER C.: This mighty arm
  Will deal out harm
  This foot will crush to powder
  These hands will tear
  And no parts spare
  No voice will ring out louder.

ADAM O.: Have you finished, sir?

MATTHEW S.: [*Getting up, goes to* WALTER C. *and gives him a shove*] This miller doth offend me.

[CRADDOCK *falls back on the others who propel him forward again.* WALTER C. *shoves the* BLACKSMITH *back.* F. CATCHPOLE *jumps up and tries to separate the pair. Suddenly everybody is involved trying to come between them*]

ADAM O.: Oh dear no—we'll have no brawling.

FRANCIS C.: Pray, masters, be still. Let us not argue so, but proceed, for I must leave you.

[*He gets completely winded by* TIMOTHY POTTLE *who is hurled through the air attached to the* BLACKSMITH'S *arm*]

[SOLOMON SLEEMAN *is already on his way out.* ADAM O. *runs after him*]

ADAM O.: Master Sleeman, pray. Stay a while longer.

SOLOMON S.: This bickering achieveth nought. [POT BOY *mimics him and gets cuffed*] I must away to my druggery.

ADAM O.: But you, sir, have the best of parts, 'tis worth the waiting. [SOLOMON S. *returns to the bench*] Jasper Muddiman, you shall play the Hobbyhorse.

[JASPER *twists his hat in his hands*]

JASPER M.: Is it a big part?

ADAM O.: No, but it is most telling.

JASPER M.: Does this Hobbyhorse have much words to say? My alphabet is still not learned.

ADAM O.: Never fear, it is all trotting and galloping, prancing and leaping, the which you know exceeding well from our ploughing.

C. CARTWRIGHT: Let him play the dragon [*pointing at Jasper*]. Let me play the hobbyhorse.

ADAM O.: You shall not play the hobbyhorse. You shall play the dragon as I said.

[*Sensing another* J. BOTTLE *leaps up*]

JEREMIAH B.: And me, sir, what part have you in mind for me?

ADAM O.: Why Beelzebub, of course!

JEREMIAH B.: The Devil?

ADAM O.: Rightly so. Something of the devil you see in me to say "of course"?

ADAM O.: Me, no, Master Bottle, do not mistake my words. As thou art a taverner dispensing spirits and ale daily and seeing the ill humor they create when taken in abundance, I thought you were the only man in our company that hath the knowledge to transfer unto this wicked creature and make believable methink.

[*During this speech* S. SLEEMAN *tries to sneak out but* ADAM O., *holding on to* J. BOTTLE *catches him and tries to seat both of them in great confusion*]

SOLOMON S.: This character I could enjoy with forked tongue and tail, with horns and blackened visage.

ADAM O.: Stay! Master Sleeeman, stay for you are to play the doctor. [*He forces him to sit on the opposite bench where he can keep an eye on him.*]

SOLOMON S.: What doctor?

ADAM O.: Why the doctor who restores St George to life.

POT BOY: When did he die? The play has not yet begun. [W. CRADDOCK *cuffs him*] Ouch!

ADAM O.: St George will die by swords and you shall bring him back to life.

JASPER M.: 'Tis not possible.

[*Suddenly everybody seems to be on the move from one bench to the other*]

ADAM O.: [*Getting exasperated*] This is a drama wherein the impossible becomes possible.

WALTER C.: Let me play the doctor. I see some magical maneuvering here.

JEREMIAH B.: You were not picked!

WALTER C.: Neither you.

FRANCIS C.: This is the silliest stuff I ever heard.

MATTHEW S.: [*Moves in on everyone, threatening them*] Sit down and be silent! Master Town Clerk, read once more your choice of man and his named part. For the rest [*he turns and makes a fist*] hold silence!

[*Everyone freezes. They don't want a broken nose*]

ADAM O.: [*Sighing*] You all do so dispute amongst yourselves, my presence here seems bootless. [*Collects his papers and leaves*]

POT BOY: [*Running after him*] Pray, Master Oliphant, take no offence, 'tis their nature to disagree.

GREGORY C.: [*Apologetically*] We will abide by your decisions and those that be contrary should leave now.

[*No-one stirs*]

POT BOY: Please come back, sir.

ALL: Please, Master Oliphant. Stay.

ADAM O.: [*Returning to his lectern*] Well, well, if I have offended, it was with good will, my intention was all for your delight. [*Reads his cast list*]

Gregory Cartwright—The Dragon

Matthew Shoesmith—The Giant

Jasper Muddiman—The Hobbyhorse

Jeremiah Bottle—The Devil

Solomon Sleeman—The Doctor

Francis Catchpole—The Tax Collector

FRANCIS C.: Master Oliphant, I am the tax collector

ADAM O.: Ah, aha, yes, Francis Catchpole, the Fool.

[*Roars of sustained laughter from the rest*]

FRANCIS C.: [*Rises*] A fool! A fool! Is that how you see me? A mawkish clown, with black ringed eyes and glowing nose? A laughing stock? A Tom-o-Bedlam, a merry Andrew?

GREGORY C.: A jester?

JEREMIAH B.: A buffoon?

SOLOMON S.: A mooncalf?

TIMOTHY P.: A donkey?

ALL: Nay. He hath not the humor!

ADAM O.: Be that as it may, I believe he hath the potential.

[FRANCIS C. *starts to go, then comes back*]

FRANCIS C.: Master Oliphant, think of my professional standing, none here will respect me after.

ADAM O.: [*Taking him forwards and speaking quietly and confidentially*] 'Tis the biggest part and the best. [FRANCIS C. *hesitates*] This merry fool holds all the strings that pull the elements of our play together. He is our master of ceremonies, our confidante, our friend.

[FRANCIS C. *hesitates, uncertain, tempted*]

FRANCIS C.: So say you?

ADAM O.: On my word, this Fool hath great standing and is much loved.

FRANCIS C.: [*Hesitates*] Well then I will abide by your decision.

[ADAM O. *heaves a sigh of relief and moves towards the villagers*]

ADAM O.: [*Nods*] Timothy Pottle, you shall play the boy.

TIMOTHY P.: [*Amazed*] I have a part?

ADAM O.: We need a boy to help the doctor with his trickery. You will do as good as any. [*He moves to others present at the back*] Various kings and queens [*Much comment from the rest at the mention of Kings and Queens*] and supernumeraries, devils, trolls and pixies will be your parts. And for myself I will undertake the role of Father Christmas whose presence is essential in this festivity. So, masters, here are your parts and I entreat you to commit them to memory by our next meeting.

[*There is a lot of pushing and shoving as they collect their respective scripts.* WALTER C. *sits aghast*]

WALTER C.: Is there no part for me?

[*The departing* VILLAGERS *stop and look back*]

ADAM O.: I did not mention you?

WALTER C.: Nay!

ADAM O.: Nor set you down?

WALTER C.: Nay!

ADAM O.: It's most heinous to have left you out in this manner. [*Consults his list*] I see no part for you.

[POT BOY *sees one part left on the lectern*]

TIMOTHY P.: [*Whispers*] You have not set the knight. [ADAM O. *cuffs him, goes through his papers, suddenly looks up.*]

ADAM O.: What say you?

TIMOTHY P.: [*Holding up the part*] St George.

MATTHEW S.: "St George".

GREGORY C.: Who is to play St George?

[ADAM O. *stands up, dismayed, realizing his mistake*]

ADAM O.: [*Slowly, unhappily, reluctantly*] Then you, Master Craddock, must play the Knight, all else is cast.

WALTER C.: [*Leaps to his feet then on to a bench*]
By my pike
I'll show my might
Evil shall not slay me
The dragon's lust
I'll turn to dust
And free you all from danger

TIMOTHY P.: You just made that up. [WALTER C. *cuffs him*]

ADAM O.: Masters, I pray you, stay with the written word, speak only what is written down. Naught shall be extemporaneous.

[*Exit all eagerly scanning their scripts, except* YOUNG VILLAGER *and several others*]

YOUNG VILLAGER: Where be my part, Master Oliphant?

ADAM O.: [*Gazing at the receding crowd*] What? Oh? Here, take mine, I fear this play will see me in my grave. [*Hands out the rest to the other Villagers*]

VILLAGER: [*Exiting*] What beard were I best to play it in? Your yellow tawny beard.

[ADAM O. *Sits down on a bench, exhausted.* TIMOTHY POTTLE *is starting after the crowd. He turns thoughtfully*]

POT BOY: Master Oliphant! Master Oliphant!

ADAM O.: Huh?

POT BOY: [*Sitting down next to* ADAM O.] His sister hath the mumps.

ADAM O.: Whose sister?

POT BOY: The one you gave the part to.

ADAM O.: Mumps you say?

POT BOY: Mumps, as in lumps. [*Indicates and blowing out his cheeks*]

ADAM O.: Go then and get it back.

POT BOY: What, sir?

ADAM O.: The part! The part!

[*Exit* POT BOY]

ADAM O.: [*Exiting, mumbling*] Mumps! Lumps! I've got enough lumps without spreading the mumps. [*Exit*]

THE PLAY

The action takes place in a village square or market place as it is done when played out of doors. A continuous banging is heard from an outside door. It stops. We hear 3 single knocks, followed by a fanfare which leads into a dance music.

[*Enter* FOOL—*leading* THE MORRIS DANCERS *who dance a traditional hankie dance which is circular. It is very gay and lively and at the end the* FOOL *breaks into the circle*]

FOOL: Room, room, brave gallants, all!
　　　Pray, give us room to rhyme.
　　　We've come to show activity
　　　Upon this wintertime. [*EXIT* DANCERS]
　　　Such activity as you've ever seen
　　　Upon an open stage!
　　　Though some of us be little,
　　　And some of a middle sort,
　　　We all desire your favor
　　　To see our pleasure sport.

[*Enter* FATHER XMAS, *leaning on a staff which is decorated with holly and ivy and wearing a headdress of the same*]

OLD FATHER CHRISTMAS: Here come I, Old Father Christmas.
　　　Welcome, or welcome no
　　　I hope Old Father Christmas
　　　Will never be forgot.
　　　Christmas comes but once a year,
　　　And when it comes it brings good cheer.
　　　Roast beef, plum pudding, strong ale and mince pie,
　　　Who likes that better than I?

Good master and good mistress,
I see you are all within
For I've come this merry Christmas time
To see your kith and kin.
I hope you won't get angry,
Nor still take no offence.
For if you do, pray tell me,
And we'll be gone before we commence:

FOOL: [*singing*] Deck the Hall with boughs of holly,
Fa la la la la la la la la
'Tis the season to be jolly
Fa la, etc.
Fill the mead cup, drain the barrel.
Fa la etc. Troll the ancient Christmas carol. Fa la, etc.

[*During this the* FOOL *and* FATHER CHRISTMAS *move upstage to the ceremonial chair which* FATHER CHRISTMAS *now sits on*]

KNOCKING [*as before*]

[FOOL, *holding on high his cap and bells stick, which has a fools puppet head on it, decorated with ribbons and bells. He speaks in a squeaky puppet voice*]

FOOL: A Room, Room, brave gallants all.
Give us room to reign.
We've come to show our story
At Christmas, it is plain.
These merry actors that travel the street.
These merry actors that fight for their meat.
Have come here to greet you and perform here today.

[*Enter* KINGS *and* QUEENS *to music in a procession. They take their places on the circle facing the audience.*]

ALL KINGS AND QUEENS: Good people all, we've come today,
To meet with you and show our play.
The majesty we here present
We bring forth now for your consent.

[*They take poses, which they only break when they speak*]

KING ALFRED: I am King Alfred, the brave and the bold,
I never forget whatever I'm told.
Away from my enemies to the forest I ran
To the house of a woman with cakes in a pan.
Watch my cakes, they're baking and steaming,

But I forgot cause I was day-dreaming.
The cakes were too hard to cut with a knife.
Heaven help me I said, Keep this news from my wife.

ALFRED'S QUEEN: I'm Alfred's Queen, so charming and shy,
But not so stupid as to burn a big pie.
Alfred, stop snoring, and don't be a pig!
He's dumb as a fruit cake and fat as a fig!
Back to my mother I'm going today.
Don't try to stop me, get out of my way.
No longer I'm charming, no longer I'm shy.
Unless you repent now it's Alfred good-bye!

KING WILLIAM: King William the Conqueror of England, I am
The first Norman monarch to conquer this land.
The Britons joined forces and raised me on high
Because of an arrow in poor Harold's eye.

WILLIAM'S QUEEN: I'm William's Queen from that land over there.
The weather here drives me to rage and despair.
To you he's a hero, a jolly good fella,
But he never remembers to bring my umbrella!

KING CHARLES: King Charles I am, a merry man
Who reigned for many a year.
But I lost my head
For fear, some said,
Oliver Cromwell's sneer.

CHARLES' QUEEN: And so you should, you wretched man,
I know your cunning ways.
Your queen I am for all these years
And all these wretched days.

KING CHARLES: If it was so, I'd surely know.
Oh, how you nag and blame me so!

[KINGS *and* QUEENS *take their places on the benches during the second verse of the* FOOL's *carol which follows*]

FOOL: [*singing*] See the flowing bowl before us,
Fa la, etc.
Strike the harp and join the chorus.
Fa la, etc.
Follow me in merry measure,
Fa la, etc.
While I sing of beauty's treasure.

Fa la, etc.

[FOOL *brings in the* MORRIS MEN]

[*2ND MORRIS DANCE, a robust and lively stick dance. At the end they freeze, terrified by the roaring of* BLUNDERBORE *offstage*]

BLUNDERBORE: Fee, Fie, Foe, Fum.

[*A* CHILD, *sitting on* BLUNDERBORE'*s shoulders, holding a big club above its head is covered by an enormous cloak giving the impression of great height. Under the cloak other gnomes and trolls hide as the giant lumbers on stage. They throw the cloak off as he begins to speak*]

BLUNDERBORE: In comes Giant Blunderbore, fee fie foe fum.
    Ready to fight you all—so I says, Come!
    If I could meet St George here,
    I'd stick a spear in through his ear.
    I'd cut him, I'd slash him as little as flies,
    And send him to Jamaica to make into mince pies.

FOOL AND GNOMES: Mince pies hot,
    Mince pies cold.
    Send him to Jamaica 'ere he's nine days old.

TROLLS AND GNOMES: [*Using cackling voices and weird spooky movements*]
    Misty foggy mountain tops,
    Swampy streams and molding crops,
    There we dance and taunt and tease
    Wafting down a smelly breeze
    To those who do not leave us sweets,
    Spicy cakes and tasty meals.

[*They advance slowly and menacingly on the audience*]

TROLLS AND GNOMES: We will make you writhe and retch,
    Cough and heave with sickly bletch
    The message to you all is this
    Do as you're told
    Then your spirits won't be sold
    To the Devil.

[*Giant* BLUNDERBORE *rushes at the* FOOL *who dodges him, dances around and taunts him*]

BLUNDERBORE: A battle, a battle betwixt you and I,
    To see who will fall on the ground and just die.

GNOMES: [*Poking and smacking the* FOOL] Mince pies hot,
    Mince pies cold,

Send him to Jamaica 'ere he's nine days old.

[*During this the* KINGS, ALFRED, WILLIAM *and* CHARLES *quietly take the cloak, arrange it between themselves then fling it over the giant trying to capture him. He struggles to throw it off.*]

BLUNDERBORE: I'll fight King Alfred.
King William and King Charles.
To each a big thump on his rump [*He does it*]
And a whack on his back.
I'm ready to fight any mortal soul
And if he were here now, I'd fight King Cole.

[KING COLE *has been trying to hide, but now, takes courage and tackles the giant*]

KING COLE: So saying here be I, King Cole.
Avaunt there, Giant Blunderbore,
I'll smite you down upon the floor.
I hear you want to strike me dead.
You won't touch me. I'll use my head.
Your aim is worsening every blow
And my advice is that you go
On fighting me until you're old,
Then to the devil you'll be sold.

[GIANT BLUNDERBORE *chases* KING COLE *who retreats.* BLUNDERBORE *goes for* KING COLE *and* QUEEN COLE *rescues him*]

QUEEN COLE: How dare you treat my husband so,
You great big oaf, don't sink so low.
Why do you fight and aim to kill
When all that's here is true goodwill?
You need a wife to shape you up,
To stop your evil ways
I'd sort you out [BLUNDERBORE *roars*]
Don't scream and shout,
Your nights are numbered and your days.

[BLUNDERBORE *pins them to the wall.*]

KING AND QUEEN COLE: Come in, come in, thou Hobby Horse!

HOBBY HORSE: [*Dressed and moving as a horse*] Over mire and over moss
In comes I, the hobby hoss.
Make room, make room, my boys and girls,
Pray give me room to ride.
I've come to show activity.

> This merry Christmastide.
> A Dragon you shall see,
> A wild worm for to flee.

[*He indicates the entrance of the* DRAGON]

> Come in, come in, thou Dragon stout,
> And take thy compass round about.

[*Offstage* DRAGON *roars,* KINGS *and* QUEENS *react*]

[*Enter* DRAGON, *roaring. Directs his action at the children in the audience*]

DRAGON: Watch my head, feel my heat!
> I want meat for to eat.
> I am the Dragon, here are my claws.
> I am the Dragon, here are my jaws.

[DRAGON *roars and beckons in* BEELZEBUB, *who flies in on a trapeze out of hell*]

BEELZEBUB: [*on each of his lines a little devil leaps out of hell.*]
> Fire and Flintstone
> Smoke and Brimstone
> Thunder and Lighting

ALL: The devil himself!

[*The* LITTLE DEVILS *threaten everyone on stage and in the audience.*]

BEELZEBUB: Some people call me Beelzebub,
> It really doesn't matter.
> My devilish form and devilish ways
> Were never meant to flatter.

DEVILS: We are so evil,
> We are so quick,
> See how we scare you
> With our tails that go flick,
> Don't try to catch us.
> You'll fall flat on your face,
> Then the devil will take you
> To that fiery place.

[BEELZEBUB *beckons in other trolls who intimidate bystanders and dance round in a circle*]

GNOMES & DEVILS & FOOL: We're mean, we're evil,
> We aim to kill.

We conquer all people
And destroy good will.
We're scratchers and stingers,
We're able to scare you
Through days and through nights.   [*Exit screaming*]

[*Each of the* THREE MALEFACTORS *now starts to assert his authority*]

BLUNDERBORE: By my club I use my might,
Few there are come back to fight
I'll take my victims back on high
To stew and bake into a pie.

BEELZEBUB: Hell's fires will blaze
And the ovens will bake.
Such succulent smells
Will make your stom-ache.

DRAGON: I am the strongest!
I am the worst!
Neither of these two
Has my burning force.

BLUNDERBORE: I will destroy all Christmas cheer,
And those who fight will lose one ear.

DRAGON: I'll cover you all with muck and with mire.

BEELZEBUB: I'll throw you into Hell's raging fire.

[*A battle ensues between the* GIANT, DEVIL, *and* DRAGON. FOOL *watches frightened, intrigued, then cheekily mimicking them*]

FOOL: A dragon, a devil, a giant so big,
In conflict together, I don't give a fig!
I'll taunt them and tease them and dance round about.
Their efforts to catch me will all come to nought.

[*They capture him in a series of comic kicks, hits and falls, and lean over him triumphant*]

DRAGON: I'll catch him and scratch him
And blood you will see.
Then into a pot
With some beans for my tea.

FOOL: [*terrified*] Oh help me, oh save me!
My life it is done.
No more will I caper
Or dance for your fun.

[*The 4* KINGS *and* QUEENS *cry out*]

ALL: St George! Find St George!
Bring St George.

SONG—VERSE 1

A shining knight we need here now
To save us from this terror.
Of all the men in Christendom
St George must be our saviour.

CHORUS

On a fine white horse
With his righteous sword
He will rescue us from danger.
On a fine white horse
With his righteous sword
He will rescue us from danger.

VERSE 2

St George must come and see our plight
With right and might to defend us.
Of all the men in Christendom
St George must be our saviour.

CHORUS

On a fine white horse
With his righteous sword
He will rescue us from danger.
On a fine white horse
With his righteous sword
He will rescue us from danger.

[OLD FATHER CHRISTMAS *steps forth and raises his hand. Silence*]

OLD FATHER CHRISTMAS: [*Whispers*] St George shall come
And die by swords
Which circle round his neck.
As Winter dies so shall he die,
And rise again, as Spring.
A fanfare is heard and jubilant music.

[ST GEORGE *rides in on his hobby horse, heroically, dramatically and impressively. He is dressed in a suit of armor bearing a shining sword. He is attended at all times by his* PAGE]

ST GEORGE: Here come I, St George, from Britain did I spring.
　　　　I'll fight the dragon bold, my wonders to begin.
　　　　I'll clip his wing, he shall not fly,
　　　　I'll cut him down or else I die.

DRAGON: Who's he that seeks the dragon's blood
　　　　And calls so angry and so loud?
　　　　With my long teeth and scurvy jaws,
　　　　I'll tear the flesh from off his nose.

ST GEORGE: Stand off, stand off, thou dragon bold,
　　　　Or by my sword thou'lt die.
　　　　I'll pierce thy body full of holes
　　　　And make thy buttons fly.

[*They circle about one another*]

DRAGON: My body's made of iron,
　　　　My head is made of steel;
　　　　My claws are made of beaten brass.
　　　　No man can make me feel.

ST GEORGE: No one could ever frighten me,
　　　　For many I have slain.
　　　　I long to fight, 'tis my delight
　　　　To battle o'er again.

ST GEORGE: Bring in the Morris men, bring in the band,
　　　　These are our tricks—Ho men ho
　　　　These are our sticks—whack men so!

[MORRIS MEN *enter and form a circle round the three and follow* ST
GEORGE's *instructions. It is a very menacing and dramatic action. They
fight alongside* ST GEORGE, *and each in turn,* BLUNDERBORE, BEELZE-
BUB *and the* DRAGON *are killed*]

OLD FATHER CHRISTMAS: Step forth, St George, thou champion.
　　　　The finest in the land.
　　　　For you have slain the dragon,
　　　　And banished evil by your hand.

ST GEORGE: The evil that was here about
　　　　Is soundly beat, is down and out,
　　　　He fell from this my righteous hand
　　　　and peace can now spread on this land.

OLD FATHER CHRISTMAS: But stay —
　　　　Even though the dragon's dead,
　　　　He may come back to life.

I beg you sir, oh please, oh please,
Take thou this golden knife.

ST GEORGE: Old Father Christmas, never fear.
First comes Christmas, then comes Spring.
Like Winter I must die,
Then to life again like Spring.

[*3rd MORRIS DANCE*]

[*Sword Dance*]

[*The* MORRIS MEN *perform the traditional dance which results in the locking of swords round the victim's neck—a ritual killing. St George falls down dead*]

FOOL: [*Quietly*] I thought that this was all in fun.
We have cut him down like the evening sun.
To kill the hero, ends the play.

[*He indicates the audience*]

They can't go now. They're here to stay!

OLD FATHER CHRISTMAS: Horrible! Terrible! What have you done?
You have killed my dearly beloved son.
Oh, is there a doctor to be found
To cure this deep and deadly wound?

[*ALL* ACTORS *shouting ad lib to the audience*]

ALL: A doctor! A doctor! Please, a doctor!

FOOL: [*Staring into distance*] See, sir, a doctor here!

[*Enter* DOCTOR BALL *riding on a hobby horse*]

DOCTOR BALL: Here I am, old Doctor Ball
The best quack doctor you can call.
I am the doctor come from Spain
To fetch the dead to life again.
Ten pounds be my fee,
But if thou be an honest man
I'll only take five of thee.

FOOL: Who is this man?
I know that face
I've seen that horse
No doctor case?

DOCTOR: Here's a fellow
See's me through

I wonder who he's
talking to.

[*Turns to the* FOOL]

Hold my horse!

FOOL: Will he bite?

DOCTOR BALL: No

FOOL: Will he kick?

DOCTOR BALL: No.

FOOL: Take two to hold him?

DOCTOR BALL: No.

FOOL: Then hold him yourself.

DOCTOR BALL: What's that, you saucy rascal?

FOOL: I'll hold him, sir.
I've got fast hold of his tail.

DOCTOR BALL: Bring me my spy-glass, Boy! . . . . Boy!

[*Enter* POT BOY, *an exact version of* DR BALL—*top hat, rail coat, etc., on a small hobby horse, carrying a large and very heavy doctor's bag which is full of* DR BALL's *paraphernalia*]

DOCTOR BALL: Bring me my spy-glass and my instruments.

OLD FATHER CHRISTMAS: How cam'st thou to be a doctor?

DOCTOR BALL: By my travels.

OLD FATHER CHRISTMAS: Where have you travelled?

DOCTOR BALL: Italy, Spittaly,
France, and Spain,
Germany, Iceland,
and back again.

FOOL: What no farther?

DOCTOR BALL: Oh yes, a great deal farther.
From the fireside and cupboard.
Upstairs and into bed
Pottle, don't rattle the bottle.

OLD FATHER CHRISTMAS: But can you cure my son?

DOCTOR BALL: Can I cure your son?

[*To the audience*]

Can I cure his son?
Take these, my pills.
They cure the young, the old,
The hot, the cold,
The living and the dead.

[DOCTOR *stumbles over the corpse*]

DOCTOR BALL: What the devil's the matter here?

FOOL: A man's dead seven minutes.
Can you cure him?

DOCTOR BALL: If he's dead seven hours I can cure him.

FOOL: Pray, Doctor, what sort of diseases can you cure?

DOCTOR BALL: The allsorts.

OLD FATHER CHRISTMAS AND FOOL: The allsorts. What's the allsorts?

DOCTOR BALL: All sorts of diseases, whatever you pleases.
I am the doctor that can cure all ills,
Only gulp up my potions and swallow my pills.

FOOL: Particular skills for particular ills?

DOCTOR BALL: I can cure the itch, the stitch, the palsy, and the gout. Here's a box of my pills. Take one tonight, and two in the morning, and swallow the box at dinnertime. If the box don't cure you, the lid will.

FOOL: You must be a clever doctor.

OLD FATHER CHRISTMAS: You'd better try your skill.

DOCTOR BALL: Thank you, sir, and that I will.

[DOCTOR *goes to* ST GEORGE *and lifts his feet*]

DOCTOR BALL: Come, old fellow, raise your head.

FOOL: That ain't his head.

DOCTOR BALL: What is it then?

FOOL: Them's his feet.

DOCTOR BALL: Come, old fellow, raise your head.

FOOL: That ain't his head.

DOCTOR BALL: What is it then?

FOOL: Them's his stommicks.

DOCTOR BALL: Boy! Boy! Let him take a drop of my inkum-pinkum . . .

BOY: Inkum-pinkum?

DOCTOR BALL: Inkum-pinkum . . . Mixed up with cat's feathers.

BOY: Cat's feathers?

DOCTOR BALL: Cat's feathers!

[BOY *makes a great show of mixing the potion and hands it to* DOCTOR BALL]

DOCTOR BALL: Let's have a drop in his eye, a drop in his nose, and a drop in his mouth. Any better, old fellow?

FOOL: You silly man, the dead man never stirs.

DOCTOR BALL: Oh look, I have quite forgot. I've taken the right cork off the wrong bottle. Let's take a drop of another bottle.

DOCTOR BALL: Timothy Pottle,
>   Bring me a bottle
>   Of physic,
>   the strongest of brews

[BOY *looks for it*]

DOCTOR BALL: Come along, Pottle
>   Don't tittle and tottle
>   This knight here
>   Could die from the flu.

TIMOTHY POTTLE: They said sir,
>   He's dead, sir,
>   He isn't in bed, sir
>   So how can he swallow
>   Your brew?

DOCTOR BALL: Don't argue and rottle.
>   Just bring me the bottle
>   Allow me to show them
>   My skills.

TIMOTHY POTTLE: (Aside) He's the one who talks rottle.

DOCTOR BALL: The bottle! The bottle!

TIMOTHY POTTLE: His potions don't cure
>   They just kills.

DOCTOR BALL: That'll go down your thrittle-throttle. Open thy flip-flop
>   And take this slip-slop.

OLD FATHER CHRISTMAS: Well, Doctor, he's a long time coming back to life.

FOOL: Stand aside a fair distance;
> This man's not dead but in a trance.
> If I can fetch him back by chance,
> We'll raise him up and have a dance.
> There's this for that
> And that for this.
> There's hokum and pokum.
> Smack 'im and tickle 'im.
> Blow on 'im and sing to 'im.
> Jump over him and
> Whistle at him.

[ST GEORGE *begins to awaken*]

> Aha
> Ahem
> Oh lor!

[ST GEORGE *arises as if from a deep sleep*]

ST GEORGE: Good morning, gentlemen, a-sleeping have I been.
> I've had such a sleep as the world was never seen.
> But now I am awake, alive unto this day.
> Our dancers shall have a dance, and the Doctor take his pay.

[*The* FOOL *rushes in between* DOCTOR BALL *and* FATHER CHRISTMAS *and snatches up the money bag*]

FOOL: 'Twas I who brought you back to life
> And not the Doctor here.
> Let him revive the Dragon now
> And then we'll make good cheer.

DOCTOR BALL: If these pills don't work on man,
> Upon each beast I'll try.

[DRAGON *revives with a roar, the* DEVIL *with a cry,* GIANT *stirs*]

DOCTOR BALL: Aha, you see! Some truth there be.
> My claims to cure don't lie.

ST GEORGE: We must all shake hands,
> Never fight no more.
> Be all of us brothers,
> As we ever were before.

[*Enter all the characters and dancers shaking hands and making a chain formation*]

ALL: [*song*] God Bless the master of this house,
   Likewise the mistress too,
   And all the little children
   That round the table go

CHORUS

   Love and joy come to you
   And to you your wassail too,
   And God bless you, and send you
   A happy New Year
   And God send you a Happy New Year
   We are not daily beggars
   That beg from door to door
   But we are neighbors' children
   Whom you have seen before.

CHORUS

   Love and joy come to you
   And to you your wassail too,
   And God bless you, and send you
   A happy New Year
   And God send you a Happy New Year

[KINGS, QUEENS, TROLLS, GNOMES, DEVILS, DANCERS *exit. The* MAJOR CHARACTERS *form a tableau*]

BLUNDERBORE: We wish you a merry Christmas
   And a joyful New Year,

BEELZEBUB: And spring comes soon to fill
   Us all with good cheer.

HOBBY HORSE: A pocket full of money
   And a cellar full of beer,
   And a good fat pig
   To last you all the year.

OLD FATHER CHRISTMAS: Be there bread in your locker
   And sheep in your fold,
   A fire on the hearth.
   And good luck for your lot,
   Money in the pocket,
   And a pudding in the pot.

ST GEORGE: We fought as foes
>   With bloody blows
>   Through centuries of hatred.

DRAGON: I chaffed my teeth
>   On bones and meat
>   From victims I devoured.

TOGETHER: But now we'll retire
>   And sit by the fire
>   Eating hot tea cakes and butter
>   We'll sing and be merry
>   And drink the best sherry
>   And only the yule log will splutter.

FOOL: Our play is done, we must be gone.
>   We stay no longer here.
>   We wish you all, both great and small,
>   A happy bright New Year.

[*sings*]

>   Fast away the old year passes
>   Fa la, etc.
>   Hail the new, ye lads and lasses,
>   Fa la, etc [*Laughing, quaffing all together*]
>   Heedless of the wind and weather,
>   Fa la, etc

[*During this carol, the lights fade to one small hard circle, into which the* BOY *comes. He puts the bag down and sits on it, shivering. The snow starts to fall as* DOCTOR BALL *moves to the edge of the circle. He wraps a scarf around the* BOY'S *neck*]

DOCTOR BALL: On to the next town?

[*There is a long pause before the* BOY *nods. They mount their hobby-horses and ride off into the night*]

Fade out lights; fade in sound [*carols*].

END

Part Two:

RELIGIOUS PLAYS

BLACK NATIVITY

A Gospel-Song-Play

by Langston Hughes

CHARACTERS

(In order of appearance)

WOMAN

MAN

SINGERS [Townsfolk.]

NARRATOR

OLD WOMAN

FOUR SHEPHERDS [NED, ZED, TED, JED.]

Non-speaking roles:

JOSEPH

MARY

THREE WISE MEN [BALTHAZAR, MELCHIOR, CASPAR.]

TIME: *When Christ was born.*
SETS: *None—only a platform of various levels and a star, a single glowing star over a place that might be manger.*
MOODS: *reverence, awe, joy and jubilation.*

SONGS:
Act One: The Child Is Born
Joy To The World
My Way Is Cloudy
No Room At The Inn
Most Done Travelling
Oh, Jerusalem In The Morning
Poor Little Jesus
What You Gonna Name Your Baby?
Wasn't That A Mighty Day!
Joy To The World—Reprise
Christ Is Born
No-Good Shepherd Boy
Go Tell It On The Mountain
Rise Up, Shepherd, And Follow!
What Month Was Jesus Born In?
Sweet Little Jesus Boy
Oh, Come All Ye Faithful

Act Two: The Word Is Spread
Meetin' Here Tonight

Holy Ghost, Don't Leave Me
We Shall Be Changed
The Blood Saved Me
Leak In The Building
Nobody Like The Lord
His Will Be Done
Said I Wasn't Gonna Tell Nobody
Get Away Jordan
Packin' Up
God Be With You

ACT ONE

[*Prelude: Organ Music. Voices are heard offstage as* MAN *and* WOMAN *enter.*]

[SONG: "JOY TO THE WORLD"]

WOMAN: JOY TO THE WORLD!

THE LORD HAS COME!

LET EARTH RECEIVE HER KING.

LET EVERY HEART PREPARE HIS ROOM.

MAN: LET HEAVEN AND NATURE SING.

(PILGRIMS *enter down aisles to join* WOMAN *and* MAN *on stage.*]

SINGERS: JOY TO THE WORLD!

THE LORD HAS COM—

LET EARTH RECEIVE HER KING...

[*Light spots* NARRATOR *at side of stage.*]

NARRATOR: IT CAME TO PASS IN THOSE DAYS, that there went out a decree from Caesar Augustus that all the world should be taxed. And this taxing was first made when Cyrenius was governor of Syria. And all went to be taxed, everyone into his own city.
[*The sunset lights left stage as* MARY *and* JOSEPH *enter.*]

And Joseph also went up from Galilee to be taxed—out of the city of Nazareth into Judea, unto the city of David which is called

Bethlehem—with his wife, Mary, being great with child…"I think—oh, Joseph—I think my time's most come."

(SONG: "MY WAY'S CLOUDY"]

SINGERS: OH BRETHREN, MY WAY'S CLOUDY

SEND ONE ANGEL DOWN!

WOMAN: THERE'S FIRE IN THE EAST,

THERE'S FIRE IN THE WEST,

THERE'S FIRE AMONG

THE METHODISTS.

SATAN'S MAD AND I'M SO GLAD

HE MISSED THE SOUL HE THOUGHT HE HAD

THIS IS THE YEAR OF JUBILEE,

THE LORD HATH COME TO SET US FREE.

SINGERS: OH BRETHREN, MY WAY'S CLOUDY,

SEND ONE ANGEL DOWN!

[*Almost, but not quite beneath the star,* JOSEPH *knocks repeatedly at the door.* MARY, *too tired to stand any longer, sinks to the roadway. An irate* INNKEEPERS's *words are heard.*]

NARRATOR: "I have no room! Didn't I tell you no, before? Why do you come back? What do you keep knocking for? My inn's full. I've got no room for you and that woman there. This is no hospital. I keep no midwives about. I'm sorry, but there's no place here. No room! No, I say, no!"

SINGERS: OH BRETHREN, MY WAY'S CLOUDY.

SEND ONE ANGEL DOWN!

NARRATOR: No room! No room at the inn! No room at the rich fine hotel. No room!

[JOSEPH *lifts* MARY *to her feet. They struggle on, wandering through street after street searching for a place to stay.*

OLD WOMAN: Did you hear about it—a woman named Mary, they won't let her in the hotel?

WOMAN: Ain't that a shame?

OLD WOMAN: Did you hear about it? Big, rich, free place-and no room for a poor woman to have her child! Did you-all hear?

WOMAN: Ain't it a shame!

[SONG: "NO ROOM AT THE INN"]

WOMAN: IT WAS ACCORDING TO THE WORD,

THERE WAS A VIRGIN GIRL.

YOU KNOW THE MOTHER OF JESUS,

SHE WAS WANDERING AROUND AT NIGHT.

SHE WAS TRYING TO FIND A HOME

FOR THE SAVIOUR TO BE BORN,

BUT THERE WAS NO ROOM AT THE HOTEL.

SINGERS: NO ROOM, THERE WAS NO ROOM

AT THE HOTEL! NO ROOM!

OH, LORD, NO ROOM!

IT WAS THE TIME FOR THE SAVIOUR TO BE BORN

BUT THERE WAS NO ROOM AT THE HOTEL.

NARRATOR: No room. No room for Mary anywhere! No room for Joseph. No room. In all the great city of Bethlehem, no room. The night is late. The air is cold. The doors are locked. The lights are out. Good folks have gone to bed. The streets are deserted. "I can't! Oh, Joseph, I can't go on."

[SONG: "MOST DONE TRAVELLING"]

SINGERS: POOR MARY'S ON THE ROAD-

MOST DONE TRAVELING!

I'M BOUND TO CARRY

MY SOUL TO THE LORD!

NARRATOR: They are strangers here. Her time has almost come. Joseph does not know what to do, and in this place he has no friends. "Joseph! Joseph, I must lie down now. I must! Oh, I...Oh, no! I can't go farther! No! No...I can't."Joseph begs, "Wait! Wait here, I'll find a place."

SINGERS: POOR JOSEPH'S ON THE ROAD-

MOST DONE TRAVELLING!

I'M BOUND TO CARRY

MY SOUL TO THE LORD!

[MARY *sits alone on the curb as the song dies and a new song begins.*]

[SONG: "OH, JERUSALEM IN THE MORNING"]

SINGERS: MARY, MARY, WHAT IS THE MATTER?

OH, JERUSALEM IN THE MORNING!

OH, POOR JOSEPH, WHAT IS THE MATTER?

OH, JERUSALEM IN THE MORNING!

NIGHT IS CHILLY, WHAT IS THE MATTER?

OH, JERUSALEM IN THE MORNING!

OH, POOR MARY, WHAT IS THE MATTER?

OH, JERUSALEM IN THE MORNING!

COWS A-LOWING, WHAT IS THE MATTER?

OH, JERUSALEM IN THE MORNING!

SHEEP A-BAAING! WHAT IS THE MATTER?

OH, JERUSALEM IN THE MORNING!

OXEN A-BAWLING! WHAT IS THE MATTER?

OH, JERUSALEM IN THE MORNING!

OH, POOR MARY, WHAT IS THE MATTER?

OH, JERUSALEM IN THE MORNING!

NARRATOR: And so it was that her days were accomplished that she should be delivered. And she brought forth her first born son, wrapped him in swaddling clothes, and laid him in a manger—for there was no room for them in the inn.

[*The* WOMEN *among the* SINGERS *appear in the shadows lamenting.*]

[SONG: "POOR LITTLE JESUS"]

WOMEN: POOR LITTLE JESUS,

BORN ON CHRISTMAS

AND LAID IN A MANGER

WASN'T THAT A PITY AND A SHAME?

POOR LITTLE JESUS, SON OF MARY,

DIDN'T HAVE NO CRADLE.

WASN'T THAT A PITY AND A SHAME?

LORD, WASN'T THAT A PITY AND A SHAME?

NARRATOR: For unto us a Child is born, unto us a Son is given and the government shall be upon His shoulders, and His name shall be called Wonderful, Counselor, All Mighty God, The Everlasting Father, The Prince of Peace.

[SONG: "WHAT YOU GONNA NAME YOUR BABY?"]

WOMAN: MARY, MARY WHAT YOU GONNA NAME

THAT PRETTY LITTLE BABY?

GLORY BE TO THE NEW BORN KING!

NARRATOR: Some call Him one thing—she's gonna call Him Jesus.

WOMAN: SOME CALL HIM ONE THING.

SHE'S GONNA CALL HIM JESUS.

SINGERS: GLORY BE TO THE NEW BORN KING!

NARRATOR: Some call Him Jesus—she's gonna call Him Emanuel.

WOMAN: SOME CALL HIM JESUS.

SHE'S GONNA CALL HIM EMANUEL.

SINGERS: GLORY BE TO THE NEW BORN KING.

NARRATOR: Some call Him Emanuel—she's gonna call Him Wonderful.

WOMAN: SOME CALL HIM EMANUEL.

SHE'S GONNA CALL HIM WONDERFUL.

SINGERS: GLORY BE TO THE NEW BORN KING!

NARRATOR: Some call Him Wonderful—she's gonna call Him the Prince of Peace.

WOMAN: SOME CALL HIM WONDERFUL.

SHE'S GONNA CALL HIM PRINCE OF PEACE.

SINGERS: GLORY BE TO THE NEW BORN KING!

NARRATOR: Some call Him Prince of Peace— she's gonna call Him Jesus.

WOMAN: SOME CALL HIM PRINCE OF PEACE.

SHE'S GONNA CALL HIM JESUS.

SINGERS: GLORY TO THE NEW BORN KING!

NARRATOR: And his name shall be called Jesus.

[*Enter a group of* PILGRIMS.]

[SONG:"WASN'T THAT A MIGHTY DAY!"]

SINGERS: WASN'T THAT A MIGHTY DAY,

WHEN JESUS CHRIST WAS BORN!

STAR SHONE IN THE EAST,

WHEN JESUS CHRIST WAS BORN!

THE ANGEL CAME FROM ABOVE,

WHEN JESUS CHRIST WAS BORN.

NARRATOR: Yes, His name shall be called Jesus.

[SONG: "JOY TO THE WORLD" REPRISE]

SINGERS: JOY TO THE WORLD,

SO GLAD THE LORD IS COME!

LET EARTH RECEIVE HER KING.

LET EVERY HEART PREPARE HIS ROOM,

AND HEAVEN AND NATURE SING.

JOY TO THE WORLD,

HALLELUJAH, THE SAVIOUR REIGNS!

LET WE THEIR SONGS EMPLOY,

WHILE FIELDS AND FLOODS,

ROCKS, HILLS, AND PLAINS,

REPEAT THE SOUNDING JOY.

JOY TO THE WORLD,

THE LORD IS COME.

NARRATOR: Rejoice! Rejoice, for the Lord is come!

[SONG: "CHIRST IS BORN"]

SINGERS: CHRIST IS BORN IN THE LAND OF JUDEA

    CHRIST IS BORN! CHRIST IS BORN!

    BORN OF THE HOLY VIRGIN MARY!

    CHRIST IS BORN! CHRIST IS BORN!

    PRETTY LITTLE HOLY BABY!

    CHRIST IS BORN! CHRIST IS BORN!

    WHY DON'T YOU COME ON TO THE MANGER?

    COME AND ADORE THE LITTLE STRANGER

    BABY WHO NEVER HAD NO CRADLE,

    AND HIS ONLY BED A MANGER

    SEE THE WISE MEN FROM AFAR,

    ALL WERE GUIDED BY A STAR.

    HERALD ANGELS LEFT FROM GLORY

    AND CAME TO EARTH TO TELL THE STORY.

    TELL THE STORY OF HIS GLORY—

    CHRIST IS BORN! CHRIST IS BORN!

    [A roadside leading to the pastures. Four SHEPHERDS *enter; their talk leads into song.]*

NED: My wife wonders why I have to tend sheep at night.

JED: So does mine. The old shepherds always get the best shifts—the day shift.

ZED: It's cold, dag-nab it! And I've got no coat.

JED: You're ragged as a goat herd without a goat.

    [Song-speech into song.]

NED: I've got a coat—

[SONG: "NO-GOOD SHEPHERD BOY!"]

NED: BUT YOU WON'T GET MINE-

WASTING ALL YOUR MONEY
ON WOMEN AND WINE.
NO-GOOD SHEPHERD!

JED: NO-GOOD SHEPHERD!

TRIO: NO-GOOD SHEPHERD BOY!

ZED: Aw, get off of it! Are you not your brother's keeper?

NED: No, not when my brother—
AIN'T NOTHING BUT A SLEEPER
YOU RUN AROUND ALL DAY,
SLEEP ON YOUR JOB ALL NIGHT.

JED: IF YOU GONNA BE A SHEPHERD,
BE A SHEPHERD RIGHT.

TED: I hear you lost a ewe and a lamb?

ZED: I LOST MORE THAN THAT-
I LOST A RAM.

TED: What you gonna do when Master counts his sheep?

ZED: JUST GET UNDER A TREE
AND GO TO SLEEP.

TED: WHAT GOOD IS A SHEPHERD
THAT GOES TO SLEEP?
SUPPOSE A WOLF WOULD COME,
AND STEAL YOUR LAMBS AWAY,
WHAT YOU GONNA TELL
YOUR MASTER NEXT DAY?

NED: IF YOU TELL A LIE
YOUR TONGUE MIGHT SLIP.

JED: IF YOU TELL THE TRUTH,
HE MIGHT BUST YOU IN THE LIP.

TRIO: NO-GOOD SHEPHERD!

NED: SLEEPY-HEADED SHEPHERD!

TRIO: NO-GOOD SHEPHERD BOY!

NED: YOU CAN'T PREACH ONE THING
THEN UP AND DO ANOTHER,

TRIO: LOOK OUT FOR YOURSELF
BUT TRY TO CON YOUR BROTHER.
NO-GOOD SHEPHERD!
NO-GOOD SHEPHERD!

ZED: I'm a—

ALL: NO NO-GOOD SHEPHERD BOY!

TRIO: WHAT GOOD IS A SHEPHERD
THAT CAN'T HERD SHEEP?.

TED: FOR IF YOU LOSE A EWE
THEN YOU CAN LOSE A LAMB.

NED: IF YOU LOSE A LAMB
YOU CAN LOSE A RAM.

JED: IF YOU DO NOT GET
YOUR LOST SHEEP BACK,
THEN YOUR MASTER MIGHT
GET MAD AND GIVE YOU THE SACK.

TRIO: NO-GOOD SHEPHERD!
LAZY OLD SHEPHERD!
NO-GOOD SHEPHERD BOY!
YOU CAN'T SIT AROUND
AND NEVER DO YOUR WORK WELL,
SAY YOU'RE HEAVEN BOUND
WHEN YOU KNOW YOU'RE BOUND FOR HELL!
NO-GOOD SHEPHERD!
NO-GOOD SHEPHERD!
NO-GOOD SHEPHERD BOY!

ZED: JUST A NO-GOOD SHEPHERD BOY!

[ZED *shrugs his shoulders, sits down and pulls a flute from the folds of his ragged clothing. But his melody is a series of screeches. The other* SHEPHERDS *put their hands over their ears in protest and cry aloud.*]

NED: WHAT GOOD IS A SHEPHERD
    WHO CAN'T PLAY A FLUTE?
JED: AND HOW IN THE WORLD
    CAN YOU ATTRACT A GIRL
    WHEN YOU SMELL LIKE SHEEP
    AND YOUR FLUTE, IT WON'T BEEP?
NED: AND WHAT GOOD'S THE MOON
    OR NIGHTS IN JUNE
    WHEN YOU'RE OUT OF KEY
    AND YOUR FLUTE'S OUT OF TUNE?
TRIO: NO-GOOD SHEPHERD!
    RAGGEDY SHEPHERD,
    NO-GOOD SHEPHERD BOY,
    YOU CAN'T SWEET-TALK GIRLS,
    PULL TRICKS YOU KNOW AIN'T NICE
    BE A SNAKE IN THE GRASS,
    UNLESS YOU PAY THE PRICE.
    NO-GOOD SHEPHERD!
    NO-GOOD SHEPHERD!
    NO-GOOD SHEPHERD BOY!
ZED: Oh, poor me!
    [ZED *rises to sing dolefully.*]
    WHAT GOOD IS A SHEPHERD
    THAT'S GOT NO GIRL?
    MARY AND HER LAMB
    HAD FLEECE AS WHITE AS SNOW.
    I SAID, *LOVE ME BABE.*
    BUT SHE SAID, *NO! NO! NO!*
    SAID, YOU'LL HOLD MY HAND,
    YOU'LL KISS MY EAR—
    BUT WHEN I'M IN NEED

I CAN'T FIND YOU NOWHERE NEAR!

NO-GOOD SHEPHERD!

JIVE-TALKING SHEPHERD!

TRIO: NO-GOOD SHEPHERD BOY!

ZED: She said—

YOU MEN SWEET-TALK GIRLS,

DO THINGS YOU KNOW AIN'T NICE-

DIRTY SNAKES IN THE GRASS,

YOU MAKE A GIRL THINK TWICE!

NO-GOOD SHEPHERD!

she said—

TRIO: HEART-BREAKING SHEPHERD!

ZED: NO! NO-GOOD SHEPHERD BOY!

Oh, she gave me down-the-country—that woman did!

TED: It's a sin to betray a girl, Zed.

NED: And you are nothing but a sinner! Zed, you're a sinner!

[ZED *hangs his head in shame as* TED *becomes serious.*]

TED: WHAT GOOD IS A SHEPHERD

THAT DON'T KNOW GOD?

TRIO: WHEN OLD DEATH WILL COME

TO TAKE YOUR SOUL AWAY,

HOW YOU GONNA FACE

SAINT PETER THAT DAY?

TED: IF YOU LIVE IN SIN

WHEN LIFE DOTH END,

THEN WHO WILL YOU HAVE BUT

THE DEVIL FOR YOUR FRIEND?

TRIO: NO-GOOD SHEPHERD!

SIN-LOVING SHEPHERD!

NO-GOOD SHEPHERD BOY!

YOU CAN'T DANCE AND BALL

AND HOLLER, *HUH! COME SEVEN!*

THEN WHEN DEATH COMES BY,

EXPECT TO GO TO HEAVEN.

NO-GOOD SHEPHERD!

NO-GOOD SHEPHERD!

NO-GOOD SHEPHERD BOY!

[*There is sudden thunder, a flash of light. Then a distant trumpet sounds. The* SHEPHERDS *are astounded.* ZED *backs away in fright and* ALL *flee.* BLACKOUT. *The spotlight centers on the* NARRATOR *as the scene changes. Lights fade, only* NARRATOR *is visible.*]

NARRATOR: Hear again the Christmas story—

Christ is born in all His glory.

Baby laid in manger dark,

Lighting ages with the spark

Of innocence that is the Child,

Trusting all within His smile.

Tell again the Christmas story

With the halo of His glory;

Halo born of humbleness

By the breath of cattle blest,

By the poverty of stall

Where a bed of straw is all,

By a door closed to the poor.

Christ is born on earthen floor

In a stable with no lock—

Yet kingdoms tremble at the shock

Of a King in swaddllling clothes

At an address no one knows

Because there is no hotel sign—

Nothing but a star divine,

Nothing but a halo bright

About His young head in the night.

Mary's Son in manger born!

Music of the Angel's horn!

Mary's Son in straw and glory!

Wonder of the Christmas story!

[Now the Star shines very brightly.]

[SONG: "GO TELL IT ON THE MOUNTAIN"]

WOMAN: GO TELL IT ON THE MOUNTAIN,

OVER THE HILLS AND EVERYWHERE!

GO TELL IT ON THE MOUNTAIN

THAT JESUS CHRIST IS BORN!

[*The* WOMAN *carries the news to the whole city and everyone joins in the jubilation.*]

SINGERS: GO TELL IT ON THE MOUNTAIN,

OVER THE HILLS AND EVERYWHERE!

GO TELL IT ON THE MOUNTAIN

THAT JESUS CHRIST IS BORN!

WOMAN: AN ANGEL CAME FROM GLORY

TO HAIL THE SAVIOUR'S BIRTH,

AND THEN A LIGHT FROM HEAVEN

SHONE ON THE HEAVENLY PLACE.

SINGERS: GO TELL IT ON THE MOUNTAIN,

OVER THE HILLS AND EVERYWHERE!

GO TELL IT ON THE MOUNTAIN

THAT JESUS CHRIST IS BORN!

[*The light fades to a spot on a* SHEPHERD *alone on a hilltop.*]

NARRATOR: And there were in the same country shepherds abiding in the field, keeping watch over their flocks by night. And lo, the angel of the Lord came upon them, and the glory of the Lord shown round about them, and they were sore afraid. And the angel said unto them, "Fear not for behold, I bring you good tidings of your great joy which shall be to all people. For unto you is born this day in the city of David, a Savior which is Christ the Lord."

SINGERS: WHILE SHEPHERDS KEEP THEIR WATCH
O'ER SILENT FLOCKS BY NIGHT,
BEHOLD THROUGHOUT THE HEAVENS
THERE SHONE A HOLY LIGHT.
GO TELL IT ON THE MOUNTAIN
OVER THE HILLS AND EVERYWHERE
GO TELL IT ON THE MOUNTAIN
THAT JESUS CHRIST IS BORN.

WOMAN: THE SHEPHERDS FEARED AND TREMBLED
WHEN, LO, ABOVE THE EARTH
RANG OUT THE ANGELS' CHORUS
THAT HAILED THE SAVIOUR'S BIRTH.

SINGERS: GO TELL IT ON THE MOUNTAIN
OVER THE HILLS AND EVERYWHERE
GO TELL IT ON THE MOUNTAIN
THAT JESUS CHRIST IS BORN.

NARRATOR: And this shall be a sign unto you: Ye shall find the Babe wrapped in swaddling clothes, lying in a manger. And suddenly there was with the angel a multitude of heavenly hosts praising God, and saying: "Glory be to God in the highest, and on earth, peace, good will toward men!"

[SONG: "RISE UP, SHEPHERD, AND FOLLOW!"]

SINGERS: THERE'S A STAR IN THE EAST
ON CHRISTMAS MORN.
RISE UP, SHEPHERD, AND FOLLOW!
IT WILL LEAD TO THE PLACE
WHERE THE SAVIOUR'S BORN.
RISE UP, SHEPHERD, AND FOLLOW!
IF YOU TAKE GOOD HEED
TO THE ANGEL'S WORDS AND
RISE UP, SHEPHERD, AND FOLLOW

YOU'LL FORGET YOUR FLOCKS,
YOU'LL FORGET YOUR HERDS.
RISE UP, SHEPHERD, AND FOLLOW!
LEAVE YOUR SHEEP, LEAVE YOUR LAMBS.
LEAVE YOUR EWES, AND LEAVE YOUR RAMS
RISE UP, SHEPHERD, AND FOLLOW—
FOLLOW THE STAR OF BETHLEHEM.
RISE UP, SHEPHERD, AND FOLLOW!

NARRATOR: Look! Look there at the star!

I—I, just a poor shepherd-
I, among the least,
I will arise and take
A journey to the East.
But what shall I bring.
As a gift for the King?
Shall I bring a song,
A song that I will sing?
A song for the King,
In the manger?
Watch out for my flocks!
Do not let them stray.
I am going on a journey
Far, far away.
But what shall I bring.
As a gift for the Child?
What. shall I bring to the Manger?
Shall I bring a lamb,
Gentle, meek and mild,
A lamb for the Child
In the manger?
Very poor I am

But I know there is

A King in Bethlehem.

What shall I bring

As a gift just for Him?

What shall I bring

To the manger?

Shall I bring my heart—

And give my heart to Him?

I will bring my heart

To the manger.

[*Light fades as the* SHEPHERD *begins his journey toward the star. The* SINGERS *continue joyously in darkness.*]

[SONG: "WHAT MONTH WAS JESUS BORN IN?"]

SINGERS: JUST TELL ME WHEN WAS JESUS BORN?
THE LAST MONTH OF THE YEAR.
WAS IT JANUARY, FEBRUARY, MARCH, APRIL, MAY
JUNE, JULY, AUGUST, SEPTEMBER, OCTOBER, NOVEMBER,
THE TWENTY-FIFTH DAY OF DECEMBER-
THE LAST MONTH OF THE YEAR.
HE WAS BORN OF THE VIRGIN MARY,
WRAPPED IN SWADDLING CLOTHES
AND LAIN IN A HOLY MANGER
ON THE TWENTY-FIFTH DAY OF DECEMBER-
THE LAST MONTH OF THE YEAR.

[*The* VIRGIN *enters with the* CHILD.]

NARRATOR: And so the news spread, and the people heard, and the people came to see Him—sweet little Jesus Boy, sleeping in a stable among the swine.

[*A* WOMAN *stands above the seated* MOTHER *and* CHILD.]

[SONG: "SWEET LITTLE JESUS BOY"]

WOMAN: SWEET LITTLE JESUS BOY,
    THEY MADE YOU BE BORN IN A MANGER,
    SWEET LITTLE HOLY CHILD,
    DIDN'T KNOW WHO YOU WAS
    DIDN'T KNOW YOU COME TO SAVE US, LORD,
    TO TAKE OUR SINS AWAY.
    OUR EYES WERE BLIND,
    WE COULDN'T SEE—
    WE DIDN'T KNOW WHO YOU WAS.
    LONG TIME AGO YOU WAS BORN,
    BORN IN A MANGER LOW.
    SWEET LITTLE HOLY CHILD!
    THE WORLD TREATS YOU MEAN, LORD,
    TREATS ME MEAN, TOO—
    BUT THAT'S HOW THINGS IS DOWN HERE.
    WHERE WE DON'T KNOW WHO YOU IS.
    YOU DONE TOLD US HOW,
    AND WE BEEN TRYING.
    MASTER, YOU DONE SHOWED US HOW
    EVEN WHEN YOU WAS DYING.
    JUST SEEMS LIKE WE CAN'T DO RIGHT.
    LOOK HOW WE DONE TREATED YOU.
    WELL, PLEASE, FORGIVE US, LORD.
    WE DIDN'T KNOW IT WAS YOU.
    SWEET LITTLE JESUS BOY,
    BORN LONG TIME AGO.
    SWEET LITTLE HOLY CHILD,
    WE DIDN'T KNOW WHO YOU WAS.

NARRATOR: They shall call His name Jesus, for he shall save His people
    from their sins. They shall call His name which being interpreted is,

God is with us, Jesus, Lord, Emanuel. Now when Jesus was born in Bethlehem of Judea in the days of Herod the King, behold, there came Men from the East saying, "Where is He that is Born King Of the Jews? For we have seen His star in the East and have come to worship Him."

[*The* THREE KINGS *enter down the aisle as the* SINGERS *burst into song and there is a glare of light.*]

[SONG: "OH, COME ALL YE FAITHFUL"]

WOMAN: OH, COME ALL YE FAITHFUL,

JOYFUL AND TRIUMPHANT!

OH, COME YE, OH, COME YE, TO BETHLEHEM.

COME AND BEHOLD HIM,

BORN THE KING OF ANGELS.

[*The* WISE MEN, *presenting their gifts, bow down before the* CHILD *as song fills the night and the* SINGERS *surround the manger.*]

SINGERS: OH, COME LET US ADORE HIM!

OH, COME LET US ADORE HIM!

OH, COME LET US ADORE HIM-

CHRIST THE LORD!

NARRATOR: It all began that first Christmas in Bethlehem when the star shone over the manger and there was born in the city of David, a Savior whose name was Christ the Lord.

SINGERS: AMEN!...AMEN!....AMEN!

End Act One

ACT TWO

[*The lights come up on two bands of* CHRISTIANS *entering from either side, marching in time to the music, as the* NARRATOR *sits to one side.*]

[SONG: "MEETIN' HERE TONIGHT"]

SINGERS: THERE'S A MEETIN' HERE TONIGHT,

MEETIN' HERE TONIGHT,

MEETIN' ON THE OLD CAMPGROUND.

NARRATOR: And so the star of Bethlehem became a symbol. The manger became a church. The three kings became Princes of the Church. Wise men became its ministers. The heavenly hosts became the singers of God's praises all over the world—for almost two thousand years ago now in the Bethlehem of Judea, Christ was born—born to preach to the elders in the temple—to pass the miracle of the loaves and fishes—to turn the water into wine—to heal the sick and raise the dead—to cause the lame to walk and the blind to see. He was crucified, dead, and was buried, and on the third day arose from the dead, ascended into heaven and sitteth at the right hand of God, the Father—who gave His only begotten Son that man might have eternal life. Now, today, here in this place, nineteen centuries removed from Bethlehem—in a land far across the sea from Judea-we sing His songs and glorify His name. This church where you see us gathered—this gospel church where HIS word is spread—is but an extension of His manger. Those gathered here are His worshippers who have come tonight to make—as the Bible says—a joyful noise unto the Lord.

[*Exit* NARRATOR *as the* ELDER *comes to center.*]

SINGERS: THIS IS THE WAY WE SING ON THE OLD CAMPGROUND.

THIS IS THE WAY WE SING ON THE OLD CAMPGROUND.

ELDER: Praise God' Bless His name! There's a meeting here tonight, oh, yes! We've come to spread His word and glorify His name. And what shall we tell the world? Tell the world that Jesus was born in Bethlehem! Tell the world that Christ was born to save this earth from sin. Tell the world that this sweet little Jesus-Boy was born to save you-and to save me—to show us how to find the path of salvation, earn a right to the tree of life—to show us how to turn our eyes to God—to show the nations how to beat their swords into plowshares. Yes! That's why He came! He came to make the lion lie down with the lamb, the mighty to be meek, and the meek to be lifted up! Oh yes! Jesus came to ride me on the wings of His glory, to take me up in the Chariot of His love, to wrap me in His glorious glory.

[SONG: "HOLY GHOST, DON'T LEAVE ME"]

SINGERS: OH, HOLY GHOST, PLEASE DON'T LEAVE ME,
GUIDE ME ON MY WAY.
HOLY GHOST, DON'T LEAVE ME,—
JUST GUIDE ME ON MY WAY.

WOMAN: We're going to Sing for you now, "We Shall Be, Changed—In The Twinkling Of An Eye!" Changed from mortal to immortality.

[SONG: "WE SHALL BE CHANGED"]

SINGERS: WE SHALL BE CHANGED! WE SHALL BE
CHANGED!
CHANGED FROM MORTALS TO IMMORTALITY
IN THE TWINKLING OF AN EYE.
I'LL SHOW YOU A MYSTERY—
WE SHALL NOT ALL SLEEP,
BUT BE CHANGED IMMEDIATELY—
IN THE TWINKLING OF AN EYE.
WHEN THAT FIRST TRUMPET SOUNDS,
ALL THE DEAD IN CHRIST SHALL RISE
WE'LL MEET JESUS IN THE SKIES-
IN THE TWINKLING OF AN EYE.
WE'LL SHAKE OFF MORTAL,
PUT ON IMMORTALITY.
DEATH WILL BE SWALLOWED UP IN
VICTORY—
IN THE TWINKLING OF AN EYE.
IF A MAN DIES
AND HE DIES SERVING THE LORD
HE SHALL LIVE AGAIN—
IN THE TWINKLING OF AN EYE
I TELL YOU, WE SHALL BE CHANGED!

WE SHALL BE CHANGED! CHANGED FROM MORTALS
TO IMMORTALITY
IN THE TWINKLING OF AN EYE!

WOMAN: One day when I was lost Jesus bled and died upon the cross.
That's why I know it was His blood—yes, it was—that saved me.

[SONG: "THE BLOOD SAVED ME"]

SINGERS: I KNOW IT WAS THE BLOOD,
I KNOW IT WAS THE BLOOD SAVED ME.
ONE DAY WHEN I WAS LOST,
JESUS DIED UPON THE CROSS.
I KNOW IT WAS THE BLOOD SAVED ME.
HE SET THE SINNER FREE FROM SIN.
JESUS CAME AND TOOK US IN.
I KNOW IT WAS THE BLOOD SAVED ME.
WHEN THEY WHIPPED HIM UP THE HILL,
HE NEVER SAID A WORD.
THE DAY THE WORLD STOOD STILL,
HE NEVER SAID A WORD
WHEN THEY HUNG HIM WAY UP HIGH,
JESUS NEVER SAID A WORD.
THEN THEY PIERCED HIM IN THE SIDE.
OH, HE NEVER SAID A WORD.
CAN'T YOU SEE HIM HANGING THERE?
HE WAS IN PAIN AND IN DESPAIR.
I KNOW IT WAS THE BLOOD,
I KNOW IT WAS THE BLOOD SAVED ME.

ELDER: Jesus died upon the cross that I might have life, and have it more
abundantly. Yes, he did! But we ought to try harder to deserve God's
love, and goodness. We ought to look inside ourselves and see if we
need fixing, need any personal repair work done. I examined myself
one day, myself and my surrounding, and—

[SONG: "'LEAK IN THE BUILDING"]

SINGERS: I FOUND A LEAK IN MY BUILDING
 AND MY SOUL HAS GOT TO MOVE—
 BUT I THANK GOD I HAVE ANOTHER BUILDING
 NOT MADE BY HANDS.

ELDER: ONE DAY AS I WAS WALKING ALL ALONE
 I HEARD A VOICE SPEAK TO. ME,
 LOOKED ALL AROUND BUT I SAW NO ONE
 THEN HE TOLD ME, "BEFORE I'M THROUGH
 I'M GOING TO TELL YOU WHAT TO DO."

SINGERS: OH, I THANK GOD I HAVE ANOTHER BUILDING.
 NOT MADE BY HANDS.

ELDER: FIXED MY LEAK IN THE BUILDING.
 I WENT ON MY KNEES IN PRAYER.
 I LAID MY FOUNDATION WHILE I WAS THERE.
 OH, YES! OH, YES! OH, YES! OH, YES!
 AND I BUILT MY WALLS WITH GRACE,
 I COVERED MY ROOF WITH FAITH,
 AND I BUILT MY DOORS WITH LOVE,
 AND I PLACED GOD'S NAME ABOVE,
 AND ABOUT THAT TIME,
 MY LANDLORD CAME.
 YOU OUGHT TO KNOW WHO I MEAN-
 MY GOD AND YOUR GOD!
 MY LORD AND YOUR LORD!
 HE SAID, "I'M PLEASED WITH WHAT YOU'VE DONE.
 AND YOUR RACE HAS BEEN WON.
 I'M HERE WITH YOUR KEY,
 AND I'VE GOT YOUR DEEDS WITH ME."

SINGERS: OH, I THANK GOD I HAVE ANOTHER BUILDING
 NOT MADE BY HANDS, NOT MADE BY HANDS.*

ELDER: Oh, yes, my soul had to move—but I moved with my hand in the hand of the Lord. I moved knowing that I may search the whole world over, but there's nobody like Him.

[SONG: "NOBODY LIKE THE LORD"]

SINGERS: THERE'S NOBODY LIKE THE LORD-

NOBODY LIKE THE LORD.*

YOU MAY SEARCH THIS WIDE WORLD

OVER AND OVER AGAIN,

BUT YOU WON'T FIND NOBODY LIKE HIM.

MOTHER'S MY FRIEND, FATHER'S MY FRIEND,

SISTER AND BROTHER, THEY ARE MY FRIENDS

BUT THEY CAN'T GO WITH ME EACH DAY

PROTECTING ME UNTIL THE END.

YES, YOU MAY SEARCH THE WIDE WORLD

OVER AND OVER AGAIN BUT YOU WON'T FIND NO-

BODY LIKE HIM.

NOBODY, NOBODY LIKE THE LORD!

ELDER: There's nobody like the Lord! No matter what we try to do, God is God all by himself. Sometimes we think he don't come when he ought to, but He's God, and he knows what we need, so he's always there on time. We tried him a long time ago and we know him. He supplied our every need. There's so many of us that are too busy complaining about things we already have that we should be thanking God for. We are so busy complaining that we overlook his goodness. There's so much to thank Him for—for the blood still running warm in our bodies when we get up each morning, for our loved ones, for the joy and beauty of living. If I were you, I'd thank Him while I have a chance. There was a man who complained about his shoes until he saw a man who had no feet. There was a woman who complained about her clothes until she saw someone on a bed of affliction and she thanked God for what she had. No matter what you think about things, God knows all, and His will must be done. Tell it in song, sister, tell it in song!

[SONG: "HIS WILL BE DONE"]

WOMAN: IT MATTERS NOT TO ME
IF AGAIN I NEVER SEE.
HIS WILL MUST BE DONE.
HE IS MY STAFF, HE IS MY ROD
WHEREVER MY FOOTSTEPS TROD,
HIS WILL MUST BE DONE.
IN THIS ETERNAL DARKNESS
THAT COVERS ME TODAY, I LIVE FOR MY SAVIOUR.
AND I'LL LET HIM HAVE HIS WAY.
MY LIFE IS IN GOD'S HANDS
AND I'LL MOVE AT HIS COMMAND,
HIS WILL MUST BE DONF,
IF AGAIN I NEVER SEE
GOD KNOWS WHAT'S BEST FOR ME.
HIS WILL MUST BE DONE,
LORD, WHEN I HAVE DONE ALL I CAN
I'LL BE STANDING RIGHT HERE
WAITING FOR YOU—
YOUR WILL MUST BE DONE.

ELDER: Let everything that has breath praise the Lord! Put your trust in Him. Talking about religion may kill your faith. People who really believe don't worry about it—because the Lord is going to make a way. Yes, He will! You know when I first got religion way back yonder in Alabama, I never will forget the day, seems like the trees were praising the Lord that day, seems like the sun was shining just for me. I don't know how it happened to happen so fast, but when I came to myself, I was seven and a half miles down the road. I don't know how I got there, but I was full of the spirit. The hand of God had touched me. I meant to keep my happiness to myself, but I couldn't.

[SONG: "SAID I WASN'T GONNA TELL NOBODY"]

SINGERS: I SAID I WASN'T GONNA TELL NOBODY-

BUT I JUST COULDN'T KEEP IT TO MYSELF,
WHAT THE LORD HAS DONE FOR ME.
YOU OUGHT TO HAVE BEEN THERE WHEN HE SAVED
MY SOUL
THAT SUNDAY MORNING
WHEN HE PUT MY NAME ON THE ROLL,
AND I STARTED WALKING,
AND I STARTED TALKING,
AND I STARTED SINGING,
AND I STARTED SHOUTING
ABOUT WHAT THE LORD HAS DONE FOR ME.

ELDER: I SAID I WASN'T GONNA TESTIFY—
BUT I COULDN'T KEEP IT TO MYSELF
WHAT THE LORD HAS DONE FOR ME.

WOMAN: I SAID I WASN'T GONNA SHOUT FOR JOY
BUT I COULDN'T KEEP IT TO MYSELF
WHAT THE LORD HAS DONE FOR ME.

SINGERS: I SAID I WASN'T GONNA SING MY SONG
BUT I COULDN'T KEEP IT TO MYSELF
WHAT THE LORD HAS DONE FOR ME.

[*General shouting.*]

VOICES: Bless God Hallelujah! Amen! Yes!

SINGERS: IF IT WASN'T FOR JESUS
MY SOUL, YOUR SOUL WOULD BE LOST.

WOMAN: Is everybody happy? Praise the Lord! I want to tell you tonight that God is real in my life. And I'm thanking Him this evening for keeping me. For one of these days, we all will come to the end of our journey. And when we come to the end of our journey, we must come down to the chilly banks of Jordan. And when I get there I don't want nobody to stop me. I want to be able to cross over to see my Lord.

[SONG: "GET AWAY, JORDAN"]

SINGERS: GET AWAY! GET AWAY, JORDAN!

GET AWAY! GET AWAY, CHILLY JORDAN!

GET BACK, GET WAY BACK, JORDAN.

I WANT TO CROSS OVER TO SEE MY LORD.

WOMAN: ONE DAY I WAS WALKING ALONE.

I HEARD A VOICE BUT I SAW NO ONE.

THE VOICE I HEARD SOUNDED SO SWEET,

IT RAN FROM MY HEAD TO THE SOLE OF MY
FEET.

IF YOU DON'T BELIEVE I'VE BEEN REDEEMED,

JUST FOLLOW ME DOWN TO JORDAN STREAM.

JORDAN WATER IS CHILLY AND COLD,

MAY CHILL THE BODY BUT NOT MY SOUL!

GET AWAY! GET AWAY, JORDAN!

I WANT TO CROSS OVER TO SEE MY LORD!

WOMAN: I know there's nothing for Christians to be afraid of when we
come to Jordan and cross over into the Promised Land. That's why
I'm packing up—getting ready to go, ahead of time—because I'm
ready, and I have no fear.

[SONG: "PACKING UP"]

SINGERS: I'M ON MY WAY TO NEW JERUSALEM

WHERE THE SUN NEVER GOES DOWN.

EVERY DAY IN PREPARATION-

PACKING UP GETTING READY TO GO.

I'M PACKING, PACKING, GETTING READY TO
GO.

I GOT MY SWORD, I GOT MY SHIELD...

GOT MY TICKET, SIGNED AND SEALED,

SO I'M PACKING UP, GETTING READY,

PACKING UP, GETTING READY TO GO.

ELDER: And it all began with that first Star in Bethlehem almost two thousand years ago—the Star that brought us to the Manger to kneel at the feet of Christ.

[SONG: "GOD BE WITH YOU"]

SINGERS: GOD BE WITH YOU, GOD BE WITH YOU,

GOD BE WITH YOU UNTIL WE MEET AGAIN.

IF WE NEVER MEET HERE AGAIN,

WE SHALL MEET IN THE END.

GOD BE WITH YOU UNTIL WE MEET AGAIN.

GOOD-NIGHT!

CURTAIN

The Shepherds of Saint Francis
The Story of the First Christmas Pageant in 1223

by Lowell Swortzell

THE SHEPHERDS OF SAINT FRANCIS

CHARACTERS

BROTHER FRANCIS	the famous Friar, in his early 40s
LEONE	a villager, just turning 20
A SHEPHERD	in his 20s
HIS WIFE	about the same age
THE SQUIRE	a robust man of middle years or older
THE LORD OF THE MANOR	in his late 50s or early 60s
THE LADY OF THE MANOR	his wife of similar age
A FARMER'S WIFE	in her 40s

Roles in the Pageant

JOSEPH	played by the Shepherd
MARY	played by the Shepherd's Wife
AN ANGEL OF THE LORD	played by the Farmer's Wife
SHEPHERD ONE	played by Leone
*SHEPHERD TWO	
*THE THREE WISE MEN	
KING HEROD	played by the Squire
SHEEP, COWS, DONKEYS, and GOATS	played by members of the audience

*These roles may be played either by actors cast by the director or by members of the audience recruited as they arrive for the performance. If the latter choice is made, Leone will guide them on stage, place them in their positions for the pageant and speak their lines. When members of the audience are used in these roles, they should not be costumed but appear in the clothes they are presently wearing.

TIME AND PLACE

December 1223

Near, in and around the town of Greccio, Italy.

THE SCENES

Scene One: In a church in a small Italian town

Scene Two: On the road to Greccio

Scene Three: In the Shepherd's hut

Scene Four: The council chamber of the Lord of the Manor

Scene Five: Inside and outside of the Shepherd's hut

SCENE ONE

AT RISE: Down the center aisle of a church, or of the space in which the play is being performed a FRIAR *sweeps his way toward the high altar. His broom is made of dried rushes, with a handle of a gnarled and knotted stick.* BROTHER FRANCIS, *now in his early forties, clearly enjoys what he is doing—sweeping vigorously.*

When he gets about halfway, LEONE, *a young native of the town, enters from the back and hurries to* BROTHER FRANCIS. *Over one shoulder he carries a bundle of clothes and in his arms he holds a pack of candles tied together by a heavy piece of string. His face is flushed with excitement and an eagerness to share some important news*

LEONE: Brother Francis, what are you doing?

FRANCIS: Isn't it apparent? Sweeping, vigorously.

LEONE: You mustn't.

FRANCIS: The congregation will be arriving in a few minutes. We aren't ready.

LEONE: Others can clean. Not you.

FRANCIS: I want to. Nothing pleases me more than a spotless church [*Sweeping faster.*]

LEONE: Then give me the broom.

FRANCIS: [*playfully*] Get your own. [*Using the broom as a weapon to hold* LEONE *off*] This one's mine.

LEONE: But I must talk to you, Brother Francis, before everyone gets here.

FRANCIS: After the service, my son, we'll have a nice long visit.

LEONE: It's *very* important.

FRANCIS: But can wait, I'm sure.

LEONE: No, Brother, I'm desperate to tell you something.

FRANCIS: What can be more important than to re-open this church after so many years?

LEONE: Yes, I know. A new building has risen from the ruins. [*Looking about and pointing.*] The walls freshly painted. The roof sealed and safe. Doors repaired. Windows replaced. The altar restored. It's a miracle.

FRANCIS: Of God's love and mankind's hard work. And no one in the village has done more than you, my son. You've earned my everlasting thanks.

LEONE: Do you really believe that, Brother Francis?

FRANCIS: Leone, have you ever known me to lie?

LEONE: Of course not. But—

FRANCIS: Something does trouble you!

LEONE: That's why we must talk. NOW. Before they come. It can't wait.

FRANCIS: Very well. But place those candles on the altar while I sweep here.

LEONE: [*as he inserts candles in holders throughout the altar*] Are you ready? Brace yourself.

FRANCIS: My broom will support me if I feel faint. Go ahead, tell me.

LEONE: Very well. Last night the Lord spoke to me in my dreams.

FRANCIS: No doubt to thank you for all you've done in His service. He must be very pleased to see this house is His own again.

LEONE: Perhaps He is. He didn't say so, at least not exactly in those words. Well, maybe He did. I'm not sure.

FRANCIS: What did He say, exactly? Tell me. *His* words.

LEONE: [*laboring each word*] He said that when you leave here today . . .

FRANCIS: I didn't know I was leaving . . . Today? Are you certain?

LEONE: Yes, right after the service . . . you're to move on to find others who need you. [*Proudly*] And *I* am to go with you.

FRANCIS: YOU! YOU!

LEONE: I was afraid you'd have this reaction.

FRANCIS: You're only a boy! Wet behind the ears.

LEONE: I'm as old as you were when you were called.

FRANCIS: You can't be, still living at home with your parents.

LEONE: You were living at home with your parents. It's no reason to refuse me.

FRANCIS: But I had no choice. God spoke to me. I had to obey.

LEONE: He's spoken to me, too. That's what I'm telling you!

FRANCIS: You're not even a priest!

LEONE: Neither were you when you began, Brother Francis. Have you forgotten?

FRANCIS: [*angered, he shakes his broom at* LEONE] Now just one minute, young man. What's going on here? How do you know so much about me?

LEONE: Your fame has spread far from Assisi, even to small towns like this. And the rest God told me.

FRANCIS: So you want to be famous? That's it! You want people to say, "Here comes the man from Assisi and his followers." "Aren't they weird?" "Aren't they strange?" "Just look at them."

LEONE: No, I want to come with you, and if I prove worthy, become one of your Brothers and do the Lord's work. You said I had earned your everlasting thanks.

FRANCIS: And so you have, dear boy. I'm touched by your offer to join me. And I must appear ungrateful when I say you can't accompany me. Yet I must.

LEONE: You couldn't possibly refuse the Lord. Not you, Brother Francis. [*He's on the verge of tears.*]

FRANCIS: Come over here, son. You're right. This is much more important than a well-swept floor. [*He puts his broom aside and places his arm around* LEONE'*s shoulder, comforting him.*] You must understand that you're needed here, to keep *this* church open and to keep *this* congregation coming, day after day, week after week. That's how you can help me.

LEONE: Others can do that. Now that you have showed them how.

FRANCIS: But you don't know what you ask. Just look at you, in your fine suit with gold buttons.

LEONE: The tailor will take it back I know him. [*He unbuttons and removes his jacket, stripping as fast as he can.*]

FRANCIS: You'd be embarrassed to go about dressed as I am.

LEONE: No, I wouldn't. I'll hold my head high, just as you do.

FRANCIS: My robe is patched on the inside as well as the outside. All over.

LEONE: So is mine. [*He takes a similar robe from the bundle and quickly puts it on, removing his trousers at the same time.*] And with this piece of string as a belt, I must look the way you did twenty years ago when you left home. [*He ties the string that had bound the candles around his waist and stands before* FRANCIS.]

FRANCIS: Amazing! My youthful mirror.

LEONE: And what do you see when you look at me?

FRANCIS: A young man, well fed, well supported by his parents, well respected *by* his friends, well adjusted to his world . . . a young man who deserves to remain so.

LEONE: Not at all. Look again. Before you stands a young man ready to give up his past for a life of poverty, to serve God by serving the poor, as a beggar . . .

FRANCIS: You don't know what it is to beg.

LEONE: Don't I? Then how did I get these candles? This altar has not been graced with candles since before I was born. Now look at them. Aren't they beautiful? [*Placing the last of them.*] God told me to get them, just as He once told you.

FRANCIS: What do you mean? He once told me?

LEONE: The first time you ever begged it was for candles to light a church.

FRANCIS: You know that? I've never told that to anyone. Did God really speak to you, Leone?

LEONE: [*imitating the way* FRANCIS *stated this earlier*] Have I ever lied to you, Brother Francis?

FRANCIS: Of course not. I'm ashamed to have doubted you, my boy. Forgive me.

LEONE: Now will you let me accompany you?

FRANCIS: My life's not always so easy as it's been here. Sometimes my brothers and I are stoned, driven off like thieves. Sometimes laughed at and called fools. Sometimes locked up in an asylum. Leone, there are those who think we're crazy.

LEONE: It doesn't matter. I don't care. I'll go where you go, and if it happens, I will suffer your pain. Gladly. And, also, like today, share your joy. Do whatever I must to make your message known far and wide.

FRANCIS: Not *my* message. I have no message but to obey God's command, fully, strictly, purely.

LEONE: [*kneeling before him*] That's all I ask. Please, Brother Francis. I'll give my best.

FRANCIS: All you ask? *All*, you understand, is nothing. My brothers and I have nothing and want nothing, nothing but hard work. We seek nothing except that we give to the poor. Keep nothing but the patches which cover our patches. We possess nothing but the peace of God. That's our all, our nothing that becomes our everything.

LEONE: You play with words. Remember I'm a village boy with much to learn.

FRANCIS: As I was a cloth merchant's son who learned from bolts of brocades and embroidery.

LEONE: What did they teach you?

FRANCIS: Vanity, pride and all the other deadly sins. Until one day when I was almost lost forever, God spoke to me.

LEONE: Just as He has spoken to me.

FRANCIS: Yes, I'm convinced He has. Then say farewell to your village and bid good-bye to your church. We'll set out as soon as the service ends. [*Shaking his hand.*] Welcome!

LEONE: Thank you, Brother Francis, thank you.

FRANCIS: God must have a special job for us. Did He give you any indication what it might be?

LEONE: Just to go with you. Nothing more.

FRANCIS: Clearly He thinks I need help. So, it must be something significant. [*Bells ring in the tower of the church. And soon murmuring voices can
be heard approaching.*]

LEONE: Listen, the people are coming to worship. To claim this church as
their own.

FRANCIS: Leone, let's open the doors and welcome them. But, first, take a
look at your work and be grateful.

LEONE: [*turning toward the altar*] I am. [*Bows.*]

FRANCIS: Thank you, Leone. Thank you, God. [*Bows. Then he picks up the
broom and takes it to the altar.*]

LEONE: What are you doing, Brother Francis? It's too late to sweep the
altar. They're here.

FRANCIS: Giving them the only thing I have. In honor of this great
moment. [*Kisses the broom and stands it upright on the altar.*]

LEONE: Look, it's your statue. The people will know it comes from you
and will think of you, always.

FRANCIS: Use it in good faith, my brethren. And pray for me and Leone
as we seek our new assignment. [*Bowing, they back away from the altar,
then turn and run down the aisle towards the doors and the gathering congregation As the bells continue to ring louder and louder, the lights fade,
leaving only the broom illuminated like a statue. After a few seconds, it, too,
disappears into the darkness.*]

SCENE TWO

*SCENE: A road through the hilly countryside, outside the small town of
Greccio, Italy. A cold, dark night. In the silence, we hear occasional "baas"
from the sheep occupying these slopes.*

AT RISE: BROTHER FRANCIS *and* LEONE *emerge out of the inkiness,
clearly not certain of their way. They pause, looking about.*

LEONE: Brother, the road divides just ahead. Which direction shall we
take?

FRANCIS: Let's go where we're needed most. [*Pauses to consider.*] What do you think? Left or right?

LEONE: Among the shepherds of these hills, both left *and* right, I suspect.

FRANCIS: Be patient. Something will tell us. You'll see.

LEONE: When I'm with you I don't doubt we'll find our way. But it's quiet now . . . [*Shivers*] . . . and cold . . .

FRANCIS: Cold, Leone?

LEONE: [*quickly changing his tune*] Not me, of course. No, no, no! I'm not complaining . . . not for a minute. How can I, when you wear no sandals at all? Forgive me.

FRANCIS: I simply tell my feet they're warm and they believe me.

LEONE: Mine are harder to convince. Even in sandals.

FRANCIS: Just walk like the animals. It's simple.

LEONE: But, Brother, animals have hooves to protect them.

FRANCIS: And I have the skin and bones God gave me. That's enough.

LEONE: You'll catch cold, my friend.

FRANCIS: Do sheep sneeze? Do cows cough? Neither do I.

LEONE: I gladly follow you throughout all of Italy and beyond, dear Brother, but, thus far, I must keep my sandals on.

FRANCIS: And so you should . . . until your feet feel God's warmth.

LEONE: [*shivering again*] Well, that doesn't seem likely on this December night.

FRANCIS: Don't be too certain. God may amaze you. He constantly astounds me.

LEONE: Has He told you which way to go? [*Points to the two roads ahead.*]

FRANCIS: He will. He will. Be patient. [*At this point, a small rock is thrown at them. It misses but nonetheless takes them by surprise.*]

LEONE: What was that?

FRANCIS: A stone. [*Picking it up.*] From over there.

LEONE: [*covering* FRANCIS] I'll stand in front of you, Brother.

FRANCIS: Why should you?

LEONE: Let them strike me.

FRANCIS: I'm used to withstanding stones, my friend.

LEONE: [*looking about*] I don't see anyone.

FRANCIS: Someone must be here. [*Another stone is thrown.*] Watch out! [*Stands aside to miss it.*]

LEONE: Brother, I think we should run.

FRANCIS: [*calling out*] Who's there?

LEONE: I don't want to know.

FRANCIS: Friend or foe?

LEONE: It's a strange friend who pummels us with stones.

FRANCIS: If I have an enemy in these hills, I want to face him. [*Calling.*] Step forward, whoever you are. [*From out of the shadows appears a* SHEPHERD.]

FRANCIS: Why do you want to harm us?

SHEPHERD: You'll not steal my sheep. [*Lifts his arm to throw another stone.*]

FRANCIS: Do we look like thieves?

SHEPHERD: Who else would come this way? At this time of night?

LEONE: We're friars, bringing peace to the countryside.

FRANCIS: This is my friend Leone, we mean no harm.

SHEPHERD: I'll protect my sheep, all the same. Thieves come in many disguises. [*Lifts arm again.*]

FRANCIS: Throw away your stones.

LEONE: Over there. [*Pointing.*] Way over there.

FRANCIS: And join us.

SHEPHERD: How do I know I can trust you?

LEONE: Recognize my brother and you will.

SHEPHERD: I can't see his face.

LEONE: My fellow friar is known as the French one because once, long ago he learned a little French.

SHEPHERD: Francis? Brother Francis?

FRANCIS: Yes, you need no stones for us.

SHEPHERD: [*now greatly concerned and apologetic*] I hope I didn't hurt you. My wife comes from Assisi and often speaks about you.

FRANCIS: She's not said I'm a thief, I hope.

SHEPHERD: She tells me you beg for bricks to repair the churches and for oil to light them.

FRANCIS: I beg for everything, my friend, and I steal nothing.

SHEPHERD: Surely you know it's dangerous to travel these roads at night.

FRANCIS: Now we do.

SHEPHERD: Forgive me, Brother Francis. I just wanted to frighten you.

LEONE: You succeeded.

SHEPHERD: To chase you away. Not harm you.

FRANCIS: We're quite all right, I assure you.

SHEPHERD: Why don't you stay here and continue your journey after sunrise? When it's safe.

FRANCIS: I want to find a church where we can celebrate Christmas. Is this the road to Greccio?

SHEPHERD: Yes, but you needn't hurry. Christmas is just another day there.

LEONE: Why is that?

SHEPHERD: We have our work to do . . . and we can't take our sheep to church, can we?

FRANCIS: I suppose not. Although they might enjoy it.

SHEPHERD: The Lord of the Manor needs his wool, his money. Besides, we wouldn't understand the service if we went. They speak Latin.

FRANCIS: You know the Christmas story, surely?

SHEPHERD: I'm a simple man, Brother Francis, who lives for my flocks and my family. I have no time for stories.

FRANCIS: It's a special story and a special day. You can feel it approaching, it's in the air. In the morning's first rays of sun. Look there. [*Points off* as *the sky begins to lighten, gradually gaining color.*]

SHEPHERD: [*shaking his head*] Like any other, to me and my sheep. How can it be anything else?

FRANCIS: And to your family?

SHEPHERD: My wife and baby live in a hut inside a cave. We're too poor to celebrate anything.

FRANCIS: Flies!

SHEPHERD: I beg your pardon?

FRANCIS: Flies!

SHEPHERD: [*to* LEONE] What does he mean? Flies?

LEONE: That's what he calls money.

SHEPHERD: Flies?

FRANCIS: That's all money is. A nuisance that gets in our way, complicates our lives and causes us trouble.

SHEPHERD: I don't have that difficulty. There are no flies on me.

FRANCIS: Look around you. These valleys are full of beauty, these rich Umbrian hills . . . this is your wealth.

SHEPHERD: [*looking off*] They're hills, just hills. What's so beautiful about them?

FRANCIS: Open your eyes, my son.

SHEPHERD: I see rocks that must be picked up and mud that must be cleared away.

FRANCIS: Rocks and mud are beautiful, too, in their own way, for they are created by God.

SHEPHERD: Then it is God who makes me work on Christmas day?

FRANCIS: No, I didn't say that . . . or I didn't mean to.

SHEPHERD: I would like to behold what you call my wealth. But that will never happen. Not to a poor shepherd.

FRANCIS: There must be a way to let you appreciate the beauty of it all . . . the earth, the sky, the glory of God.

SHEPHERD: I tell you we shepherds will be working on Christmas day, like any other. We have no choice.

LEONE: Brother, you wondered where we're needed most. Right here, I would say. In Greccio. [*He points to the road.*]

FRANCIS: What do you think I can do?

LEONE: Find a way to let the shepherds see as they never have before.

FRANCIS: Is that possible? [*Takes a deep breath.*] I don't know.

SHEPHERD: I wish you could.

FRANCIS: It may take a miracle!

LEONE: Well, it won't be your first, Brother Francis.

FRANCIS: [*pleased to be reminded*] *Very* well! Good shepherd, lead us to Greccio. And a miracle, perhaps—[*As they follow, the lights fade.*]

SCENE THREE

SCENE: In the dark, we hear a baby cry.

AT RISE: As the lights come up, we are inside the Shepherd's hut, where his WIFE *hurries to a cradle and gathers the baby in her arms. She soothes the infant and hums a bit of a lullaby.*

WIFE: I'm here. And your father will be home soon. [*She paces back and forth with the baby who soon stops crying.*] Now that the morning light has arrived, he'll be coming down from the hills. And we'll be together, won't we? For a little while. Let me put you down. [*She does so.*] Go back to sleep. The straw will keep you warm. [*She arranges the baby in the straw. Her face brightens as she suddenly remembers something.*] I wonder if they're still there. [*She runs to the stack of straw piled near the stable and digs deep inside it.*] I put them here when they were hard and green, just before the first frost. Yes, here's one right. [*She pulls out a bright red plum.*] Just look! [*She brings forth another.*] And this one, too! [*She runs to the cradle. Showing the baby.*] Aren't they beautiful? Your father will be so surprised. I have a gift to make him happy.

> [*Suddenly into the hut bursts* THE SQUIRE, *a portly middle-aged man whose red nose suggests he is drunk. So does his unruly, unstable and clearly threatening behavior.* WIFE *not happy to see him, immediately becomes uncomfortable.*]

SQUIRE: Well, good morning, dear lady.

WIFE: Squire, what brings you out so early?

SQUIRE: I'm looking for a thief.

WIFE: No one has passed this way. I would have heard.

SQUIRE: Where's your husband?

WIFE: On his way down from the hills, I hope. [*Looking at the sun through the door.*] Yes, any minute now. How can he help you?

SQUIRE: He can return the wool he's stolen, that's how.

WIFE: Oh, you're mistaken.

SQUIRE: I think not. I'm here to take it back.

WIFE: He would never steal.

SQUIRE: His supply to the Lord of the Manor is one bundle short.

WIFE: He works hard out there, protecting the sheep from the wolves and thieves.

SQUIRE: And I work hard here protecting the Landlord from the likes of your husband.

WIFE: We have no wool.

SQUIRE: It's here somewhere. Hidden. You shepherds are clever that way.

WIFE: We're not thieves.

SQUIRE: Then where did you get these plums?

WIFE: From the tree outside our door. Just before the frost came I put them deep in the straw to ripen.

SQUIRE: [*takes a plum and examines it*] Looks delicious!

WIFE: They're for my husband, for Christmas.

SQUIRE: Not any more. [*He bites into the plum.*]

WIFE: [*close to tears*] You mustn't. They're all I have to give him.

SQUIRE: Oh, yes, I must. Red, ripe and ready to eat. [*He devours both plums.*] The best I've ever had. Thank you. [*He wipes his mouth with his sleeve.*] Magnificent!

WIFE: Now I have nothing.

SQUIRE: You have the Landlord's wool. And, if I must, I'll tear this hut apart to find it. [*Knocks over a stool.*]

WIFE: Please stop! You can see everything we own.

[SHEPHERD *enters, eager to speak to his wife.*]

SHEPHERD: Wife, I have a surprise for you. Someone I met in the hills this morning . . . He's just behind me on the road.

SQUIRE: So, the pilferer returns . . .

SHEPHERD: What are you doing here, Squire? Why are your men outside?

SQUIRE: We await the pilferer . . .

SHEPHERD: What do you mean?

SQUIRE: And what fills your pockets this morning, pilferer?

SHEPHERD: I don't understand. Wife, what's he calling me?

WIFE: He accuses you of taking wool from the Lord of the Manor.

SHEPHERD: Stealing, you mean?

SQUIRE: See, you *do* understand. When you hold back wool that belongs to the Master, you pilfer.

SHEPHERD: [*ironically*] Look around you, Squire. If I steal, what good does it do me? We live in a cave that's been a stable.

SQUIRE: You hide your pilferage, of course.

WIFE: Where?

SHEPHERD: We have no hiding place and nothing to hide.

SQUIRE: You hid the plums! Didn't you?

SHEPHERD: What plums?

WIFE: A surprise for you.

SQUIRE: The surprise is I ate them. Merry Christmas! [*Roars with laughter.*]

WIFE: How can you? [*She cries.*]

SHEPHERD: You have no right to upset my wife.

SQUIRE: Don't speak to me of rights. You're a shepherd who owns nothing. Not even this pitiful squalor. You're the property of the Landowner, just like his sheep.

SHEPHERD: Not exactly! The sheep are better looked after.

SQUIRE: So give me the Landlord's wool. I know it's here. Perhaps you'll remember when chained to a stone wall for your crimes.

WIFE: [*screaming*] He has committed no crime. [*The baby cries.*] Now see what you've made me do. [*She goes to the cradle.*]

SHEPHERD: [*anxiously*] Wife, leave the baby.

WIFE: But I must comfort him.

SHEPHERD: [*growing more apprehensive*] Leave him, I say.

SQUIRE: [*becoming suspicious*] No, pick him up.

SHEPHERD: He's stopping. Leave him.

SQUIRE: Pick him up. PICK HIM UP! I say.

WIFE: Come to me, sweet one. [*She takes the baby.*]

SQUIRE: And what do we have here? [*He pulls the straw off the top and looks underneath.*] The Landowner's wool!

SHEPHERD: Just enough to keep the baby warm. No more.

SQUIRE: I knew it!

WIFE: Husband, how did it get here?

SQUIRE: How do you think, dear lady? A miracle.

WIFE: I believe in miracles . . .

SQUIRE: Then I suggest you start praying for one now. Your husband needs it.

[FRANCIS *and* LEONE *enter.*]

FRANCIS: What's wrong here? We heard you shouting. And those men outside.

WIFE: Brother Francis! Is it really you?

FRANCIS: Yes, my dear. We wanted to surprise you. This is my friend Leone. [LEONE *and* WIFE *exchange greetings.*]

WIFE: [*to* SQUIRE] Look, here's my miracle! Brother Francis has come to help us. [*She embraces him.*]

FRANCIS: And who's this? [*Points to* SQUIRE.]

SQUIRE: The squire of this estate. But who are you to be called a miracle?

WIFE: Brother Francis of Assisi.

SQUIRE: The crazy one? Who talks to the animals?

FRANCIS: The same.

WIFE: He's our friend . . . And he's not crazy.

SQUIRE: No, he just walks about barefoot in December. Keeps you on your toes, I suppose. And wears nothing but a sack tied with a piece of rope. Likes to travel light, I guess, Especially in the head. [*Laughs louder.*]

WIFE: He's a good man.

SQUIRE: Now I could understand if you stole a sheep or two, to keep warm.

FRANCIS: I need nothing more than I have.

WIFE: He's a friend of the poor. He understands us.

SQUIRE: What's to understand? You have no money. You don't have to go barefoot in December to grasp that. It's easy. You have no money.

SHEPHERD: No, but . . .

SQUIRE: I hear it coming, so don't tell me you have each other. Because there's a dungeon waiting for you, Shepherd, and who knows what will happen to your wife and baby.

WIFE: Brother Francis, help us, please.

FRANCIS: Leone and I will do whatever we can.

SQUIRE: [*mockingly*] Yes, Brother Francis, why don't you check it out with that wolf over in Gubbio, the one that went around killing children and terrifying housewives? Until you convinced it that it's really a dog, man's best friend!

FRANCIS: It hasn't attacked anyone since. Has it?

SQUIRE: Maybe not. But one day, mark me, that "puppy dog" of yours is going to come to its senses and say, "Look, I'm a wolf, I'm supposed to be bad. People should be afraid of me. What's going on here? How'd I get so messed up?" And then he's going to come after you and make such a fricassee of you that we'll never see your rags again. [*He is convulsed by his own story.*]

WIFE: Pay no attention to him, Brother Francis. He doesn't know what he's saying.

SQUIRE: I know the difference between a wolf and a dog. [*He laughs anew.*]

WIFE: Brother Francis loves all animals.

SQUIRE: I understand you even talk to bugs and insects.

FRANCIS: Happy to say I do.

SQUIRE: I do, too, after I step on them. I say, "Good riddance, pests." [*Laughs again.*]

SHEPHERD: Francis is called the brother of all living things, large and small.

SQUIRE: Right now, Shepherd man, you are God's smallest creature—a thief. Come. My master will determine your punishment. Move along. My men are waiting.

WIFE: [*gathering up the baby*] Brother Francis, come with us. Help us.

FRANCIS: Leone and I will be at your side, of course.

SQUIRE: [*to* FRANCIS] The Lord of the Manor will get a laugh out of you, all right.

FRANCIS: I'm not a court jester but a friar. Please try to remember that.

SQUIRE: [*ignoring his request*] Show him one of your tricks, how you talk to the animals, for instance.

FRANCIS: If he's interested, I will, happily.

WIFE: It's not a trick; he really does it.

SQUIRE: [to FRANCIS] The Lord of the Manor won't find you so funny. He dislikes thieves.

FRANCIS: It's Christmastide. His heart will open wide.

SQUIRE: Not his heart, but his dungeon doors. That's where you'll spend Christmas. Locked away. All of you.

LEONE: [deeply alarmed] We have our work to do. We can't go to jail.

FRANCIS: I warned you, Leone, there could be disappointments on this journey. Brace yourself

LEONE: [trying to convince himself] I have no regrets. I'm happy to be in your service.

FRANCIS: Good, then don't be frightened, my son.

LEONE: I'll be all right in a minute. As you said, God constantly astounds you. I think at the moment I'm somewhat astounded, myself!

FRANCIS: God isn't finished with this Squire and neither am I.

SQUIRE: Oh, no? Outside! My men will take you away. And, please, Brother Francis, spare us any miracles along the way.

FRANCIS: I'll save them all until later, I promise.

SQUIRE: He believes it. That's what gets me. He really thinks he performs miracles.

FRANCIS: And so will you someday.

SQUIRE: And now out with all of you. [Pushes SHEPHERD through the door, as the others follow.]

FRANCIS: [looking Heavenward as he leaves] Is this some kind of joke or are you serious? Forgive me for asking, but I can't tell which. [And he's gone. The lights dim.]

SCENE FOUR

SCENE: Out of the darkness, a loud chorus of cackling hens is heard, ad nauseam.

AT RISE: The lights come up on a corner of the council chamber of the

Lord of Manor. THE LORD, *dressed in long, flowing, and rich fur-lined robes, sits behind a large table with his hands covering his ears. His wife, the* LADY OF THE MANOR *rushes in and shouts at her husband*

LADY: Husband, the castle is turned into a barnyard. I've never seen so many chickens.

LORD: What are you saying? [*Shouting.*] I can't hear you.

LADY: [*pulling his hands away from his ears*] Get them to stop!

LORD: I wish I could! They've given me a headache.

LADY: I can't concentrate on my needlework with all this commotion. Do something!

LORD: It's the egg tax. Every farmer's wife must bring me her best hen.

LADY: They've brought their loudest, that's for certain.

LORD: [*rises, crosses and calls off*] Guards, shut the door.

[*From just out of view, we hear the sound of a door slamming. Immediately, the cackling subsides.*]

LADY: That's better! Thank you! But you can't just close the door. This is no solution. There are chickens everywhere. In the hallways, on the stairs, in my sewing room. You've got to get rid of them.

LORD: I will, dear wife. In a moment. [*He sits down, as if in pain.*]

LADY: What's the matter?

LORD: I can't face those women. It's the hardest job I have, to collect their chickens. I dread it.

LADY: Don't do it, then. Tell them to go home and take their chickens with them. And as quickly and quietly as possible.

LORD: I wish I could.

LADY: What's to stop you? You're the Lord of the Manor.

LORD: Tradition. The past says the Landlord receives one chicken from each household each year.

LADY: Then proceed and be done with it, so we can have some peace and order.

LORD: You don't have to look into their eyes. You don't have to play the role of the oppressor.

[*Suddenly, we hear the door open and the sound of cackling resumes; then,*] *just as quickly, dies out again as the door slams closed.* A FARMER'S WIFE *dashes into the chamber and kneels before* THE LORD *and* LADY.]

FARMER'S WIFE: Sire, I must speak to you in private. I'm sorry but I can't give you a hen this year.

LORD: If you keep chickens, you must present one hen to the Lord of the Manor. Everyone does.

FARMER'S WIFE: A wicked fox attacked our hen house, Sire, and we have only a few left.

LORD: What makes you think I will allow a fox to deprive me of what is mine? Surrender one hen or my stewards will take away all your chickens. It's the law.

FARMER'S WIFE: Spare us this once, Sire, and I'll give you two next year.

LORD: [*quickly becoming the tyrannical figure he hates so much*] Woman, for all I know you may be a fox, trying to trick me.

FARMER'S WIFE: You know perfectly well who I am. My poor husband's in your service, Sire. His entire life.

LORD: I cannot exempt him.

FARMER'S WIFE: We have five children to feed three times a day. You know that as well.

LORD: They'll never miss a few eggs less.

FARMER'S WIFE: And you'll never notice a few more.

LORD: Enough! I'm not listening to a sentimental story about hungry children, wicked foxes, and promises for next year.

FARMER'S WIFE: Faithfully, I've given you hens, Sire, for the last thirteen years.

LORD: [*now fully playing the tyrant*] As you will again today or henceforth you'll own no chickens whatsoever.

LADY: Husband, don't; you'll make yourself sick!

LORD: [*shouting*] It's the law!

FARMER'S WIFE: Yours, not mine. And I cannot obey it.

LORD: Woman, I warn you. Don't anger me. Do you remember what happened to the man who stole sixteen eggs?

FARMER'S WIFE: Of course, Sire. I can see him hanging there still.

LORD: I'm glad you do.

LADY: Husband, how can you say that?

FARMER'S WIFE: I haven't stolen anything.

LORD: You steal from me if you withhold my due. Can't you understand that?

FARMER'S WIFE: Very well. Have your hen. [*Bowing, as she rises and begins to back out.*] But I hope, as you eat its eggs, you'll see the faces of my children looking up at you from your plate. And know that it is you who makes them starve.

LADY: [*to herself*] Poor, poor children!

LORD: [*coming from his seat in an attempt to drive her out*] Silence! You disgusting, nauseating witch! Your words have put a curse on my appetite. [*Clutching his stomach.*] I may never eat an egg again. [*In pain.*] I hate eggs!

FARMER'S WIFE: [*triumphantly*] In that case, I'll give you my best layer. Good day!

LORD: [*shouting*] Out of my sight! [*She leaves.*]

LADY: Let me go after her and tell her to keep her hen.

LORD: You mustn't. I forbid it! [*He is nearly out of control*]

LADY: Don't punish yourself this way. Here, sit down. [*She helps him.*]

LORD: [*he sits at his desk in agony*] She, and all the others, make my stomach knot, tighter and tighter, each time I see them.

LADY: Stay here. I'll take care of the farmer's wives and their chickens. You rest.

LORD: [*wincing*] I have no choice. Thank you, dear wife.

[*As* THE LADY *leaves and we hear the chickens once more,* THE SQUIRE *enters and bows.* THE LORD *sits up, trying to pretend he's recovered but clearly he hasn't.*]

SQUIRE: Master, I've caught the thief. [*Sensing his distress.*] This will cheer you I know. The shepherd who stole the wool from you is outside. He needs to learn his lesson. You'll feel much better once you've sentenced him.

LORD: What are you rambling on about?

SQUIRE: We were one bundle short. Remember? Well, here it is. [*Proudly placing the wool on his desk*]

LORD: What am I supposed to do with this?

SQUIRE: The thief must be punished. I've got him here. And you'll never guess who's with him.

LORD: What are you talking about?

SQUIRE: That crazy friar over in Assisi, the one who talks to animals and walks around barefoot and looks funny.

LORD: Brother Francis?

SQUIRE: He's here, with the shepherd.

LORD: Did he steal the wool?

SQUIRE: No, he's a friend of the shepherd and his wife. They stole the wool.

LORD: What did Brother Francis steal?

SQUIRE: He has nothing and he needs nothing. So why would he steal?

LORD: He must be a happy man.

SQUIRE: Happy and crazy.

LORD: Perhaps to be happy you must be crazy.

SQUIRE: You look pale. May I get you something? Should I call your wife?

LORD: She's busy right now. Then she has her sewing; that's what makes her happy. But bring Brother Francis to me. Perhaps he can help me.

SQUIRE: You'll get a good laugh out of him. Ask him to tell you the one about the wolf of Gubbio. It breaks me up every time.

LORD: I'm in no mood for jokes.

SQUIRE: Then why do you want to meet the crazy one?

LORD: To discover what makes him happy. And perhaps what makes me unhappy.

SQUIRE: You see, he claims he tamed a wolf into behaving like a dog. [*Laughing.*] The poor boob doesn't know the difference. [*Roaring.*]

LORD: And what is the difference?

SQUIRE: Everyone knows. A wolf is—well—a wolf. And a dog is, doggone it, a dog.

LORD: And a boob is a boob.

SQUIRE: Exactly. That's just what he is, all right. You can spot one every time.

LORD: I certainly can. [*Shakes his head in dismay.*] Still, I want to see Brother Francis.

SQUIRE: Of course, Sire. But what about the thief. Aren't you going to hang him?

LORD: Not today. My nerves couldn't take it.

SQUIRE: At least, chain him up in the dungeon, with a little torture, to set an example?

LORD: I've heard enough screaming for one day. Bring the friar here. [*Shouting.*] How many times do I have to tell you?

SQUIRE: I'm going. [*Running out.*] He's just outside. Wait 'til you see him; you're going to die laughing. [*He's off.*]

LORD: No one ever does, do they? Die laughing? [*Puts his head down on his desk.*]

[THE SQUIRE *ushers in* BROTHER FRANCIS, *and points to his tunic.*]

SQUIRE: How's this for fashion? [*Laughs.*] Did you ever behold so pathetic a creature?

LORD: I have, Squire, and so have you if only you could recognize him.

SQUIRE: I've seen them all: dwarfs, humpbacks, six toes on one foot, you name it, but this friar takes the cake. What gets me is he did it to himself. You know his father had money and this one renounced it. Even gave back the clothes his parents had bought him, to go about the countryside looking like this.

LORD: Your introduction is overlong. Wait outside.

SQUIRE: I can't leave you here with a lunatic, my Lord.

LORD: Outside, I say. [*Sharply.*] And don't make me repeat it.

SQUIRE: Call if he begins to act weird. I'll be right here.

LORD: Squire, if you don't leave, I may change my mind about a hanging today.

SQUIRE: I wish you would. We can make the arrangements in no time. And everybody would come to watch. It'd be a lovely Christmas present from you to the peasants.

LORD: [*pulling him by the ear and shoving him out*] Go torture the thief with your talk. [*Returning.*] Brother Francis, I don't think we've met.

FRANCIS: Not that I can recall, Your Grace. [*Bows.*]

LORD: Won't you sit down?

FRANCIS: I prefer to stand, thank you, for I have foresworn creature comforts.

LORD: Very well. [*Looking him over, carefully.*] They call you "the new man," I understand.

FRANCIS: Some do, those who take me seriously.

LORD: I must tell you, you don't look "new" to me.

FRANCIS: I became "new" more than twenty years ago when I rejected a youth of wealth, wine and women to live a life of poverty, penance and prayer, as you see me now.

LORD: You make a convincing beggar, all right.

FRANCIS: Our Lord said, "If you will be perfect, go and sell what you have and give the money to the poor, and you will have treasure in Heaven. Come and follow me." This is my purpose, the determination that keeps me "new."

LORD: You restore churches, I hear.

FRANCIS: Our Lord spoke to me, "Francis, go, repair my house, which you see is falling to ruin." And I did as He asked, first one and then, with the help of my followers, many more.

LORD: Is it true you whip yourself until you bleed?

FRANCIS: I have done so, Your Grace.

LORD: Why?

FRANCIS: To make myself worthy of God's blessings.

LORD: Must one bleed?

FRANCIS: To feel God in the pain, yes.

LORD: What if one bleeds inside? In the mind? In the heart?

FRANCIS: Perhaps it's much the same. If one sees God.

LORD: Then it's not the same. At least, for me.

FRANCIS: But, Sire, what reasons have you to bleed?

LORD: My fortunes are vast but I find no reward in their value. My estate thrives but I take no pride in its success. I am surrounded by hundreds of shepherds, farmers and their families but I have no friends. I am a model of a modern medieval man but I find no happiness in it. So I bleed. This is how I whip myself.

FRANCIS: And you grow more and more miserable?

LORD: I am the richest and most powerful person in this region but I cannot help myself. Every day the pain is worse.

FRANCIS: Perhaps I can find a way to help you.

LORD: If only you could. [*Abruptly changing the subject.*] But enough of my complaints. That's not what brought you here. How may I help you?

FRANCIS: I met one of your shepherds in the hills who led me to believe there would be no Christmas service in Greccio. Is this true?

LORD: No one would come.

FRANCIS: But how will the people of this estate know the meaning of Christmas?

LORD: Oh, I think they already know, from years back They remember.

FRANCIS: The shepherd doesn't. Do you?

LORD: [*indignant*] Well, of course. How can you ask me that? Everybody does, one way or another.

FRANCIS: It appears the people of Greccio don't. The Squire wants to hang the shepherd on Christmas day. I heard you call the farmer's wife a witch. And look at you, your personal misery is crippling your strength.

LORD: Perhaps I have forgotten the story.

FRANCIS: Some never knew it. And worse, they don't care. The shepherd has no idea of what beauty is.

LORD: Then he can't miss it, as I do, can he?

FRANCIS: But he should know. [*As if speaking to himself.*] I must help him. [*To* THE LORD.] We need a Christmas service, Your Grace.

LORD: Very well. If you think it's so important, we'll open the church.

FRANCIS: I need more than that. Something different. Something to grasp their attention.

LORD: My stewards will drag everyone to hear you preach. And make them listen, if necessary.

FRANCIS: I don't preach.

LORD: They say your words can burn like fire.

FRANCIS: I simply speak in my own voice, as I do now. But this time I must do more . . . to make them see God's glories, to renew their faith in the Holy Church, in the world, in themselves.

LORD: That's exactly what we need, my shepherds, the farmers, the Squire . . .

FRANCIS: Especially the Squire . . .

LORD: . . . and most of all, myself . . . But it's too much to expect of any-one . . .

FRANCIS: [*deep in thought*] Something they've never seen before . . . which they can share . . . [*Suddenly remembering.*] I understand the shepherds must be in the fields on Christmas Day.

LORD: That's true.

FRANCIS: No, I want them here and their sheep, too.

LORD: [*surprised*] Here? [*Not understanding.*] Well, yes, if you say so.

FRANCIS: And the farmers with their goats and cows . . .

LORD: Here? Goats and cows? [*Again, perplexed.*] Very well.

FRANCIS: And the peasants with their donkeys . . .

LORD: I can't imagine what for. Very well. But where? The church won't hold them all, not even the marketplace.

FRANCIS: On the hillside, then. Yes, there's plenty of room near the cave where the shepherd and his wife dwell. The entire town can gather there.

LORD: I'll make a proclamation. [*Still confused.*] What should I say?

FRANCIS: No matter, just get them there.

LORD: You'll have an audience, I promise.

FRANCIS: Oh, yes, I need the shepherd, his wife and baby to assist me. May I ask Leone to bring them in?

LORD: The shepherd must go to prison.

FRANCIS: He means no harm. Let him do this, I beg you. He has much to learn.

LORD: Very well, help him, if you can. Along with the rest of us. [*He exits.*]

FRANCIS: [*quietly contemplating*] "How?" is the question. How can I teach you?

[LEONE *enters, escorting the* SHEPHERD *and his* WIFE, *carrying the baby. They gather around* FRANCIS *eager to learn what has happened.*]

WIFE: Are you all right, Brother Francis?

SHEPHERD: What's going to happen?

FRANCIS: I don't know. Let me think.

LEONE: We've been put in your care . . . to do anything you ask.

FRANCIS: Something they've never seen before. That's what we need. To open their eyes . . . to startle . . . to make them react . . . to think . . .

LEONE: Like your broom did when you placed it on the altar and the people thought it was a statue? They will never forget it standing there.

FRANCIS: Exactly. That's just the result we want. But we have no statues.

LEONE: Yes, we do!

FRANCIS: Where? What do you mean?

LEONE: Human statues! Us!

FRANCIS: Of course, that's it! Leone, you're brilliant.

LEONE: I am? [*Then seizing the moment.*] Yes, I am. What did I say?

FRANCIS: You've answered my question.

LEONE: What question?

FRANCIS: It doesn't matter. But thank you. Now I know what we're going to do. And we must begin at once. Let's go.

WIFE: Where?

FRANCIS: Your house.

SHEPHERD: The cave?

FRANCIS: That's where it will take place.

SHEPHERD: We've no room.

FRANCIS: Everyone in Greccio is coming. At the sound of the bells.

WIFE: Where will we put them?

FRANCIS: On the hillside, the people and their animals.

SHEPHERD: Animals?

FRANCIS: They're all coming. Sheep, cows, donkeys, and goats . . .

SHEPHERD: To our house?

FRANCIS: Yes.

SHEPHERD: You're going to speak to goats?

FRANCIS: And what's more, they're going to listen. Come, we've got work to do. [*Ushering them off.*] Hurry! Hurry!

SHEPHERD: [*shocked and bewildered, but caught up in the excitement of the moment, calls out as they leave*] Everybody, come to our house. I don't know why. But come.

FRANCIS: Yes, come. Come to the first Christmas pageant!

[*The lights fade.*]

SCENE FIVE

SCENE: In the darkness we hear bells ringing, and, gradually, just as at the end of Scene One, voices of people approaching grow louder and louder. Only this time, the voices are accompanied by sounds of sheep, cows, donkeys and goats. [These are taped, not yet produced by the audience.] We also hear Shepherds calling to their sheep to keep them in line; farmers to their cows, donkeys and goats, as they climb the hillside.

AT RISE: When the lights come up, BROTHER FRANCIS *is seen standing in front of the shepherd's cave which is now closed to view by screens or by a painted cover. He raises his arms to silence the gathering.*

FRANCIS: Welcome, everyone! What you are about to see is a simple story . . . short and easy to follow. The animals will understand, each in its own way. [*Looking at one section of the audience and moving to it.*] Of course, you will. Won't you, sheep? [THE SHEEP *"Baa-a" gently.*] I'm so glad you're here, for as you'll see, sheep and shepherds are important to our tale. You were the first to hear the glad tidings. [*Moves to another part of the audience.*] And you, my cud-chewing cows! Hear me! [THE COWS *"moo-o" softly.*] You bring warmth and serenity to the manger. Thank you for coming. [*Crosses to another section.*] And over here, our dear donkeys. There is no story without you. For one of you carried Mary on the long journey here. Bless you, kind and gentle donkeys. [THE DONKEYS *bray quietly.*] Sweet music! And one of you will carry her away with her baby in the days to come. [*Going to the last section.*] And here, let me see. Oh, yes, the smelly goats. Make no mistake about it! I'm glad to see you, too. Although the sheep did ask to stay as far away as possible. You bring sparkling eyes and the wisdom of the ages to our story. [THE GOATS *bleat respectively.*] Of course, you do!

[THE SQUIRE *pokes his head in from the side and speaks to the audience.* FRANCIS *ignores him.*]

SQUIRE: Did you see that? He talked to the animals. And they spoke back! All of them. I can never get my horse to understand anything I say. Always does just the opposite of what I ask. Stupid brute. [*He retreats.*]

FRANCIS: And to our human friends, we say thank you for lighting the torches to find your way before this cave.

[THE LORD *and* LADY *arrive and take their seats in two huge chairs that face the cave.* FRANCIS *bows to them.*]

LORD: Brother Francis, we gather here to listen to your message.

LADY: I hope you have found a way to help my husband.

FRANCIS: I think we have, my lady. If everyone is ready, we'll begin.

[THE SQUIRE *re-emerges at the side and whispers loudly to* THE LORD.]

SQUIRE: My Lord, I've got the best part. Just wait until you see me. You'll be amazed by my talent.

LORD: I certainly will, Squire, I certainly will.

LADY: Be off with you, so Brother Francis can commence.

[THE SQUIRE *departs.*]

FRANCIS: [*kneels to pray*] Dear Lord, give us the imagination to tell your story in a way that will touch this audience. For this ability, we pray. Amen. [*He rises. To the audience.*] And now the story of the first Christmas. [*The lights shift to the playing area of the pageant, although the cave is still closed from view.*] "When Mary was engaged to wed Joseph, the son of David, she was found to be with child, a child of the Holy Spirit. Joseph, a just man who dearly loved Mary, did not want her to suffer shame."

[THE SHEPHERD, *costumed as* JOSEPH, *enters, talking to himself.*]

SHEPHERD: How can I help Mary? Yes, send her away from here, quietly, at night so no one will see

FRANCIS: "But then an Angel of the Lord spoke to him."

[THE FARMER'S WIFE, *dressed as the* ANGEL, *enters.*]

FARMER'S WIFE: Joseph, do not fear your marriage to Mary, for she will bear a son of the Holy Spirit. You will call this son—Jesus. And someday he will save his people from their sins. [*She exits.*]

SHEPHERD: Very well, I will marry her immediately. [*He rushes out.*]

FRANCIS: "And Joseph went in search of Mary and soon they were married. And in that region, shepherds watched their flocks by night."

[TWO SHEPHERDS *enter. The first is played by* LEONE.]

LEONE: How quiet these hills are tonight . . . and dark.

FRANCIS: "When suddenly an angel stood before them in dazzling light."

[THE FARMER'S WIFE *enters and stands illuminated.*]

LEONE: What is this light?

SHEPHERD TWO: You frighten us. Who are you?

FARMER'S WIFE: Don't be afraid, for I bring you news of great joy, a joy that is everyone's to share. Today is born a savior who is Christ the Lord. If you search, you will find him in a manger. Glory to God in the highest and on earth peace among humankind. [*The light dims and* THE ANGEL *disappears.*]

FRANCIS: "And the Shepherds were no longer frightened."

LEONE: Let's go to Bethlehem and see this miracle that has happened.

SHEPHERD TWO: There are hundreds of mangers in Bethlehem. How will we know the right one?

LEONE: The power of the Angel will tell us. We'll find it, I know. [*They move off quickly.*]

FRANCIS: "And they hurried towards Bethlehem. Now all this that I have said happened in the days of Herod, the King of Judea." [*He gestures towards the entrance, to herald the King.*]

[THE SQUIRE, *wearing the crown of Judea, blusters in and takes his place.*]

SQUIRE: That's me. King Herod. See this. [*Pointing to his Crown.*] Real gold. A rich king, powerful, too, and mean. Not a bit nice. [*Snarls at the audience.*] Who's this coming before me? Three wise men. Wise men bore me but these may have some news. [*Grandly.*] I give you permission to enter and bow.

[THREE WISE MEN *enter and bow.*]

SQUIRE: What news have you?

WISE MAN ONE: We have heard that a newborn baby may be found in your country.

SQUIRE: Not in Bethlehem, surely?

WISE MAN TWO: Precisely in Bethlehem.

SQUIRE: No, I forbid it. This must not be. You are mistaken.

WISE MAN THREE: Why, what troubles you so greatly?

SQUIRE: Have you not heard? A prophet has foretold that a new King would be born in Bethlehem. This is what I fear the most. A King who could replace me, take my crown. But I'm too clever by far to let this happen.

WISE MAN ONE: It already has, King Herod.

WISE MAN TWO: You're too late to stop it.

WISE MAN THREE: Even now we are on our way to see the baby, bearing gifts.

SQUIRE: Your gifts should be for me, not for some baby. I'm the King.

WISE MAN ONE: But for how long?

SQUIRE: Don't say that!

WISE MAN TWO: You can't outsmart a prophet.

SQUIRE: Of course, I can. I'M THE KING!

WISE MAN THREE: Then try and see what happens.

SQUIRE: Listen to this and discover how bright I am.

THE WISE MEN: We're listening . . .

SQUIRE: [fishing for words] This is what I want to do . . .

THE WISE MEN: We're listening . . .

SQUIRE: Search and find this child, will you . . . ?

THE WISE MEN: Go on . . . we're listening . . .

SQUIRE: And when you do, send word here to me, so that I, too, may come and worship him.

THE WISE MEN: Is that all?

SQUIRE: Isn't that enough? Once I find him, I'll "worship" him all right. You can count on it. And then I'll never have to worry again.

WISE MAN ONE: King Herod, you wouldn't . . .

SQUIRE: Don't try to reason with me, especially on behalf of some baby, squawking away somewhere, just waiting to take my place. No, I won't have it. You may be wise but you're no match for me. Not King Herod.

FRANCIS: Squire, you're carried away.

SQUIRE: [responding in character of Herod to FRANCIS] How dare you speak like that to a King!

FRANCIS: We must go on with the story.

SQUIRE: Very well. [To THE WISE MEN.] You have heard my demands. Let me know where to find that baby. Now be on your way. [As he is stomping off; to THE LORD and LADY.] Don't go away. I have another scene.

FRANCIS: "They journeyed on, and, yes, the star they had seen in the east moved before them, guiding them until it came to rest over the place where the child was. When they saw the star, they rejoiced and arrived at a house much like this." [*Points to the cave.*] "And soon they were joined by the shepherds who also wanted to see the Child."

[THE SHEPHERDS *re-enter and gather near.*]

FRANCIS: "This house was really a stable for that is all Joseph could find since there was no place in the inn." [THE SHEPHERDS *remove the screens that have covered the cave.*] "The Baby lay in a manger, wrapped in swaddling clothes, with Mary, his Mother, seated beside him and Joseph standing watch just behind them." [*Indeed, this is exactly the picture we see before us.*] "And they fell down and worshipped him." [THE WISE MEN *and* THE SHEPHERDS *kneel in honor.*] "But they were not the first to do so. For the animals were present from the beginning. The sheep gently baa-ed." [THE SHEEP *do so.*] "The cows softly moo-ed." [THE COWS *do so.*] "The donkeys sweetly brayed." [THE DONKEYS *bray.*] "And the smelly goats bleated their praise." [THE GOATS *bleat.*] "It was a warm and wonderful sight. The Wise Men cried at its beauty. The Shepherds, seeing what they had heard was true, repeated the words of the Angel."

SHEPHERDS: Glory to God in the highest, and on earth, peace and good will.

FRANCIS: "And indeed the Babe was called Jesus."

WISE MAN ONE: In celebration, I offer the child gifts of gold. [*He places them in the straw before the manger.*]

WISE MAN TWO: In celebration, I offer the gift of frankincense. [*Places his gift*]

WISE MAN THREE: In celebration, I offer the gift of myrrh. [*Puts the myrrh at the foot of the manger.*]

FRANCIS: "And then a most remarkable thing happened. A light in the form of a halo appeared over the heads of the Baby and his Mother. And the manger glowed brilliantly in the night."

[THE ANGEL *enters and gives the halos to* THE LORD. *She escorts him from his seat and leads him to the crib, where he places the halos on the heads of Mary and the Baby. As he stands there, the cave is illuminated in gold and amber light.*]

FRANCIS: "The animals had nothing to offer but their own presence. But they, too, were awed by the transformation of the stable and sang their praises. The sheep baa-ing." [*Yes, they do.*] "The cows, the donkeys and the smelly goats, all joining in a chorus of thanks." [*He allows*

the sounds to rise and then cuts them off. To the SHEPHERD *playing Joseph.*]
Do you see the beauty of it now, gentle Shepherd?

SHEPHERD: I can't believe this is my home. In this golden light, everything is beautiful. Yes, I can see beauty all around me. My eyes are
open. Thank you. [*He returns to playing* JOSEPH.]

FRANCIS: And what about you, noble Sire, what do you feel?

LORD: You have brought Bethlehem to Greccio. I never dreamed this
possible but here it is on a hillside in a stable in a cave, for all my people to experience. A miracle that makes this story live before us.

FRANCIS: But you have not answered my question.

LORD: Haven't I?

FRANCIS: I want to know what you feel inside. Is the emptiness gone

LORD: This living picture fills me with warmth. And helps to drive away
my sorrows.

FRANCIS: But is your faith restored?

LORD: I am stronger after seeing this. And more secure.

FRANCIS: But still doubting, not entirely sure?

LORD: I have tears in my eyes for the first time in many years. They must
count for something.

FRANCIS: Keep looking.

LORD: The halos make me want to believe again. But I can't be certain.
Why is that?

FRANCIS: Don't give up. The answer is here in this manger scene, in the
light of our lives. Keep looking.

LORD: What are you telling me?

FRANCIS: Look at these faces. At this serenity. At the adoration of the
Wise Men. At the joy of the Shepherds. And translate that happiness
to your life, your being.

LORD: I'm trying. I'm trying.

FRANCIS: We'll help you, show you the way.

LORD: I want so desperately to find that peace of which the Angel spoke.

FRANCIS: They have found it.

LORD: Who?

FRANCIS: The animals. Look into their eyes. What do you see? [*He leads him, looking into the eyes of the audience.*]

LORD: Gentleness.

FRANCIS: Yes.

LORD: Innocence.

FRANCIS: Yes.

LORD: Kindness.

FRANCIS: In abundance.

LORD: Sweetness.

FRANCIS: Everywhere. And listen to them. [*He cues the animals to softly produce their sounds.*] What do they say? Those moo-s, those baa-s, those brays, those bleats . . .

LORD: They say . . . they say . . . they say . . . [*He chokes.*]

FRANCIS: Say it.

LORD: They say they love this manger. [*He is wrought, not having said the word "love" in so long a time.*]

FRANCIS: Yes, love. And, if you can hear it in these sounds of the beasts, surely you can hear it in yourself as well.

LORD: Yes, I do. However faint from lack of use.

FRANCIS: It will return. Loud and clear. The light that engulfs the manger now begins to glow in you.

LORD: I'm changing even as I speak [*A golden light falls on him.*]

FRANCIS: Let it run deeply through your being.

LORD: [*in a new voice, as if a new person*] Shepherd, keep your wool to warm your baby.

SHEPHERD: I'll return it when winter ends, I promise.

SHEPHERD'S WIFE: [*still posed as Mary*] My husband's not a thief, please believe me.

LORD: I do, dear lady. He's a free man, as of now.

SHEPHERD'S WIFE: Bless you, my Lord.

SHEPHERD: I'm most grateful, Sire.

LORD: And you, Farmer's Wife and Angel, you shall have your hen back and a hundred more besides.

FARMER'S WIFE: That's too generous, Sire. But, on the other hand, yes, I'll take them and share them with the others. Thank you. And may you enjoy your breakfast eggs tomorrow morning.

LORD: And, Brother Francis, here is a bag of gold to help you restore the next church you come upon. [*Hands him a bag of gold.*]

FRANCIS: I am grateful, Your Grace. [*Gives the bag to* LEONE.]

LEONE: Brother Francis, just think of the brooms we can buy with this!

LORD: And to my people, I shall no longer be the Lord of the Manor but your neighbor. And I hope, a friend, if that is possible. [*There is applause to suggest that it is.* THE LORD *smiles, clearly pleased.*]

LADY: [*to* FRANCIS] Look, he's happy, for the first time in many years. Thank you, Brother Francis. You have saved him from his own despair.

[THE SQUIRE, *poking his head out from the side, calls to* BROTHER FRANCIS.]

SQUIRE: Brother Francis, I haven't played my big scene yet. What's going on out there?

FRANCIS: [*to* THE LORD] What shall we do?

LORD: Better let him finish or we'll never hear the end of it.

FRANCIS: Please, everyone, our story isn't over. We seem to have forgotten King Herod and he's very upset. [THE LORD *takes his seat. Everyone else settles down and the pageant resumes.* THE SQUIRE *disappears.*] "You remember that the Wise Men here were supposed to report back to Herod and tell him the whereabouts of the child."

WISE MAN ONE: Absolutely not!

WISE MAN TWO: He'll come here with his soldiers . . .

WISE MAN THREE: . . . and take the child and destroy it.

WISE MAN ONE: What shall we do?

WISE MAN TWO: If we're not going to tell him . . .

WISE MAN THREE: . . . there's only one thing we can do . . .

THE WISE MEN: GO HOME!

FRANCIS: "And they made plans to return to their own country. And then the Angel appeared and spoke to Joseph once more."

FARMER'S WIFE: Take the Child and his Mother and flee to Egypt and remain there until I tell you it is safe to return.

FRANCIS: "And Joseph prepared to do so. Now when Herod heard about this, well, you can imagine . . . "

[THE SQUIRE *bursts in.*]

SQUIRE: Nothing of the sort. I'll show you. [*Coming C.*] Lord and Lady, my mad scene. Watch this. [*He goes into character of Herod.*] I will have the messenger killed who brings this news. How dare he? So, they have run out of the country and not told me the location of the Child. How dare they? And now the Father has gone into Egypt with the Mother and Child? How dare they? Dare me, will they? No, I'll dare them. Double dare. Triple dare. Quadruple dare. It makes me furious that the Child got away! It drives me insane, mad, crazy. [*Shaking his head and screaming in rage.*] CRAZY! CRAZY! CRAZY!

LORD: Squire, like everything else, you take too long to die. Get on with it.

SQUIRE: [*outrageously over-acting*] My brain bursts with anger. My heart bursts with hate. My tongue bursts with vengeance. My soul bursts with . . .

LORD: I'd say, you're pretty well bursted.

SQUIRE: I'm just getting started.

LORD: No, my friend, you're finished. Otherwise, my sword will see your stomach burst. Lie down and die. NOW!

SQUIRE: [*realizing he's serious*] Very well. [*He stretches out on the floor before them.*] How's this?

LORD: Splendid. We're all touched. Now close your eyes.

SQUIRE: Do I look dead?

LORD: For the full effect, you must put your feet close together and clasp your hands as if in prayer.

SQUIRE: Yes, sire. [*He does so.* THE LORD *signals to* FRANCIS *and* LEONE. *One quickly ties the* SQUIRE'*s feet, the other his hands.*] Just one last word . . .

LORD: And that was it. [*He bends over and places a gag in his mouth.* THE SQUIRE *squirms and kicks but to no avail*] Now, Brother Francis, is the pageant ended?

FRANCIS: I have this to add, as we depart. [*He steps forward and speaks to everyone, including the audience, his most famous words.*]

> Praise to the Lord God for all creatures,
> Above all our Brother Sun,
> Who brings us day and lends us light.

Glorious is he, radiant with splendor.
Praise to the Lord for Sister Moon.
And for the stars
Set in heaven, clear, precious and bright.
Praise to the Lord for Brother Wind and
Cloud who give us weather;
And for the air that gives all creatures life.
Praise to the Lord for Sister Water
Who is so clean and pure and useful to us.
Praise to the Lord for Brother Fire
Who brings light into darkness.
He is warm, mighty and strong.
Praise to the Lord for our Mother Earth.
Who sustains us with fruits and vegetables
of many colors.
Praise to the Lord for those who pardon
one another and for those who endure
sickness and frustration.
Praise to the Lord. Thank him.
Praise to the Lord. Serve him with humility.
Amen.

LORD: Thank you, Brother Francis, for reminding us of our blessings. [*Now addressing everyone.*] So that others will not forget the story of Christmas, as I did, I decree that such an enactment as we see before us shall take place in the years to come. In this way, wherever we are, the beauty of Bethlehem will come alive to illustrate the Angel's words.

FARMER'S WIFE: Glory to God in the highest, and on earth, peace and goodwill.

FRANCIS: And now, Leone and I must be off to continue our work. [*They start to leave.*]

LEONE: Brother Francis, do you notice anything different about me?

FRANCIS: You've changed, my friend?

LEONE: Yes, the golden light of the manger shines in me, too. Now my faith is so strong, I don't have to wear sandals anymore. My feet have got the message.

FRANCIS: [*delighted*] This means you're a true friar, my son. Come, Brother Leone, we go barefoot together in the service of the Lord.

[*With* THE LORD *and* LADY *leading, everyone, including the audience, waves good-bye. Church bells chime in the distance, announcing the arrival of Christmas.*]

LORD: Listen, my friends, Christmas is here. [*Everyone kneels, facing the manger, as above the hut a large star appears in the sky, one of its radiant points extending a beam of light down upon the scene below. The remaining lights dim, leaving only the star and the two halos glowing in the darkness as the play ends.*]

CURTAIN

Note: *After the actors have bowed,* BROTHER FRANCIS *runs to each section of the audience, saying, "A special hand for the animals." And the performers applaud the audience.*

FRANCIS: [*going to the* SHEEP] You were wonderful. You followed, well, just like sheep. [*He applauds them and goes to the* COWS.] And our splendid cows could not have been more contented. [*After applauding, he runs to the* DONKEYS.] And you're the best donkeys I've seen, well, in donkey years. [*Applauds them and runs to the* GOATS.] And the smelly goats, very convincing, I'd say! No, no goats ever smelled sweeter. Thank you. Thank you, all. [THE SQUIRE *is still tied and twisting on the floor.* BROTHER FRANCIS *bends over him.*] You have one final word? [SQUIRE *nods that he does.*] Very well. [*He unties ropes about his feet and hands and removes gag.*] What is it? [SQUIRE *Jumps to his feet*] MERRY CHRISTMAS! [*Everyone, joining hands, bows one last time.*]

FINAL CURTAIN—END OF PLAY

The following should be filled in and distributed to members of the audience as they enter the performance space:

PLEASE NOTE

Dear Audience Member:

CONGRATULATIONS!

You have been cast to play the role of a _____* at this performance of *The Shepherds of St. Francis*. You will participate in the final scene and during the curtain calls. When asked, you are requested to reply in character, giving the proper response this animal would make under the circumstances.

Please stay in character and speak only when your cues are given. Silliness, giggling or lack of sincerity can result in the loss of your role. We wouldn't want this to happen and spoil your holidays!

The director and cast look forward to your participation and thank you for sharing your talents with us in this performance of *The Shepherds of St. Francis*.

BREAK A LEG!

The Management

*Fill in one: Sheep, Cow, Donkey, Goat

Directors: Please Note

A member of the cast or an usher should briefly rehearse the proper animal sounds with each section of the audience just before the play begins. This should be done softly so as not to spoil the effect when the voices are needed in the performance itself.

AMAHL AND THE NIGHT VISITORS

by Gian-Carlo Menotti

CHARACTERS

AMAHL   a crippled boy of about 12

HIS MOTHER

KASPAR slightly deaf ⎫   THE

MELCHOIR   ⎬   THREE

BALTHAZAR   ⎭   KINGS

THE PAGE

CHORUS OF SHEPHERDS AND VILLAGERS

DANCERS

The curtain rises. It is night. The crystal-clear winter sky is dotted with stars, the Eastern Star flaming amongst them. Outside the cottage, not far from its door, AMAHL, *wrapped in an oversized cloak, sits on a stone, playing his shepherd's pipe. His crudely-made crutch lies on the ground beside him. Within,* THE MOTHER *works at household chores. The room is lighted only by the dying fire and the low flame of a tiny oil lamp.*

THE MOTHER: [*She pauses in her work to listen to the piping, then calls:*] Amahl! Amahl!

AMAHL: Oh!

THE MOTHER: Time to go to bed!

AMAHL: Coming! [AMAHL *does not stir. After a moment he begins to play again.*]

THE MOTHER: Amahl!

AMAHL: Coming! [*With a shrug of his shoulders,* AMAHL *continues to play. Impatiently,* THE MOTHER *goes to the window, opens it sharply, and leans out.*]

THE MOTHER: How long must I shout to make you obey?

AMAHL: I'm sorry, Mother.

THE MOTHER: Hurry in! It's time to go to bed.

AMAHL: But Mother, let me stay a little longer!

THE MOTHER: The wind is cold.

AMAHL: But my cloak is warm, let me stay a little longer!

THE MOTHER: The night is dark.

AMAHL: But the sky is light, let me stay a little longer!

THE MOTHER: The time is late.

AMAHL: But, the moon hasn't risen yet, let me stay a little . . .

THE MOTHER: [*Clapping her hands*] There won't be any moon tonight. But there will be a weeping child very soon, if he doesn't hurry up and obey his mother.

[THE MOTHER *closes the window with a sharp little bang.*]

AMAHL: Oh, very well.

[*Reluctantly,* AMAHL *rises, takes up his crutch, and hobbles into the house. On the pegs to one side of the door he hangs his heavy cloak and shepherd's cap. His pipe he places carefully in the corner.* THE MOTHER *kneels at the fireplace, trying to coax a flame from the few remaining twigs.* AMAHL *returns to the open door and leans against it, looking up to the sky.*]

THE MOTHER: What was keeping you outside?

AMAHL: Oh, Mother, you should go out and see! There's never been such a sky! Damp clouds have shined it and soft winds have swept it as if to make it ready for a King's ball. All its lanterns are lit, all its torches are burning, and its dark floor is shining like crystal. Hanging over our roof there is a star as large as a window, and the star has a tail, and it moves across the sky like a chariot on fire.

THE MOTHER: [*wearily*] Oh! Amahl, when will you stop telling lies? All day long, you wander in and out in a dream. Here we are with nothing to eat, not a stick of wood on the fire, not a drop of oil in the jug and all you do is to worry your mother with fairy tales. Oh! Amahl, have you forgotten your promise never, never to lie to your mother again?

AMAHL: Mother, darling, I'm not lying. Please, do believe me. [*He tugs at her skirt.*] Come outside and let me show you. See for yourself . . . See for yourself . . . .

THE MOTHER: [*She brushes his hand aside*] Stop bothering me! Why should I believe you? You come with a new one every day! First it was a leopard with a woman's head. Then it was a tree branch that shrieked and bled. Then it was a fish as big as a boat, with whiskers like a cat and wings like a bat and horns like a goat. And now it is a star as large as a window . . . or was it a carriage . . . And if that weren't enough, the star has a tail and the tail is of fire!

AMAHL: But there is a star and it has a tail this long.

[AMAHL *measures the air as wide as his arms can reach. At her frown, he reduces the size by half.*]

Well, maybe only . . . this long. But it's there!

THE MOTHER: Amahl!

AMAHL: Cross my heart and hope to die.

THE MOTHER: [*Clasping* AMAHL *in her arms*] Poor Amahl! Hunger has gone to your head. Dear God, what is a poor widow to do when her cupboards and pockets are empty and everything sold?

[*She moves disconsolately to the fireplace.*]

Unless we go begging how shall we live through tomorrow? My little son, a beggar!

[*She sinks, weeping, onto a little stool.* AMAHL *goes to her and embraces her tenderly, stroking her hair.*]

AMAHL: Don't cry, Mother dear, don't worry for me. If we must go begging, a good beggar I'll be. I know sweet tunes to set people dancing. We'll walk and walk from village to town, you dressed as a gypsy and I as a clown. At noon we shall eat roast goose and sweet almonds, at night we shall sleep with the sheep and the stars. I'll play my pipes, you'll sing and you'll shout. The windows will open and people lean out. The King will ride by and hear your loud voice and throw us some gold to stop all the noise. At noon we shall eat roast goose and sweet almonds, at night we shall sleep with the sheep and the stars.

THE MOTHER: My dreamer, good night. You're wasting the light. Kiss me good night.

AMAHL: Good night.

[THE MOTHER *rises and bends to receive the good-night kiss.* AMAHL *goes to his pallet of straw at one side of the fireplace.* THE MOTHER *secures the door, takes* AMAHL'S *cloak and spreads it over him, touches his head tenderly, then, having snuffed out the tiny oil lamp, she lies down on the bench. The lights die from the room except for a faint glow in the fireplace and the radiance of the sky through the window.*

[*In the distance among the hills, we see a tiny winking light from a lantern, then the small figures of* THE THREE KINGS *and* THE PAGE, *wending their way along the mountain road.* AMAHL *raises himself on one elbow and listens with astonishment to the distant singing. The figures disappear at a turn in the road.* AMAHL *throws back his cloak and, leaning on his crutch, hobbles over to the window. At the left, on the road, appear* THE THREE KINGS: *first* MELCHIOR, *bearing the coffer of gold, then* BALTHAZAR *bearing the chalice of myrrh, and finally* KASPAR *bearing the urn of incense. All are preceded by* THE PAGE *who walks heavily, bent beneath the load of many bundles, among them a rich Oriental rug, a caged parrot, and an elaborate jeweled box. In one hand* THE PAGE *carries a heavy lantern to light the way.*]

MELCHIOR, BALTHAZAR: From far away we come and farther we must go. How far, how far, my crystal star? The shepherd dreams inside the fold. Cold are the sands by the silent sea. Frozen the incense in our frozen hands, heavy the gold. How far, how far, my crystal star? By silence-sunken lakes the antelope leaps. In paper-painted oasis the drunken gypsy weeps. The hungry lion wanders, the cobra sleeps. How far, how far, my crystal star?

[*As the travelers approach the door of the cottage,* THE PAGE *steps aside to let* KING MELCHIOR *knock upon the door.*]

THE MOTHER: [*Without stirring from her bed*] Amahl, go and see who's knocking at the door.

AMAHL: Yes, Mother.

[AMAHL *goes to the door and opens it a crack. He quickly closes the door and rushes to his* MOTHER.]

Mother, Mother, Mother, come with me. I want to be sure that you see what I see.

THE MOTHER: [*Raising herself on her elbow*] What is the matter with you now? What is all this fuss about? Who is it then?

AMAHL: [*Hesitatingly*] Mother . . . outside the door there is . . . there is a King with a crown.

THE MOTHER: What shall I do with this boy, what shall I do? If you don't learn to tell the truth, I'll have to spank you!

[*Knocks. After a pause she sinks back on the bed.*]

Go back and see who it is and ask them what they want.

[AMAHL *hurries to the door, again opens it just a crack, and stares. He closes it once more and returns to his* MOTHER.]

AMAHL: Mother, Mother . . . Mother, come with me. I want to be sure that you see what. I see.

THE MOTHER: What is the matter with you now, what is all this fuss about?

AMAHL: Mother . . . I didn't tell the truth before.

THE MOTHER: That's a good boy.

AMAHL: There is not a King outside.

THE MOTHER: I should say not!

AMAHL: There are two Kings!

THE MOTHER: What shall I do with this boy? What shall I do? Hurrry back and see who it is and don't you dare make up tales!

[AMAHL *repeats again the action to the door and back.*]

AMAHL: Mother . . . Mother . . . Mother, come with me. If I tell you the truth, I know you won't believe me.

THE MOTHER: Try it for a change!

AMAHL: But you won't believe me.

THE MOTHER: I'll believe you if you tell the truth.

AMAHL: Sure enough, there are not two Kings outside.

THE MOTHER: That is surprising.

AMAHL: The Kings are three, and one of them is black.

THE MOTHER: Oh! What shall I do with this boy! If you were stronger I'd like to whip you.

AMAHL: I knew it!

THE MOTHER: I'm going to the door myself, and then, young man, you'll have to reckon with me!

[THE MOTHER *rises wearily and moves determinedly to the door.* AMAHL *follows, holding onto her skirt. As the door swings open, she beholds* THE THREE KINGS. *In utter amazement, she bows to them.*]

KASPAR, MELCHIOR, BALTHAZAR: Good evening!

AMAHL [*Whispering*] What did I tell you?

THE MOTHER: [*To* AMAHL] Sh! [*To* THE KINGS.] Noble sires!

BALTHAZAR: May we rest a while in your house and warm ourselves by your fireplace?

THE MOTHER: I am a poor widow. A cold fireplace and a bed of straw are all I have to offer you. To these you are welcome.

KASPAR [*cupping his ear*] What did she say?

BALTHAZAR: That we are welcome.

KASPAR: [*excitedly*] Oh, thank you, thank you, thank you!

[MELCHIOR *and* BALTHAZAR *tap* KASPAR'S *shoulder to restrain him.*]

KASPAR, MELCHIOR, BALTHAZAR: Oh, thank you!

THE MOTHER: Come in, come in!

[*Still bowing,* THE MOTHER *makes way for* THE KINGS *to enter,*

pulling AMAHL *with her.* THE PAGE *enters first, places his lantern on the stool beside the fireplace, and drops his bundles. Immediately,* KING KAS-PAR *proceeds at a stately march to his place on the bench.* THE PAGE *hurries to hold* KING KASPAR'S *train. Once* KASPAR *has placed himself,* BALTHAZAR *enters and proceeds to a place beside him.* MELCHIOR *is the last to take his place.* THE PAGE *runs back and forth to carry the trains of each. When* THE THREE KINGS *are together, they sit as one.* THE PAGE *spreads the rug before them and sets upon it the gifts* THE KINGS *bear for the Child.* AMAHL *watches the procession with growing wonder and excitement.*]

MELCHIOR: It is nice here.

THE MOTHER: I shall go and gather wood for the fire. I've nothing in the house.

[THE MOTHER *takes her shawl from the peg and goes to the door.*]

MELCHIOR: We can stay only for a little while. We must not lose sight of our star.

THE MOTHER: Your star?

AMAHL. [*whispering to his mother*] What did I tell you?

THE MOTHER: Sh!

MELCHIOR: We still have a long way to go.

THE MOTHER: I shall be right back . . . and Amahl don't be a minute. [*She goes quickly.*]

AMAHL: No, Mother.

[*The moment his* MOTHER *is gone,* AMAHL *goes to* BALTHAZAR. KASPAR *goes to the corner of the fireplace where* THE PAGE *has placed the parrot and the jeweled box. During the following scene he feeds the parrot bits of food from his pocket.*]

Are you a real King?

BALTHAZAR: Yes.

AMAHL: Have you regal blood?

BALTHAZAR: Yes.

AMAHL: Can I see it?

BALTHAZAR: It is just like yours.

AMAHL: What's the use of having it, then?

BALTHAZAR: No use.

AMAHL: Where's your home?

BALTHAZAR: I live in a black marble palace full of black panthers and white doves. And you, little boy, what do you do?

AMAHL: [*Sadly*] I was a shepherd, I had a flock of sheep. But my mother sold them. Now there are no sheep left. I had a black goat who gave me warm sweet milk. But she died of old age. Now there is no goat left. But Mother says that now we shall both go begging from door to door. Won't it be fun?

BALTHAZAR: It has its points.

[AMAHL *crosses to* KASPAR, *who continues to feed the parrot.*]

AMAHL: Are you a real King, too?

KASPAR: Eh?

[AMAHL *looks wonderingly at* BALTHAZAR *who indicates that* KASPAR *is deaf.* AMAHL *repeats the question, shouting.*]

AMAHL: ARE YOU A REAL KING, TOO?

KASPAR: Oh, truly, truly, yes. I am a real King . . . am I not?

[KASPAR *looks questioningly at* BALTHAZAR.]

BALTHAZAR: Yes, Kaspar.

AMAHL: What is that?

KASPAR: Eh?

AMAHL: WHAT IS THAT?

KASPAR: A parrot.

AMAHL: Does it talk?

KASPAR: Eh?

AMAHL: DOES IT TALK?

KASPAR: [*Indicating his deaf ears*] How do I know?

AMAHL: Does it bite?

KASPAR: Eh?

AMAHL: DOES IT BITE?

[KASPAR *displays a heavily bandaged finger.*]

KASPAR: Yes.

AMAHL: [*Pointing at the jeweled box*] And what is this?

[*With great excitement,* KASPAR *opens one drawer at a time, concealing its contents from* AMAHL *until he lifts the jewels, the beads, and finally the licorice before the boy's amazed eyes.*]

KASPAR: This is my box, this is my box. I never travel without my box. In the first drawer I keep my magic stones. One carnelian against all evil and envy. One moonstone to make you sleep. One red coral to heal your wounds. One lapis lazuli against quartern fever. One small jasper to help you find water. One small topaz to soothe your eyes. One red ruby to protect you from lightning. This is my box, this is my box. I never travel without my box. In the second drawer, I keep all my beads. Oh, how I love to play with beads, all kinds of beads. This is my box, this is my box. I never travel without my box. In the thrid drawer . . . Oh, little boy! Oh, little boy . . . In the third drawer I keep . . . licorice . . . Black, sweet licorice. Have some.

[AMAHL *seizes the candy and gobbles it down as his* MOTHER *enters from the outside, bearing a few sticks.*]

THE MOTHER: Amahl, I told you not to be a nuisance!

AMAHL: But it isn't my fault!

[*Going to his mother,* AMAHL *whispers discreetly.*]

They kept asking me questions.

THE MOTHER: I want you to go and call the other shepherds. Tell them about our visitors, and ask them to bring whatever they have in the house, as we have nothing to offer them. Hurry on!

AMAHL: Yes, Mother.

[AMAHL *grabs up his cloak, claps his hat on his head, and hurries out as fast as his crutch will carry him.* THE MOTHER *crosses to the fireplace to set down the wood she has gathered. Suddenly she sees the coffer of gold, and the rich chalices of incense and myrrh which sit before* THE KINGS. *Irresistibly drawn, she moves toward them.*]

THE MOTHER: Oh, these beautiful things, and all that gold!

MELCHIOR: These are the gifts to the Child.

THE MOTHER: [*With great excitement*] The child? Which child?

MELCHIOR: We don't know. But the Star will guide us to Him.

THE MOTHER: But perhaps I know him. What does he look like?

BALTHAZAR: Have you seen a Child the color of wheat, the color of dawn? His eyes are mild, His hands are those of a King, as King He was born. Incense, myrrh, and gold we bring to His side and the Eastern Star is our guide.

THE MOTHER: [*as if to herself*] Yes, I know a child the color of wheat, the color of dawn. His eyes are mild, his hands are those of a King, as King he was born. But no one will bring him incense or gold, though sick and poor and hungry and cold. He's my child, my son, my darling, my own.

MELCHIOR, BALTHAZAR: Have you seen a Child the color of earth, the color of thorn? His eyes are sad, His hands are those of the poor, as poor He was born. Incense, myrrh, and gold we bring to His side, and the eastern star is our guide.

THE MOTHER: Yes, I know a child the color of earth, the color of thorn. His eyes are sad, his hands are those of the poor, as poor he was born. But no one will bring him incense or gold, though sick and poor and hungry and cold. He's my child, my son, my darling, my own.

MELCHIOR: The Child we seek holds the seas and the winds on His palm.

KASPAR: The Child we seek has the moon and the stars at His feet.

BALTHAZAR: Before Him the eagle is gentle, the lion is meek.

[*Absorbed in her own thoughts,* THE MOTHER *moves slowly downstage.*]

THE MOTHER: The child I know on his palm holds my heart. The child I know at his feet has my life. He's my child, my son, my darling, my own, and his name is Amahl.

KASPAR, MELCHIOR, BALTHAZAR: Choirs of angels hover over His roof and sing Him to sleep. He's warmed by breath, He's fed by Mother who is both Virgin and Queen. Incense, myrrh, and gold we bring to His side, and the Eastern Star is our guide.

[*The call of* THE SHEPHERDS *falls sharp and clear on the air, breaking the hushed silence of the room.*]

SHEPHERDS: Shepherds! Shepherdesses! Who's calling, who's calling? Oh! Oh!

[THE MOTHER *looks instinctively to see if her room is ready to receive her neighbors, then she goes to the door and opens it wide.*]

THE MOTHER: The shepherds are coming!

MELCHIOR: [*He nudges the dozing* KASPAR] Wake up, KASPAR!

[*First singly, then in twos and threes,* THE SHEPHERDS *begin to appear. They come from all directions. On the hills in the distance lantern lights pierce the darkness. Slowly they converge and move down the road toward the hut, led by a radiant* AMAHL.]

SHEPHERDS: Emily, Emily, Michael, Bartholomew, how are your children and how are your sheep? Dorothy, Dorothy, Peter, Evangeline, give me your hand, come along with me, All the children have mumps. All the flocks are asleep. We are going with Amahl, bringing gifts to the Kings. Benjamin, Benjamin, Lucas, Elizabeth, how are your children and how are your sheep? Carolyn, Carolyn, Matthew, Veronica, give me your hand, come along with me.

[*Ragged and joyous,* THE SHEPHERDS *approach the hut, bearing their baskets of fruit and vegetables.*]

Brrr! How cold is the night! Brrr! How icy the wind! Hold me very, very, very tight. Oh, how warm is your cloak! Katherine, Katherine, Christopher, Babila, how are your children and how are your sheep? Josephine, Josephine, Angela, Jeremy, come along with me. Oh! look!. Oh! look!

[THE SHEPHERDS *crowd together in the frame of the door of the hut, struck dumb by the sight of* THE KINGS, *not daring to enter.* AMAHL, *however, slips through the crowd to take his place beside his* MOTHER.]

THE MOTHER: Come in, come in! What are you afraid of?

[*Shy and embarrassed, everyone tries to push his neighbor in ahead of him, until all of them are crowded into one corner of the room.*]

Don't be bashful, silly girl! Don't be bashful, silly boy! They won't eat you. Show what you brought them.

[*At last one shepherd boldly marches forward and lays his gifts before* THE KINGS *then, bowing shyly, he retreats to his place.*]

SHEPHERDS: Go on, go on, go on! No! You go on! Olives and quinces, apples and raisins, nutmeg and myrtle, medlars and chestnuts, this is all we shepherds can offer you.

KASPAR, MELCHIOR, BALTHAZAR: Thank you, thank you, thank you kindly. Thank you. Thank you, thank you kindly, too.

[*A second shepherd crosses to* THE KINGS, *presents his gifts, and returns, bowing, to his place.*]

SHEPHERDS: Citrons and lemons, musk and pomegranates, goat-cheese and walnuts, figs and cucumbers, this is all we shepherds can offer you.

KASPAR, MELCHIOR, BALTHAZAR: Thank you, thank you, thank you kindly. Thank you, thank you, thank you kindly, too.

[*Taking courage from the others, a third shepherd presents his gifts and returns to his place.*]

SHEPHERDS: Hazelnuts and camomile, mignonettes and laurel, honeycombs and cinnamon, thyme, mint, and garlic, this is all we shepherds can offer you.

KASPAR, MELCHIOR, BALTHAZAR: Thank you, thank you, thank you kindly. Thank you, thank you, thank you kindly, too,

SHEPHERDS: Take them, eat them, you are welcome. [*To* THE PAGE.] Take them, eat them, you are welcome, too.

THE MOTHER: [*Beckoning to the young people*] Now won't you dance for them?

[*One young girl tries to flee. The young men pull her back, and after much embarrassed nudging and pushing, she returns. Meanwhile,* AMAHL *fetches his shepherd's pipe and sits at the fireplace beside an old bearded shepherd who already holds his pipe. The two begin to play and the dance follows.*]

SHEPHERDS: Don't be bashful, silly girl! Don't be bashful, silly boy! They won't eat you!

[*The dance of* THE SHEPHERDS *which may include two or more dancers, should combine the qualities of primitive folk dancing and folk ritual. It is both an entertainment and a ceremony of welcome and hospitality. The dancers are at first shy and fearful at the realization that they are in the presence of three great* KINGS *and their movements are at times faltering and hesitant. But later, the dance assumes the character of a tarantella, gaining in pace and sureness and ending in a joyous frenzy.* BALTHAZAR *rises to thank the dancers, then resumes his seat.*]

BALTHAZAR: Thank you, good friends, for your dances and your gifts. But now we must bid you good night. We have little time for sleep and a long journey ahead.

SHEPHERDS: Good night, my good Kings, good night and farewell. The pale stars foretell that dawn is in sight. Good night, my good Kings, good night and farewell. The night wind foretells the day will be bright.

[THE SHEPHERDS *pass before* THE KINGS, *bowing as they depart.* THE

MOTHER *bids them good night at the door and for a moment watches them down the road. After all have gone their voices are still heard on the winter air.*]

ALL: Good night.

[*Having closed the door,* AMAHL *and* THE MOTHER *bid* THE KINGS *good night. While* THE MOTHER *prepares for herself a pallet of sheepskins on the floor,* AMAHL *seizes his opportunity and speaks to* KING KASPAR.]

AMAHL: Excuse me, sir, amongst your magic stones is there . . . is there one that could cure a crippled boy?

KASPAR: Eh?

[*Defeated by* KASPAR'S *deafness,* AMAHL *goes sadly to his pallet of straw.*]

AMAHL: Never mind . . . good night.

SHEPHERDS: [*From off-stage*] Good night, good night, The dawn is in sight. Good night, farewell, good night.

[THE MOTHER *and* AMAHL *have lain down on their pallets.* THE KINGS, *still sitting on the rude bench, settle themselves to sleep, leaning against each other.* THE PAGE *curls himself up at their feet, his arms laid protectively over the rich gifts. His lantern has been placed on the floor by the fireplace, leaving only a dim glow in the room. The lights in the hut are lowered completely to denote the passage of time. On the last chords of the interlude the interior of the hut is slowly lighted by the first pale rays of the dawn from the hills.*]

THE MOTHER. [*Still sitting on her pallet,* THE MOTHER *cannot take her eyes from the treasure guarded by* THE PAGE] All that gold! All that gold! I wonder if rich people know what to do with their gold! Do they know how a child could be fed? Do rich people know? Do they know that a house can be kept warm all day with burning logs? Do rich people know? Do they know how to roast sweet corn on the fire? Do they know? Do they know how to fill a courtyard with doves? Do they know? Do they know how to milk a clover-fed goat? Do they know how to spice hot wine on cold winter nights? Do they know? All that gold! All that gold! Oh, what I could do for my child with that gold! Why should it all go to a child they don't even know? They are asleep. Do I dare? If I take some they'll never miss it.

[*Slowly she draws herself across the floor, dragging her body with her hands. Her words become a hushed whisper.*]

For my child . . . for my child . . . for my child . . .

[*As* THE MOTHER *touches the gold,* THE PAGE *is instantly aroused. He seizes her arm, crying to his masters.* THE MOTHER *pulls frantically to free herself, dragging* THE PAGE *into the center of the room. She still clutches the gold and jewels she has seized.*]

THE PAGE: Thief! Thief!

[THE KINGS *awaken in confusion and rise.*]

MELCHIOR, BALTHAZAR: What is it? What is it?

THE PAGE: I've seen her steal some of the gold. She's a thief! Don't let her go! She's stolen the gold!

KASPAR, MELCHIOR, BALTHAZAR: Shame! Shame!

THE PAGE: Give it back or I'll tear it out of you!

[AMAHL *awakens, at first completely bewildered. When he sees his* MOTHER *in the hands of* THE PAGE *he helps himself up with his crutch and awkwardly hurls himself upon* THE PAGE *beating him hysterically and pulling his hair, in an effort to force the man to release* THE MOTHER]

KINGS, THE PAGE: Give it back! Give it back!

AMAHL: Don't you dare! Don't you dare, ugly man, hurt my mother! I'll smash in your face! I'll knock out your teeth! Don't you dare! Don't you dare, ugly man, hurt my mother!

[*Rushing to* KING KASPAR *and tugging at his robe.*]

Oh, Mister King, don't let him hurt my mother! My mother is good. She cannot do anything wrong. I'm the one who lies. I'm the one who steals.

[*Rushing back to attack* THE PAGE.]

Don't you dare! Don't you dare, ugly man, hurt my mother! I'll break all your bones! I'll bash in your head!

[*At a sign from* KASPAR, THE PAGE *releases* THE MOTHER. *Still kneeling, she raises her arms toward her son. Choked by tears,* AMAHL *staggers toward her and, letting his crutch fall, collapses, sobbing, into his* MOTHER'S *arms.*]

MELCHIOR: Oh, woman, you may keep the gold. The Child we seek doesn't need our gold. On love, on love alone He will build His kingdom. His pierced hand will hold no scepter. His haloed head will wear no crown. His might will not be built on your toil. Swifter than lightning He will soon walk among us. He will bring us new life and receive our death, and the keys to His city belong to the poor.

[*Turning to the other* KINGS.]

Let us leave, my friends.

[*Freeing herself from* AMAHL'S *embrace,* THE MOTHER *throws herself on her knees before* THE KINGS, *spilling the gold she has taken from her hands onto the carpet. Meanwhile,* AMAHL *is on his feet, leaning on his crutch.*]

THE MOTHER: Oh, no, wait . . . take back your gold! For such a King I've waited all my life. And if I weren't so poor I would send a gift of my own to such a child.

AMAHL: But, Mother, let me send him my crutch. Who knows, he may need one, and this I made myself.

THE MOTHER: But that you can't, you can't!

[THE MOTHER *moves to stop him as he starts to raise the crutch.* AMAHL *lifts the crutch. There is a complete hush in the room. The boy takes one step toward* THE KINGS, *then realizes that he has moved without the help of his crutch.*]

AMAHL: [*in a whisper*] I walk, Mother . . . I walk, Mother!

KASPAR: He walks . . .

MELCHIOR: He walks . . .

BALTHAZAR: He walks . . .

THE MOTHER: He walks . . .

[*Step by step,* AMAHL *very slowly makes his way toward* THE KINGS, *the crutch held before him in his outstretched hands.* THE MOTHER *rises and draws back, almost fearful of the miracle she beholds.*]

KASPAR, MELCHIOR, BALTHAZAR: It is a sign from the Holy Child. We must give praise to the newborn King. We must praise Him. This is a sign from God!

[*Having placed the crutch in the outstretched hands of* KING KASPAR, AMAHL *moves uncertainly to the center of the room. With growing confidence,* AMAHL *begins to jump and caper about the room.*]

AMAHL: Look, Mother, I can dance, I can jump, I can run!

KASPAR, MELCHIOR, BALTHAZR: Truly, he can dance, he can jump, he can run!

[THE MOTHER *and* THE KINGS *follow* AMAHL *breathlessly, fearing that he may fall. At last, as he turns a clumsy pirouette,* AMAHL *does stumble and fall to the floor.*]

THE MOTHER: [*She goes quickly to* AMAHL *and lifts him from the floor*] Please, my darling, be careful now. You must take care not to hurt yourself.

KASPAR, MELCHIOR, BALTHAZAR: Oh, good woman, you must not be afraid. For he is loved by the Son of God.

KASPAR: Oh, blessed child, may I touch you?

MELCHIOR: Oh, blessed child, may I touch you?

BALTHAZAR: Oh, blessed child, may I touch you?

[*One at a time,* THE KINGS *pass before* AMAHL *and lay their hands upon him. Then each goes across to take up his gift to the Child, ready to begin the departure.* THE PAGE *comes last, prostrating himself on the floor before* AMAHL.]

THE PAGE: Oh, blessed child, may I touch you?

AMAHL: [*Enjoying a first taste of self-importance*] Well, I don't know if I'm going to let you touch me.

THE MOTHER: [*In gentle reproof*] Amahl!

AMAHL: Oh, all right . . . but just once. Look, Mother, I can fight, I can work, I can play! Oh Mother, let me go with the Kings. I want to take the crutch to the Child myself.

KASPAR, MELCHIOR, BALTHAZAR: Yes, good woman, let him come with us! We'll take good care of him, we'll bring him back on a camel's back.

[AMAHL *and his* MOTHER *are together apart from the others, she kneeling before him.*]

THE MOTHER: Do you really want to go?

AMAHL: Yes, Mother.

THE MOTHER: Are you sure, sure, sure?

AMAHL: I'm sure!

THE MOTHER: Yes, I think you should go, and bring thanks to the Child yourself.

AMAHL: [*Not quite believing his ears*] Are you sure, sure, sure?

THE MOTHER: Go on, get ready.

KASPAR: What did she say?

BALTHAZAR: She said he can come.

KASPAR: Oh, lovely, lovely, lo . . .

[*Again* BALTHAZAR *restrains* KASPAR'S *exuberance.*]

BALTHAZAR: Kaspar!

THE MOTHER: What to do with your crutch?

AMAHL: You can tie it to my back.

THE MOTHER: Don't forget to wear your hat!

AMAHL: I shall always wear my hat.

THE MOTHER: So, my darling, goodbye!

AMAHL, THE MOTHER: So, my darling, goodbye! I shall miss you very much.

THE MOTHER: Wash your ears!

AMAHL: Yes, I promise.

THE MOTHER: Don't tell lies!

AMAHL: No, I promise. Feed my bird!

THE MOTHER: Yes, I promise.

AMAHL: Watch the cat!

THE MOTHER: Yes, I promise.

AMAHL: I shall miss you very much.

SHEPHERDS: [*From off-stage*] Shepherds, arise!

MELCHIOR: Are you ready?

AMAHL: Yes, I'm ready.

MELCHIOR: Let's go then.

[*Led by* THE PAGE, *who has taken up his burdens and the heavy lamp,* THE THREE KINGS *start their stately procession out of the cottage.*]

SHEPHERDS: Come, oh, shepherds, come outside. All the stars have left the sky. Oh, sweet dawn, oh, dawn of peace.

[AMAHL *rushes into his* MOTHER'S *arms, bidding her goodbye, then hurries to catch up with the departing* KINGS. *Having taken his place at the end of the procession,* AMAHL *begins to play his pipes as he goes. Outside, the soft colors of dawn are brightening the sky, and a few great flakes of snow have begun to fall upon the road.* THE MOTHER *stands alone in the doorway of the cottage. Then she goes outside to wave once more to* AMAHL, *as he turns to her, just before he disappears at the bend in the road. The curtain falls very slowly.*]

Part Three:

NON-RELIGIOUS PLAYS

THE NUTCRACKER AND THE MOUSE-KING

A SCENARIO OF THE ORIGINAL 1816 TALE TO BE IMPROVISED AS A PLAY, MIME OR DANCE, WITH OR WITHOUT TCHAIKOVSKY'S MUSIC

by E.T.A. Hoffman

CHARACTERS

FRITZ   aged twelve or thereabouts

MARIE   his sister, eleven or thereabouts

DROSSELMEIER   their godfather, a clockmaker and a judge

MOTHER   their kind mother

FATHER   their father, a doctor

THE MOUSE-KING   a horror

THE NUTCRACKER   a hero

AN ARMY OF MICE   more or less

AN ARMY OF TOY SOLDIERS   less, unfortunately

DROSSELMEIER'S NEPHEW   thirteen or thereabouts

SETTINGS: *Christmas Eve in the parlor of Dr. Stahlbaum's house and the hallway just outside*

TIME: *a hundred years ago or thereabouts.*

At rise: The living room or parlor is separated from the hallway by double doors which at the moment are closed. But inside we see the magnificently decorated tree around which are spread brightly ribboned gifts. At one side of the room stands a glass case filled with toys, rows of dolls and soldiers. Plates of candies and bowls of nuts fill the table tops. The hall is dominated by a tall grandfather's clock with the carved figure of an owl residing on top. The hands of the clock move during the play and its insides will be exposed later on. Right now it is ticking as a normal clock should.

Fritz and Marie enter, excited that Christmas Eve finally has arrived. They rush to open the parlor doors, only to discover they are firmly locked. Fritz twists the doorknobs, Marie pounds her fists against the wood. There is no reply from within. They look at each other puzzled and disappointed. Marie starts to leave when Fritz decides, "No, we'll stay right here and wait. Someone's bound to come sooner or later. After all, it's Christmas Eve!"

They settle on the floor, directly in front of the doors, staring straight ahead when suddenly from the side appears the figure of a short man carrying a large box.

Fritz and Marie jump up and run to greet their Godfather, the Judge Drosselmeier, an old family friend. An unusual sight in his flowing white wig and black eye patch, he wears a long cape that nearly touches the floor.

Fritz and Marie hug him and point to the box. "Is this for us?" "What have you made?" "Let me see!" "Let me see!" "We like your presents best."

The old man raises the box above their heads, out of reach. "No, you must wait for the music and for the party to begin," he reminds them.

And at once, as if by magic, music is heard, the double doors fly open and bright light pours from within. There in the middle of parlor stand Mother and Father, beckoning the children to enter and see the many gifts piled around the base of the Christmas tree.

Marie shouts with joy; Fritz leaps high into the air. They scurry about looking at the presents, shaking several to see if they can guess what may be inside. But they return each package unopened because there is one they wish to see most of all. Yes, the box is still under the arm of old Drosselmeier. When the parents give their permission, the Judge makes the children stand back while he unwraps the box, as slowly as possible, each layer of tissue paper revealing another beneath, until the suspense is almost more than they can bear. Realizing he has teased them enough, he pulls back the final wrapping and takes out a large carved figure.

"How handsome!" Marie exclaims. "How unusual," Fritz proclaims. Then looking at each other and shrugging their shoulders, they ask, "What is it?"

"A soldier," their Godfather replies by marching about the room in a very military manner.

Inspecting the soldier — a Hussar, actually, which means he is a light horseman in the Hungarian manner — Marie indicates that he looks the way she imagines Drosselmeier did when he was young. The old man, honored with this compliment, bows to her.

Fritz, somewhat curious about this present, examines it closely. "What does it do?" he asks.

"Let me show you," the old man replies, reaching for a nut in a large bowl on the table. He places it in the mouth of the Hussar and slaps down the handle in the back of the figure. "Here." He hands a kernel to each of them.

"A nutcracker!" "Let me try it!" "Let me try it," they beg, becoming even more excited when each extracts from the wooden white teeth of the soldier — whole nutmeats, which they proudly present to their parents.

"I want him, Godfather!" cries Marie.

"He's mine," counters Fritz. "He's mine."

And a shouting match ensues which finally has to be stopped by Father: "Children, listen to me. Marie, you shall be the Nutcracker's nurse and look after him but Fritz may use him at any time he desires. That's fair."

Marie begins to crack one small nut after another while Fritz waits to get his turn. Becoming impatient, he grabs the Nutcracker and sticks an extra large nut into its mouth. He slams down the handle and then lifts upwards. The uncracked nut falls out along with three white teeth!

"Oh, look what you've done!" Marie sobs, scooping up the figure. His jaw is broken. "My dear nutcracker!"

"He just lost some teeth. But who cares anyway?" Fritz responds, defensively. "I do," Marie reminds him. "He looks so unhappy with those missing teeth. How can you be so mean?"

"He's mine as much as yours," Fritz reminds her. "Father said so," He glances at their parents who have been conversing quietly with Drosselmeier at the side.

Marie wraps the Nutcracker in her shawl, assuring that she will give him the best care. Sitting on the floor, she rocks him in her arms.

Leaving his sister and the Nutcracker alone, Fritz plays with his toy soldiers.

Godfather Drosselmeier, touched by the picture of the little girl holding the Nutcracker he has carved, stands over her, asking how she can make such a fuss about this little fellow. She replies that if he were dressed in the same sort of uniform as the Nutcracker, he would look as handsome. The old man is charmed by this and taps her on the head, affectionately.

The clock ticks loudly, then chimes.

The parents say goodnight to Drosselmeier who seeing the children are each involved in their separate worlds blows them a farewell kiss and tiptoes out. Mother and Father put out most of the candles and likewise retire after tapping Marie and Fritz on their shoulders and pointing upstairs to their bedrooms. The children nod that they soon will be on their ways to bed. And indeed Fritz, after watching the dying light reflect from the fireplace, does place his last soldier into the case and drags himself, already half asleep, out into the hall and off.

The second he is gone, Marie is on her feet at the table where she unwraps the Nutcracker. She rolls up the shawl to make a soft bed for him. "I'll take good care of you, dear Nutcracker," Marie assures her friend. She hugs the carved figure, carefully placing him in the improvised bed.

The tall clock begins to move as the owl carved at the top drops its wings down over the face. The ticking becomes louder and louder, followed by twelve bonging chimes that are unlike any Marie has heard before.

She runs to the clock to discover what is wrong when she notices that instead of the owl on top her Godfather is sitting there with his coattails hanging down. She jumps back, startled.

"Godpapa, how did you get up there?" she exclaims. "Come down to me. Something strange is happening. I'm frightened."

But he doesn't hear her over the increasing noise brought about by the feet of little Mice who enter and run about the room, their eyes glittering in the light. Then with a royal fanfare, the Mice stand at attention to herald the arrival of the Mouse-king, a strange sight indeed!

Marie gulps as he approaches for here is a mouse as large as a man. But this is not what makes him unusual. No, his seven heads do! Yes, that's right, a mouse with seven heads, each wearing a shining bright crown.

Marie staggers in disbelief. "Godpapa Drosselmeier," she cries, "Tell me what to do."

From top of the clock, he points to the toy cabinet where Fritz has stored his soldiers. And from within we hear them speaking in unison:

"Arise, arise

On to battle, tonight, tonight,

Ready to fight,

Ready to fight"

And a line of toy soldiers — now life-sized — march forth, reciting their battle cry, over and over.

Standing directly between them, and the Mice, Marie realizes that only she separates the two armies. Once more she looks to the clock. "Godpapa, I can't move," she quivers, not knowing what to do.

Drosselmeier directs her attention to the sleeping Nutcracker who to her amazement throws off his blanket, rises life-sized and brandishes his sword for everyone to see.

"My fellows, good soldiers all, are you with me," he shouts. "Will you help me defend this lady?" The soldiers reply in unison:

"Ready to fight; ready to fight!

We're ready to fight!"

Then escorting Marie to the side where she can watch, he adds, "I will be grateful forever for the kindness you have shown me." He bows to her and returns to lead the soldiers. "Beat the march," he commands, and the drums begin. He runs back and forth through the ranks of soldiers, inspecting them and giving words of encouragement.

Flags unfurl and trumpets blare adding to the tension as the Mice under the leadership of their King also prepare for the first encounter.

At the command of the Nutcracker who orders "Ready, Aim, Fire," the soldiers throw objects at the Mice battalions. These are sugar-plums taken from a plate on the table. Instead of harming the Mice, they cover them in white sugar powder. Insulted by the indignity, the Mice start throwing their ammunition which they take from a candy jar.

Marie, standing on a chair, sees what is happening and warns the soldiers, "Be careful, they're going to bombard you with jawbreakers!"

Indeed, the air quickly fills with brightly colored balls of sweetness. Several soldiers are hit and stagger about as if wounded.

Marie calls to the Nutcracker, "They're winning." As they advance, the Mice make hissing noises of victory. "Use that bowl of nuts," Marie advises, adding, "Uncracked!"

"Uncracked?" The Nutcracker is shocked to think that anyone would serve a nut uncracked, even in the time of war. He overcomes his pride and realizes the importance of the moment, shouting, "Ready, aim, fire!" The nuts bring down the front ranks of Mice who scurry about in great distress.

The Mouse-king runs to the wounded, "Back on your feet." Quickly, he rallies his dazed forces. "Back on you feet. Stop your squeaking and get ready to use your weapons."

Marie, hearing this, warns the Nutcracker who strides amidst his men, ordering them to prepare their arms. "Are you men or mice?" he demands. "Men" is the response, quite firmly. "Well, it's time to prove it?"

The Mouse-king likewise parades up and down his lines, "Are you mice or men?" "Mice," they reply, quite proudly. "Very well, show me...in all my fourteen eyes."

Both leaders give the signal for hand-to-hand combat and once more music blasts forth and flags are flared. As the armies advance toward each other, they both produce their weapons —large candy canes — which they wield as swords. The stage fills in colorful combat with Marie cheering the soldiers onward.

The Nutcracker and the Mouse-king parry but the match becomes uneven when the many heads and eyes of the mouse prove a great distraction to the swordplay. "Bring out the reserves," the Nutcracker shouts in growing desperation. The soldiers reply there are no reserves, retreating closer and closer to the glass case which is their home.

Pressed against the door, the Nutcracker bellows in his best Shakespearean voice, "A horse! A horse! My kingdom for a horse!"

"There is no horse," Marie replies. "And watch out." She indicates that he is about to be seized by two mice who indeed do pin him against the glass case.

Jumping and clapping with delight, the Mouse-king sings out of all seven heads, "I've won. The mice are the winners. We've won!"

"Oh, my dear Nutcracker, what can I do to help you?" She looks up at Godfather for assistance but he shrugs that this time he has no solution.

The Mouse-king triumphs over the Nutcracker who gives one last cry, "Marie, think, please think of something."

She panics for a half-second, then bends down and removes her left shoe which she hurls at the King in a direct hit on his back. He freezes. Instantly, the lights flicker and go out.

When they return the stage is empty except for the figure of Marie who has fainted and fallen to the floor, motionless.

The face of the clock has blown off and all of the internal works are hanging out, broken and dangling.

Mother and Father come dashing into the room. They see Marie, revive her and help her to the sofa where they cover her with the same shawl that had served as the Nutcracker's blanket. "Mother, is the Nutcracker safe?" she whimpers. "Where are the mice?"

"Calm yourself! And don't talk nonsense!" they say as they ignore her questions. Fritz now joins them. "Marie, what's happened to you?" Fritz asks. "You look different."

"You should have seen the battle here between the Nutcracker and the Mouse-king. It was horrible!" she attempts to tell them.

They indicate that there are no mice now and the toy soldiers are standing safely in their case.

"Look who's here. Now you'll feel better." They usher in Godfather Drosselmeier who comes to comfort Marie.

"Godpapa, why didn't you get down from the clock and help me? That wasn't very nice of you. It's your fault that I'm lying here now."

"What is she talking about?" Mother demands.

Drosselmeier doesn't answer but begins to tick like a clock, chiming and ringing, dancing about, singing:

"Ding dong, cling clang;
    Bing bong loud and long
    To chase the mice away.
    Bing bong loud and long
    To stop the Mouse-King's song;
    To chase the mice away.

During this song he puts the clock back together and soon it is ticking happily away, as good as new.

"Dear Judge," Mother says, "you make no more sense than Marie. What is the meaning of all this tick-tocking?"

"Marie understands," he insists and then whispering in her ear, "Don't be cross with me for not fighting the Mouse-king. You did that beautifully on you own. I know you will forgive me when you see what I've brought." And from under his cape he produces the wooden Nutcracker.

Marie sits up, joyously embracing the toy. "Look, Fritz, Godfather has replaced his missing teeth and mended his broken jaw. Oh, thank you, Godfather. He looks so handsome," she sighs.

"You see how kind Godfather Drosselmeier is to you and your Nutcracker," Mother says.

"Indeed, I do forgive you, Godpapa," Marie agrees. "But I hope I never see that Mouse-king again with his seven heads and seven crowns."

"Marie, no more of this Mouse-king nonsense, please. You're safe now with all of us here," her father assures her.

"Yes, my bright new Nutcracker will protect me. Won't you?" she asks the toy. Then Drosselmeier interrupts, "I almost forgot, I have another surprise for you, dear Marie. Standing in the hallway, waiting to be announced." He goes to the door, opening it with great fanfare. "My nephew wants to meet you."

There stands a young man just a bit older than Marie who is as handsome as the Nutcracker when he came to life in the previous scenes (and, in fact, is played by the same actor). As he approaches, Marie rises from the sofa almost like a marionette, reaching out her arm to receive him. He kneels before her and quite formally kisses her hand.

"I'm pleased to meet you," Marie beams.

"I've brought you a small gift, Miss Marie," The young man says, drawing forth a handkerchief tied into a small bundle.

"Open it," orders old Drosselmeier.

Marie unties the red ribbon and looks inside.

Amazed, her face registers astonishment.

Impatiently, Fritz demands to know what she holds. But Marie is too overcome to answer.

Finally, Father asks softly, "Are none of us to know?"

Drosselmeier, after another pause, reassures Marie, "It's all right to show them, even if they may not understand."

"He...he...he...," she stammers, ...has given me..."

"Yes, dear?" Mother and Father say in unison.

"Seven little crowns made of gold," she proclaims and opens the handkerchief wide for everyone to see. They, of course, resemble exactly those worn by the Mouse-king.

"How beautiful!" Mother exclaims.

"Pure gold, it looks to me" Father adds.

"Absolutely," Drosselmeier exclaims, "good enough for a king."

"Seven kings," Fritz corrects him.

"Yes, seven," Marie smiles, then realizes she has not thanked him. "I don't know what to say."

"They are but charms to wear on your bracelet, Miss Marie," the young man assures her.

"Thank you, dear Nutcracker, thank you" Marie blurts out.

Fritz bursts into wild laughter. "Did you hear what she called him?" he asks everyone. "Dear Nutcracker! Oh, Sister, you are a silly goose!" He bends over, convulsed in giggles.

"Dear Master Nutcracker, such a kind gentleman," Marie begins, almost as in a trance. "And, yes, I accept you as my betrothed."

"Mother, Father, she's crazy. We must take her to the mad house at once," Fritz spurts out, still half laughing. "Poor girl!"

Mother instructs Fritz to be quiet and takes the situation under her control. "Now, Master Drosselmeier, if you will escort Marie, we will go into Christmas breakfast and then begin to open our gifts."

Mother and Father lead the exit, followed by Godfather and Fritz, then Marie and Master Drosselmeier who perform a bit of a waltz on their way out.

As the music swells, the lights dim except for a circle engulfing the figure of the wooden Nutcracker who has been left behind.

CURTAIN

A CHRISTMAS CAROL:
SCROOGE AND MARLEY

adapted from Charles Dickens

by Israel Horovitz

THE PEOPLE OF THE PLAY

JACOB MARLEY, a spectre

EBENEZER SCROOGE, not yet
dead, which is to
say still alive

BOB CRATCHIT, Scrooge's
clerk

FRED, Scrooge's nephew

THIN DO-GOODER

PORTLY DO-GOODER

SPECTRES (Various), carrying
money-boxes

THE GHOST OF CHRISTMAS
PAST

FOUR JOCUND TRAVELERS

A BAND OF SINGERS

A BAND OF DANCERS

LITTLE BOY SCROOGE

YOUNG MAN SCROOGE

FAN, Scrooge's little sister

THE SCHOOLMASTER

SCHOOLMATES

FEZZIWIG, a fine and fair
employer

DICK, young Scrooge's co-
worker

YOUNG SCROOGE

A FIDDLER

MORE DANCERS

SCROOGE'S LOST LOVE

SCROOGE'S LOST LOVE'S
DAUGHTER

SCROOGE'S LOST LOVE'S HUS-
BAND

THE GHOST OF CHRISTMAS
PRESENT

SOME BAKERS

MRS. CRATCHIT, Bob
Cratchit's wife

BELINDA CRATCHIT, a daughter

MARTHA CRATCHIT, another
daughter

PETER CRATCHIT, a son

TINY TIM CRATCHIT, another
son

SCROOGE'S NIECE, Fred's wife

THE GHOST OF CHRISTMAS
FUTURE, a mute
Phantom

THREE MEN OF BUSINESS

DRUNKS, SCOUNDRELS

WOMEN OF THE STREETS

A CHARWOMAN

MRS. DILBER

JOE, an old second-hand
goods dealer

A CORPSE, very like Scrooge

AN INDEBTED FAMILY

ADAM, a young boy

A POULTERER

A GENTLEWOMAN

SOME MORE MEN OF BUSINESS

THE PLACE OF THE PLAY

Various locations in and around the City of London, including SCROOGE's *Chambers and Offices; the* CRATCHIT *Home;* FRED's *Home;* SCROOGE's *School;* FEZZIWIG's *Offices;* OLD JOE's *Hide-a-Way.*

THE TIME OF THE PLAY

The entire action of the play takes place on Christmas Eve, Christmas Day, and the morning after Christmas, 1843.

ACT ONE

SCENE 1

Ghostly mist in auditorium. A single spotlight on JACOB MARLEY. *He is ancient; awful, dead-eyed. He speaks straight out to auditorium.*

MARLEY: [*Cackle-voiced.*] My name is Jacob Marley and I am dead. [*He laughs.*] Oh, no, there's no doubt that I am dead. The register of my burial was signed by the clergyman, the clerk, the undertaker...and by my chief mourner...Ebenezer Scrooge...[*Pause; remembers*] I am dead as a door-nail.

[A spotlight fades up on SCROOGE, *in his counting-house, counting. Lettering on the window behind* SCROOGE *reads:* "SCROOGE AND MAR-LEY, LTD." *The spotlight is tight on* SCROOGE's *head and shoulders. We shall not yet see into the offices and setting. Ghostly music continues, under.* MARLEY *looks across at* SCROOGE; *pitifully. After a moment's pause.]*

MARLEY: [*Cont'd.*] I present him to you: Ebenezer Scrooge...England's most tightfisted hand at the grindstone, Scrooge! A squeezing, wrenching, grasping, scraping, clutching, covetous, old sinner! Secret, and self-contained, and solitary as an oyster. The cold within him freezes his old features, nips his pointed nose, shrivels his cheek, stiffens his gait; makes his eyes red, his thin lips blue; and speaks out shrewdly in his grating voice. Look at him. Look at him...

[SCROOGE *counts and mumbles.*]

SCROOGE: They owe me money and I will collect. I will have them jailed, if I have to. They owe me money and I will collect what is due me.

[MARLEY *moves toward* SCROOGE; *two steps. The spotlight stays with him.*]

MARLEY: [*Disgusted.*] He and I were partners for I don't know how many years. Scrooge was my sole executor, my sole administrator, my sole assign, my sole residuary legatee, my sole friend and my sole mourner. But Scrooge was not so cut up by the sad event of my death, but that he was an excellent man of business on the very day of my funeral, and solemnized it with an undoubted bargain. [*Pauses again in disgust.*] He never painted out my name from the window. There it stands, on the window and above the warehouse door: Scrooge and Marley. Sometimes people new to our business call him Scrooge and sometimes they call him Marley. He answers to both names. It's all the same to him. And it's cheaper than painting in a new sign, isn't it? [*Pauses; moves closer to* SCROOGE.] Nobody has ever stopped him in the street to say, with gladsome looks, "My dear Scrooge, how are you? When will you come to see me?" No beggars implored him to bestow a trifle, no children ever ask him what it is o'clock, no man or woman now, or ever in his life, not once, inquire the way to such and such a place.

[MARLEY *stands next to* SCROOGE *now. They share, so it seems, a spotlight.*]

MARLEY: [*Cont'd.*] But what does Scrooge care of any of this? It is the very thing he likes! To edge his way along the crowded paths of life, warning all human sympathy to keep its distance.

[*A ghostly bell rings in the distance.* MARLEY *moves away from* SCROOGE, *now. As he does, he "takes" the light:* SCROOGE *has disappeared into the black void beyond.* MARLEY *walks, talking directly to the audience. Pauses.*]

MARLEY: [*Cont'd.*] The bell tolls and I must take my leave. You must stay a while with Scrooge and watch him play out his scroogey life. It is now the story: the once-upon-a-time. Scrooge is in his counting house. Where else? Christmas eve and Scrooge is busy in his counting-house. It is cold, bleak, biting weather outside: foggy withal: and, if you listen closely, you can hear the people in the court go wheezing up and down, beating their hands upon their breasts, and stamping their feet upon the pavement stones to warm them...

[*The clocks outside strike three.*]

MARLEY: [*Cont'd.*] Only three! and quite dark outside already: it has not been light all day this day.

[*This ghostly bell rings in the distance again.* MARLEY *looks about him. Music in.* MARLEY *flies away.*]

SCENE 2

Christmas music in, sung by a live chorus, full. At conclusion of song, sound fades under and into distance. Lights up in set: offices of SCROOGE AND MARLEY, LTD. SCROOGE *sits at his desk, at work. Near him is a tiny fire. His door is open and in his line of vision, we see* SCROOGE's *clerk,* BOB CRATCHIT, *who sits in a dismal tank of a cubicle, copying letters. Near* CRATCHIT *is a fire so tiny as to barely cast a light: perhaps it is one pitifully glowing coal? Cratchit rubs his hands together, puts on a white comforter and tries to heat his hands around his candle.* SCROOGE's *nephew enters, unseen.*

SCROOGE: What are you doing, Cratchit? Acting cold, are you? Next, you'll be asking to replenish your coal from my coal-box, won't you? Well, save your breath, Cratchit! Unless you're prepared to find employ elsewhere!

NEPHEW: [*Cheerfully; surprising* SCROOGE.] A Merry Christmas to you, Uncle! God save you!

SCROOGE: Bah! Humbug!

NEPHEW: Christmas a "humbug," Uncle? I'm sure you don't mean that.

SCROOGE: I do! Merry Christmas? What right do you have to be merry? What reason have you to be merry? You're poor enough!

NEPHEW: Come, then. What right have you to be dismal? What reason have you to be morose? You're rich enough.

SCROOGE: Bah! Humbug!

NEPHEW: Don't be cross, Uncle.

SCROOGE: What else can I be? Eh? When I live in a world of fools such as this? Merry Christmas? What's Christmas time to you but a time of paying bills without any money; a time for finding yourself a year older, but not an hour richer. If I could work my will, every idiot who goes about with "Merry Christmas" on his lips, should be boiled with his own pudding, and buried with a stake of holly through his heart. He should!

NEPHEW: Uncle!

SCROOGE: Nephew! You keep Christmas in your own way and let me keep it in mine.

NEPHEW: Keep it! But you don't keep it, Uncle.

SCROOGE: Let me leave it alone, then. Much good it has ever done you!

NEPHEW: There are many things from which I have derived good, by which I have not profited, I daresay. Christmas among the rest. But I am sure that I always thought of Christmastime, when it has come round—as a good time: the only time I know of when men and women seem to open their shut-up hearts freely and to think of people below them as if they really were fellow passengers to the grave, and not another race of creatures bound on other journeys. And therefore, Uncle, though it has never put a scrap of gold or silver in my pocket, I believe that it has done me good, and that it will do me good; and I say, God bless it!

[*The* CLERK *in the tank applauds, looks at the furious* SCROOGE *and pokes out his tiny fire, as if in exchange for the moment of impropriety.* SCROOGE *yells at him.*]

SCROOGE: [*To the* CLERK.] Let me hear another sound from you and you'll keep your Christmas by losing your situation. [*To the* NEPHEW.] You're quite a powerful speaker, sir. I wonder you don't go into Parliament.

NEPHEW: Don't be angry, Uncle. Come! Dine with us tomorrow.

SCROOGE: I'd rather see myself dead than see myself with your family!

NEPHEW: But, why? Why?

SCROOGE: Why did you get married?

NEPHEW: Because I fell in love.

SCROOGE: That, sir, is the only thing that you have said to me in your entire lifetime which is even more ridiculous than "Merry Christmas"! [*Turns from* NEPHEW.] Good afternoon.

NEPHEW: Nay, Uncle, you never came to see me before I married either. Why give it as a reason for not coming now?

SCROOGE: Good afternoon, Nephew!

NEPHEW: I want nothing from you; I ask nothing of you: why cannot we be friends?

SCROOGE: Good afternoon!

NEPHEW: I am sorry with all my heart, to find you so resolute. But I have made the trial in homage to Christmas, and I'll keep my Christmas humor to the last. So A Merry Christmas, Uncle!

SCROOGE: Good afternoon!

NEPHEW: And A Happy New Year!

SCROOGE: Good afternoon!

NEPHEW: [*He stands facing* SCROOGE.] Uncle, you are the most... [*Pauses.*] no, I shan't. My Christmas humor is intact [*Pause.*] God bless you, Uncle...[NEPHEW *turns and starts for the door; he stops at* CRATCHIT's *cage.*] Merry Christmas, Bob Cratchit.

CRATCHIT: Merry Christmas to you, sir, and a very, very happy New Year.

SCROOGE: [*Calling across to them.*] Oh, fine, a perfection, just fine...to see the perfect pair of you: husbands, with wives and children to support...my clerk there earning fifteen shillings a week...and the perfect pair of you, talking about a Merry Christmas! [*Pauses.*] I'll retire to Bedlam!

NEPHEW: [*To* CRATCHIT.] He's impossible!

CRATCHIT: Oh, mind him not, sir. He's getting on in years, and he's alone. He's noticed your visit. I'll wager your visit has warmed him.

NEPHEW: Him? Uncle Ebenezer Scrooge? Warmed? You are a better Christian than I am, sir.

CRATCHIT: [*Opening the door for* NEPHEW; *two* DO-GOODERS *will enter, as* NEPHEW *exits.*] Good day to you, sir, and God bless.

NEPHEW: God bless...

[*One man who enters is portly, the other thin. Both are pleasant.*]

CRATCHIT: Can I help you, gentlemen?

THIN MAN: [*Carrying papers and books; looks around* CRATCHIT *to* SCROOGE.] Scrooge and Marley's, I believe. Have I the pleasure of addressing Mr. Scrooge, or Mr. Marley?

SCROOGE: Mr. Marley has been dead these seven years. He died seven years ago this very night.

PORTLY MAN: We have no doubt his liberality is well represented by his surviving partner...[*Offers his calling card.*]

SCROOGE: [*Handing back the card; unlooked at.*] Good afternoon.

THIN MAN: This will take but a moment, sir...

PORTLY MAN: At this festive season of the year, Mr. Scrooge, it is more than usually desirable that we should make some slight provision for the poor and destitute, who suffer greatly at the present time. Many thousands are in want of common necessities; hundreds of thousands are in want of common comforts, sir.

SCROOGE: Are there no prisons?

PORTLY MAN: Plenty of prisons.

SCROOGE: And aren't the Union workhouses still in operation?

THIN MAN: They are. Still. I wish that I could say that they art not.

SCROOGE: The Treadmill and the Poor Law are in full vigor then?

THIN MAN: Both very busy, sir.

SCROOGE: Ohhh, I see. I was afraid, from what you said at first that something had occurred to stop them from their useful course. [*Pauses.*] I'm glad to hear it.

PORTLY MAN: Under the impression that they scarcely furnish Christian cheer of mind or body to the multitude, a few of us are endeavoring to raise a fund to buy the Poor some meat and drink and means of warmth. We choose this time, because it is a time, of all others, when Want is keenly felt, and Abundance rejoices [*Pen in hand; as well as notepad.*] What shall I put you down for, sir?

SCROOGE: Nothing!

PORTLY MAN: You wish to be left anonymous?

SCROOGE: I wish to be left alone! [*Pauses; turns away; turns back to them.*] Since you ask me what I wish, gentlemen, that is my answer. I help to support the establishments that I have mentioned: they cost enough: and those who are badly off must go there.

THIN MAN: Many can't go there; and many would rather die.

SCROOGE: If they would rather die, they had better do it, and decrease the surplus population. Besides—excuse me—I don't know that.

THIN MAN: But you might know it!

SCROOGE: It's not my business. It's enough for a man to understand his own business, and not to interfere with other people's. Mine occupies me constantly. Good afternoon, gentlemen [SCROOGE *turns his back on the gentlemen and returns to his desk.*]

PORTLY MAN: But, sir, Mr. Scrooge...think of the poor.

SCROOGE: [*Turns suddenly to them. Pauses.*] Take your leave of my offices, sirs, while I am still smiling.

[*The* THIN MAN *looks at the* PORTLY MAN. *They are undone. They shrug. They move to door.* CRATCHIT *hops up to open it for them.*]

THIN MAN: Good day, sir. [*To* CRATCHIT.] A merry Christmas to you, sir...

CRATCHIT: Yes. A Merry Christmas to both you...

PORTLY MAN: Merry Christmas...

[CRATCHIT *silently squeezes something into the hand of the* THIN MAN.]

THIN MAN: What's this?

CRATCHIT: Shhhh...

[CRATCHIT *opens the door; wind and snow whistle into the room.*]

THIN MAN: Thank you, sir, thank you.

[CRATCHIT *closes the door and returns to his workplace.* SCROOGE *is at his own counting table. He talks to* CRATCHIT *without looking up.*]

SCROOGE: It's less of a time of year for being merry, and more a time of year for being loony...if you ask me.

CRATCHIT: Well, I don't know, sir...[*The clock's bell strikes 6 o'clock.*] Well, there it is, eh, sir?

SCROOGE: Saved by six bells, are you?

CRATCHIT: I must be going home...[*He snuffs out his candle and puts on his hat.*] I hope you have a...very very lovely day tomorrow, sir.

SCROOGE: Hmmm. Oh, you'll be wanting the whole day tomorrow, I suppose?

CRATCHIT: If quite convenient, sir.

SCROOGE: It's not convenient, and it's not fair. If I was to stop half-a-crown for it, you'd think yourself ill-used, I'll be bound?

[CRATCHIT *smiles faintly.*]

CRATCHIT: I don't know, sir...

SCROOGE: And yet, you don't think me ill-used, when I pay a day's wages for no work.

CRATCHIT: It's only but once a year...

SCROOGE: A poor excuse for picking a man's pocket every 25th of December! But I suppose you must have the whole day. Be here all the earlier the next morning!

CRATCHIT: Oh, I will, sir, I will. I promise you. And, sir...

SCROOGE: Don't say it, Cratchit.

CRATCHIT: But let me wish you a…

SCROOGE: Don't say it, Cratchit. I warn you…

CRATCHIT: Sir!

SCROOGE: Cratchit!

[CRATCHIT *opens the door.*]

CRATCHIT: All right, then, sir…well…[*Suddenly.*] Merry Christmas, Mr. Scrooge!

[*And he runs out the door, shutting same behind him.* SCROOGE *moves to his desk; gathering his coat, hat, etc. A* BOY *appears at his window.*]

BOY: [*Singing.*] "Away in a manger…"

[SCROOGE *seizes his ruler and whacks at the image of the* BOY *outside. The* BOY *leaves.*]

SCROOGE: Bah! Humbug! Christmas! Bah! Humbug! [*He shuts out the light.*]

A NOTE ON THE CROSSOVER, FOLLOWING SCENE 2

Scrooge will walk alone to his rooms from his offices. As he makes a long slow cross of the stage, the scenery should change, Christmas music will be heard, various people will cross by Scrooge, often smiling happily.

There will be occasional pleasant greetings tossed at him. Scrooge, in contrast to all, will grump and mumble. He will snap at passing boys, as might an old horrid hound.

In short, Scrooge's sounds and movements will define him in contrast from all other people who cross the stage: he is the misanthrope, the malcontent, the miser. He is Scrooge.

This statement of Scrooge's character, by contrast to all other characters, should seem comical to the audience.

During Scrooge's crossover to his rooms, snow should begin to fall. All passers-by will hold their faces to the sky, smiling, allowing snow to shower them lightly. Scrooge, by contrast, will bat at the flakes with his walking-stick, as might an insomniac swat at a sleep-stopping, middle-of-the-night swarm of mosquitoes. He will comment on the blackness of the night, and, finally, reach his rooms and his encounter with the magical spectre: Marley, his eternal mate.

SCENE 3

SCROOGE: No light at all...no moon...that is what is at the center of a Christmas Eve: dead black: void...

[SCROOGE *puts his key in the door's keyhole. He has reached his rooms now. The door knocker changes and is now* MARLEY's *face. A musical sound; quickly: ghosty.* MARLEY's *image is not at all angry, but looks at* SCROOGE *as did the old* MARLEY *look at* SCROOGE. *The hair is curiously stirred; eyes wide open, dead: absent of focus.* SCROOGE *stares wordlessly here. The face, before his very eyes, does deliquesce: it is a knocker again.* SCROOGE *opens the door and checks the back of same, probably for* MARLEY's *pigtail. Seeing nothing but screws and nuts,* SCROOGE *refuses the memory.*]

SCROOGE: [*Cont'd.*] Pooh, pooh!

[*The sound of the door closing resounds throughout the house as thunder. Every room echoes the sound.* SCROOGE *fastens the door and walks across the hall to the stairs, trimming his candle as he goes: and then he goes slowly up the staircase. He checks each room: sitting room, bedroom, lumber-room. He looks under the sofa, under the table: nobody there. He fixes his evening gruel on the hob; changes his jacket.* SCROOGE *sits near the tiny low-flamed fire, sipping his gruel. There are various pictures on the walls: all of them now show likenesses of* MARLEY. SCROOGE *blinks his eyes.*]

SCROOGE: [*Cont'd.*] Bah! Humbug!

[SCROOGE *walks in a circle about the room. The pictures change back into their natural images. He sits down at the table in front of the fire. A bell hangs overhead. It begins to ring, of its own accord. Slowly, surely, begins the ringing of every bell in the house. They continue ringing for nearly half a minute.* SCROOGE *is stunned by the phenomenon. The bells cease their ring- ing all at once. Deep below* SCROOGE, *in the basement of the house, there is the sound of clanking, of some enormous chain being dragged across the floors; and now up the stairs. We hear doors flying open.*]

SCROOGE: [*Cont'd.*] Bah still! Humbug still! This is not happening! I won't believe it!

[MARLEY's *Ghost enters the room. He is horrible to look at: pigtail, vest, suit as usual, but he drags an enormous chain now, to which is fastened cash- boxes, keys, padlocks, ledgers, deeds, and heavy purses fashioned of steel. He is transparent. If possible, we should now, in faithfulness to Dickens' story, be able to see that* MARLEY *has no bowels.* MARLEY *stands opposite the strick- ened* SCROOGE.]

SCROOGE: [*Cont'd.*] How now! What do you want of me?

MARLEY: Much!

SCROOGE: Who are you?

MARLEY: Ask me who I was.

SCROOGE: Who were you then?

MARLEY: In life, I was your business partner: Jacob Marley.

SCROOGE: I see…can you sit down?

MARLEY: I can.

SCROOGE: Do it then.

MARLEY: I shall. [MARLEY *sits opposite* SCROOGE, *in the chair across the table, at the front of the fireplace.*] You don't believe in me.

SCROOGE: I don't.

MARLEY: Why do you doubt your senses?

SCROOGE: Because every little thing affects them. A slight disorder of the stomach makes them cheat. You may be an undigested bit of beef, a blot of mustard, a crumb of cheese, a fragment of an underdone potato. There's more of gravy than of grave about you, whatever you are!

[*There is a silence between them.* SCROOGE *is made nervous by it. He picks up a toothpick.*]

SCROOGE: [*Cont'd.*] Humbug! I tell you: humbug!

[MARLEY *opens his mouth and screams a ghosty, fearful scream. The scream echoes about each room of the house. Bats fly, cats screech, lightning flashes.* SCROOGE *stands and walks backwards against the wall.* MARLEY *stands and screams again. This time, he takes his head and lifts it from his shoulders. His head continues to scream.* MARLEY's *face again appears on every picture in the room: all screaming.* SCROOGE, *on his knees before* MARLEY.]

SCROOGE: [*Cont'd.*] Mercy! Dreadful apparition, mercy! Why, O! why do you trouble me so?

MARLEY: Man of the worldly mind, do you believe in me, or not?

SCROOGE: I do. I must. But why do spirits such as you walk the earth? And why do they come to me?

MARLEY: It is required of every man that the spirit within him should walk abroad among his fellow-men, and travel far and wide; and if that spirit goes not forth in life, it is condemned to do so after death. [MARLEY *screams again: a tragic scream from his ghosty bones.*] I wear the chain I forged in life. I made it link by link, and yard by yard. Is its pattern strange to you? Or would you know, you, Scrooge, the weight and length of the strong coil you bear yourself? It was full and heavy and long as this, seven Christmas Eves ago. You have labored on it, since. It is a ponderous chain.

[*Terrified that a chain will appear about his body,* SCROOGE *spins and waves the unwanted chain away. None, of course, appears. Sees* MARLEY *watching him dance about the room.* MARLEY *watches* SCROOGE; *silently.*]

SCROOGE: Jacob. Old Jacob Marley, tell me more. Speak comfort to me, Jacob.

MARLEY: I have none to give. Comfort comes from other regions, Ebenezer Scrooge, and is conveyed by other ministers, to other kinds of men. A very little more, is all that is permitted to me. I cannot rest, I cannot stay, I cannot linger anywhere…[*He moans again.*] my spirit never walked beyond our counting-house—mark me!—in life my spirit never roved beyond the narrow limits of our money-changing hole; and weary journeys lie before me!

SCROOGE: But you were always a good man of business, Jacob.

MARLEY: [*Screams word "business"; a flashpot explodes with him.*] BUSI-NESS!!! Mankind was my business. The common welfare was my business; charity, mercy, forbearance, benevolence, were, all, my business.

[SCROOGE *is quaking.*]

MARLEY: [*Cont'd.*] Hear me, Ebenezer Scrooge! My time is nearly gone!!

SCROOGE: I will, but don't be hard upon me. And don't be flowery, Jacob! Pray!

MARLEY: How is it that I appear before you in a shape that you can see, I may not tell. I have sat invisible beside you many and many a day. That is no light part of my penance. I am here tonight to warn you that you have yet a chance and hope of escaping my fate. A chance and hope of my procuring, Ebenezer.

SCROOGE: You were always a good friend to me. Thank'ee!

MARLEY: You will be haunted by Three Spirits.

SCROOGE: Would that be the chance and hope you mentioned, Jacob?

MARLEY: It is.

SCROOGE: I think I'd rather not.

MARLEY: Without their visits, you cannot hope to shun the path I tread. Expect the first one tomorrow, when the bell tolls one.

SCROOGE: Couldn't I take 'em all at once, and get it over, Jacob?

MARLEY: Expect the second on the next night at the same hour. The third upon the next night when the last stroke of twelve has ceased to vibrate. Look to see me no more. Others may, but you may not. And look that, for your own sake, you remember what has passed between us!

[MARLEY *places his head back upon his shoulders. He approaches the window and beckons to* SCROOGE *to watch. Outside the window, spectres fly by, carrying money-boxes and chains. They make a confused sound of lamentation.* MARLEY, *after listening a moment, joins into their mournful dirge. He leans to the window and floats out into the bleak, dark night. He is gone.*]

SCROOGE: [*Rushing to the window.*] Jacob! No, Jacob! Don't leave me! I'm frightened!

[*He sees that* MARLEY *has gone. He looks outside. He pulls the shutter closed, so that the scene is blocked from his view. All sound stops. After a pause, he re-opens the shutter and all is quiet, as it should be on a Christmas Eve. Carolers carol out of doors, in the distance.* SCROOGE *closes the shutter and walks down the stairs. He examines the door by which* MARLEY *first entered.*]

SCROOGE: [*Cont'd.*] No one here at all! Did I imagine all that? Humbug! [*He looks about the room.*] I did imagine it. It only happened in my foulest dream-mind, didn't it? An undigested bit of...

[*Thunder and lightning in the room, suddenly.*]

SCROOGE: [*Cont'd.*] Sorry! Sorry!

[*There is silence again. The lights fade out.*]

SCENE 4

Christmas music, choral, "Hark the Herald Angels Sing," sung by an on-stage choir of children. Above, SCROOGE, *in his bed, dead to the world, asleep, in his darkened room. It should appear that the choir is singing somewhere outside of the house. When the singing is ended, the choir should fade out of view and* MARLEY *should fade into view, in their place.*

MARLEY: [*Directly to audience.*] From this point forth...I shall be quite visible to you, but invisible to him. [*Smiles.*] He will feel my presence, nevertheless, for, unless my senses fail me completely, we are—you and I—witness to the changing of a miser: that one, my partner in life, in business, and in eternity: that one: Scrooge. [*Moves to staircase, below* SCROOGE.] See him now. He endeavors to pierce the darkness with his ferret eyes. [*To audience.*] See him, now. He listens for the hour.

[*The bells toll.* SCROOGE *is awakened and quakes as the hour approaches one o'clock, but, the bells stop their sound at the hour of twelve.*]

SCROOGE: [*Astonished.*] Midnight! Why this isn't possible. It was past two when I went to bed. An icicle must have gotten into the clock's works! I couldn't have slept through the whole day and far into another night. It isn't possible that anything has happened to the sun, and this is twelve at noon. [*He runs to window; unshutters same; it is night.*] Night, still. Quiet, normal for the season, cold. It is certainly not noon. I cannot in any way afford to lose my days. Securities come due, promissary notes, interest on investments: these are things that happen in the daylight! [*He returns to his bed.*] Was this a dream?

[MARLEY *appears in his room. He speaks to the audience.*]

MARLEY: You see? He does not, with faith, believe in me fully, even still! Whatever will it take to turn the faith of a miser from money to men?

SCROOGE: Another quarter and it'll be one and Marley's ghosty friends will come. [*Pauses, listens.*] Where's the chime for one?

[*Ding, dong.*]

SCROOGE: [*Cont'd.*] A quarter past!

[*Repeats.*]

SCROOGE: [*Cont'd.*] Half-past!

[*Repeats.*]

SCROOGE: [*Cont'd.*] A quarter to it! But where's the heavy bell of the hour one? This is a game in which I lose my senses! Perhaps, if I allowed myself another short doze .

MARLEY: Doze, Ebenezer, doze.

[*A heavy bell thuds its one ring: dull and definitely one o'clock. There is a flash of light.* SCROOGE *sits up, in a sudden. A hand draws back the curtains by his bed. He sees it.*]

SCROOGE: A hand! Who owns it? Hello!

[*Ghosty music again, but of a new nature to the play. A strange figure stands before* SCROOGE—*like a child, yet at the same time like an old man: white hair, but unwrinkled skin; long, muscular arms, but delicate legs and feet. Wears white tunic; lustrous belt cinches waist. Branch of fresh green holly in its hand, but has its dress trimmed with fresh summer flowers. Clear jets of light spring from the crown of its head. Holds cap in hand. The* SPIRIT *is called* PAST.]

SCROOGE: [*Cont'd.*] Are you the Spirit, Sir, whose coming was foretold to me?

PAST: I am.

MARLEY: Does he take this to be a vision of his green grocer?

SCROOGE: Who, and what are you?

PAST: I am the Ghost of Christmas Past.

SCROOGE: Long past?

PAST: Your past.

SCROOGE: May I ask, please, sir, what business you have here with me?

PAST: Your welfare.

SCROOGE: Not to sound ungrateful, sir, and really, please do understand that I am plenty obliged for your concern, but, really, kind spirit, it would have done all the better for my welfare to have been left alone altogether, to have slept peacefully through this night.

PAST: Your reclamation, then. Take heed!

SCROOGE: My what?

PAST: [*Motioning to* SCROOGE *and taking his arm.*] Rise! Fly with me! [*He leads* SCROOGE *to the window.*]

SCROOGE: [*Panicked.*] Fly, but I am a mortal and cannot fly!

PAST: [*Pointing to his heart.*] Bear but a touch of my hand here and you shall be upheld in more than this!

[SCROOGE *touches the* SPIRIT'*s heart and the lights dissolve into sparkly flickers. Lovely crystals of music are heard. The scene dissolves into another. Christmas music again.*]

SCENE 5

SCROOGE *and the* GHOST OF CHRISTMAS PAST *walk together across an open stage. In the background, we see a field that is open; covered by a soft, downy snow: a country road.*

SCROOGE: Good Heaven! I was bred in this place. I was a boy here!

[SCROOGE *freezes, staring at the field beyond.* MARLEY'*s ghost appears be-*

side him; takes SCROOGE's *face in his hands, and turns his face to the audience.*]

MARLEY: You see this Scrooge: stricken by feeling. Conscious of a thousand odors floating in the air, each one connected with a thousand thoughts, and hopes, and joys, and cares long, long forgotten. [*Pause.*] This one—this—Scrooge—before your very eyes, returns to life, among the living. [*To audience, sternly.*] You'd best pay your most careful attention. I would suggest rapt.

[*There is a small flash and puff of smoke and* MARLEY *is gone again.*]

PAST: Your lip is trembling, Mr. Scrooge. And what is that upon your cheek?

SCROOGE: Upon my cheek? Nothing…a blemish on the skin from the eating of overmuch grease…nothing…[*Suddenly.*] Kind Spirit of Christmas Past, lead me where you will, but quickly! To be stagnant in this place is, for me, unbearable!

PAST: You recollect the way?

SCROOGE: Remember it! I would know it blindfolded! My bridge, my church, my winding river! [*Staggers about, trying to see it all at once. He weeps again.*]

PAST: These are but shadows of things that have been. They have no consciousness of us.

[*Four jocund travelers enter, singing a Christmas song in 4-part harmony— "God Rest Ye Merry Gentlemen."*]

SCROOGE: Listen! I know these men! I know them! I remember the beauty of their song!

PAST: But, why do you remember it so happily? It is Merry Christmas that they say to one another! What is Merry Christmas to you, Mr. Scrooge! Out upon Merry Christmas, right? What good has Merry Christmas ever done you, Mr. Scrooge?

SCROOGE: [*After a long pause.*] None. No good. None…[*He bows his head.*]

PAST: Look, you, sir, a school ahead. The schoolroom is not quite deserted. A solitary child, neglected by his friends, is left there still.

[SCROOGE *falls to the ground; sobbing as he sees, and we see, a small boy, the* YOUNG SCROOGE, *sitting and weeping, bravely, alone at his desk: alone in a vast space, a void.*]

SCROOGE: I cannot look on him!

PAST: You must, Mr. Scrooge, you must.

SCROOGE: It's me. [*Pauses; weeps.*] Poor boy. He lived inside his head...alone...[*Pauses; weeps.*] poor boy. [*Pauses; stops his weeping.*] I wish...[*Dries his eyes on his cuff.*] ah! it's too late!

PAST: What is the matter?

SCROOGE: There was a boy singing a Christmas Carol outside my door last night. I should like to have given him something: that's all.

PAST: [*Smiles; waves his hand to* SCROOGE.] Come. Let us see another Christmas.

[*Lights out on little boy. A flash of light. A puff of smoke. Lights up on older boy.*]

SCROOGE: Look! Me, again! Older now! [*Realizes.*] Oh, yes still alone.

[*The boy—a slightly older* SCROOGE—*sits alone in a chair, reading. The door to the room opens and a young girl enters. She is much, much younger than this slightly older* SCROOGE. *She is, say, six, and he is, say, twelve.* EL-DER SCROOGE *and the* GHOST OF CHRISTMAS PAST *stand watching the scene, unseen.*]

FAN: Dear, dear brother, I have come to bring you home.

BOY: Home, little Fan?

FAN: Yes! Home, for good and all! Father is so much kinder than he ever used to be, and home's like heaven! He spoke so gently to me one dear night when I was going to bed that I was not afraid to ask him once more if you might come home; and he said "yes"...you should; and sent me in a coach to bring you. And you're to be a man and are never to come back here, but first, we're to be together all the Christmas long, and have the merriest time in the world.

BOY: You are quite a woman, little Fan!

[*Laughing; she drags at* BOY, *causing him to stumble to the door with her. Suddenly we hear a mean and terrible voice in the hallway, Off. It is the* SCHOOLMASTER.]

SCHOOLMASTER: Bring down Master Scrooge's travel box at once! He is to travel!

FAN: Who is that, Ebenezer?

BOY: O! Quiet, Fan. It is the Schoolmaster, himself!

[*The door bursts open and into the room bursts with it the* SCHOOLMASTER.]

SCHOOLMASTER: Master Scrooge?

BOY: Oh, Schoolmaster, I'd like you to meet my little sister, Fan, sir...

[*Two boys struggle on with* SCROOGE's *trunk.*]

FAN: Pleased, sir. [*She curtsies.*]

SCHOOLMASTER: You are to travel, Master Scrooge.

SCROOGE: Yes, sir. I know, sir...

[*All start to exit, but* FAN *grabs the coattail of the mean old* SCHOOLMAS-TER.]

BOY: Fan!

SCHOOLMASTER: What's this?

FAN: Pardon, sir, but I believe that you've forgotten to say your good bye to my brother, Ebenezer, who stands still now awaiting it...[*She smiles, curtsies, lowers her eyes.*] Pardon, sir.

SCHOOLMASTER: [*Amazed.*] I...uh...harumph...uhh...well, then... [*Outstretches hand.*] Goodbye, Scrooge.

BOY: Uh, well, goodbye, Schoolmaster...

[*Lights fade out on all but* BOY *looking at* FAN; *and* SCROOGE *and* PAST *looking at them.*]

SCROOGE: Oh, my dear, dear little sister, Fan...how I loved her.

PAST: Always a delicate creature, whom a breath might have withered, but she had a large heart.

SCROOGE: So she had.

PAST: She died a woman, and had, as I think, children.

SCROOGE: One child.

PAST: True. Your nephew.

SCROOGE: Yes.

PAST: Fine, then. We move on, Mr. Scrooge. That warehouse, there? Do you know it?

SCROOGE: Know it? Wasn't I apprenticed there?

PAST: We'll have a look.

[*They enter the warehouse. The lights crossfade with them, coming up on an old man in Welsh wig:* FEZZIWIG.]

SCROOGE: Why, it's old Fezziwig! Bless his heart; it's Fezziwig, alive again!

[FEZZIWIG *sits behind a large, high desk, counting. He lays down his pen; looks at the clock: seven bells sound.*] Quittin' time...

FEZZIWIG: Quittin' time…[*He takes off his waistcoat and laughs; calls off.*] Yo ho, Ebenezer! Dick!

[DICK WILKINS *and* EBENEZER SCROOGE—*a young man version—enter the room.* DICK *and* EBENEZER *are* FEZZIWIG's *apprentices.*]

SCROOGE: Dick Wilkins, to be sure! My fellow-'prentice! Bless my soul, yes. There he is. He was very much attached to me, was Dick. Poor Dick! Dear, dear!

FEZZIWIG: Yo ho, my boys. No more work tonight. Christmas Eve, Dick. Christmas, Ebenezer!

[*They stand at attention in front of* FEZZIWIG; *laughing.*]

FEZZIWIG: [*Cont'd.*] Hilli-ho! Clear away, and let's have lots of room here! Hilli-ho, Dick! Chirrup, Ebenezer!

[*The young men clear the room, sweep the floor, straighten the pictures, trim the lamps, etc. The space is clear now. A* FIDDLER *enters, fiddling.*]

FEZZIWIG: [*Cont'd.*] Hi-ho, Matthew! Fiddle away…where are my daughters?

[*The* FIDDLER *plays. Three young daughters of* FEZZIWIG, *followed by six young male suitors are dancing to the music. All employees come in: workers, clerks, housemaids, cousins, the baker, etc. All dance. Full number wanted here. Throughout the dance, food is brought into the feast. It is "eaten" in dance, by the dancers.* EBENEZER *dances with all three of the daughters, as does* DICK. *They compete for the daughters, happily, in the dance.* FEZZIWIG *dances with his daughters.* FEZZIWIG *dances with* DICK *and* EBENEZER. *The music changes:* MRS. FEZZIWIG *enters. She lovingly scolds her husband. They dance. She dances with* EBENEZER, *lifting him and throwing him about. She is enormously fat. When the dance is ended, they all dance off, floating away, as does the music.* SCROOGE *and the* GHOST OF CHRISTMAS PAST *stand alone now. The music is gone.*]

PAST: It was a small matter, that Fezziwig made those silly folks so full of gratitude.

SCROOGE: Small!

PAST: Shhh!

[*Lights up on* DICK *and* EBENEZER.]

DICK: We are blessed, Ebenezer, truly, to have such a master as Mr. Fezziwig!

YOUNG SCROOGE: He is the best, best, the very and absolute best! If ever I own a firm of my own, I shall treat my apprentices with the same dignity and the same grace. We have learned a wonderful lesson from the master, Dick!

DICK: Ah, that's a fact, Ebenezer. That's a fact!

PAST: Was it not a small matter, really? He spent but a few pounds of his mortal money on your small party. Three or four pounds, perhaps. Is that so much that he deserves such praise as you and Dick so lavish now?

SCROOGE: It isn't that! It isn't that, Spirit. Fezziwig had the power to make us happy or unhappy; to make our service light or burdensome; a pleasure or a toil. The happiness he gave is quite as great as if it cost him a fortune.

PAST:. What is the matter?

SCROOGE: Nothing particular.

PAST: Something, I think.

SCROOGE: No, no. I should like to be able to say a word or two to my clerk just now! That's all!

[EBENEZER *enters the room and shuts down all the lamps. He stretches and yawns.* THE GHOST OF CHRISTMAS PAST *turns to* SCROOGE; *all of a sudden.*]

PAST: My time grows short! Quick!

[*In a flash of light,* EBENEZER *is gone, and in his place stands an* OLDER SCROOGE, *this one a man in the prime of his life. Beside him stands a* YOUNG WOMAN *in a mourning dress. She is crying. She says to the* MAN, *with hostility.*]

WOMAN: It matters little...to you, very little. Another idol has displaced me.

MAN: What idol has displaced you?

WOMAN: A golden one.

MAN: This is an even-handed dealing of the world. There is nothing on which it is so hard as poverty; and there is nothing it professes to condemn with such severity as the pursuit of wealth!

WOMAN: You fear the world too much. Have I not seen your nobler aspirations fall off one by one, until the master-passion, Gain, engrosses you? Have I not?

SCROOGE: No!

MAN: What then? Even if I have grown so much wiser, what then? Have I changed towards you?

WOMAN: No…

MAN: Am I?

WOMAN: Our contract is an old one. It was made when we were both poor and content to be so. You are changed. When it was made, you were another man.

MAN: I was not another man: I was a boy.

WOMAN: Your own feeling tells you that you were not what you are. I am. That which promised happiness when we were one in heart is fraught with misery now that we are two…

SCROOGE: No!

WOMAN: How often and how keenly I have thought of this, I will not say. It is enough that I have thought of it, and can release you…

SCROOGE: [*Quietly.*] Don't release me, madame…

MAN: Have I ever sought release?

WOMAN: In words. No. Never.

MAN: In what then?

WOMAN: In a changed nature; in an altered spirit. In everything that made my love of any worth or value in your sight. If this has never been between us, tell me, would you seek me out and try to win me now? Ah, no!

SCROOGE: Ah, yes!

MAN: You think not?

WOMAN: I would gladly think otherwise if I could, heaven knows! But if you were free today, tomorrow, yesterday, can even I believe that you would choose a dowerless girl—you who in your very confidence with her weigh everything by Gain; or, choosing her, do I not know that your repentance and regret would surely follow? I do; and I release you. With a full heart, for the love of him you once were.

SCROOGE: Please, I…I…

MAN: Please, I…I…

WOMAN: Please. You may—the memory of what is past half makes me hope you will—have pain in this. A very, very brief time, and you will dismiss the memory of it, as an unprofitable dream, from which it happened well that you awoke. May you be happy in the life that you have chosen for yourself.

SCROOGE: No!

WOMAN: Yourself...alone...

SCROOGE: No!

WOMAN: Goodbye, Ebenezer...

SCROOGE: Don't let her go!

MAN: Goodbye.

SCROOGE: No!

[*She exits.* SCROOGE *goes to* YOUNGER MAN: *himself.*]

You fool!. Mindless loon! You fool!

MAN: [*To exited* WOMAN.] Fool. Mindless loon. Fool...

SCROOGE: Don't say that! Spirit, remove me from this place.

PAST: I have told you these were shadows of the things that have been. They are what they are. Do not blame me, Mr. Scrooge.

SCROOGE: Remove me! I cannot bear it!

[*The faces of all who appeared in this scene are now projected for a moment around the stage: enormous, flimsy, silent.*]

SCROOGE: [*Cont'd.*] Leave me! Take me back! Haunt me no longer!

[*There is a sudden flash of light: a flare.* THE GHOST OF CHRISTMAS PAST *is gone.* SCROOGE *is, for the moment, alone onstage. His bed is turned down, across the stage. A small candle burns now in* SCROOGE's *hand. There is a child's cap in his other hand. He slowly crosses the stage to his bed, to sleep.* MARLEY *appears behind* SCROOGE, *who continues his long, elderly cross to bed.* MARLEY *speaks directly to the audience.*]

MARLEY: Scrooge must sleep now. He must surrender to the irresistible drowsiness caused by the recognition of what was. [*Pauses.*] The cap he carries is from ten lives past: his boyhood cap...donned atop a hopeful hairy head...askew, perhaps, or at a rakish angle. Doffed now in honor of regret. Perhaps even too heavy to carry in his present state of weak remorse...

[SCROOGE *drops the cap. He lies atop his bed. He sleeps. To audience.*]

MARLEY: [*Cont'd.*] He sleeps. For him, there's even more trouble ahead. [*Smiles.*] For you? The play house tells me there's grog and cider, both hot, as should be your anticipation for the spectres Christmas Present and Future, for I promise you both. [*Smiles again.*] So, I pray you hurry back to your seats refreshed and ready for a miser—to turn his coat of gray into a blazen Christmas holly-red.

[*A flash of lightning. A clap of thunder. Bats fly. Ghosty music.* MARLEY *is gone.*]

CURTAIN

ACT TWO

SCENE 1

Lights. Choral music is sung. Curtain. SCROOGE, *in bed, sleeping, in spot-light. We cannot yet see the interior of his room.* MARLEY, *opposite, in spot-light equal to* SCROOGE's. MARLEY *laughs. He tosses his hand in the air and a flame shoots from it, magically, into the air. There is a thunder clap, and then another; a lightning flash, and then another. Ghostly music plays under. Colors change.* MARLEY's *spotlight has gone out and now reappears, with* MARLEY *in it, standing next to the bed and the sleeping* SCROOGE. MARLEY *addresses the audience directly.*

MARLEY: Hear this snoring Scrooge! Sleeping to escape the nightmare that is his waking day. What shall I bring to him now? I'm afraid nothing would astonish old Scrooge now. Not after what he's seen. Not a baby boy, not a rhinoceros, nor anything in between would as-tonish Ebenezer Scrooge just now. I can think of nothing... [*Suddenly.*] that's it! Nothing! [*He speaks confidentially.*] I'll have the clock strike one and, when he awakes expecting my second messen-ger, there will be no one...nothing. Then I'll have the bell strike twelve. And then one again...and then nothing. Nothing...[*Laughs.*] nothing will...astonish him. I think it will work.

[*The bell tolls one.* SCROOGE *leaps awake.*]

SCROOGE: One! One! This is it: time! [*Looks about the room.*] Nothing!

[*The bell tolls midnight.*]

SCROOGE: [*Cont'd.*] Midnight! How can this be? I'm sleeping backwards.

[*One again.*]

SCROOGE: [*Cont'd.*] Good heavens! One again! I'm sleeping back and forth! [*A pause.* SCROOGE *looks about.*] Nothing! Absolutely nothing!

[*Suddenly, thunder and lightning.* MARLEY *laughs and disappears. The room shakes and glows. There is suddenly spring like music.* SCROOGE *makes a run for the door.*]

MARLEY: Scrooge!

SCROOGE: What?

MARLEY: Stay you put!

SCROOGE: Just checking to see if anyone is in here.

[*Lights and thunder again: more music.* MARLEY *is of a sudden gone. In his place sits the* GHOST OF CHRISTMAS PRESENT—*to be called in the stage directions of the play,* PRESENT—*Center of room. Heaped up on the floor, to form a kind of throne, are turkeys, geese, game, poultry, brawn, great joints of meat, suckling pigs, long wreaths of sausages, mince-pies, plum puddings, barrels of oysters, red hot chestnuts, cherry-cheeked apples, juicy oranges, luscious pears, immense twelfth cakes, and seething bowls of punch, that make the chamber dim with their delicious steam. Upon this throne sits* PRESENT, *glorious to see. He bears a torch, shaped as a Horn of Plenty.* SCROOGE *hops out of the door, and then peeks back again into his bedroom.* PRESENT *calls to* SCROOGE.]

PRESENT: Ebenezer Scrooge. Come in, come in! Come in and know me better!

SCROOGE: Hello. How should I call you?

PRESENT: I am the Ghost of Christmas Present. Look upon me.

[PRESENT *is wearing a simple green robe. The walls around the room are now covered in greenery, as well. The room seems to be a perfect grove now: leaves of holly, mistletoe and ivy reflect the stage lights. Suddenly, there is a mighty roar of flame in the fire place and now the hearth burns with a lavish, warming fire. There is an ancient scabbard girdling the* GHOST's *middle, but without sword. The sheath is gone to rust.*]

PRESENT: [*Cont'd.*] You have never seen the like of me before?

SCROOGE: Never.

PRESENT: You have never walked forth with younger members of my family; my elder brothers born on Christmases Past?

SCROOGE: I don't think I have. I'm afraid I've not. Have you had many brothers, Spirit?

PRESENT: More than eighteen hundred.

SCROOGE: A tremendous family to provide for!

[PRESENT *stands.*]

SCROOGE: [*Cont'd.*] Spirit, conduct me where you will. I went forth last night on compulsion, and learnt a lesson which is working now. Tonight, if you have aught to teach me, let me profit by it.

PRESENT: Touch my robe.

[SCROOGE *walks cautiously to* PRESENT *and touches his robe. When he does, lightning flashes, thunder claps, music plays.*]

[*Blackout.*]

SCENE 2

PROLOGUE

MARLEY *stands spotlit. He speaks directly to the audience.*

MARLEY: My ghostly friend now leads my living partner through the city's streets.

[*Lights up on* SCROOGE *and* PRESENT.]

MARLEY: [*Cont'd.*] See them there and hear the music people make when the weather is severe, as it is now.

[*Winter music. Choral group behind scrim, sings. When the song is done and the stage is re-set, the lights will fade up on a row of shops, behind the singers. The choral group will hum the song they have just completed now and mill about the streets, carrying their dinners to the bakers' shops and restaurants. They will, perhaps, sing about being poor at Christmas time, whatever.*]

PRESENT: These revellers, Mr. Scrooge, carry their own dinners to their jobs, where they will work to bake the meals the rich men and women of this city will eat as their Christmas dinners. Generous people these...to care for the others, so...

[PRESENT *walks among the choral group and a sparkling incense falls from his torch on to their baskets, as he pulls the covers off of the baskets. Some of the choral group become angry with each other.*]

MAN #1: Hey, you, watch where you're going.

MAN #2: Watch it yourself, mate!

[PRESENT *sprinkles them directly, they change.*]

MAN #1: I pray go in ahead of me. It's Christmas. You be first!

MAN #2: No, no, I must insist that YOU be first!

MAN **#1:** All right, I shall be, and gratefully so.

MAN **#2:** The pleasure is equally mine, for being able to watch you pass, smiling.

MAN **#1:** I would find it a shame to quarrel on Christmas Day...

MAN **#2:** As would I.

MAN **#1:** Merry Christmas then, friend!

MAN **#2:** And a Merry Christmas straight back to you!

[*Church bells toll. The choral group enters the buildings; the shops and restaurants; they exit the stage, shutting their doors closed behind them. All sound stops.* SCROOGE *and* PRESENT *are alone again.*]

SCROOGE: What is it you sprinkle from your torch?

PRESENT: Kindness.

SCROOGE: Do you sprinkle your kindness on any particular people or on all people?

PRESENT: To any person kindly given. And to the very poor most of all.

SCROOGE: Why to the very poor most?

PRESENT: Because the very poor need it most. Touch my heart...here, Mr. Scrooge. We have another journey.

[SCROOGE *touches the* GHOST's *heart and music plays, lights change color, lightning flashes, thunder claps. A choral group appears on the street, singing Christmas carols.*]

SCENE 3

MARLEY *stands spotlit in front of a scrim on which is painted the exterior of* CRATCHIT's *four-roomed house. There is a flash and a clap and* MAR-LEY *is gone. The lights shift color again, the scrim flies away, and we are in the interior of the* CRATCHIT *family home.* SCROOGE *is there, with the* SPIRIT [PRESENT], *watching* MRS. CRATCHIT *set the table, with the help of* BELINDA CRATCHIT *and* PETER CRATCHIT, *a baby, pokes a fork into the mashed potatoes on his high-chair's tray. He also chews on his shirt collar.*

SCROOGE: What is this place, Spirit?

PRESENT: This is the home of your employee, Mr. Scrooge. Don't you know it?

SCROOGE: Do you mean Cratchit, Spirit? Do you mean this is Cratchit's home?

PRESENT: None other.

SCROOGE: These children are his?

PRESENT: There are more to come presently.

SCROOGE: On his meagre earnings! What foolishness!

PRESENT: Foolishness, is it?

SCROOGE: Wouldn't you say so? Fifteen shillings a week's what he gets!

PRESENT: I would say that he gets the pleasure of his family, fifteen times a week times the number of hours in a day! Wait, Mr. Scrooge. Wait, listen and watch. You might actually learn something.

MRS. CRATCHIT: What has ever got your precious father then? And your brother, Tiny Tim? And Martha wasn't as late last Christmas by half an hour!

[MARTHA *opens the door, speaking to her mother as she does.*]

MARTHA: Here's Martha, now, Mother!

[*She laughs. The* CRATCHIT CHILDREN *squeal with delight.*]

BELINDA: It's Martha, Mother! Here's Martha!

PETER: Marthmama, Marthmama! Hullo!

BELINDA: Hurrah! Martha! Martha! There's such an enormous goose for us, Martha!

MRS. CRATCHIT: Why, bless your heart alive, my dear, how late you are!

MARTHA: We'd a great deal of work to finish up last night, and had to clear away this morning, Mother.

MRS. CRATCHIT: Well, never mind so long as you are home. Sit ye down before the fire, my dear, and have a warm, Lord bless ye!

BELINDA: No, no! There's Father coming. Hide, Martha, hide!

[MARTHA *giggles and hides herself.*]

MARTHA: Where? Here?

PETER: Hide, hide!

BELINDA: Not there! THERE!

[MARTHA *is hidden.* BOB CRATCHIT *enters, carrying* TINY TIM *atop his shoulder. He wears a threadbare and fringeless comforter hanging down in front of him.* TINY TIM *carries small crutches and his small legs are bound in an iron frame brace.*]

BOB AND TINY TIM: Merry Christmas.

BOB: Merry Christmas my love, Merry Christmas, Peter; Merry Christmas, Belinda. Why, where is Martha?

MRS. CRATCHIT: Not coming.

BOB: Not coming? Not coming upon Christrnas Day?

MARTHA: [*Pokes head out.*] Ohhh, poor Father. Don't be disappointed.

BOB: What's this?

MARTHA: 'Tis I!

BOB: Martha! [*They embrace.*]

TINY TIM: Martha! Martha!

MARTHA: Tiny Tim!

[TINY TIM *is placed in* MARTHA's *arms.* BELINDA *and* PETER *rush him off-stage.*]

BELINDA: Come, brother! You must come hear the pudding singing in the copper.

TINY TIM: The pudding? What flavor have we?

PETER: Plum! Plum!

TINY TIM: Oh, Mother! I love plum!

[*The* CHILDREN *exit the stage, giggling.*]

MRS. CRATCHIT: And how did little Tim behave?

BOB: As good as gold, and even better. Somehow he gets thoughtful sitting by himself so much, and thinks the strangest things you ever heard. He told me, coming home, that he hoped people saw him in the church, because he was a cripple, and it might be pleasant to them to remember upon Christmas Day, who made lame beggars walk and blind men see. [*Pauses.*] He has the oddest ideas sometimes, but he seems all the while to be growing stronger and more hearty...one would never know.

[*Hears* TIM's *crutch on floor outside door.*]

PETER: The goose has arrived to be eaten!

BELINDA: Oh, mama, mama, it's beautiful.

MARTHA: It's a perfect goose, Mother!

TINY TIM: To this Christmas goose, Mother and Father, I say...[*Yells.*] Hurrah! Hurrah!

OTHER CHILDREN: [*Copying* TIM.] Hurrah! Hurrah!

[*The family sits round the table.* BOB *and* MRS. CRATCHIT *serve the trimmings, quickly. All sit; all bow heads, all pray.*]

BOB: Thank you, dear Lord, for your many gifts...our dear children; our wonderful meal; our love for one another; and the warmth of our small fire— [*Looks up at all.*] A merry Christmas to us, my dear: God bless us!

ALL: [*Except* TIM.] Merry Christmas! God bless us!

TINY TIM: [*In a short silence.*] God bless us every one.

[*All freeze. Spotlight on* PRESENT *and* SCROOGE.]

SCROOGE: Spirit, tell me if Tiny Tim will live.

PRESENT: I see a vacant seat...in the poor chimney corner, and a crutch without an owner, carefully preserved. If these shadows remain unaltered by the future, the child will die.

SCROOGE: No, no, kind Spirit! Say he will be spared!

PRESENT: If these shadows remain unaltered by the future, none other of my race will find him here. What then? If he be like to die, he had better do it, and decrease the surplus population.

[SCROOGE *bows his head. We hear* BOB's *voice speak* SCROOGE's *name.*]

BOB: Mr. Scrooge...

SCROOGE: Huh? What's that? Who calls?

BOB: [*His glass raised in a toast.*] I'll give you Mr. Scrooge, the Founder of the Feast!

SCROOGE: Me, Bob? You toast me?

PRESENT: Save your breath, Mr. Scrooge. You can't be seen or heard.

MRS. CRATCHIT: The Founder of the Feast, indeed! I wish I had him here, that miser Scrooge. I'd give him a piece of my mind to feast upon, and I hope he'd have a good appetite for it!

BOB: My dear! Christmas Day!

MRS. CRATCHIT: It should be Christmas Day, I am sure, on which one drinks the health of such an odious, stingy, unfeeling man as Mr. Scrooge...

SCROOGE: Oh, Spirit, must I?

MRS. CRATCHIT: You know he is, Robert! Nobody knows it better than you do, poor fellow!

BOB: This is Christmas Day, and I should like to drink to the health of the man who employs me and allows me to earn my living and our support and that man is Ebenezer Scrooge...

MRS. CRATCHIT: I'll drink to his health for your sake and the day's, but not for his sake...a Merry Christmas and a Happy New Year to you, Mr. Scrooge, wherever you may be this day!

SCROOGE: Just here, kind madam...out of sight, out of sight...

BOB: Thank you, my dear. Thank you.

SCROOGE: Thank you, Bob...and Mrs. Cratchit, too. No one else is toasting me...not now...not ever. Of that I am sure...

BOB: Children...

ALL: Merry Christmas to Mr. Scrooge.

BOB: I'll pay you six-pence, Tim, for my favorite song.

TINY TIM: Oh, Father, I'd so love to sing it, but not for pay. This Christmas goose—this feast—you and Mother, my, brother and sisters close with me: that's my pay—

BOB: Martha, will you play the notes on the lute, for Tiny Tim's song.

BELINDA: May I sing, too, Father?

BOB: We'll all sing.

> [*They sing a song about a tiny child lost in the snow, probably from Wordsworth's poem. TIM sings the lead vocal; all chime in for the chorus. Their song fades under, as* THE GHOST OF CHRISTMAS PRESENT *speaks.*]

PRESENT: Mark my words, Ebenezer Scrooge. I do not present the Cratchits to you because they are a handsome, or brilliant family. They are not handsome. They are not brilliant. They are not well-dressed, or tasteful to the times. Their shoes are not even water-proofed by virtue of money or cleverness spent. So when the pavement is wet, so are the insides of their shoes and the tops their toes. These are the Cratchits, Mr. Scrooge. They are not highly special. They are happy, grateful, pleased with one another, contented with the time and how it passes. They don't sing very well, do they? But, nonetheless, they do sing...[*Pauses.*] think of that, Scrooge. 15 shillings a week and they do sing...hear their song until its end.

SCROOGE: I am listening.

[*The chorus sings full volume now, until...the song ends here.*]

SCROOGE: [*Cont'd.*] Spirit, it must be time for us to take our leave. I feel in my heart that it is... that I must think on that which I have seen here...

PRESENT: Touch my robe again...

[SCROOGE *touches* PRESENT's *robe. The lights fade out on the* CRATCHITS, *who sit, frozen, at the table.* SCROOGE *and* PRESENT *in a spotlight now. Thunder, lightning, smoke. They are gone.*]

SCENE 4

MARLEY *appears in single spotlight. A storm brews. Thunder and lightning.* SCROOGE *and* PRESENT *"fly" past. The storm continues, furiously, and, now and again,* SCROOGE *and* PRESENT *will zip past in their travels.* MARLEY *will speak straight out to the audience.*

MARLEY: The Ghost of Christmas Present, my co-worker in this attempt to turn a miser, flies about now with that very miser, Scrooge, from street to street, and he points out partygoers on their way to Christmas parties. If one were to judge from the numbers of people on their way to friendly gatherings, one might think that no one was left at home to give anyone welcome...but that's not the case, is it? Every home is expecting company and...[*He laughs.*] Scrooge is amazed.

[SCROOGE *and* PRESENT *zip past again. The lights fade up around them. We are in the* NEPHEW's *home, in the living room,* PRESENT *and* SCROOGE *stand watching the* NEPHEW: FRED *and his* WIFE, *fixing the fire.*]

SCROOGE: What is this place? We've moved from the mines!

PRESENT: You do not recognize them?

SCROOGE: It is my nephew!...and the one he married...

[MARLEY *waves his hand and there is a lightning flash. He disappears.*]

FRED: It strikes me as sooooo funny, to think of what he said...that Christmas was a humbug, as I live! He believed it!

WIFE: More shame for him, Fred!

FRED: Well, he's a comical old fellow, that's the truth.

WIFE: I have no patience with him.

FRED: Oh, I have! I am sorry for him; I couldn't be angry with him if I tried. Who suffers by his ill whims? Himself, always...

SCROOGE: It's me they talk of, isn't it, Spirit?

FRED: Here, wife, consider this. Uncle Scrooge takes it into his head to dislike us, and he won't come and dine with us. What's the consequence?

WIFE: Oh...you're sweet to say what I think you're about to say, too, Fred...

FRED: What's the consequence? He don't lose much of a dinner by it, I can tell you that!

WIFE: Ooooooo, Fred! Indeed, I think he loses a very good dinner, ask my sisters, or your lecherous bachelor friend, Topper...ask any of them. They'll tell you what old Scrooge, your uncle, missed a dandy meal!

FRED: Well, that's something of a relief, wife. Glad to hear it!

[*He hugs his* WIFE. *They laugh. They kiss.*]

FRED: [*Cont'd.*] The truth is, he misses much yet. I mean to give him the same chance every year, whether he likes it or not, for I pity him. Nay, he is my only uncle and I feel for the old miser...but, I tell you, wife: I see my dear and perfect mother's face on his own wizened cheeks and brow: brother and sister they were, and I cannot erase that from each view of him I take...

WIFE: I understand what you say, Fred, and I am with you in your yearly asking. But he never will accept, you know. He never will.

FRED: Well, true, wife. Uncle may rail at Christmas till he dies. I think I shook him some with my visit yesterday...[*Laughing.*] I refused to grow angry...no matter how nasty he became...[*Whoops.*] It was HE who grew angry, wife!

[*They both laugh now.*]

SCROOGE: What he says is true, Spirit.

FRED AND WIFE: Bah humbug!

FRED: [*Embracing his* WIFE.] There is much laughter in our marriage, wife. It pleases me. You please me.

WIFE: And you please me, Fred. You are a good man...

[*They embrace.*]

WIFE: [*Cont'd.*] Come now. We must have a look at the meal...our guests will soon arrive...my sisters, Topper...

FRED: A toast first...[*He hands her glass.*] A toast to Uncle Scrooge... [*Fills their glasses.*]

WIFE: A toast to him?

FRED: Uncle Scrooge has given us plenty of merriment, I am sure, and it would be ungrateful not to drink to his health. And I say...Uncle Scrooge!

WIFE: [*Laughing.*] You're a proper loon, Fred...and I'm a proper wife to you...[*She raises her glass.*] Uncle Scrooge!

[*They drink. They embrace. They kiss.*]

SCROOGE: Spirit, please, make me visible! Make me audible! I want to talk with my nephew and my niece!

[*Calls out to them. The lights that light the room and* FRED *and* WIFE *fade out.* SCROOGE *and* PRESENT *are alone spotlit.*]

PRESENT: These shadows are gone to you now, Mr. Scrooge. You may return to them later tonight in your dreams. [*Pauses.*] My time grows short, Ebenezer Scrooge. Look you on me. Do you see how I've aged?

SCROOGE: Your hair has gone grey! Your skin, wrinkled! Are spirits' lives so short?

PRESENT: My stay upon this globe is very brief. It ends tonight.

SCROOGE: Tonight?

PRESENT: At midnight. The time is drawing near! [*Clock strikes 11:45.*] Hear those chimes? In a quarter hour, my life will have been spent! Look, Scrooge, man, look you here.

[*Two gnarled baby dolls are taken from* PRESENT's *skirts.*]

SCROOGE: Who are they?

PRESENT: They are Man's children, and they cling to me, appealing from their fathers. The boy is Ignorance; the girl is Want. Beware them both, and all of their degree, but most of all beware this boy, for I see that written on his brow which is doom, unless the writing is erased.

[*He stretches out his arms. His voice now amplified: lowly and oddly.*]

SCROOGE: Have they no refuge or resource?

PRESENT: Are there no prisons? Are there no workhouses?

[*Twelve chimes.*]

PRESENT: [*Cont'd.*] Are there no prisons? Are there no workhouses?

[*A* PHANTOM, *hooded, appears in dim light.*]

PRESENT: [*Cont'd.*] Are there no prisons? Are there no workhouses?

[PRESENT *begins to deliquesce.* SCROOGE *calls after him.*]

SCROOGE: Spirit, I'm frightened! Don't leave me! Spirit!

PRESENT: Prisons? Workhouses? Prisons? Workhouses...

[*He is gone.* SCROOGE *is alone now with the* PHANTOM, *who is, of course, the* GHOST OF CHRISTMAS FUTURE. *The* PHANTOM *is shrouded in black. Only its outstretched hand is visible from under his ghostly garment.*]

SCROOGE: Who are you, Phantom? Oh, yes, I think I know you! You are, are you not, the Spirit of Christmas Yet to Come?

[*No reply.*]

SCROOGE: [*Cont'd.*] And you are about to show me the shadows of the things that have not yet happened, but will happen in time before us. Is that not so, Spirit?

[*The* PHANTOM *allows* SCROOGE *a look at his face. No other reply wanted here. A nervous giggle here.*]

SCROOGE: [*Cont'd.*] Oh, Ghost of the Future, I fear you more than any Spectre I have seen! But, as I know that your purpose is to do me good, and as I hope to live to be another man from what I was, I am prepared to bear you company

[FUTURE *does not reply, but for a stiff arm, hand and finger set, pointing forward.*]

SCROOGE: [*Cont'd.*] Lead on, then, lead on. The night is waning fast, and it is precious time to me. Lead on, Spirit!

[FUTURE *moves away from* SCROOGE *in the same rhythm and motion employed at its arrival.* SCROOGE *falls into the same pattern, a considerable space apart from the* SPIRIT. *In the space between them,* MARLEY *appears. He looks to* FUTURE *and then to* SCROOGE. *He claps his hands. Thunder and lightning.* THREE BUSINESSMEN *appear, spotlighted singularly. Thus, six points of the stage should now be spotted in light.* MARLEY *will watch this scene from his position.*]

FIRST BUSINESSMAN: Oh, no, I don't know much about it either way, I only know he's dead.

SECOND BUSINESSMAN: When did he die?

FIRST BUSINESSMAN: Last night, I believe.

SECOND BUSINESSMAN: Why, what was the matter with him? [*He uses snuff here; sneezes, etc.*] I thought he'd never die, really...

FIRST BUSINESSMAN: [*Yawning.*] God knows, God knows...

THIRD BUSINESSMAN: What has he done with his money?

SECOND BUSINESSMAN: I haven't heard. Have you?

FIRST BUSINESSMAN: Left it to his Company, perhaps. Money to money: you know the expression...

THIRD BUSINESSMAN: He hasn't left it to me. That's all I know...

FIRST BUSINESSMAN: [*Laughing.*] Nor to me...[*Looks at* SECOND BUSINESSMAN.] you, then? You got his money???

SECOND BUSINESSMAN: [*Laughing.*] Me, me, his money? Nooooo!

[*They all laugh.*]

THIRD BUSINESSMAN: It's likely to be a cheap funeral, for upon my life, I don't know of a living soul who'd care to venture to it. Suppose we make up a party and volunteer?

SECOND BUSINESSMAN: I don't mind going if a lunch is provided, but I must be fed, if I make one.

FIRST BUSINESSMAN: Well, I am the most disinterested among you, for I never wear black gloves, and I never eat lunch. But I'll offer to go, if anybody else will. When I come to think of it, I'm not all sure that I wasn't his most particular friend; for we used to stop and speak whenever we met. Well, then...bye, bye!

SECOND BUSINESSMAN: Bye, bye...

THIRD BUSINESSMAN: Bye, bye...

[*They glide offstage in three separate directions. Their lights follow them.*]

SCROOGE: Spirit, why did you show me this? Why do you show me businessmen from my streets as they take the death of Jacob Marley. That is a thing past. You are future!

[JACOB MARLEY *laughs a long, deep laugh. There is a thunder clap and lightning flash, and he is gone.* SCROOGE *faces* FUTURE, *alone on stage now.* FUTURE *wordlessly stretches out his arm-hand-and-finger-set, pointing into the distance. There, above them,* DRUNKS *and* SCOUNDRELS *and* WOMEN OF THE STREETS *"fly" by, half-dressed and slovenly. [*N,B. *There could be a dance number here, showing the seamier side of London city life.] When the scene has passed, a woman enters the playing area. She is almost at once fol-*

lowed a second woman; and then a man in faded black; and then, suddenly, an old man, who smokes a pipe. The old man scares the other three. They laugh, anxious.]

FIRST WOMAN: Look here, old Joe, here's a chance! If we haven't all three met here without meaning it!

OLD JOE: You couldn't have met in a better place. Come into the parlor. You were made free of it long ago, you know; and the other two an't strangers. [*He stands; shuts a door. Shrieking.*] We're all suitable to our calling. We're well matched. Come into the parlor. Come into the parlor…

[*They follow him.* SCROOGE *and* FUTURE *are now in their midst, watching; silent. A truck comes in on which is set a small wall with fireplace and a screen of rags, etc. All props for the scene.*] Let me just rake this fire over a bit…[*He does. He trims his lamp with the stem of his pipe. The* FIRST WOMAN *throws a large bundle on to the floor. She sits beside it, crosslegged; defiantly.*]

FIRST WOMAN: What odds then? What odds, Mrs. Dilber? Every person has a right to take care of themselves, HE always did!

MRS. DILBER: That's true indeed! No man more so!

FIRST WOMAN: Why, then, don't stand staring as if you was afraid, woman! Who's the wiser? We're not going to pick holes in each other's coats, I suppose?

MRS. DILBER: No, indeed! We should hope not!

FIRST WOMAN: Very well, then! That's enough. Who's the worse for the loss of a few things like these? Not a dead man, I suppose?

MRS. DILBER: [*Laughing.*] No, indeed!

FIRST WOMAN: If he wanted to keep 'em after he was dead, the wicked old screw, why wasn't he natural in his lifetime? If he had been, he'd have had somebody to look after him when he was struck with Death, instead of lying gasping out his last there, alone by himself.

MRS. DILBER: It's the truest word that was ever spoke. It's a judgement on him.

FIRST WOMAN: I wish it were a heavier one, and it should have been, you may depend on it, if I could have laid my hands on anything else. Open that bundle, old Joe, and let me know the value of it. Speak out plain. I'm not afraid to be the first, nor afraid for them to see it. We knew pretty well that we were helping ourselves; before we met here, I believe. It's no sin. Open the bundle, Joe.

FIRST MAN: No, no, my dear! I won't think of letting you be the first to show what you've…earned…earned from this. I throw in mine. [*He takes a bundle from his shoulder; turns it upside down and empties its contents out on to the floor.*] It's not very extensive, see…seals…a pencil case…sleeve buttons

MRS. DILBER: Nice sleeve buttons, though…

FIRST MAN: Not bad, not bad…a brooch there…

OLD JOE: Not really valuable, I'm afraid…

FIRST MAN: How much, old Joe?

OLD JOE: [*Writing on the wall with chalk.*] A pitiful lot, really. Ten and six and not a sixpence more!

FIRST MAN: You're not serious!

OLD JOE: That's your account and I wouldn't give another sixpence if I was to be boiled for not doing it. Who's next?

MRS. DILBER: Me! [*Dumps out contents of her bundle.*] Sheets, towels, silver spoons, silver sugar-tongs…some boots…

OLD JOE: [*Writing on wall.*] I always give too much to the ladies. It's a weakness of mine and that's the way I ruin myself. Here's your total comin' up…two pounds-ten…if you asked me for another penny, and made it an open question, I'd repent being so liberal and knock off half a-crown.

FIRST WOMAN: And now do MY bundle, Joe.

OLD JOE: [*Kneeling to open knots on her bundle.*] So many knots, madam…[*He drags out large curtains; dark.*] What do you call this? Bed curtains!

FIRST WOMAN: [*Laughing.*] Ah, yes, bed curtains!

OLD JOE: You don't mean to say you took 'em down, rings and all, with him lying there?

FIRST WOMAN: Yes, I did, why not?.

OLD JOE: You were born to make your fortune and you'll certainly do it.

FIRST WOMAN: I certainly shan't hold my hand, when I can get anything in it by reaching it out, for the sake of such a man as he was, I promise you, Joe. Don't drop that lamp oil on those blankets, now!

OLD JOE: His blankets?

FIRST WOMAN: Whose else's do you think? He isn't likely to catch cold without 'em, I daresay.

OLD JOE: I hope that he didn't die of anything catching? Eh?

FIRST WOMAN: Don't you be afraid of that. I ain't so fond of his company that I'd loiter about him for such things if he did. Ah! You may look through that shirt till your eyes ache, but you won't find a hole in it, nor a threadbare place. It's the best he had, and a fine one, too. They'd have wasted it, if it hadn't been for me.

OLD JOE: What do you mean "They'd have wasted it?"

FIRST WOMAN: Putting it on him to be buried in, to be sure. Somebody was fool enough to do it, but I took it off again [*She laughs, as do they all, nervously.*] If calico an't good enough for such a purpose, it isn't good enough then for anything. It's quite as becoming to the body. He can't look uglier than he did in that one!

SCROOGE: [*A low-pitched moan emits from his mouth; from the bones.*] OOOOOOOoooooOOOOOooooooOOOOOOOOOooooooOOOOOOooooo0O!

OLD JOE: One pound six for the lot.

[*He produces a small flannel bag filled with money. He divvies it out. He continues to pass around the money as he speaks. All are laughing.*]

OLD JOE: [*Cont'd.*] That's the end of it, you see! He frightened every one away from him while he was alive, to profit us when he was dead! Hah ha ha!

ALL: HAHAHAHHAhahahahahahah!

SCROOGE: OOOooo0OOooo000ooo000ooo00ooo00ooo0OooOOOonn! [*He screams at them.*] Obscene demons! Why not market the corpse itself, as sell its trimming??? [*Suddenly.*] Oh, Spirit, I see it, I see it! This unhappy man—this stripped-bare corpse could very well be my own. My life holds parallel! My life ends that way now!

[SCROOGE *backs into something in the dark behind his spotlight.* SCROOGE *looks at* FUTURE, *who points to the corpse.* SCROOGE *pulls back the blanket: The corpse is, of course,* SCROOGE, *who screams. He falls aside the bed; weeping.*]

SCROOGE: [*Cont'd.*] Spirit, this is a fearful place. In leaving it, I shall not leave its lesson, trust me. Let us go!

[FUTURE *points to the corpse.*]

SCROOGE: [*Cont'd.*] Spirit, let me see some tenderness connected with a death, or that dark chamber, which we just left now, Spirit, will be forever present to me.

[FUTURE *spreads his robes again. Thunder and lightning. Lights up in the* CRATCHIT *home setting.* MRS. CRATCHIT *and her daughters, sewing.*]

TINY TIM'S VOICE: [*Off.*] And He took a child and set him in the midst of them.

SCROOGE: [*Looking about the room; to* FUTURE.] Huh? Who spoke? Who said that?

MRS. CRATCHIT: [*Puts down her sewing.*] The color hurts my eyes. [*Rubs her eyes.*] That's better. My eyes grow weak sewing by candlelight. I shouldn't want to show your father weak eyes when he comes home...not for the world! It must be near his time...

PETER: [*In corner, reading. Looks up from book.*] Past it, rather. But I think he's been walking a bit slower than usual these last few evenings, Mother.

MRS. CRATCHIT: I have known him walk with...[*Pauses.*] I have known him walk with Tiny Tim upon his shoulder and very fast indeed...

PETER: So have I, Mother! Often!

DAUGHTER: So have I!

MRS. CRATCHIT: But he was very light to carry and his father loved him so, that it was no trouble—no trouble.

[BOB, *at door.*]

MRS. CRATCHIT: [*Cont'd.*] And there is your father at the door.

[BOB CRATCHIT *enters. He wears a comforter. He is cold, forlorn.*]

PETER: Father!

BOB: Hello, wife, children...

[*The* DAUGHTER *weeps; turns away from* CRATCHIT.]

BOB: [*Cont'd.*] Children! How good to see you all! And you, wife. And look at this sewing! I've no doubt, with all your industry, we'll have a quilt to set down upon our knees in church on Sunday!

MRS. CRATCHIT: You made the arrangements today, then, Robert, for the...service...to be on Sunday.

BOB: The funeral. Oh, well, yes, yes, I did. I wish you could have gone. It would have done you good to see how green a place it is. But you'll see it often, I promised him that I would walk there on Sunday, after the service. [*Suddenly.*] My little, little child! My little child!

ALL CHILDREN: [*Hugging him.*] Oh, Father...

BOB: [*He stands.*] Forgive me. I saw Mr. Scrooge's nephew, who you know I'd just met once before, and he was so wonderful to me, wife...he is the most pleasant-spoken gentleman I've ever met...he said "I am heartily sorry for it and heartily sorry for your good wife. If I can be of service to you in any way, here's where I live." And he gave me this card.

PETER: Let me see it!

BOB: And he looked me straight in the eye, wife, and said, meaningfully, "I pray you'll come to me, Mr. Cratchit, if you need some help. I pray you do." Now it wasn't for the sake of anything that he might be able to do for us, so much as for his kind way. It seemed as if he had known our Tiny Tim and felt with us.

MRS. CRATCHIT: I'm sure that he's a good soul.

BOB: You would be surer of it, my dear, if you saw and spoke to him. I shouldn't be at all surprised, if he got Peter a situation.

MRS. CRATCHIT:. Only hear that, Peter!

MARTHA: And then, Peter will be keeping company with someone and setting up for himself!

PETER: Get along with you!

BOB: It's just as likely as not, one of these days, though there's plenty of time for that, my dear. But however and whenever we part from one another, I am sure we shall none of us forget poor Tiny Tim—shall we?—or this first parting that was among us?

ALL CHILDREN: Never, Father, never!

BOB: And when we recollect how patient and mild he was, we shall not quarrel easily among ourselves, and forget poor Tiny Tim in doing it.

ALL CHILDREN: No, Father, never!

LITTLE BOB: I am very happy, I am, I am, I am very happy.

[BOB *kisses his little son, as does* MRS. CRATCHIT, *as do the other children. The family is set now in one sculptural embrace. The lighting fades to a gentle pool of light, tight on them.*]

SCROOGE: Spectre, something informs me that our parting moment is at hand. I know it, but I know not how I know it.

[FUTURE *points to the other side of the stage. Lights out on* CRATCHITS. FUTURE *moves slowing, gliding.* SCROOGE *follows.* FUTURE *points opposite.* FUTURE *leads* SCROOGE *to a wall and a tombstone. He points to the stone.*]

SCROOGE: [*Cont'd.*] Am I that man those ghoulish parasites so gloated over? [*Pauses.*] Before I draw nearer to that stone to which you point, answer me one question. Are these the shadows of things that will be, or the shadows of things that MAY be, only?

[FUTURE *points to the gravestone.* MARLEY *appears in light. He points to grave as well. Gravestone turns front and grows to ten feet high. Words upon it:* EBENEZER SCROOGE. *Much smoke billows now from the grave. Choral music here.* SCROOGE *stands looking up at gravestone.* FUTURE *does not at all reply in mortals' words, but points once more to the gravestone. The stone undulates and glows. Music plays, beckoning* SCROOGE. SCROOGE, *reeling in terror.*]

SCROOGE: [*Cont'd.*] Oh, no, Spirit! Oh, no, no!

[FUTURE's *finger still pointing.*]

SCROOGE: [*Cont'd.*] Spirit! Hear me! I am not the man I was. I will not be the man I would have been but for this intercourse. Why show me this, if I am past all hope?

[FUTURE *considers* SCROOGE's *logic. His hand wavers.*]

SCROOGE: [*Cont'd.*] Oh, Good Spirit, I see by your wavering hand that your good nature intercedes for me and pities me. Assure me that I yet may change these shadows that you have shown me by an altered life!

[FUTURE's *hand trembles; pointing has stopped.*]

SCROOGE: [*Cont'd.*] I will honor Christmas in my heart and try to keep it all the year. I will live in the Past, the Present, and the Future. The Spirits of all Three shall strive within me. I will not shut out the lessons that they teach. Oh, tell me that I may sponge away the writing that is upon this stone!

[SCROOGE *makes a desperate stab at grabbing* FUTURE's *hand. He holds it firm for a moment, but* FUTURE, *stronger than* SCROOGE, *pulls away.* SCROOGE *is on his knees, praying.*]

SCROOGE: [*Cont'd.*] Spirit, dear Spirit, I am praying before you. Give me a sign that all is possible. Give me a sign that all hope for me is not lost. Oh, Spirit, kind Spirit, I beseech thee: give me a sign…

[FUTURE *deliquesces, slowly, gently. The* PHANTOM's *hood and robe drop gracefully to the ground in a small heap. Music in. There is nothing in them. They are mortal cloth. The* SPIRIT *is elsewhere.* SCROOGE *has his sign.* SCROOGE *is alone. Tableau. The lights fade to black.*]

SCENE 5

The end of it. MARLEY, *spotlighted, opposite* SCROOGE, *in his bed, spot-lighted.* MARLEY *speaks to audience, directly.*

MARLEY: [*He smiles at* SCROOGE.] The firm of Scrooge and Marley is doubly blessed: two misers turned; one, alas, in Death, too late; but the other miser turned in Time's penultimate nick. Look you on my friend, Ebenezer Scrooge…

SCROOGE: [*Scrambling out of bed; reeling in delight.*] I will live in the Past, in the Present, and in the Future! The Spirits of all Three shall strive within me!

MARLEY: [*He points and moves closer to* SCROOGE'*s bed.*] Yes, Ebenezer, the bedpost is your own. Believe it! Yes, Ebenezer, the room is your own. Believe it!

SCROOGE: Oh, Jacob Marley! Wherever you are, Jacob, know ye that I praise you for this! I praise you…and heaven…and Christmas time! [*Kneels facing away from* MARLEY.] I say it to ye on my knees, old Jacob, on my knees! [*He touches his bed curtains.*] Not torn down. My bed curtains are not at all torn down! Rings and all, here they are! They are here: I am here: the shadows of things that would have been, may now be dispelled. They will be, Jacob! I know they will be! [*He chooses clothing for the day. He tries different pieces of clothing and settles, perhaps, on a dress suit, plus a cape of the bed clothing: something of color.*] I am light as a feather, I am happy as an angel, I am as merry as a schoolboy. I am as giddy as a drunken man! [*Yells out window and then out to audience:*] Merry Christmas to everybody! Merry Christmas to everybody! A Happy New Year to all the world! Hallo here! Whoop! Whoop! Hallo! Hallo! I don't know what day of the month it is! I don't care! I don't know anything! I'm quite a baby! I don't care! I don't care a fig! I'd much rather be a baby than be an old wreck like me or Marley! (Sorry, Jacob, wherever ye be!) Hallo! Hallo there!

[*Church bells chime in Christmas Day. A small boy, named* ADAM, *is seen now as a light fades up on him.*]

SCROOGE: [*Cont'd.*] Hey, you, boy! What's today? What day of the year is it?

ADAM: Today, sir? Why, it's Christmas Day!

SCROOGE: It's Christmas Day, is it? Whoop! Well, I haven't missed it after all, have I? The Spirits did all they did in one night. They can do anything they like, right? Of course they can! Of course they can!

ADAM: Excuse me, sir?

SCROOGE: Huh? Oh, yes, of course, what's your name, lad?

[SCROOGE *and* ADAM *will play their scene from their own spotlights.*]

ADAM: Adam, sir.

SCROOGE: Adam! What a fine, strong name! Do you know the poulterer's in the next street but one, at the corner?

ADAM: I certainly should hope I know him, sir!

SCROOGE: A remarkable boy! An intelligent boy! Do you know whether the poulterer's have sold the prize turkey that was hanging up there? I don't mean the little prize turkey, Adam, I mean the big one!

ADAM: What, do you mean the one they've got that's as big as me?

SCROOGE: I mean, the turkey the size of Adam: that's the bird!

ADAM: It's hanging there now, sir.

SCROOGE: It is? Go and buy it! No, no, I am absolutely in earnest. Go and buy it and tell 'em to bring it here, so that I may give them the directions to where I want it delivered, as a gift. Come back here with the man, Adam, and I'll give you a shilling. Come back here with him in less than five minutes, and I'll give you half-a-crown!

ADAM: Oh, my, sir! Don't let my brother in on this.

[ADAM *runs off stage.* MARLEY *smiles.*]

MARLEY: An act of kindness is like the first green grape of summer: one leads to another and another and another. It would take a queer man indeed to not follow an act of kindness with an act of kindness. One simply whets the tongue for more…the taste of kindness is too too sweet. Gifts—goods—are lifeless. But the gift of goodness one feels in the giving is full of life. It…is…a…wonder.

[*Pauses; moves closer to* SCROOGE, *who is totally occupied with his dressing and arranging of his room and his day. He is making lists, etc.* MARLEY *reaches out to* SCROOGE.]

ADAM: [*Calling, off.*] I'm here! I'm here!

[ADAM *runs on with a man, who carries an enormous turkey.*]

ADAM: [*Cont'd.*] Here I am, sir. Three minutes flat! A world record! I've got the poultryman and he's got the poultry! [*He pants, out of breath.*] I have earned my prize, sir, if I live…

[*He holds his heart, playacting.* SCROOGE *goes to him and embraces him.*]

SCROOGE: You are truly a champion, Adam

MAN: Here's the bird you ordered, sir.

SCROOGE: Oh, my, MY!!! Look at the size of that turkey, will you! He never could have stood upon his legs, that bird! He would have snapped them off in a minute, like sticks of sealingwax! Why you'll never be able to carry that bird to Camden-Town. I'll give you money for a cab...

MAN: Camden-Town's where it's goin', sir?

SCROOGE: Oh, I didn't tell you? Yes, I've written the precise address down just here on this...[*Hands paper to him.*] Bob Cratchit's house. Now he's not to know who sends him this. Do you understand me? Not a word...[*Handing out money and chuckling.*]

MAN: I understand, sir, not a word.

SCROOGE: Good. There you go then...this is for the turkey... [*Chuckle.*] and this is for the taxi. [*Chuckle.*]...and this is for your world-record run, Adam.

ADAM: But I don't have change for that, sir.

SCROOGE: Then keep it, my lad. It's Christmas!

ADAM: [*He kisses* SCROOGE's *cheek, quickly.*] Thank you, sir Merry, Merry Christmas! [*He runs off.*]

MAN: And you've given me a bit overmuch here, too, sir...

SCROOGE: Of course I have, sir. It's Christmas!

MAN: Oh, well, thanking you, sir, I'll have this bird to Mr. Cratchit and his family in no time, sir. Don't you worry none about that. Merry Christmas to you, sir, and a very happy New Year, too...

[*The man exits.* SCROOGE *walks in a large circle about the stage, which is now gently lit. A chorus sings Christmas music far in the distance. Bells chime as well, far in the distance. A* GENTLEWOMAN *enters and passes.* SCROOGE *is on the streets now.*]

SCROOGE: Merry Christmas, madam

WOMAN: Merry Christmas, sir...

[*The* PORTLY BUSINESSMAN *from the first act enters.*]

SCROOGE: Merry Christmas, sir.

PORTLY MAN: Merry Christmas, sir.

SCROOGE: Oh, you! My dear sir! How do you do? I do hope that you succeeded yesterday! It was very kind of you. A Merry Christmas.

PORTLY MAN: Mr. Scrooge?

SCROOGE: Yes, Scrooge is my name though I'm afraid you may not find it very pleasant. Allow me to ask your pardon. And will you have the goodness to— [*He whispers into the man's ear.*]

PORTLY MAN: Lord bless me! My dear Mr. Scrooge, are you serious!?!

SCROOGE: If you please. Not a farthing less. A great many back-payments are included in it, I assure you. Will you do me that favor?

PORTLY MAN: My dear sir, I don't know what to say to such munifi—

SCROOGE: [*Cutting him off.*] Don't say anything, please. Come and see me. Will you?

PORTLY MAN: I will! I will! Oh, I will, Mr. Scrooge! It will be my pleasure!

SCROOGE: Thank'ee, I am much obliged to you. I thank you fifty times. Bless you!

[PORTLY MAN *passes offstage.* SCROOGE *now comes to the room of his* NEPHEW *and* NIECE. *He stops at the door, begins to knock on it, loses his courage, tries again, loses his courage again, tries again, fails again, and then backs off and runs at the door, causing a tremendous bump against it. The* NEPHEW *and* NIECE *are startled.* SCROOGE, *poking head into room.*] Fred!

NEPHEW: Why, bless my soul! Who's that?

NEPHEW AND NIECE: [*Together.*] How now? Who goes?

SCROOGE: It's I. Your Uncle Scrooge.

NIECE: Dear heart alive!

SCROOGE: I have come to dinner. May I come in, Fred?

NEPHEW: May you come in???!!! With such pleasure for me you may, Uncle!!! What a treat!

NIECE: What a treat, Uncle Scrooge! Come in, come in!

[*They embrace a shocked and delighted* SCROOGE. FRED *calls into the other room.*]

NEPHEW: Come in here, everybody, and meet my Uncle Scrooge! He's come for our Christmas party!

[*Music in. Lighting here indicates that day has gone to night and gone to day again. It is early, early morning.* SCROOGE *walks alone from the party, exhausted, to his offices, opposite side of the stage. He opens his offices. The offices are as they were at the start of the play.* SCROOGE *seats himself with his door wide open so that he can see into the tank, as he awaits* CRATCHIT, *who enters, head down, full of guilt.* CRATCHIT *starts writing almost before he sits.*]

SCROOGE: What do you mean by coming in here at this time of day, a full eighteen minutes late, Mr. Cratchit? Hallo, sir? Do you hear me?

BOB: I am very sorry, sir. I am behind my time.

SCROOGE: You are? Yes, I certainly think you are. Step this way, sir, if you please...

BOB: It's only but once a year, sir...it shall not be repeated. I was making rather merry yesterday and into the night.

SCROOGE: Now, I'll tell you what, Cratchit. I am not going to stand this sort of thing any longer. And therefore...[*He stands and pokes his finger into* BOB's *chest.*] I am...about...to...raise...your salary.

BOB: Oh, no, sir, I...[*Realizes.*] what did you say, sir?

SCROOGE: A Merry Christmas, Bob [*He claps* BOB's *back.*] A merrier Christmas, Bob, my good fellow than I have given you for many a year. I'll raise your salary and endeavor to assist your struggling family and we will discuss your affairs this very afternoon over a bowl of smoking bishop, Bob! Make up the fires and buy another coal scuttle before you dot another I, Bob. It's too damned cold in this place! We need warmth and cheer, Bob Cratchit! Do you hear me? DO... YOU...HEAR...ME?

[BOB CRATCHIT *stands, smiles at* SCROOGE. BOB CRATCHIT *faints. Blackout. As the main lights black out, a spotlight appears on* SCROOGE, *another on* MARLEY. *He talks directly to the audience.*]

MARLEY: Scrooge was better than his word. He did it all and infinitely more; and to Tiny Tim, who did NOT die, he was a second father. He became as good a friend, as good a master, as good a man, as the good old city knew, or any other good old city, town, or borough in the good old world. And it was always said of him that he knew how to keep Christmas well, if any man alive possessed the knowledge. [*Pauses.*] May that be truly said of us, and all of us: And so, as Tiny Tim observed...

TINY TIM: [*Atop* SCROOGE's *shoulder.*] God Bless Us, Every One...

[*Lights up on chorus, singing final Christmas Song.* SCROOGE *and* MARLEY *and all spirits and other characters of the play join in.*]

[*The play has ended.*]

A VISIT FROM ST. NICHOLAS or THE NIGHT BEFORE CHRISTMAS

A Full Length Comedy For Two Men and Four Women

by Lowell Swortzell

CHARACTERS

MARGARET.. age ten or eleven
BENJAMIN..age nine
CHARITY...age eight
HARRIET BUTLER...............................a holiday house guest, early 20s
FATHER (Clement Clarke Moore)...in his 40s
MOTHER (Alice Moore)..in her early 30s

PLACE: *"Chelsea," the Moore homestead in Manhattan, New York.*

TIME: *Late Christmas eve, 1822, and early the next morning.*

The action is continuous.

SCENE: *Clement Clarke Moore's house, late Christmas Eve, 1822.*

AT RISE: THE FAMILY, *except for* MOTHER *is gathered in the living room, listening to* FATHER *finish reading a poem he wrote earlier in the day and which he is now speaking aloud for the first time. He stands by the fireplace while* EVERYONE *else is seated, the* CHILDREN *on pillows and* HARRIET BUTLER *sitting at a nearby table. Their rapt attention is totally focused upon* FATHER *who delivers the poem in a commanding voice with dramatic feeling.* EVERYONE *is elegantly dressed for bed, wearing colorful robes and appropriate slippers*

FATHER: "He spoke not a word, but went straight to his work,

And filled all the stockings; then turned with a jerk,

And laying his finger aside of his nose,

And giving a nod, up the chimney he rose.

He sprang up to his sleigh, to his team gave a whistle,

And away they all flew like the down of a thistle.

But I heard him exclaim, ere he drove out of sight,

Happy Christmas to all, and to all a good night!' '

[*As* FATHER *lowers the pages from which he has been reading,* ALL *applaud vigorously.*]

CHARITY: Is that the end?

FATHER: It's the end of his visit, Charity, so it's the end of the poem, too.

BENJAMIN: That's why it's called "A Visit from St. Nicholas," silly.

MARGARET: Father, this is your very best poem.

FATHER: [p*leased*]. Why, thank you, Margaret.

MARGARET: The others are so...[*Searching for the correct word*]...serious...

FATHER: They're about serious subjects, Margaret. But you can say "boring" if you like. I won't mind.

MARGARET: I wouldn't be so cruel.

CHARITY: I would. They bore me.

FATHER: [*to* HARRIET]. Despite her name, Charity's my severest critic, in all things. [*He laughs.*]

CHARITY: But I love this one. Lots and lots.

BENJAMIN: Will you write some more for us?

FATHER: This was just an improvisation.

CHARITY: What does that mean? "Improvisation.'

FATHER: Cousin Harriet, you're a teacher, you explain.

HARRIET: It's something that happens on the spur of the moment... quickly made up.

CHARITY: Then that's the way you should write all your poems instead of locked in your study with all your books...where we can't see you...

BENJAMIN: Charity's right, "improvisation" is best.

FATHER: But my poems are about life and death, religion and philosophy...they come from deep reading...and deep thinking...

CHARITY: That's why they put us to sleep...deep sleep.

FATHER: I must say I've never seen you so attentive as just now.

MARGARET: Because it was about something important...

CHARITY: St. Nicholas! I want to hear it again.

MARGARET: Father, would you please?

CHARITY: [*excited*]. Read it again! Read it again!

BENJAMIN: Please, Father!

FATHER: I will--next year.

MARGARET: Next year!

FATHER: Yes, I wrote it to be read on Christmas Eve.

CHARITY: Well, it's Christmas Eve.

FATHER: Only barely. The midnight chimes will be ringing any minute now. Remember we got ready for bed hours ago. And look, we're still up, all of us!

CHARITY: I want to stay and see St. Nicholas come down the chimney.

FATHER: You just did, young lady, in the poem.

MARGARET: Did you ever see him, Father?

FATHER: [*not quite certain how to answer this and looking at* HARRIET *for help*]. Well, I must have...to have written the poem...mustn't I?

HARRIET: And you made us see him, too, so clearly. I believed he was right here in this room.

CHARITY: Dressed in red...

BENJAMIN: With a big beard...

MARGARET: And his suit trimmed in white fur.

HARRIET: You did see him! Oh, Mr. Moore, it's a wonderful poem.

FATHER: Some simple rhymes, that's all.

MARGARET: Father, this is the first time you've written anything for us. Thank you!

FATHER: You're welcome, Margaret.

HARRIET: [*tentatively*]. Mr. Moore...?

FATHER: Yes, Cousin Harriet.

HARRIET: [*carefully feeling her way, not knowing how he will respond*]. I'm wondering...if I might have a copy of the poem...to take home with me...

FATHER: Oh, no, it's just for the children...

HARRIET: But that's why I want it...for the children...the children I know in Troy...my students...

FATHER: [*firmly*]. I wrote it for the children in this house alone.

HARRIET: I loved it and I'm no child!

FATHER: You're just being kind...

HARRIET: I can get it published in Troy's best newspaper where everyone can read it.

FATHER: [*not taking her seriously, he laughs*]. No, no, no!

HARRIET: You'll be famous!

FATHER: [*sharply*]. No! [*Now taking her very seriously.*] That must never happen. Never! I can be famous only as a professor of classical languages. That's my profession, not as a poet for children. Do you understand?

HARRIET: Surely, it would do no harm.

FATHER: [*clearly annoyed*]. Cousin, it's quite out of the question!

HARRIET: [*recognizing his answer as final*]. I don't mean to anger you, sir, especially on Christmas Eve. Forgive me, please.

FATHER: Certainly. [*Changing the subject and returning to his normal voice.*] Now, children, where is your Mother? It's time for you to say good night.

MARGARET: She's in the dining room.

BENJAMIN: Setting the table for tomorrow's dinner.

FATHER: We need her to tuck you in.

CHARITY: Harriet will do it. Won't you, Harriet?

HARRIET: Of course. I always do when I come to visit.

CHARITY: Let Harriet do it, please.

FATHER: [*to* HARRIET]. Do you mind?

HARRIET: It's my pleasure, sir.

FATHER: Very well then. Now to make it easy for Cousin Harriet, let's be certain everyone, and I mean *everyone* is in bed by the time the last bell chimes.

BENJAMIN: Does that include you and Mother?

CHARITY: You said everyone!

[MOTHER *enters. She is in her early thirties, most attractive and self-assured. She runs the household and, usually without letting him know,* FATHER *as well.*]

MOTHER: Does what include me?

FATHER: If she's willing to join in, it does.

MOTHER: Oh, dear, surely it's too late for games. We've got to go to bed.

MARGARET: That's just it!

FATHER: Everyone must be in bed, with all lamps and

candles out by the twelfth chime of midnight.

MOTHER: Sounds like an excellent game to me. I'm happy to play.

FATHER: I'll fix the fire for the night. [*He works at the fireplace.*]

HARRIET: [*to* MOTHER]. I'll go with the children.

MOTHER: Thank you, dear. They always do everything you say.

CHARITY: Harriet's our favorite cousin.

MARGARET: Her visit is the best Christmas present you could give us.

HARRIET: Thank you, but I think your Father's poem is the best gift you...or...[*Pointedly.*]...anyone...could receive.

FATHER: [*ignoring her compliment and returning from the fireplace*]. Is everyone ready to go upstairs?

CHILDREN: Yes, I am. All ready.

BENJAMIN: I'll be the first one in bed.

CHARITY: No, you have to carry the candle, Benjamin.

MOTHER: A very good suggestion. [*Handing him a lighted candle.*] Be careful on the stairs, please.

[*The first chime is heard*]

FATHER: We must go. Time's running out.

MOTHER: Sleep well. Tomorrow's a long, long adventure.

FATHER: Good night, everyone.

EVERYONE: Good night, Father. Good night, Mother. [Etc.]

> [*As the chimes ring, they file through the imaginary door and into the hallway, then climb the imaginary stairs. There is much giggling and laughter from the* CHILDREN, *as the* ADULTS *loudly count the chimes. Once upstairs,* EVERYONE *waves good night, the* CHILDREN *and* HARRIET *going one way,* FATHER *and* MOTHER *the other. The* CHILDREN *remove their bathrobes and slippers and climb into bed.* HARRIET *tucks them in, blows out candle, and then exits.* FATHER *and* MOTHER *turn down the lamp and go to bed. The chimes have continued throughout their movement. This action is timed so they all are in bed and simultaneously pulling up covers exactly as* FATHER *and* MOTHER *say "twelve." In unison* EVERYONE *says. "Good night," and they immediately go to sleep. The lights have dimmed with a low glow still burning in the fireplace. There is a pause during which we can hear the soft sounds of their sleeping. Then the chimes are heard again, now ringing four times.* A VOICE *is heard speaking through the theatre 's sound system.*]

VOICE: "'Twas the night before Christmas, when all through the house

Creatures were stirring, each as quiet as a mouse."

[CHARITY *pulls back her covers, creeps out of bed, and quietly moves to* BENJAMIN *and* MARGARET, *awaking them. Quick to find their robes and slippers, they soon are ready to proceed. Looking at each other and placing a finger over their lips to indicate that no one should speak, they tiptoe to the door. The first one there opens it as silently as possible and they* ALL *slip through, the last one closing the door behind them. They make their way into the hallway and slowly descend the staircase. At the living room door, they pause to discern if their movements have been heard by anyone else in the house. Satisfied that everyone is still asleep, they proceed by opening the door and sneaking through, with ever increasing suspense. Once inside, they move even more cautiously until...*]

BENJAMIN: [*stubbing his toe on a chair, he cries out*] Ouch!

[*Immediately,* ALL *three huddle together, afraid to move. They remain frozen throughout the following.*]

VOICE: "'Twas the night before Christmas, when all through the house

Several creatures were stirring, though not so silently as a mouse."

[HARRIET *enters carrying a lighted candle. She comes into the upstairs hallway and heads to the children's bedroom, carefully opening the door. Moving towards the beds, she bends over the first bench and whispers softly.*]

HARRIET: Margaret, wake up. I need your help. [*Not waiting for an answer, she goes to the second bed.*] Benjamin, get up and come with me. Quickly! [*Again, not lingering, she proceeds to the third bed.*] Charity, don't cry out, dear. Just find your slippers and robe and follow the others. We have work to do. [*Now addressing all three.*] Well, why don't you move? [*She returns to the first bed and shakes the covers.*] Margaret, this is important...What on earth? [*From under the covers she extracts a large doll.*] Not here in the middle of the night? [*Returns to second bed.*] Benjamin, why isn't Margaret in bed? [*She pulls back the blankets to find a large ball on the pillow and a jacket rolled up to resemble a body.*] Charity, where are your brother and sister? I need them. [*Pulls covers away to find another doll.*] What's happening? You're up to something...that's clear. Well, so am I.

[HARRIET *opens door, slips into the hallway and disappears into the darkness, as the lights come up dimly in the living room.*]

VOICE: "'Twas the night before Christmas, when in another part of the house

Several frightened creatures stood frozen as if they had seen a mouse."

MARGARET: What's the matter?

BENJAMIN: I bumped my toe on the leg of the chair.

MARGARET: Why don't you look where you're going?

BENJAMIN: I can't see in the dark, silly!

MARGARET: I haven't bumped my toe, have I?

BENJAMIN: No.

MARGARET: Then don't you. [*She begins to feel her* way.] Ouch!

BENJAMIN: Don't *you!*

CHARITY: Quiet, both of you. Ouch!

MARGARET AND BENJAMIN: *You*, too!

BENJAMIN: We're going to get caught if we're not quiet. Let's hide here where we can watch the fireplace.

MARGARET: The embers are still glowing.

[*The fireplace glimmers in an orange-and-red light.*]

CHARITY: Benjamin, you better put out the fire.

BENJAMIN: Why?

CHARITY: So his feet won't get burned.

MARGARET: Very good, Charity. [*To* BENJAMIN] But do it quietly, please.

BENJAMIN: You can't put out a fire without making some noise. [*He pokes the fire and rattles the grill.*] See, it's impossible.

MARGARET: Sh-h-h! I'll do it. Just watch. [*She gently pokes at the fire which immediately dims.*] There. See.

BENJAMIN: It's too dark to see anything.

CHARITY: What are we going to do now?

MARGARET: Wait.

CHARITY: How long?

MARGARET: I don't know. Just listen for him.

BENJAMIN: All I hear is you two talking.

MARGARET: Very well, we won't say anything for an entire minute.

[*With effort, they remain silent.*]

VOICE: "'Twas the night before Christmas, which was rather nice,

Until suddenly in the bedroom, Mother thought she heard mice."

[*In the parents' bedroom,* MOTHER *suddenly sits up and listens intently.*]

MOTHER: Father! [*Reaches over and pokes him.*]

FATHER: Mother, what is it?

MOTHER: Sit up a minute! I heard something.

FATHER: The house settling.

MOTHER: No, it isn't. Someone's in the parlor...moving about.

FATHER: The servants cleaning up, most likely.

MOTHER: They went to bed hours ago. It must be three or four in the morning.

FATHER: Perhaps it's snowing.

MOTHER: The moon is streaming through the windows, crystal clear.

FATHER: I know, then.

MOTHER: What?

FATHER: What we usually hear at this time of night.

MOTHER: I thought so at first, but mice don't talk.

FATHER: They're wishing each other "Happy Christmas."

MOTHER: I thought I head one of them say "ouch."

FATHER: A clumsy mouse, no doubt. Go back to sleep

MOTHER: And another one rake the fire.

FATHER: A cold mouse, no doubt. Stop worrying.

MOTHER: And another say, "Sh-h-h!"

FATHER: Because he wants to sleep. A wise mouse, I'd say. [*He pulls up the covers.*]

MOTHER: I tell you it's not a mouse stirring in this house, Mr. Moore.

FATHER: Then why are you so upset, Mrs. Moore?

MOTHER: Because something is.

FATHER: Is what?

MOTHER: Talking and walking about downstairs.

FATHER: Even robbers stay at home on Christmas Eve.

MOTHER: Then who is it?

FATHER: St. Nicholas perhaps.

MOTHER: If so, I think we should say "hello."

FATHER: Go ahead. Give him my regards.

MOTHER: [*taking no more of his nonsense*]. Father!

FATHER: [*imitating her stand*]. Mother!

MOTHER: I think we better see for ourselves.

FATHER: Must we?

MOTHER: I can't stop worrying.

FATHER: Very well. Hand me my robe. [*He gets up.*]

MOTHER: Oh, thank you, Father. I feel better already.

FATHER: You're coming, too, of course.

MOTHER: But why?

FATHER: You don't think after what you heard I'm going down there by myself, do you?

MOTHER: Oh, very well! Anything to get you to look. [*She rises and puts on her robe.*]

FATHER: And no screams, please, if it's only a mouse.

MOTHER: You can be certain I won't scream. I don't want to wake the children.

[*Lighting two candles, they go out, disappearing into the hallways.*]

[HARRIET *reappears at the opposite side of the house from which we last saw her. She stops before an imaginary door at the extreme side of the stage which she thrusts open. She goes through, closing it behind her, and whispers loudly.*]

HARRIET: Are you in the kitchen tasting the Christmas pudding? Well, take one last raisin and one last plum and follow me. And don't make any noise, please. We mustn't wake your parents. [*Pause.*] Children, come out from your hiding places. You've always trusted me. I won't tell where I found you. [*She waits for an answer.*] You can't be here and keep this quiet. Oh, dear! I wish this house weren't so big. If I don't find you soon, it's going to be too late! [*She closes the kitchen door and continues her search, crossing to the living room area. Here she opens the door and steps inside.*] Children, I know you're somewhere. If you're not in the library, the nursery or the kitchen, you must be here. Will you help me? Please, I can't wait any longer.

MARGARET: [*meekly from their hiding place in the dark*]. Neither can we.

CHARITY: We're getting tired.

BENJAMIN: And cold.

HARRIET: Where are you?

BENJAMIN: Over here.

HARRIET: [*going to them*]. What are you doing here?

CHARITY: Waiting for St. Nicholas. Where is he?

HARRIET: [*pointing towards the windows*]. Out there somewhere. Don't worry, he'll find his way here.

BENJAMIN: I want to see him come down the chimney.

MARGARET: I want to hear him laugh.

CHARITY: I want to see his round little belly.

HARRIET: That's exactly what I need to talk to you about.

CHARITY: His belly?

MARGARET: Does it really shake like a bowl full of jelly?

HARRIET: Of course! I should have known. You're here because of your father's poem. Aren't you?

MARGARET: We want to watch it happen.

BENJAMIN: [*quickly reciting*]. "'Twas the night before Christmas, when all through the house

Not a creature was stirring, not even a mouse."

CHARITY: I never knew what St. Nicholas looked like before.

MARGARET: Or that he travels through the air with eight reindeer.

BENJAMIN: Or that he can go up and down chimneys.

HARRIET: No one ever saw St. Nicholas like that before. When I was your age, I thought he was an ancient old man with a beard that touched the ground.

MARGARET: I like Father's description better.

BENJAMIN: So do I.

HARRIET: And so would everyone else. But when I asked him for a copy of the poem you heard him say, "No, absolutely not!"

MARGARET: He's strict.

BENJAMIN: And likes lots of rules.

CHARITY: We're breaking all of them right now. [*She giggles with excitement at the thought.*]

MARGARET: If he finds us out of bed, St. Nicholas may not come to this house for years and years.

HARRIET: That's why you must help me as fast as possible, and get right back to bed.

BENJAMIN: How?

HARRIET: We're going to copy the poem. He left it stuck in a book on the table. I'll light the candles and find some paper. If we each take a section, we should be able to get the whole thing written down in a few minutes.

MARGARET: Won't Father be upset?

HARRIET: If he finds out, yes, but I wasn't planning to tell him--at least, not tonight--and I'm hoping you won't either.

CHARITY: We're good at secrets.

MARGARET: But isn't it a bit like stealing to copy his poem?

HARRIET: No, I don't think so. We'll be sharing, so that others can enjoy it, too.

MARGARET: I certainly wouldn't want to be selfish. [To BENJAMIN *and* CHARITY.] Would you?

BENJAMIN: Not at all.

CHARITY: Let's share it with everybody.

HARRIET: I knew you'd understand. Now take these pens. Here's paper for each of us

[MOTHER *and* FATHER *have entered the area and stand just outside the door.*]

HARRIET: Do each letter, as neatly as we can. And, please, let's not spill any ink on the tablecloth. [*She gives them quills and paper.*] Here's the poem. When we're finished, I'll put it back in the book and your father will never know.

CHARITY: And we'll never, never, never tell.

VOICE: "The children were nestled busily at work

Unaware that outside two creatures lurk'd

Who they were about to discover

Were none other than Father and Mother."

[FATHER *and* MOTHER *burst into the room. The* CHILDREN, *seeing them, drop their pens.*]

CHARITY: Oh, no!

MARGARET: You scared us!

HARRIET: Mr. and Mrs. Moore!

BENJAMIN: What a surprise!

FATHER: [*to* MOTHER]. Why, it's not St. Nicholas, after all!

MOTHER: [*to* FATHER]. And, as I said, these are not mice, are they?

FATHER: [*shivering*]. Who let the fire go out? It's freezing in here. [*He goes to the fireplace and puts logs on the fire.*] I'll get it going in no time.

BENJAMIN: [*urgently pleading*]. Please don't!

CHARITY: We're warm enough.

MARGARET: We really don't need it.

FATHER: Your mother and I need it!

MOTHER: [*gently to* FATHER]. Don't include me, Father, please.

FATHER: Very well. I need a fire and I'll have a fire [*He lights the fire with the candle he has been carrying and soon flames are leaping up, considerably brightening the room.*] There!

BENJAMIN: [*softly to* CHARITY *and* MARGARET *who also whisper*]. Now he'll never come!

CHARITY: If he does, he'll burn his feet!

MARGARET: He'll go back up the chimney in a hurry!

MOTHER: Children, what are you whispering about? You should be sound asleep. Why are you out of bed?

FATHER: And, Cousin Harriet, what are you up to? Walking in your sleep, no doubt?

HARRIET: [*politely*]. No, I'm very much awake, thank you, sir. [*A long pause.*]

FATHER: Well, isn't anyone going to tell us?

MARGARET: What do you want to know?

FATHER: That's obvious.

CHARITY: Not to me.

BENJAMIN: Can't imagine, myself.

FATHER: I don't want to imagine. I want to know! What all three of you, and Cousin Harriet, too, are doing here in the middle of the night?

MARGARET: Trying to be quiet so no one would hear us, that's what.

CHARITY: We didn't breathe for one whole minute.

BENJAMIN: And we didn't talk.

MOTHER: Someone said "ouch!" I distinctly heard "ouch" all the way upstairs.

MARGARET: That was Benjamin.

BENJAMIN: That was Charity.

CHARITY: That was Margaret.

CHILDREN: We bumped our toes.

FATHER: Just what should happen to prowlers. Serves you right.

MOTHER: Harriet, dear, can you shed any light on these creatures of the night?

HARRIET: Well, the truth is you've caught us.

FATHER: I should say we have. But at what, is the question.

BENJAMIN: [*thinking quickly*]. At our lessons, that's what.

MARGARET: Yes, see; we're writing away.

CHARITY: Trying to get ahead.

BENJAMIN: And Harriet is helping us. She's a good teacher, too.

FATHER: I should think so, to be holding classes so attentively at four a.m. on Christmas morning. What is it you're studying?

[*There is a long pause, as the* CHILDREN *look from one to another to see who can come up with an answer. When no one does,* HARRIET *steps forth.*]

HARRIET: Let me explain, Mr. Moore. The children are helping me, at my request.

BENJAMIN: We were up anyway.

CHARITY: When Harriet found us hiding here.

MARGARET: So don't blame her.

FATHER: [*exasperated*]. For WHAT? Cousin Harriet, before I become any more confused, will you please explain this mystery.

HARRIET: Yes, sir. You remember last evening that I asked you if I might have a copy of the poem you wrote.

FATHER: I do. And I explained that was not possible.

HARRIET: Well, that's why we're here.

BENJAMIN: We're making a copy for Cousin Harriet.

CHARITY: We'll be finished in a few minutes. [*Picks up her pen.*]

FATHER: [*firmly*]. No, not another word!

HARRIET: Please, don't be upset with us, Mr. Moore.

FATHER: I don't want anyone else to see this. What would my colleagues at the college say if they knew I spent my time writing poems for children...about St. Nicholas?

MOTHER: Father, you needn't worry about your reputation as a scholar. Everyone knows you wrote the first Hebrew dictionary published in the United States. And ever so much more.

FATHER: But a professor of my standing doesn't write jingles. Much less publish them.

MOTHER: Only because the other professors have no talent for poetry.

FATHER: This isn't poetry. [*Picking up the original manuscript.*] Just some simple rhymes. You can be certain that when I publish my real verse, these lines will not be included. Which is all the more reason they must be suppressed now.

CHARITY: What does "suppressed" mean?

FATHER: I'll show you, Charity. [*He takes their copy and tears it into small pieces.*]

BENJAMIN: But you wrote it for us. It's our poem.

MARGARET: That's what you said last night.

CHARITY: Didn't you?

FATHER: Yes, and only for you. To be read in this house and nowhere else.

HARRIET: Mr. Moore, I beg you to reconsider.

CHILDREN: Please, Father, please!

FATHER: I can't. And it's for your good as well as mine. I must protect our name, our family name. That of your grandfather, the Bishop of New York who assisted at George Washington's inauguration and conducted Alexander Hamilton's funeral. None of us must ever do anything to tarnish his distinguished name.

HARRIET: [*to* FATHER]. But surely, the Bishop, of all people, would have loved the poem as much as the children.

FATHER: I see I am alone in this. But all the same I stand firm. The poem must not leave this house.

MARGARET: Father! Please! Let's share it!

BENJAMIN: Cousin Harriet is right!

MOTHER: Father, if it will make others happy...

FATHER: I could never live down the embarrassment. So, there's only one thing to do. Harriet, give me those pages you've copied, please.

HARRIET: [*shocked*]. Oh, Mr. Moore, you wouldn't!

FATHER: The poem, Cousin Harriet. I have no choice.[*He takes the poem and the copy and moves to the fireplace and throws them in. A flame leaps up with a puff of smoke as the poem burns.*] Now no copy remains to concern any of us.

CHARITY: [*crying*]. But it's ours!

BENJAMIN: Going up in smoke. Look at it burning.

MARGARET: Gone forever, in a few seconds. Oh, Father, do you realize what you've done?

FATHER: Those words are better off as smoke.

MARGARET: You're cruel!

FATHER: Margaret, on the contrary, I'm a kind and generous man, as you have every reason to know, but in this instance I have done what I must.

BENJAMIN: [*shouting*]. You burned our poem!

FATHER: Benjamin, you will not speak to me like that. I will not allow it.

CHARITY: He's right. You gave it to us. It was our poem.

FATHER: Well, it belongs to no one now. And the matter is closed. I would never have written the lines had I known the trouble they were going to cause.

MOTHER: [*taking command of the situation*]. Children, Cousin Harriet, Father, let's all go back to bed. We have guests to entertain at dinner tomorrow and must be up at the first morning chimes. So let's get our rest while we may. Harriet, dear, would you be so kind as to tuck the children in, once again?

HARRIET: Of course, Mrs. Moore, gladly.

MOTHER: Thank you. Father, come along. There's nothing more to be said. Let's forget what has happened here and think about the good times that await us tomorrow. Stringing cranberries, pulling taffy, giving the horses apples and the dogs bones, so that everyone is happy.

MARGARET: Everyone but us!

MOTHER: Margaret, dear, that's quite enough!

BENJAMIN: AND CHARITY: She's right, though.

MOTHER: You'll feel better tomorrow, I promise. Now, good night, for the second time tonight. Your father has been very kind not to punish you for being up at this hour.

FATHER: As a matter of fact, I forgot all about it. What were you doing when Cousin Harriet found you here?

MARGARET: Waiting for St. Nicholas to arrive.

BENJAMIN: To see him come down the chimney.

CHARITY: With his belly like a bowl full of jelly!

MARGARET: Just as you described in the poem.

FATHER: I should have known better than to ask.

MOTHER: [*again taking over*]. No more, no more. Now we're all off to bed. Father, lead the way.

[MOTHER *and* FATHER *go to the door.* FATHER *opens it,* MOTHER *goes through and* FATHER *turns back, trying to think of something to say.*]

FATHER: Children, I...I...I...,[*Pause.*] I hope that someday when you grow up, you'll appreciate real poetry.

MOTHER: [*Clumping in before anyone else can speak*]. Father, bring your candle, so we can see on the stairs.

FATHER: Yes, Mother.

[*He closes the door behind him and* FATHER *and* MOTHER *make their way back to their bedroom.*]

HARRIET: Charity, take Margaret's hand, please. Benjamin fetch the candle. Thank you. And we're ready to go.

BENJAMIN: We'll shiver upstairs.

MARGARET: Can't we stay here a little while longer?

CHARITY: It's warm by the fire.

HARRIET: Perhaps for a few minutes. But we don't want to upset your father any more than we already have.[*They gather about the fireplace.*] I apologize for getting you into trouble.

MARGARET: You didn't know what Father would do.

HARRIET: I certainly didn't think he'd do that...Or I never would have suggested we copy it. It's all my fault.

BENJAMIN: No, it isn't. Father burned the poem. Not you.

MARGARET: He seemed to think it was his even though he had given it to us.

HARRIET: [*quickly trying to break the gloomy mood*]. Shall I tell you a story?

CHARITY: No, thank you.

HARRIET: I know, let's play hide and seek?

BENJAMIN: That's no fun in the dark.

MARGARET: Besides, Father would hear us...

CHARITY: ...and scold us.

HARRIET: Can you think of a quiet game?

CHARITY: I don't feel like playing.

BENJAMIN: Neither do I.

HARRIET: Margaret?

MARGARET: No, thank you.

HARRIET: Then we'll just sit and watch the fire. I'll add another log.

[*She does so. They sit silently, huddled together on the floor, facing the fire.*]

[*The lights dim on the living room and come up on the bedroom area. By now,* FATHER *and* MOTHER *have returned to their room and are back in their beds.*]

MOTHER: Father, are you asleep?

FATHER: Why, what do you hear now?

MOTHER: You. Tossing and turning. Something the matter?

FATHER: I'm thinking.

MOTHER: I'm not surprised.

FATHER: They were just some silly verses.

MOTHER: Not to the children.

FATHER: Surely nothing so upsetting...

MOTHER: Yet you're upset, aren't you? Very upset. And the looks on the children's faces...I've never seen them like that...total disbelief!

FATHER: In me, I suppose.

MOTHER: You did write it for them and give it to them.

FATHER: Perhaps I shouldn't have taken it back. And then to burn it. [*He shudders.*] I don't know how to face them.

MOTHER: [*brightly*]. I do.

FATHER: Tell me. I'll do anything to overcome this blunder.

MOTHER: Simply write the poem again. As you did yesterday. Once they have it back, they'll forgive you.

FATHER: [*excited*]. That's it! Of course! Thank you, my dear.

MOTHER: Let me get you some paper. Jot it down so they see it's not lost forever.

FATHER: This time I'll make a real gift of it, in a box wrapped with ribbons.

MOTHER: [*giving him paper and pen*]. Their faces will glow when they see it.

FATHER: [*writing quickly as he talks*]. "'Twas the night before Christmas..." I'm certain that's how it began..."And all through the house..." No, it was "When all through the house...Not a creature was stirring, not even a mouse." Is that right?

MOTHER: How should I know? You wrote it!

FATHER: That was yesterday. Once I put jingles of this sort down, they vanish from my head almost instantly. Always have.

MOTHER: Keep trying.

FATHER: Next comes something about you and me. You were wearing a kerchief and I had on a cap. That much I remember.

MOTHER: Make it up new. They won't know the difference.

FATHER: Of course they will. When I read them their favorite stories, I can never change a word. They catch me every time. They remember everything.

MOTHER: Well, I'm of little help, I fear. I was in the dining room talking to Mrs. Watkins about Christmas dinner and missed the entire poem.

FATHER: [*staring at the paper*]. They were just some simple rhymes I made up as I went from shop to shop, to occupy my mind.

MOTHER: Then imagine yourself at the butcher's and the banker's and perhaps they'll come back.

FATHER: I said to Mr. Johnson, "I want the biggest Christmas roast you have!" And I wished Mr. Goldsmith a Happy Christmas and took the plum pudding you had ordered. That's all I recall. Then I drove round to buy some holly and mistletoe. And later stopped to pick up the children's gifts. And then I came home and went straight to my study. And set down the verses. Until you called to help decorate the hallways...

MOTHER: Well, doesn't any of this jog your memory?

FATHER: [*showing her the almost blank paper*]. Unless you want a poem about shopping--[*He improvises.*]

   "'Twas the night before Christmas,

   And I felt no grief

   Because I had bought the biggest

   Roast of beef!"

   It's not the same.

MOTHER: [*laughing*]. I hope not!

FATHER: [*he crunches up the piece of paper into a ball and throws it away*]. I feel dreadful.

MOTHER: Don't punish yourself, dear. It's really quite simple. The poem is locked in your head and you must find a way to let it out. [*She hands him another sheet of paper.*] Try again.

FATHER: I tell you, there's nothing in my head. [*He stares at the paper.*] I feel so guilty.

[*The lights dim on the bedroom and come up again on the living room area.*]

HARRIET: Are you warm enough, Charity?

CHARITY: Yes, thank you. I like it here.

HARRIET: And you, Margaret and Benjamin?

MARGARET: Yes, thanks.

BENJAMIN: Me, too. [*There is a long pause which* HARRIET *finally breaks.*]

HARRIET: And I've been sitting here thinking a very bad thought I shouldn't say out loud.

CHARITY: What?

BENJAMIN: Tell us.

MARGARET: Please!

HARRIET: No, because it could get us into trouble all over again. And I've caused enough already.

MARGARET: I don't think a little more will matter now.

BENJAMIN: What can Father do? Cancel Christmas?

CHARITY: Not with guests coming! He can't.

BENJAMIN: So tell us.

HARRIET: As I look into the fire I keep seeing the poem going up in smoke. I want to reach in and grab it.

MARGARET: But you saw it burn.

CHARITY: Gone for good.

HARRIET: I'm not so certain, Charity, maybe it isn't.

CHARITY: What do you mean?

HARRIET: The paper the words were written on is gone, but not the words themselves. They're what we want.

BENJAMIN: Where are they, then?

HARRIET: With us. No one can take them back or burn them because they belong to us.

MARGARET: But we don't have them.

HARRIET: Perhaps we do. Inside us.

CHARITY: I know the reindeer's names: Dasher, Dancer, Prancer, Vixen. [*Impulsively breaking into verse.*]

"On Comet, on Cupid, on Donder and Blitzen--"

HARRIET: See, that's what I mean. You've kept those names inside you since you heard them last night. But you didn't realize it until this second.

MARGARET: If I close my eyes, I can hear the lines.

BENJAMIN: And I can see St. Nicholas!

CHARITY: "He had a broad face, and a little round belly, That shook when he laughed like a bowl full of jelly."

HARRIET: You do remember. I knew it. Let me write that down. [*She rushes to table and takes up pen, paper and ink and begins to write.*]

[*The lights come up in the* PARENTS' *bedroom with the action continuing simultaneously in both areas.*]

FATHER: There were eight reindeer. And what were their names? Some rhymed and some didn't. "Dasher," That was one of them. "Basher," "Casher," "Gasher," "Sasher," "Tasher," "Washer," "Yasher?" Must be one that didn't rhyme.

MARGARET: I think the best way to remember is to act it out.

BENJAMIN: You mean like a play?

CHARITY: Father wouldn't like that.

HARRIET: An excellent idea, Margaret. Benjamin, you play the father.

BENJAMIN: [*imitating* FATHER]. "None of us must ever do anything to tarnish his distinguished name."

MARGARET: No, she means the father in the poem.

BENJAMIN: Then I get the biggest part! Splendid!

HARRIET: Charity, you play St. Nicholas.

CHARITY: I don't have a round little belly.

BENJAMIN: Just stick a pillow inside your robe and you will.

CHARITY: [*placing the pillow*]. Somehow, I don't think this is going to shake like a bowl full of jelly.

[*She shakes her new stomach and* EVERYONE *laughs.*]

HARRIET: [*to* CHARITY]. Now stand over by the fireplace for your entrance. Margaret, you be the director, and I'11 write it all down. [*She prepares to record their words.*]

MARGARET: Are you ready, Benjamin?

BENJAMIN: Yes. [*Switching to a deep voice.*]

"'Twas the night before Christmas, when all through the house

   Not a creature was stirring, not even a mouse.

   The stockings were hung by the chimney with care,

   In hopes that St. Nicholas soon would be there."

MARGARET: Point to the stockings.

BENJAMIN: Everyone can see them, plain as day. [*He points anyway, overdoing it.*] "The children were nestled all snug in their beds,"

MARGARET: We'll just pretend the children are upstairs in their beds.

CHARITY: Where Father and Mother think we are.

MARGARET: Benjamin, go ahead.

BENJAMIN: "While visions of sugar plums danced in their heads;" Margaret, you be a sugar plum and dance about.

MARGARET: I don't know what sugar plums look like.But I'll try. [*With her arms outstretched, she spins about the room.*]

HARRIET: [*glancing up from writing*]. That's exactly how they should look.

BENJAMIN: "And Mama in her kerchief, and I in my cap" We don't have a kerchief. [*He takes a doily from the table.*] Margaret, put this on and play the mother.

MARGARET: [*still spinning*]. I'm the sugar plum right now, thank you. [*She continues dancing.*]

BENJAMIN: "Had just settled our brains for a long winter's nap." [*To* MARGARET.] How are we supposed to act out settling our brains?

MARGARET: Yawn. Or scratch your head.

BENJAMIN: [*yawning and scratching his head*]. "When out on the lawn arose such a clatter,"

MARGARET: Just imagine we hear the clatter. We don't want to wake up Mother and Father.

BENJAMIN: [*establishing an imaginary window at the front of the stage*].
"I sprang from my bed to see what was the matter.

Away to the window I flew like a flash,

Tore open the shutters, and threw up the sash."

MARGARET: Now lean out the window.

BENJAMIN: [*leaning out the imaginary window and describing the night*]. This is the hard part, all about the snow. I have to see it in my imagination. [*He closes his eyes and speaks.*]
"The moon on the breast of the new-fallen snow

Gave the--something--of midday to objects below;"

There's a word missing. Does anybody remember?

MARGARET: "Lustre," I think "Gave a lustre of midday to objects below."

BENJAMIN: That's it. The next part I know I know. [*He opens his eyes.*]
"When, what to my wondering eyes should appear,

But a miniature sleigh and eight tiny reindeer.

With a little old driver, so lively and quick,

I knew in a moment it must be St. Nick!"

MARGARET: Get ready, Charity.

BENJAMIN: Not yet. This comes first:

"More rapid than eagles his coursers they came,

And he whistled and shouted, and called them by name:"

MARGARET: Now, Charity!

CHARITY: "Now, Dasher! Now, Dancer! Now, Prancer! and Vixen!

On, Comet! On, Cupid! On, Donder and Blitzen!

To the top of the porch, to the top of the wall,

Now dash away, dash away, dash away all!"

MARGARET: Good, Charity, good! [CHARITY *beams with pride*.]

BENJAMIN: This is the tricky part about leaves and wind. Let's see.

"As dry leaves that before the wild hurricane fly,

When they meet with an obstacle, mount to the sky,"

Does that sound right?

HARRIET: It looks right on paper. Keep going before you forget.

BENJAMIN: "So up to the housetop the coursers they flew,

With a sleigh full of toys--and St. Nicholas too.

And then, in a twinkling, I heard on the roof

The prancing and pawing of each little hoof.

As I drew in my head and was turning around,

Down the chimney St Nicholas came with a bound."

MARGARET: Charity, climb up on the chair. [She does so.] Now when Benjamin repeats the line, jump off.

BENJAMIN: "Down the chimney St. Nicholas came with a bound." [CHARITY *jumps*.]

He was dressed all in fur from his head to his foot,

And his clothes were all tarnished with ashes and soot;"

CHARITY: [*brushing off her sleeves and robe*]. I'm filthy!

MARGARET: No time to clean up now, St. Nicholas; get on with your work.

BENJAMIN: "A bundle of toys he had flung on his back,

And he looked like a peddler just opening his pack."

MARGARET: Open your pack and take out the gifts.

[CHARITY *does so.*]

BENJAMIN: "His eyes how they twinkled! His dimples, how merry!

His cheeks were like roses, his nose like a cherry;

[CHARITY *points to each of these features on her face.*]

His droll little mouth was drawn up like a bow.

And the beard on his chin was as white as the snow."

CHARITY: I don't have a beard.

MARGARET: Just pretend. Pull at your whiskers.

CHARITY: Is it long or short?

BENJAMIN: As long as you want.

CHARITY: Then it comes to here. [*She indicates her waist.*]

HARRIET: That's a good length, Charity.

MARGARET: I see it. I see it. [CHARITY *jumps with joy.*]

BENJAMIN: [*laughing at* CHARITY]. Shall we continue?

MARGARET: Go ahead.

BENJAMIN: "The stump of a pipe he held tight in his teeth,

And the smoke, it encircled his head like a wreath."

CHARITY: You know Father won't allow pipes in this house.

BENJAMIN: Take this pen and make believe it's a pipe.

MARGARET: And we'll imagine we see smoke all around your head. Continue, Benjamin, please.

BENJAMIN: "He had a broad face, and a little round belly

That shook, when he laughed, like a bowl full of jelly."

CHARITY: This is the best part. [*She pushes the pillow up and down*] But doesn't look like a bowl full of jelly.

MARGARET: Does to me. Go on, Benjamin.

BENJAMIN: I can't concentrate when Charity keeps interrupting.

HARRIET: But we're getting it down exactly as your father wrote it. Keep going.

BENJAMIN: Charity, listen to the words and don't worry about anything else.

CHARITY: It's not easy to play a little old man at my age.

MARGARET: When you use your imagination, it is. Let's try again.

BENJAMIN: "He was chubby and plump--a right jolly old elf,

And I laughed when I saw him, in spite of myself;"

[*At this point,* CHARITY'S *stomach falls onto the floor. Picking up the pillow, she desperately starts stuffing her robe again.* BENJAMIN, *seeing this, bursts into uncontrolled laughter.*]

HARRIET: Benjamin, you've lost your concentration.

MARGARET: [*to* BENJAMIN]. If you don't stop, we'll all be laughing.

CHARITY: [*breaking character*]. What's the matter?

MARGARET: Benjamin is having fits of the giggles.

CHARITY: I can't think why. Father didn't mean the poem to be funny, did he?

HARRIET: Not as funny as Benjamin finds it. [BENJAMIN *laughs even more.*]

MARGARET: Listen to him!

CHARITY: Look at him!

[BENJAMIN *is rolling on the floor, legs kicking in the air.*]

HARRIET: What are we going to do? He can't continue. Margaret, it's up to you.

MARGARET: Me!

HARRIET: Jump in. Take over. Say the rest.

MARGARET: I can't think with him like this.

HARRIET: Don't try. Just do it. Be spontaneous!

CHARITY:Y. What does "spontaneous" mean?

HARRIET: Margaret, show her. Show her!

MARGARET: [*jumping in*]. "A wink of his eye, and a twist of his head, Soon gave me to know I had nothing to dread."

HARRIET: Now, Charity, get back into character.

[CHARITY *does so, at once.*]

MARGARET: "He spoke not a word, but went straight to his work,

And filled all the stockings; then turned with a jerk,

And laying his finger aside of his nose,

And giving a nod, up the chimney he rose.

He sprang up to his sleigh, to his team gave a whistle,

And away they all flew like the down of a thistle.

But I heard him exclaim, ere he drove out of sight,"

CHARITY: "'Happy Christmas to all, and to all a good night!'"

MARGARET: Harriet, do you have all of it?

HARRIET: In a second; I can't write as fast as you speak.

MARGARET: Should we repeat anything?

HARRIET: No. I've got it! You were wonderful. Thank you. You've rescued "A Visit from St. Nicholas" from the fire--every word of it. You see the poem does belong to you. [*She shows them the pages.*]

MARGARET: How beautiful!

BENJAMIN: [*rising from the floor where he has finally stopped laughing*]. Nobody can take it away from us ever again.

CHARITY: Our poem!

HARRIET: Still, let's be careful not to anger your father about it.

MARGARET: I know what we should do. Give me the poem. I want to write something on it. [*She writes.*]

HARRIET: And now we really must be off to bed. I promised your mother I would tuck you in. Remember?

CHARITY: But it's almost Christmas morning.

HARRIET: Ah the more reason your father mustn't find us down here. At least let's start the day from our beds.

MARGARET: [*finishing writing*]. There. [*Placing poem on the table.*] Let's leave this here for Father to discover.

BENJAMIN: He'll tear it up all over again.

CHARITY: And burn it.

MARGARET: I don't think so. Not after this.

CHARITY: [*eagerly*]. And if he does, we'll act it out all over again. But next time I'm going to use a bigger pillow.

MARGARET: Something tells me that won't be necessary. Just be certain when Father sees this, that neither of you gives us away.

BENJAMIN: What do you mean?

MARGARET: You'll see.

CHARITY: I hate it when people say, "You'll see"! I hate it!

HARRIET: Now if everyone is ready, I'll lead the way.

[*Taking a candle, she escorts them out and back to their bedroom, opening and closing doors along the way. They return to their beds and are soon asleep.* HARRIET *then exits.*]

VOICE: "'Twas the night before Christmas, when all through the house

Creatures were settling back to their beds

With the evening's events still filling their heads."

[FATHER *is still writing, or at least still attempting to write. By now the floor around his bed is filled with sheets of paper turned into crumpled-up balls of rejected lines and words.* MOTHER *and* FATHER *are sitting up in their beds.*]

FATHER: What rhymes with Cupid?

MOTHER: "Grupid." "Lupid." "Mupid."

FATHER: No, no, no.

MOTHER: I have it "Stupid."

FATHER: I'd never call a reindeer Stupid.

MOTHER: Well, I would never name one Cupid, but you did.

FATHER: What rhymes with Comet?

MOTHER: "Domit." "Comet." "Lomet." "Romet." I've got it "Vomit."

FATHER: How disgusting! A great help you are.

MOTHER: You're the poet. Remember?

FATHER: I wish I could.

MOTHER: I really want to help but I don't know how. Can't you bring back part of it?

FATHER: [*pointing to the floor*]. Does it look like it? My memory's blocked. Completely.

MOTHER: You're trying too hard perhaps. Just relax.

FATHER: I'm in bed. How much more relaxed can I be? Perhaps my mind is punishing me for what I did last night. Perhaps I don't deserve to remember. [*Bells ring in the distance.*]

MOTHER: Listen. The chimes!

FATHER: Oh, no! Not morning already.

MOTHER: We must go downstairs immediately.

FATHER: But I don't have the poem for the children.

MOTHER: [*kindly*]. Father, I fear it's too late now. You tried and it's simply gone. So let's give the children a happy Christmas in other ways.

FATHER: I can't forget and I know they won't.

MOTHER: In time, of course, they will. Their love for you hasn't changed.

FATHER: But their respect has. I wish I'd never written the wretched poem. How could they take it so seriously?

MOTHER: Nonsense! If they love the poem so much, it can't be wretched, can it? Don't blame the poem for something you did.

FATHER: [*having to accept this verdict, he sighs*]. As always, you're right.

MOTHER: On the other hand, don't blame yourself for something that can't be helped now. I think a short, polite apology to the children and to Cousin Harriet will suffice. And then we can proceed with Christmas as if nothing happened.

FATHER: I hope so. [*He starts to pick up balls of paper.*]

MOTHER: Don't bother with that. I'll take care of it later. Let's go to the children.

[*They open the door and head towards the living room. As they do,* HARRIET *comes into the Children's room.*]

HARRIET: Margaret. Benjamin. Charity. Hear the chimes? Let's be up.

CHARITY: I don't want to.

BENJAMIN: Neither do I.

HARRIET: You're always the first ones up on Christmas morning.

MARGARET: [*sitting up and stretching*]. Not this year. We're tired.

CHARITY: And sleepy. [*She yawns.*]

BENJAMIN: And not the least bit merry. [*Facing reality.*] But I suppose we have to. [*He gets up, puts on his robe and slippers. The others slowly follow his example.*]

HARRIET: Now let's all be very pleasant about everything.

MARGARET: [*being overly polite to* CHARITY]. I hope you have a happy, happy, happy, happy, happy holiday."

CHARITY: [*also role playing*]."'Oh, you're too very, very, very, very, very kind."

BENJAMIN: You don't have to be that pleasant. I can't stand it.

HARRIET: Just be yourselves and all will be well. Everyone ready? [*They nod that they are.*] Good. Let's go.

[*She opens the door and the CHILDREN file through and onto the stairs and then to the living room.*]

VOICE: " 'Twas not the night before but Christmas morning now,

When everyone came to the living room

With faces covered in gloom."

[MOTHER *and* FATHER *are by the table, the* CHILDREN *and* HARRIET *gather about the fireplace. There is a long awkward pause during which* EVERYONE *just stands silently, staring straight ahead. Finally,* MOTHER *steps forward and breaks the silence.*]

MOTHER: Good morning, everyone. [*The* REST *mumble faint "Good mornings" in return.*] Your father has something he would like to say.

FATHER: Yes, and, as no doubt you can imagine, this is not easy for me, but put most simply: I regret any unhappiness I caused last night. And I know I did cause all of you, as well as your mother and myself, considerable unhappiness when I refused to let you copy the poem and later when I burned it. It was your poem and I had no right to take it back, much less destroy it. I hope you will find some way to forgive me. I have tried desperately to write the poem again but it simply has left me...it would seem forever. I am sorry.

MARGARET: Father, pardon the interruption, but what is that stuck in the book beside you there?

FATHER: [*picking up the book*]. Why, it looks like the poem but it can't be. We all saw it go up in flames.

MARGARET: What does it say?

FATHER: [*taking the pages out of the book, he reads the note written on the outside*]. "Thank you for writing this. It makes me very happy. Your friend, St. Nicholas." [*He examines the pages.*] Look, it's here, word for word, exactly as I wrote it.

MOTHER: Wonderful! The Christmas present we all wanted most.

MARGARET: [*with a nod and a wink at* BENJAMIN *and* CHARITY]. And brought by St. Nicholas himself!

FATHER: I'm dumbfounded! How could this happen?

CHARITY: It's quite simple. Last night when you read the poem to us, St. Nicholas was in the chimney. He heard you, and wrote it down.

BENJAMIN: And then after it was burned he brought his copy here to share with us.

FATHER: [*still perplexed*]. That makes some kind of sense, I suppose.

MOTHER: Don't try to figure it out. The important news is that we have the poem again and can proceed with Christmas. No more long faces! No more outbursts except of joy! I couldn't be happier.

MARGARET: Father, do you see how much the poem means to us?

FATHER: I didn't before but I do now.

HARRIET: And it would mean as much to other children, too, if only you'd allow me to publish it.

FATHER: Is it so important to you, Cousin Harriet?

CHARITY: Yes, we want to share it with everyone.

HARRIET: They really do! And I can make that happen... in the Troy Sentinel. You don't have to do anything. Except give me your permission.

FATHER: Very well! [*The* CHILDREN *cheer.*] As long as...

MOTHER: [*not believing there can be conditions*]. As long as what, Father?

FATHER: My name doesn't appear on it.

MOTHER: Surely, with the delight on their faces and on your own when you realized you had the poem back, you must be proud of it?

FATHER: What I took to be some simple rhymes are clearly more than that to you. Yes, you've convinced me as well.

MOTHER: [*relieved*]. Well, I'm certain everyone's glad to hear that. The poet has confessed his poem.

FATHER: Even so, if Cousin Harriet publishes it, let her say it's by Anonymous.

CHARITY: Who's that?

HARRIET: Someone unknown, dear.

CHARITY: But we know. You know. Mother knows.

MOTHER: And someday, no matter how guarded and stubborn your father is, the world will know. But for now, let him save his reputation as a scholar, as a professor, as a pedant-I'm sorry, dear, but often you are.

CHARITY: What's a "pedant"?

FATHER: Someone who takes his work seriously and maintains high standards.

MOTHER: Someone who takes his work too seriously and maintains impossible standards.

CHARITY: I see. Thank you.

MOTHER: Father, we'll let time do the rest. And when the pages of all your important books, the dictionaries, the historical studies, the philosophical essays, are yellowing and crumbling, you'll be happy to know that children everywhere are reading your poem and seeing St. Nicholas visiting this very living room.

FATHER: That would be splendid, indeed, but until I am yellow and crumbling myself, or at least until I retire from teaching, the poem must be anonymous.

MARGARET: We won't tell, will we?

CHARITY: No, just our friends.

BENJAMIN: And classmates. And everyone at church.

CHARITY: We're good at keeping secrets.

FATHER: [amused]. I can see that.

HARRIET: Your name will not appear, I promise.

FATHER: Very well then. [The CHILDREN cheer.]

HARRIET: Oh, thank you very much, Mr. Moore.

BENJAMIN: Father, you're a good sport.

FATHER: I appreciate that, Benjamin. And I'll try to live up to it in the future.

CHARITY: If you don't, we'll just call you a "pedant."

FATHER: Mother, this is your doing...

MOTHER: [quickly changing the subject]. Father, since I'm the only one here who has never heard your poem, would you read it to me, please? So I can understand what all this fuss is about.

FATHER: With great pleasure, my dear. Everyone, gather close. [They arrange themselves to hear the poem. He takes the pages and in his best voice reads the title.] "A Visit From St. Nicholas."

EVERYONE: [*except* FATHER *together in a loud stage whisper and directly to the* AUDIENCE]. By Clement Clarke Moore.

CHARITY: [*also to the* AUDIENCE]. But don't tell anyone!

FATHER: "'Twas the Night before Christmas, when all through the house

Not a creature was stirring, not even a mouse...

[*By this time the curtain is down*]

[*Suddenly during the Curtain Call with the cast lined up to take their bows, a loud noise is heard.* EVERYONE *turns towards the fireplace and there, sure enough, appears first the feet, then the legs and the rest of* ST. NICHOLAS, *dressed as described in the poem. He scurries out of the fireplace, shakes hands with* FATHER *and joins the* OTHERS *for a bow. As the Cast take their last call, they speak in unison directly to the* AUDIENCE *"Happy Christmas to all, and to all a good night!"*]

FINAL CURTAIN

THE LONG CHRISTMAS DINNER

by Thornton Wilder

THE LONG CHRISTMAS DINNER

CHARACTERS

LUCIA	Roderick's wife
RODERICK	Mother Bayard's son
MOTHER BAYARD	
COUSIN BRANDON	
CHARLES	Lucia and Roderick's son
GENEVIEVE	Lucia and Roderick's daughter
LEONORA BANNING	Charles's wife
LUCIA	Leonora and Charles's daughter, Samuel's twin
SAMUEL	Leonora and Charles's son, Lucia's twin
RODERICK	Leonora and Charles's youngest son
COUSIN ERMENGARDE	
SERVANTS	
NURSES	

SETTING

The dining room of the Bayard home.

Close to the footlights a long dining table is handsomely spread for Christmas dinner. The carver's place with a great turkey before it is at the spectator's right. A door, left back, leads into the hall. At the extreme left, by the proscenium pillar, is a strange portal trimmed with garlands of fruits and flowers. Directly opposite is another, edged and hung with black velvet. The portals denote birth and death.

Ninety years are to be traversed in this play which represents in accelerated motion ninety Christmas dinners in the Bayard household. The actors are dressed in inconspicuous clothes and must indicate their gradual increase in years through their acting. Most of them carry wigs of white hair which they adjust upon their heads at the indicated moment, simply and without comment. The ladies may have shawls concealed beneath the table that they gradually draw up about their shoulders as they grow older.

Throughout the play the characters continue eating imaginary food with imaginary knives and forks.

There is no curtain. The audience arriving at the theatre sees the stage set and the table laid, though still in partial darkness. Gradually the lights in the auditorium become dim and the stage brightens until sparkling winter sunlight streams though the dining-room windows.

Enter LUCIA. *She inspects the table, touching here a knife and there a fork. She talks to a servant girl who is invisible to us.*

LUCIA: I reckon we're ready now, Gertrude. We won't ring the chimes today. I'll just call them myself. [*She goes into the hall and calls*] Roderick. Mother Bayard. We're all ready. Come to dinner.

[*Enter* RODERICK *pushing* MOTHER BAYARD *in a wheelchair.*]

MOTHER BAYARD: . . . and a new horse too, Roderick. I used to think that only the wicked owned two horses. A new horse and a new house and a new wife.

LUCIA: Here, Mother Bayard, you sit between us.

RODERICK: Well, Mother, how do you like it? Our first Christmas dinner in the new house, hey?

MOTHER BAYARD: Tz-Tz-Tz! I don't know what your dear father would say!

[RODERICK *says grace.*]

My dear Lucia, I can remember when there were still Indians on this very ground, and I wasn't a young girl either. I can remember when we had to cross the Mississippi on a new-made raft. I can remember when Saint Louis and Kansas City were full of Indians.

LUCIA: [*Tying a napkin around* MOTHER BAYARD's *neck*] Imagine that! There! What a wonderful day for our first Christmas dinner: a beautiful sunny morning, snow, a splendid sermon. Dr. McCarthy preaches a splendid sermon. I cried and cried.

RODERICK: [*Extending an imaginary carving fork*] Come now, what'll you have, Mother? A little sliver of white?

LUCIA: Every last twig is wrapped around with ice. You almost never see that. Can I cut it up for you dear? [*Over her shoulder*] Gertrude, I forgot the jelly. You know—on the top shelf. Mother Bayard, I found your mother's gravy boat while we were moving. What was her name, dear? What were all your names? You were . . . a . . . Genevieve Wainright. Now you mother—

MOTHER BAYARD: Yes, you must write it down somewhere. I was

Genevieve Wainright. My mother was Faith Morrison. She was the daughter of a farmer in New Hampshire who was something of a blacksmith too. And she married young John Wainright—

LUCIA: [*Memorizing on her fingers*] Genevieve Wainright. Faith Morrison.

RODERICK: It's all down in a book somewhere upstairs. We have it all. All that kind of thing is very interesting. Come, Lucia, just a little wine. Mother, a little red wine for Christmas day. Full of iron. "Take a little wine for thy stomach's sake."

LUCIA: Really, I can't get used to wine! What would my father say? But I suppose it's all right.

[*Enter* COUSIN BRANDON *from the hall. He takes his place by* LUCIA.]

COUSIN BRANDON: [*Rubbing his hands*] Well, well, I smell turkey. My dear cousins, I can't tell you how pleasant it is to be having Christmas dinner with you all. I've lived out there in Alaska so long without relatives. Let me see, how long have you had this new house, Roderick?

RODERICK: Why, it must be . . .

MOTHER BAYARD: Five years. It's five years, children. You should keep a diary. This is your sixth Christmas dinner here.

LUCIA: Think of that, Roderick. We feel as though we had lived here twenty years.

COUSIN BRANDON: At all events it still looks as good as new.

RODERICK: [*Over his carving*] What'll you have, Brandon, light or dark? —Frieda, fill up Cousin Brandon's glass.

LUCIA: Oh, dear, I can't get used to these wines. I don't know what my father'd say, I'm sure. What'll you have, Mother Bayard?

[*During the following speeches* MOTHER BAYARD'*s chair, without any visible propulsion, starts to draw away from the table, turns toward the right, and slowly goes toward the dark portal.*]

MOTHER BAYARD: Yes, I can remember when there were Indians on this very land.

LUCIA: [*Softly*] Mother Bayard hasn't been very well lately, Roderick.

MOTHER BAYARD: My mother was a Faith Morrison. And in New Hampshire she married a young John Wainright, who was a congregational minister. He saw her in his congregation one day . . .

LUCIA: Mother Bayard, hadn't you better lie down, dear?

MOTHER BAYARD: . . . and right in the middle of his sermon he said to himself "I'll marry that girl." And he did, and I'm their daughter.

LUCIA: [*Half rising, looking after her with anxiety*] Just a little nap, dear?

MOTHER BAYARD: I'm all right. Just go on with your dinner. I was ten, and I said to my brother . . .

[*She goes out. A very slight pause.*]

COUSIN BRANDON: It's too bad it's such a cold dark day today. We almost need the lamps. I spoke to Major Lewis for a moment after church. His sciatica troubles him, but he does pretty well.

LUCIA: [*Dabbing her eyes*] I know Mother Bayard wouldn't want us to grieve for her on Christmas Day, but I can't forget her sitting in her wheelchair right beside us, only a year ago. And she would be so glad to know our good news.

RODERICK: [*Patting her hand*] Now, now. It's Christmas. [*Formally*] Cousin Brandon, a glass of wine with you, sir.

COUSIN BRANDON: [*Half rising, lifting his glass gallantly*] A glass of wine with you, sir.

LUCIA: Does the Major's sciatica cause him much pain?

COUSIN BRANDON: Some, perhaps. But you know his way. He says it'll be all the same in a hundred years.

LUCIA: Yes, he's a great philosopher.

RODERICK: His wife sends you a thousand thanks for her Christmas present.

LUCIA: I forget what I gave her. —Oh, yes, the workbasket!

[*Through the entrance of Birth comes a* NURSE *wheeling a perambulator rimmed with blue ribbons.* LUCIA *rushes toward it, the men following.*]

O my wonderful new baby, my darling baby! Who ever saw such a child! Quick, nurse, a boy or a girl? A boy! Roderick, what shall we call him? Really, nurse, you've never seen such a child!

RODERICK: We'll call him Charles after your father and grandfather.

LUCIA: But there are no Charleses in the Bible, Roderick.

RODERICK: Of course, there are. Surely there are.

LUCIA: Roderick! —Very well, but he will always be Samuel to me. —What miraculous hands he has! Really, they are the most beautiful hands in the world. All right, nurse. Have a good nap, my darling child.

RODERICK: Don't drop him, nurse. Brandon and I need him in our firm.

[*Exit* NURSE *and perambulator into the hall. The others return to their chairs,* LUCIA *taking the place left vacant by* MOTHER BAYARD *and* COUSIN BRANDON *moving up beside her.* COUSIN BRANDON *puts on his white hair.*]

Lucia, a little white meat? Some stuffing? Cranberry sauce, anybody?

LUCIA: [*Over her shoulder*] Margaret, the stuffing is very good today. —Just a little, thank you.

RODERICK: Now something to wash it down. [*Half rising*] Cousin Brandon, a glass of wine with you, sir. To the ladies, God bless them.

LUCIA: Thank you, kind sirs.

COUSIN BRANDON: Pity it's such an overcast day today. And no snow.

LUCIA: But the sermon was lovely. I cried and cried. Dr. Spaulding does preach such a splendid sermon.

RODERICK: I saw Major Lewis for a moment after church. He says his rheumatism comes and goes. His wife says she has something for Charles and will bring it over this afternoon.

[*Enter* NURSE *again with perambulator. Pink ribbons. Same rush toward the left.*]

LUCIA: O my lovely new baby! Really, it never occurred to me that it might be a girl. Why, nurse, she's perfect.

RODERICK: Now call her what you choose. It's your turn.

LUCIA: Looloolooloo. Aië. Aië. Yes, this time I shall have my way. She shall be called Genevieve after your mother. Have a good nap, my treasure.

[*She looks after it as the* NURSE *wheels the perambulator into the hall.*]

Imagine! Sometime she'll be grown up and say "Good morning, Mother. Good morning, Father." —Really, Cousin Brandon, you don't find a baby like that every day.

COUSIN BRANDON: *And* the new factory.

LUCIA: A new factory? Really? Roderick, I shall be very uncomfortable if we're going to turn out to be rich. I've been afraid of that for years. —However, we mustn't talk about such things on Christmas Day. I'll just take a little piece of white meat, thank you. Roderick, Charles is destined for the ministry. I'm sure of it.

RODERICK: Woman, he's only twelve. Let him have a free mind. *We* want him in the firm, I don't mind saying. Anyway, no time passes as slowly as this when you're waiting for your urchins to grow up and settle down to business.

LUCIA: I don't want time to go any faster, thank you. I love the children just as they are. —Really, Roderick, you know what the doctor said one glass a meal. [*Putting her hand over his glass*] No, Margaret, that will be all.

[RODERICK *rises, glass in hand. With a look of dismay on his face he takes a few steps toward the dark portal.*]

RODERICK: Now I wonder what's the matter with me.

LUCIA: Roderick, do be reasonable.

RODERICK: [*Tottering, but with gallant iron*] But, my dear, statistics show that we steady, moderate drinkers . . .

LUCIA: [*Rises, gazing at him in anguish*] Roderick! My dear! What . . . ?

RODERICK: [*Returns to his seat with a frightened look of relief*] Well, it's fine to be back at table with you again. How many good Christmas dinners have I had to miss upstairs? And to be back at a fine bright one, too.

LUCIA: O my dear, you gave us a very alarming time! Here's your glass of milk. —Josephine, bring Mr. Bayard his medicine from the cupboard in the library.

RODERICK: At all events, now that I'm better I'm going to start doing something about the house.

LUCIA: Roderick! You're not going to change the house?

RODERICK: Only touch it up here and there. It looks a hundred years old.

[CHARLES *enters casually from the hall.*]

CHARLES: It's a great blowy morning, Mother. The wind comes over the hill like a lot of cannon. [*He kisses his mother's hair and sits down*]

LUCIA: Charles, you carve the turkey, dear. Your father's not well. You always said you hated carving, though you are *so* clever at it.

[*Father and son exchange places.*]

And such a good sermon. I cried and cried. Mother Bayard loved a good sermon so. And she used to sing the Christmas hymns all around the year. Oh, dear, oh, dear, I've been thinking of her all morning!

CHARLES: Shh, Mother. It's Christmas Day. You mustn't think of such things. You mustn't be depressed.

LUCIA: But sad things aren't the same as depressing things. I must be getting old. I like them.

CHARLES: Uncle Brandon, you haven't anything to eat. Pass his plate, Hilda . . . and some cranberry sauce . . .

[*Enter* GENEVIEVE. *She kisses her father's temple and sits down*]

GENEVIEVE: It's glorious. Every last twig is wrapped around with ice. You almost never see that.

LUCIA: Did you have time to deliver those presents after church, Genevieve?

GENEVIEVE: Yes, Mama. Old Mrs. Lewis sends you a thousand thanks for hers. It was just what she wanted, she said. Give me lots, Charles, lots.

RODERICK: [*Rising and starting toward the dark portal*] Statistics, ladies and gentlemen, show that we steady, moderate . . .

CHARLES: How about a little skating this afternoon, Father?

RODERICK: I'll live till I'm ninety.

LUCIA: I really don't think he ought to go skating.

RODERICK: [*At the very portal, suddenly astonished*] Yes, but . . . but . . . not yet!

[*He goes out*]

LUCIA: [*Dabbing her eyes*] He was so young and so clever, Cousin Brandon. [*Raising her voice for* COUSIN BRANDON's *deafness*] I say he was so young and so clever. —Never forget your father, children. He was a good man. Well, he wouldn't want us to grieve for him today.

CHARLES: White or dark, Genevieve? Just another sliver, Mother?

LUCIA: [*Putting on her white hair.*] I can remember our first Christmas dinner in this house, Genevieve. Twenty-five years ago today. Mother Bayard was sitting here in her wheelchair. She could remember when Indians lived on this very spot and when she had to cross the river on a new-made raft.

CHARLES: She couldn't have, Mother.

GENEVIEVE: That can't be true.

LUCIA: It certainly was true—even I can remember when there was only one paved street. We were very happy to walk on boards. [*Louder; to*

COUSIN BRANDON] We can remember when there were no sidewalks, can't we, Cousin Brandon?

COUSIN BRANDON: [*Delighted*] Oh, yes! And those were the days.

CHARLES AND GENEVIEVE: [*Sotto voce, this is a family refrain*] Those were the days.

LUCIA: And the ball last night, Genevieve? Did you have a nice time? I hope you didn't waltz, dear. I think a girl in our position ought to set an example. Did Charles keep an eye on you?

GENEVIEVE: He had none left. They were all on Leonora Banning. He can't conceal it any longer, Mother. I think he's engaged to marry Leonora Banning.

CHARLES: I'm not engaged to marry anyone.

LUCIA: Well, she's very pretty.

GENEVIEVE: I shall never marry, Mother. —I shall sit in this house beside you forever, as though life were one long, happy Christmas dinner.

LUCIA: O my child, you mustn't say such things!

GENEVIEVE: [*Playfully*] You don't want me? You don't want me?

   [LUCIA *bursts into tears.*] Why, Mother, how silly you are! There's nothing sad about that —what could possibly be sad about that?

LUCIA: [*Drying her eyes*] Forgive me. I'm just unpredictable, that's all.

[CHARLES *goes to the door and leads in* LEONORA BANNING.]

LEONORA: [*Kissing* LUCIA's *temple*] Good morning, Mother Bayard. Good morning, everybody. Mother Bayard, you sit here by Charles. It's really a splendid Christmas Day today.

CHARLES: Little white meat? Genevieve, Mother, Leonora?

LEONORA: Every last twig is encircled with ice. - You never see that.

CHARLES: [*Shouting*] Uncle Brandon, another? —Rogers, fill my uncle's glass.

LUCIA: [*To* CHARLES] Do what your father used to do. It would please Cousin Brandon so. You know [*Pretending to raise a glass*] "Uncle Brandon, a glass of wine . . . "

CHARLES: [*Rising*] Uncle Brandon, a glass of wine with you, sir.

BRANDON: A glass of wine with you, sir. To the ladies, God bless them every one.

THE LADIES: Thank you, kind sirs.

GENEVIEVE: And if I go to Germany for my music I promise to be back for Christmas. I wouldn't miss that.

LUCIA: I hate to think of you over there all alone in those strange pensions.

GENEVIEVE: But, darling, the time will pass so fast that you'll hardly know I'm gone. I'll be back in the twinkling of an eye.

[*Enter left, the* NURSE *and perambulator. Green ribbons.*]

LEONORA: Oh, what an angel! The darlingest baby in the world. Do let me hold it, nurse.

[*But the* NURSE *resolutely wheels the perambulator across the stage and out the dark door.*]

Oh, I did love it so!

[CHARLES *rises, puts his arm around his wife, and slowly leads, her back to the table.*]

GENEVIEVE: [*Softly to her mother as the other two cross*] Isn't there anything I can do?

LUCIA: [*Raises her eyebrows, ruefully*] No, dear. Only time, only the passing of time can help in these things.

[CHARLES *returns to the table.*]

Don't you think we could ask Cousin Ermengarde to come and live with us here? There's plenty for everyone and there's no reason why she should go on teaching the first grade for ever and ever. She wouldn't be in the way, would she, Charles?

CHARLES: No, I think it would be fine. —A little more potato and gravy, anybody? A little more turkey, Mother?

[BRANDON *rises and starts slowly toward the dark portal.* LUCIA *rises and stands for a moment with her face in her hands.*]

COUSIN BRANDON: [*Muttering*] It was great to be in Alaska in those days . . .

GENEVIEVE: [*Half rising, and gazing at her mother in fear*] Mother, what is . . . ?

LUCIA: [*Hurriedly*] Hush, my dear. It will pass. —Hold fast to your music, you know. [*As* GENEVIEVE *starts toward her*] No, no. I want to be alone for a few minutes.

[*She turns and starts after* COUSIN BRANDON *toward the right.*]

CHARLES: If the Republicans collected all their votes instead of going off into cliques among themselves, they might prevent his getting a second term.

GENEVIEVE: Charles, Mother doesn't tell us, but she hasn't been very well these days.

CHARLES: Come, Mother, we'll go to Florida for a few weeks.

[*Exit* BRANDON.]

LUCIA: [*Smiling at* GENEVIEVE *and waving her hand*] Don't be foolish. Don't grieve.

[LUCIA *clasps her hands under her chin. Her lips move, whispering. She walks serenely into the portal.* GENEVIEVE *stares after her, frozen.*]

GENEVIEVE: [*Sinks down at the table, her face buried in her arms*] But what will I do? What's left for me to do?

[*At the same moment the* NURSE *and perambulator enter from the left. Pale yellow ribbons.* LEONORA *rushes to it.*]

LEONORA: O my darlings . . . twins . . . Charles, aren't they glorious! Look at them. Look at them.

CHARLES: [*Bending over the basket.*] Which is which?

LEONORA: I feel as though I were the first mother who ever had twins. —Look at them now! But why wasn't Mother Bayard allowed to stay and see them!

GENEVIEVE: [*Rising suddenly distraught, loudly*] I don't want to go on. I can't bear it.

CHARLES: [*Goes to her quickly. They sit down. He whispers to her earnestly, taking both her hands*] But Genevieve, Genevieve! How frightfully Mother would feel to think that . . . Genevieve!

GENEVIEVE: [*Shaking her head wildly*] I never told her how wonderful she was. We all treated her as though she were just a friend in the house. I thought she'd be here forever.

LEONORA: [*Timidly*] Genevieve, darling, do come one minute and hold my babies' hands. We shall call the girl Lucia after her grandmother —will that please you? Do just see what adorable little hands they have.

[GENEVIEVE *collects herself and goes over to the perambulator. She smiles brokenly into the basket.*]

GENEVIEVE: They are wonderful, Leonora.

LEONORA: Give him your finger, darling. Just let him hold it.

CHARLES: And we'll call the boy Samuel. —Well, now everybody come and finish your dinners. Don't drop them, nurse; at least don't drop the boy. We need him in the firm.

LEONORA: [*Stands looking after them as the* NURSE *wheels them into the hall*] Someday they'll be big. Imagine! They'll come in and say "Hello, Mother!" [*She makes clucking noises of rapturous consternation.*]

CHARLES: Come, a little wine, Leonora, Genevieve? Full of iron. Eduardo, fill the ladies' glasses. It certainly is a keen, cold morning. I used to go skating with Father on mornings like this and Mother would come back from church saying—

GENEVIEVE: [*Dreamily*] I know saying, "Such a splendid sermon. I cried and cried."

LEONORA: Why did she cry, dear?

GENEVIEVE: That generation all cried at sermons. It was their way.

LEONORA: Really, Genevieve?

GENEVIEVE: They had had to go since they were children and I suppose sermons reminded them of their fathers and mothers, just as Christmas dinners do us. Especially in an old house like this.

LEONORA: It really is pretty old, Charles. And so ugly, with all that iron-work filigree and that dreadful cupola.

GENEVIEVE: Charles! You aren't going to change the house!

CHARLES: No, no. I won't give up the house, but great heavens! It's fifty years old. This spring we'll remove the cupola and build a new wing toward the tennis courts.

[*From now on* GENEVIEVE *is seen to change. She sits up more straightly. The corners of her mouth become fixed. She becomes a forthright and slightly disillusioned spinster.* CHARLES *becomes the plain businessman and a little pompous.*]

LEONORA: And then couldn't we ask your dear old Cousin Ermengarde to come and live with us? She's really the self-effacing kind.

CHARLES: Ask her now. Take her out of the first grade.

GENEVIEVE: We only seem to think of it on Christmas Day with her Christmas card staring us in the face.

[*Enter left,* NURSE *and perambulator. Blue ribbons.*]

LEONORA: Another boy! Another boy! Here's a Roderick for you at last.

CHARLES: Roderick Brandon Bayard. A regular little fighter.

LEONORA: Goodbye, darling. Don't grow up too fast. Yes, yes. Aië, aië, aië —stay just as you are. Thank you, nurse.

GENEVIEVE: [*Who has not left the table, repeats dryly*] Stay just as you are.

[*Exit* NURSE *and perambulator. The others return to their places.*]

LEONORA: Now I have three children. One, two, three. Two boys and a girl. I'm collecting them. It's very exciting. [*Over her shoulder.*] What, Hilda? Oh, Cousin Ermengarde's come! Come in, Cousin.

[LEONORA *goes to the hall and welcomes* COUSIN ERMENGARDE, *who already wears her white hair.*]

ERMENGARDE: [*Shyly*] It's such a pleasure to be with you all.

CHARLES: [*Pulling out her chair for her.*] The twins have taken a great fancy to you already, Cousin.

LEONORA: The baby went to her at once.

CHARLES: Exactly how are we related, Cousin Ermengarde? — There, Genevieve, that's your specialty. First a little more turkey and stuffing, Mother? Cranberry sauce, anybody?

GENEVIEVE: I can work it out. Grandmother Bayard was your . . .

ERMENGARDE: Your Grandmother Bayard was a second cousin of my Grandmother Haskins through the Wainrights.

CHARLES: Well, it's all in a book somewhere upstairs. All that kind of thing is awfully interesting.

GENEVIEVE: Nonsense. There are no such books. I collect my notes off gravestones, and you have to scrape a good deal of moss—let me tell you—to find one great-grandparent.

CHARLES: There's a story that my Grandmother Bayard crossed the Mississippi on a raft before there were any bridges or ferryboats. She died before Genevieve and I were born. Time certainly goes very fast in a great new country like this. Have some more cranberry sauce, Cousin Ermengarde.

ERMENGARDE: [*Timidly*] Well, time must be passing very slowly in Europe with this dreadful, dreadful war going on.

CHARLES: Perhaps an occasional war isn't so bad after all. It clears up a lot of poisons that collect in nations. It's like a boil.

ERMENGARDE: Oh, dear, oh, dear!

CHARLES: [*With relish*] Yes, it's like a boil. —Ho! ho! Here are your twins.

[*The twins appear at the door into the hall.* SAM *is wearing the uniform of an ensign.* LUCIA *is fussing over some detail on it.*]

LUCIA: Isn't he wonderful in it, Mother?

CHARLES: Let's get a look at you.

SAM: Mother, don't let Roderick fool with my stamp album while I'm gone.

LEONORA: Now, Sam, do write a letter once in a while. Do be a good boy about that, mind.

SAM: You might send some of those cakes of yours once in a while, Cousin Ermengarde.

ERMENGARDE: [*In a flutter*] I certainly will, my dear boy.

CHARLES: If you need any money, we have agents in Paris and London, remember.

LEONORA: Do be a good boy, Sam.

SAM: Well, good-bye . . .

[SAM *goes briskly out through the dark portal, tossing his unneeded white hair through the door before him.* LUCIA *sits down at the table with lowered eyes.*]

ERMENGARDE: [*After a slight pause, in a low, constrained voice, making conversation*] I spoke to Mrs. Fairchild for a moment coming out of church. Her rheumatism's a little better, she says. She sends you her warmest thanks for the Christmas present. The workbasket, wasn't it? —It was an admirable sermon. And our stained-glass window looked so beautiful, Leonora, so beautiful. Everybody spoke of it and so affectionately of Sammy. [LEONORA'*s hand goes to her mouth*] Forgive me, Leonora, but it's better to speak of him than not to speak of him when we're all thinking of him so hard.

LEONORA: [*Rising, in anguish*] He was a mere boy. He was a mere boy, Charles.

CHARLES: My dear, my dear.

LEONORA: I want to tell him how wonderful he was. We let him go so casually. I want to tell him how we all feel about him. —Forgive me, let me walk about a minute. —Yes, of course, Ermengarde—it's best to speak of him.

LUCIA: [*In a low voice to* GENEVIEVE] Isn't there anything I can do?

GENEVIEVE: No, no. Only time, only the passing of time can help in these things.

[LEONORA, *straying about the room, finds herself near the door to the hall at the moment that her son* RODERICK *enters. He links his arm with hers and leads her back to the table*]

RODERICK: What's the matter, anyway? What are you so glum about? The skating was fine today.

CHARLES: Sit down, young man. I have something to say to you.

RODERICK: Everybody was there. Lucia skated in the corners with Dan Creighton the whole time. When'll it be, Lucia, when'll it be?

LUCIA: I don't know what you mean.

RODERICK: Lucia's leaving us soon, Mother. Dan Creighton, of all people.

CHARLES: [*Ominously*] Roderick, I have something to say to you.

RODERICK: Yes, Father.

CHARLES: Is it true, Roderick, that you made yourself conspicuous last night at the country club —at a Christmas Eve dance, too?

LEONORA: Not now, Charles, I beg of you. This is Christmas dinner.

RODERICK: [*Loudly*] No, I didn't.

LUCIA: Really, Father, he didn't. It was that dreadful Johnny Lewis.

CHARLES: I don't want to hear about Johnny Lewis. I want to know whether a son of mine . . .

LEONORA: Charles, I beg of you . . .

CHARLES: The first family of this city!

RODERICK: [*Rising*] I hate this town and everything about it. I always did.

CHARLES: You behaved like a spoiled puppy, sir, an ill-bred spoiled puppy.

RODERICK: What did I do? What did I do that was wrong?

CHARLES: You were drunk and you were rude to the daughters of my best friends.

GENEVIEVE: [*Striking the table*] Nothing in the world deserves an ugly scene like this. Charles, I'm ashamed of you.

RODERICK: Great God, you gotta get drunk in this town to forget how dull it is. Time passes so slowly here that it stands still, that's what's the trouble.

CHARLES: Well, young man, we can employ your time. You will leave the university and you will come into the Bayard factory on January second.

RODERICK: [*At the door into the hall*] I have better things to do than to go into your old factory. I'm going somewhere where time passes, my God!

[*He goes out into the hall.*]

LEONORA: [*Rising*] Roderick, Roderick, come here just a moment. —Charles where can he go?

LUCIA: [*Rising*] Shh, Mother. He'll come back. Now I have to go upstairs and pack my trunk.

LEONORA: I won't have any children left!

LUCIA: Shh, Mother. He'll come back. He's only gone to California or somewhere. Cousin Ermengarde has done most of my packing —thanks a thousand times, Cousin Ermengarde. [*She kisses her mother*] I won't be long. [*She runs out into the hall*]

[GENEVIEVE *and* LEONORA *put on their white hair.*]

ERMENGARDE: It's a very beautiful day. On the way home from church I stopped and saw Mrs. Foster a moment. Her arthritis comes and goes.

LEONORA: Is she actually in pain, dear?

ERMENGARDE: Oh, she says it'll all be the same in a hundred years!

LEONORA: Yes, she's a brave little stoic.

CHARLES: Come now, a little white meat, Mother?—Mary, pass my cousin's plate.

LEONORA: What is it, Mary? —Oh, here's a telegram from them in Paris! "Love and Christmas greetings to all." I told them we'd be eating some of their wedding cake and thinking about them today. It seems to be all decided that they will settle down in the east, Ermengarde. I can't even have my daughter for a neighbor. They hope to build before long somewhere on the shore north of New York.

GENEVIEVE: There is no shore north of New York.

LEONORA: Well, east or west or whatever it is.

[*Pause.*]

CHARLES: My, what a dark day.

[*He puts on his white hair. Pause.*]

How slowly time passes without any young people in the house.

LEONORA: I have three children somewhere.

CHARLES: [*Blunderingly offering comfort*] Well, one of them gave his life for his country.

LEONORA: [*Sadly*] And one of them is selling aluminum in China.

GENEVIEVE: [*Slowly working herself up to a hysterical crisis*] I can stand everything but this terrible soot everywhere. We should have moved long ago. We're surrounded by factories. We have to change the window curtains every week.

LEONORA: Why, Genevieve!

GENEVIEVE: I can't stand it. I can't stand it any more. I'm going abroad. It's not only the soot that comes through the very walls of this house; it's the *thoughts*, it's the thought of what has been and what might have been here. And the feeling about this house of the years *grinding away*. My mother died yesterday—not twenty-five years ago. Oh, I'm going to live and die abroad! Yes, I'm going to be the American old maid living and dying in a pension in Munich or Florence.

ERMENGARDE: Genevieve, you're tired.

CHARLES: Come, Genevieve, take a good drink of cold water. Mary, open the window a minute.

GENEVIEVE: I'm sorry. I'm sorry.

[GENEVIEVE *hurries tearfully out into the hall.*]

ERMENGARDE: Dear Genevieve will come back to us, I think.

[*She rises and starts toward the dark portal.*]

You should have been out today, Leonora. It was one of those days when everything was encircled with ice. Very pretty, indeed.

[CHARLES *rises and starts after her.*]

CHARLES: Leonora, I used to go skating with Father on mornings like this. I wish I felt a little better.

LEONORA: What! Have I got two invalids on my hands at once? Now, Cousin Ermengarde, you must get better and help me nurse Charles.

ERMENGARDE: I'll do my best.

[*She turns at the very portal and comes back to the table.*]

CHARLES: Well, Leonora, I'll do what you ask. I'll write the puppy a letter of forgiveness and apology. It's Christmas Day. I'll cable it. That's what I'll do.

[*He goes out the dark door.*]

LEONORA: [*Drying her eyes*] Ermengarde, it's such a comfort having you here with me. Mary, I really can't eat anything. Well, perhaps, a sliver of white meat.

ERMENGARDE: [*Very old*] I spoke to Mrs. Keene for a moment coming out of church. She asked after the young people. —At church I felt very proud sitting under our windows, Leonora, and our brass tablets. The Bayard aisle—it's a regular Bayard aisle and I love it . . .

LEONORA: Ermengarde, would you be very angry with me if I went and stayed with the young people a little this spring?

ERMENGARDE: Why, no. I know how badly they want you and need you. Especially now that they're about to build a new house.

LEONORA: You wouldn't be angry? This house is yours as long as you want it, remember.

ERMENGARDE: I don't see why the rest of you dislike it. I like it more than I can say . . .

LEONORA: I won't be long. I'll be back in no time and we can have some more of our readings aloud in the evening. [*She kisses her and goes into the hall*]

[ERMENGARDE *left alone, eats slowly and talks to Mary.*]

ERMENGARDE: Really, Mary, I'll change my mind. If you'll ask Bertha to be good enough to make me a little eggnog. A dear little eggnog. —Such a nice letter this morning from Mrs. Bayard, Mary. Such a nice letter. They're having their first Christmas dinner in the new house. They must be very happy. They call her Mother Bayard, she says, as though she were an old lady. And she says she finds it more comfortable to come and go in a wheelchair. —Such a dear letter . . . And Mary, I can tell you a secret. It's still a great secret, mind! They're expecting a grandchild. Isn't that good news! Now I'll read a little.

[*She props a book up before her, still dipping a spoon into a custard from time to time. She grows from very old to immensely old. She sighs. The book falls down. She finds a cane beside her, and soon totters into the dark portal, murmuring:*]

"Dear little Roderick and little Lucia."

END OF PLAY

KRINGLE'S WINDOW

by Mark Medoff

Inquiries concerning rights should be addressed to:

William Morris Agency, Inc.
1325 Avenue of the Americas
New York, NY 10018
Attn: Gilbert Parker

"Originally commissioned by Stage One: The Louisville Theatre"

CAST

MRS. ROSEN   RON

BOOMER   ALVIN LEE

BECKA   MANTHING

IRENE   SARAH

DEAN   ZELDA

DEPARTMENT STORE SANTA   KRINGLE

                                                   ELVES

ACT ONE

SCENE 1

A Currier and Ives Christmas scene. An old New Englander; a wonderful old tree almost reaches the widow's walk. It's cold and there's evidence of the last snowfall.

    The house is a study in organized clutter. People live here. Everything though not opulent, has character, speaks of having been selected with affection. One area of the living room has been given over to BECKA's *computer set-up, another has an electric keyboard. Fireplace and chimney. A rather small Christmas tree partly trimmed.*

    There's a small breakfast counter just this side of the door into the [off-stage.] kitchen.

    A studious, intelligent child, REBECCA [*Known as* BECKA.], *12, sits at her computer, staring out a window, her mind elsewhere. She wears glasses. Her sister,* BOOMER, *8, sits on the couch reading a book.*

We hear BECKA's *mother,* IRENE, *off-stage.*

IRENE: [*Off-stage.*] I'm late, guys, gotta run. You sure you want to walk into town? Who am I talking to? Is there anyone within of my voice?

BOOMER: I hear you, Mommy.

IRENE: [*Off-stage.*] Where's Rebecca?

BOOMER: She's right there.

IRENE: [*Off-stage.*] Right there where?

BOOMER: [*Pointing.*] There!

IRENE: [*Off-stage.*] Where there?

BOOMER: Sitting at the window.

IRENE: [*Off-stage.*] Oh, that there. Why doesn't she answer me?

BOOMER: Why don't you answer Mommy, Mommy wants to know.

(BECKA *stares out the window, doesn't respond. Off-stage. To her mother.*)

BOOMER: [*Cont'd.*] She didn't answer me when I asked her why she didn't answer you.

IRENE: [*Off-stage.*] Well, at least she's treating us both with equal repugnance.

BOOMER: Are you equally repugged at Mommy and me, Becka? What does that mean—repugnance?

BECKA: Repulsion, revulsion, aversion, contempt—take your pick.

BOOMER: I don't know what those words mean either, but they don't sound nice.

[IRENE WALLER, *36, comes down into the living room—in a hurry.*]

IRENE: All right, be careful when you cross the highway. Becka!

BECKA: We will, we know. You always tell us the same thing.

IRENE: That's what mothers are for: To repeat things you've heard before. After today, no more testing, no more evaluations, no more other people's kids till after the holidays. I love you bigger than the sky. Be nice to each other, just for fun, all right! Where's my briefcase? Who's seen my...

[BOOMER *points.* IRENE *finds the briefcase beside the couch.*]

IRENE: [*Cont'd.*] Ah. And, if you were my car keys?

BOOMER: Did you look in your hand yet, Mommy!

[*Indeed,* IRENE *finds the keys there.*]

IRENE: Remarkable—time after time, day after day. You'd think I'd catch on and look there first.

[IRENE *checks her briefcase,* BECKA *continues to stare out the window,* BOOMER *to watch her mother and sister as an event happens which seems to happen totally separately from them. They take no notice as...at the back of theater,* MRS. ROSEN, *eternally 49, suddenly bursts in. She seems to think she's arrived somewhere where Polish is the native tongue.*]

MRS. ROSEN: Dzien dobry. [*dzhehn dobri.*] (*Good day.*) Szczesl iwego nowego roku! [*Shenshl ivego novego rokoo.*] (*Merry Christmas, happy new year!*) Czy to jest grudzien! [*Chi to yehst groodzhehn.*] (*Is it now December?*) Czy zawsze jest tak cieplo
Warszawy! [*Chi zahvsheh yehst tahk tshehpwo zvahrshahvi.*] (*It's*

warm for Warsaw.) [*She begins to suspect she's not getting through.*] Czy pan mowi po polski! [*Chi pahn moovee po polski.*] (*Do you speak Polish?*) [*Evidently not. She tries something else.*]

Parle-vous Francais? (*Do you speak French?*) [*She tries to find a hello that brings recognition.*] Jambo! (*Swahili.*) Susrecall! (*Punjabi.*) Konichiwa! (*Japanese.*) Hello! [*Ah—recognition!*] Hello! English! I'm sorry, I've been in an elliptical orbit and you know how that is if you get your heading off by so much as a teeny, tiny, teeny, weeny, itzy bit. Never mind, why am I talking? I'm not, I'm being quiet, catching my breath.

Just one more thing: [*She rifles through* a *small notebook. She asks someone in the audience.*] Is this the United States, _____ [*Name of the city.*]*?* Yes—excellent, good, yes. Sshh, I'm being quiet—don't pay any attention to me. May I sit down with you—just the edge of your seat? Thank you. [MRS. ROSEN *shares a seat with someone in the audience.*] By my calculation, it should be just about time for the doorbell to ring.

[*On stage the phone rings.*]

MRS. ROSEN: [*Cont'd.*] Doorbell, phone, what's the difference? Excellent.

[MRS. ROSEN *unwraps her bagel, nibbles, listens...as on-stage* IRENE *closes her briefcase, throws on her coat and muffler.*]

IRENE: Becka, get the phone, please.

BECKA: [*To* BOOMER.] Get the phone.

BOOMER: She said you.

IRENE: You, Becka.

BECKA: Don't anybody move—I got it, I got the phone—keep your places. [BECKA *answers the phone.*] Hello, Waller Nut House, Nut Becka speaking....Yes, it is, but if you want Dr. Waller, he doesn't live here anymore. Call him at his office. He'll help you there....Yes, she's here.

[IRENE *waves no, she can't talk now.*] No. she's not here. [IRENE *gestures again.*]

BECKA: [*Cont'd.*] Excuse me, are you here?

IRENE: Yes, I'm here but I'm late.

BECKA: Yes, she's here, but she's late. Call her at the guidance office at the high school and she'll help you there. They both help people at their offices...You're welcome. [BECKA *hangs up.*]

IRENE: But they're basically worthless at home? Is that the extremely subtle message there? Thank you, I need a stroke like that to start my day.

BECKA: You're welcome.

IRENE: I have a student waiting, so I can't discuss my ineffectuality at this time. Let me say for the record, however, that I'm very sorry you feel that way.

BECKA: Why should you be sorry? You're living your life the best you can. Isn't that what you both tell us?

IRENE: Sounds like a familiar refrain.

BECKA: Someone living her life the best she can doesn't owe anyone any apologies.

[IRENE *is torn between obligations.*]

IRENE: I'll be happy to talk about this later, Rebecca –if you'll talk.

BECKA: Na—what's to talk about?

IRENE: —Fine—and you can wear my earrings—those are my earrings. 'Thanks, Mom." See you later.

BOOMER: Be so, so careful, whatever you do.

[*She exits.*]

BECKA: [*Mimicking* BOOMER.] "Be so, so careful, whatever you do!" Zip your jacket, let's go.

BOOMER: Don't always be so mad to Mommy— it makes me too sad.

BECKA: Why? Doesn't she always tell us that's one of her other main roles— for us to kick around.

BOOMER: She's kidding.

BECKA: Oooh. Watch out...

[BOOMER *has trouble with the zipper on her jacket*—BECKA *does it for her.*]

BECKA: [*Cont'd.*] Okay, let's move it. If we're gonna see good ole Santa Claus, let's get it over with, I gotta meet my friends.

[*They go out the front door.* BOOMER *stops a moment, stares into the sky.* MRS. ROSEN *stands.*]

MRS. ROSEN: What is this child thinking, do you imagine: Is she thinking maybe she should disappear into the sky, the clouds, the heavens beyond? So that she wouldn't have to be here to watch her family be so sad.

BECKA: [*Off-stage.*] Boom, you want to go see Santa, dumb-dumb, or not? Let's rock and roll!

[BOOMER *hurries after her sister.*]

MRS. ROSEN: The human drama in progress. Bicker, banter, barter. One has to wonder about mankind, whether we have all—or just the vast majority—of our brains in our behinds. Yes, well: a family in the process of devouring itself before our eyes, and Christmas only two days away, approaching at the speed of time.

[*She makes a sound to imitate that speed and is illuminated by a wonderful light. Her ear tuned to a great distance, she closes her eyes, reaches skyward.*]

MRS. ROSEN: [*Cont'd.*] E mon canta. Se indo macah fay hansu ma pinulta melacan. Melacan mon felicitay, felici pelicula. What a mess. It's clear there is here the classic situation. Situation most human. [*To us.*] Estupee, estupai, estupan. There was hope, there is hope, there will always be hope. Sintu belicutai belicutoe. Here I go, the future awaits, and this little girl needs a great deal of help.

[*She waves her hand and is consumed by a white light and we fade out.*]

SCENE 2

A department store. Christmas music. Christmas shoppers. A department store SANTA. *Elsewhere, the electronics sections.*

As lights come up, BOOMER *is on* RENTED SANTA's *lap and deep into her conversation with him.* BECKA *waits dourly. Another little girl,* ZELDA, *is also in line.*

BOOMER: And my mommy, she wants to be real super thin, but I don't know if you can bring that, so she wants a new briefcase. And my daddy said he didn't know what he wanted, but I think he's just sort of sad and doesn't really care, even though he'd feel better probably if he did really want something that we could give him that would make him smile, so bring him a new putter even though he hates golf because he hits so many bad shots.

RENTED SANTA: You've told me what everybody wants except you. What do you hope Santa brings you?

BOOMER: Mostly, I just want my family to be together again. But if you can't do that, then what I want is a synthesizer but I know that's a really, really big time, major present, so if you can't bring that, then I'd just like a new, atomically correct dolly.

RENTED SANTA: I'll see what the elves can do.

BECKA: Okay, let's rock 'n roll, Boom, this isn't Wheel of Fortune, babe! [BOOMER *gets off* RENTED SANTA's *lap.*]

BOOMER: Thank you, you're very nice to listen so good.

RENTED SANTA: What a nice thing to say.

BECKA: Don't let it go to your head—she thinks everybody's nice.

RENTED SANTA: [*Dryly.*] Ho, ho, ho. Next!

ZELDA: I'm next! [ZELDA *jumps on* SANTA's *lap with a huge list of requests.*] I'd like...

[*And she continues inaudibly as...the girls walk away. In the electronics section,* "MANTHING" *and* ALVIN LEE, *12-13, at a computer.* BOOMER *goes straight to an electronic keyboard. A plump, wizened and extremely officious* SALESWOMAN *intercepts* BECKA. *The* SALESWOMAN *is, needless to say,* MRS. ROSEN.]

SALESWOMAN: Hello, ma'am. May I of assistance be some?

[BECKA *fixes the* SALESWOMAN *curiously a moment. She flashes a card.*]

BECKA: I'm with them.

SALESWOMAN: Quite not so fast, dearie. That Card you're flashing is what, that card?

BECKA: Hackers' Club. Computers. We hang out here. You're new.

SALESWOMAN: Yes, I am. But to my mind, hang out with the merchandise we don't, unless a purchase we're planning to consider.

BECKA: Oh, I'm definitely a purchase planning to consider. Always a purchase am I planning to consider.

SALESWOMAN: And I believe you. And therefore it's perfectly appropriate for you to hack the machinery. I noticed your little sister yon Santa Claus visiting. How is it that you with Mr. Claus, did not confer, also, dearie?

BECKA: Because fairy tales are out, "dearie"; it's the age of the microchip.

SALESWOMAN: Ah. Yes, I see. Hard drive, hard disk, floppy, mopsy, and cottontail. Though, you must beware when certain dreams you cease to dream. Your innerface becomes a very mean face.

BECKA: Got no idea what you're talking about, but may I say with all due respect: Ho, Ho, Ho.

SALESWOMAN: Thank you for your time—I shall remember always the congeniality of our little visit.

BECKA: It's gonna stay with me a while, too, I can tell ya. [BECKA *walks away from the* SALESWOMAN, *to the two members of the Hackers' Club, side by side at the computer.*]

ALVIN LEE: Hi, Rebecca! [*Extremely polite,* ALVIN LEE *is in the habit of shaking hands whenever possible. With* BECKA, *the hand shaking is also a way of "holding"* BECKA's *hand without appearing to be as attracted to her as he is.*]

BECKA: Yo, pals and buddies, who's gonna help me clip the code, make a run-time module from T-Base to make my father think he's got a bug in his system.

ALVIN LEE: I will—if we won't get in trouble! [ALVIN LEE *politely gives up his seat at the computer to* BECKA. *The* SALESWOMAN *moves to* BOOMER.]

SALESWOMAN: And what about you, dearie? On your mind is what?

BOOMER: Can I play this synthesizer?

SALESWOMAN: Planning to purchase?

BOOMER: No, I'm sorry, I'm just a little kid, I only got about three bucks to my name.

[*The* SALESWOMAN *cocks her head at this sweet child.*]

SALESWOMAN: I'm prepared for you to an exception make.

BOOMER: You're nice, I like you.

SALESWOMAN: Well, thank you—everyone likes a little validation of self, doesn't one?

[BOOMER *isn't quite sure what this lady means but nods...as she sits at the synthesizer and plays a sweet melody of her own creation and the officious* SALESWOMAN *watches and listens as Ron Cavindish, 12-13, handsome, preppy, and convinced he knows it all enters with* SARAH, *12-13.* BECKA *is as attracted to* RON *as* ALVIN LEE *is to* BECKA.]

RON: Rebecca Waller, check out who has arrived.

BECKA: Hail, the President. [*But now she sees* SARAH *and is not at all pleased.*] Sarah...

SARAH: Hi, Becka.

RON: Manthing!

MANTHING: Studly!

RON: Al, hey, my man!

[*A good deal of high-flying greets the arrival of the eminence.* BECKA *has a hard time keeping her eyes off* SARAH, *the intruder.*]

BECKA: So, Ronny, where you been?

RON: I was just endeavoring to explain to this cute young thing here how you log on to Max/Baud and request the illegal access nullification scheme for Toy Universe, place your order, and mark 'em prepaid.

ALVIN LEE: Isn't that illegal?

[RON *stares at* ALVIN LEE *a moment as if he just arrived from outer space.*]

RON: Duh!...So, Beckerino, what're you up to?

BECKA: Writing an auto-exec file to bomb my father's system.

RON: That's great, I love it. My man, move out...

[*He sits beside* BECKA. *In her shy way, she loves it. She would do anything for him.*]

RON: [*Cont'd.*] What you should do, see, is you should interface with your mother's system. Ya freeze their files and lock 'em into single flow so they can only talk to each other. That's one way to deal with a divorce.

BECKA: [*Heatedly.*] They're not divorced. They're just separated.

RON: Okay, okay. No biggie, huh. I mean, my parents are divorced, you don't see me crying, do ya?

[*Through the following,* BECKA *encodes on the machine — with* RON's *help.*]

RON: [*Cont'd.*] We've been looking all over for ya. We gotta have an executive board meeting, discuss whether ole Alvin Lee here's ready for the, club.

ALVIN LEE: Oh, I'm ready, Ronnie, believe me I'm ready.

RON: Why don't you let me be the judge of that, Al.

MANTHING: Yeah, let Ronnie be the judge of that, Al.

RON: Uh-oh, whoa horsie, who told you to encode it this way?

BECKA: Alvin Lee.

RON: Dumb.

MANTHING: Yeah, dumb, dumb, dumb.

ALVIN LEE: Well, Ronnie, I'm not arguin' but ...

RON: Real dumb.

MANTHING: Yeah, real dumb.

RON: Get a grip, Al.

MANTHING: Yeah, get a grip.

ALVIN LEE: Sorry, Ronnie.

RON: So, where you been, Beckareeno?

BECKA: Takin' my sister to see Santa Claus.

RON: You're joshing me. The ole Boomerang still believes in Santa Claus?

BECKA: [*Trying to be cool.*] What can I tell ya — kid's your basic dipstick.

RON: Kid's livin' in the Dark Ages.

BECKA: No lie.

RON: What is she—like eight already?

MANTHING: Gotta be at least eight.

RON: Somebody oughta bring her into the present. [*Short beat.*] We oughta bring her into the present. Who's for bringing Boomer Waller into the present?

[*The Hackers respond affirmatively...except for* ALVIN LEE *and* BECKA.]

SARAH: Whatever you think, Ronnie—absolutely.

RON: Whudduya think, Beck?

BECKA: Sure, let's bring her into the present.

[*The* SALESWOMAN, *who seems to have been listening to* BECKA, RON, *and* ALVIN LEE *from a distance, turns to* BOOMER *now.*]

SALESWOMAN: That's rather a catchy little tune, dearie.

BOOMER: I wrote it.

SALESWOMAN: Oh, no, you didn't.

BOOMER: Oh, yes, I did too.

SALESWOMAN: Nooo.

BOOMER: Yep.

SALESWOMAN: You have words for it?

BOOMER: Not yet. I need one a those whachamacallits——a lyricist.

[RON, BECKA, *and* ALVIN LEE *approach* BOOMER.]

RON: [*To* SALESWOMAN.] Would you excuse me, please, miss. Hey, Boom, the guy over there in the fatboy suit, you got an I.D. on him?

BOOMER: That's Santa Claus, silly.

RON: Or, Boomer, or is the dude over there in reality your basic rental tub a guts?

BOOMER: What does that mean?

RON: Fill her in, Alvin Lee.

[ALVIN LEE *isn't totally committed to bringing* BOOMER *into the present, but neither does he want to offend the prez.*]

ALVIN LEE: [*Whispering to* RON.] Are you sure this is the right thing to do?

RON: Am I going to knowingly involve you in a criminal act, Al? Get any kind of grip, dude.

MANTHING: Yeah, dude, get some kind of grip.

ALVIN LEE: The fella over there, Boomer, he's not exactly Santa Claus.

BOOMER: Whudduya mean?

RON: Tell her, Beck.

[*And now the actual moment of destruction falls to* BECKA.]

BECKA: He means this whole Santa Claus routine, Boom, It's just a fairy tale made up by a buncha grown-ups to trick us when we're little kids into thinking the world's like a real terrific place.

BOOMER: But it is a terrific place.

RON: Can't you picture this big, fat, major dork flying through the sky, riding this sleigh pulled by eight tiny reindeer, coming down your Chimney?

BOOMER: He's not a dork!

RON: [*Whispering to* BOOMER.] Now, you wanna know who Santa Claus really is, Boom? Come on over to that computer there and I'm gonna show ya how to bust into Toy Universe and order anything ya want for F-R-E-E. I'm Santa Claus!

BOOMER: You're not Santa Claus! You're a...you're a not-nice person! [*To* BECKA.] Is he telling the truth?

[*There is still time to retreat, to not do this. But...*]

BECKA: Yes. [*Suddenly* BECKA'*s own hand smacks her own face.*]

RON: Becker, whudduya doing? What's she hitting herself for?

ALVIN LEE: Maybe she's upset about what we did to her sister.

[BOOMER's *attention goes to* RENTED SANTA. *Suddenly she takes off running.*]

ALVIN LEE: [*Cont'd.*] I think we made a big mistake, you guys.

[RENTED SANTA *has* ZELDA *just getting off his lap when* BOOMER *leaves her feet and lands on* RENTED SANTA *with a vengeance.*]

BOOMER: You're a cheat! You're a liar! You stink! [BOOMER *knocks* RENTED SANTA *backwards and over, taking the* SANTA *display down the tubes with them.*]

ZELDA: Santa! Santa! Are you okay? I'm not through with my list.

[ZELDA *tries to help* RENTED SANTA *as everyone else watches* BOOMER *run off-stage.* MRS. ROSEN *steps down toward the audience as the Hackers drift.*]

RON: Everybody, follow me: Slushies on Alvin Lee.

[BECKA *remains.*]

MRS. ROSEN: Mankind, mankind, mankind, is there any doubt whatsoever that our brains are in our behinds? Had I known there were teenagers involved in this case, I'm not sure I would have come. But I'm here, I'll give it a shot even though I would venture to guess this is going to be one of those instances where an abominable situation is going to devolve into a truly loathsome one before it has the remotest possibility of improvement.

[MRS. ROSEN *turns to look at* BECKA *who is obviously in pain...but not ready for enlightenment. This as the lights fade.*]

SCENE 3

The Waller living room. BECKA *sits at the counter.*

We see BOOMER *sitting on a branch of the big tree.*

IRENE: You and your friends thought you were doing her a *favor*? In your infinite wisdom, how did you figure ruining Christmas for an eight-year-old to be a *favor*?

BECKA: We know where the future's coming from.

IRENE: And in the future, you figure there won't be room for kids to be kids past age eight, is that it? I'm very disappointed in you if you think you did something helpful for your sister today.

BECKA: So what's new? You and your estranged husband are always disappointed in me anyway.

IRENE: That's ridiculous and you know it.

BECKA: I don't know it.

IRENE: If you don't, you should.

BECKA: Maybe I should, but I still don't.

IRENE: I'm often very proud of you. But since Daddy and I separated you've been virtually incommunicado. Don't Daddy and I have the right to be imperfect—just as you do? Whudduya think?

[BECKA *just can't quite let her frustration go and she remains silent.*]

IRENE: [*Cont'd.*] All right, Beck, so much for intimate person-to-person parenting. Now I'm the mother and you're the kid, and here's what you're gonna do. Phone!

[*Lights cross fade to* BOOMER. IRENE *comes out of the house.* BOOMER *is talking to herself, sitting in the tree.*]

BOOMER: Mainly what they would do, see, my mom and dad, is they would talk at the same time but say the same thing—except they didn't know they were agreeing with each other *because* they were talking at the same time, telling the other person that the *other* person wasn't listening to the *other* person, so how could they know they were agreeing? They couldn't. Why do I think what I just said didn't make any sense whatsoever?

IRENE: Come in the house, baby, I don't want you to catch pneumonia.

BOOMER: I wanna catch pneumonia! And a cold! And I wanna get a real bad, really, really gigantic blister on my lip! Right here where it'd look really gross!

IRENE: Then let's both sit out here and catch pneumonia and a cold and get a gigantic blister.

BOOMER: No, I don't want you to get sick—just me. Let's go inside. [BOOMER *holds her arms open to her mother.* IRENE *lifts her down.*] I'll come see you later if you don't go bye-bye.

IRENE: Who are you talking to?

BOOMER: The nice lady inside the tree.

IRENE: What nice lady inside the...

[*Above* BOOMER *in the tree,* MRS. ROSEN *pops up.*]

IRENE: [*Cont'd.*] Excuse me. Can I help you?

MRS. ROSEN: Though I have my doubts, I certainly hope so.

BOOMER: This is Mrs. Rosen, she's been living in our tree.

MRS. ROSEN: And I must say it's one of the nicest domiciles I've had in a very long time.

BOOMER: Except, you know what? What if it snowed?

MRS. ROSEN: But it did not.

BOOMER: But what if it did?

MRS. ROSEN: Well, I would have gotten snowed upon, I suppose. And then when it stopped snowing, I would have dried out.

BOOMER: If you didn't get really disgustingly sick or something and die.

MRS. ROSEN: Oh, I don't die. Of anything. [*Suddenly there's a bolt of lightning and then a clap of thunder.*]

IRENE: How odd?

MRS. ROSEN: What's that, dear?

IRENE: Lightning in the winter.

MRS. ROSEN: Really?

BOOMER: Mrs. Rosen can stay the night with us, in the house, right, Mommy?

IRENE: [*Reluctant.*] .Well, I'm not sure Mrs. Rosen would–

BOOMER: You'd like to stay in a nice warm, soft bed tonight, wouldn't you?

MRS. ROSEN: Well, I wouldn't want to cause any–

BOOMER: And tomorrow. You can't live in somebody's tree on Christmas Eve. Right, Mommy?

IRENE: Well, there's a shelter downtown, sweetheart, for people who... Absolutely, she should stay with us. Please, come in.

SCENE 4

They've come from the kitchen into the living room. BECKA *goes to the computer alcove, puts on headphones, opens up her machine.* IRENE *and* MRS. ROSEN *carry cups and saucers.*

MRS. ROSEN: Well, that was delicious. More than delicious, it was positively salubrious. [*Her old coat off, we see that* MRS. ROSEN *is wearing an*

African necklace, has a Hebrew letter and a cross on a chain around her neck, Caribbean bracelets on one wrist, middle eastern charms on the other; rings of hammered silver from Mexico and soapstone from Kenya; in short, she wears the world on her in trinkets.]

BOOMER: You just have so much neat junk. I mean, I don't mean junk junk. It's just all such neat...

MRS. ROSEN: Junk.

BOOMER: Yeah! Where's your real home when you don't have to live in people's tree?

MRS. ROSEN: Wherever I am when I am no longer where I was.

BOOMER: So where did you live before you left where you were to come to where you are?

MRS. ROSEN: A place where people were not kind to other people—that is where last I was.

BOOMER: And you left because they kept on not being kind to each other?

MRS. ROSEN: Oh no. No, I left because they stopped.

BOOMER: You wanna see people not being kind to each other, you should come visit here sometime.

MRS. ROSEN: But I am visiting here. [*Lightning. Thunder.* BOOMER *senses that something very unusual is going on here.* MRS. ROSEN'*s bracelets begin to jangle melodiously.*]

BOOMER: How are they doing that?

IRENE: That's a wonderful trick. Yoga, yes?

MRS. ROSEN: Yogurt? Oh no, no thank you. Later perhaps.

IRENE: I'm sorry, no–yoga. I have a friend who teaches yoga. She can initiate vibrations through her body, just sheer force of will.

MRS. ROSEN: Isn't that remarkable? Who plays the piano? [*She looks at* BOOMER.]

BOOMER: I do.

MRS. ROSEN: Play. Please. But something unfamiliar. I tire of the familiar.

IRENE: Why don't you play Mrs. Rosen something of your own.

MRS. ROSEN: So long as it's not familiar.

BOOMER: What if she laughs?

MRS. ROSEN: What if I do laugh?

BOOMER: I could be deeply traumatized.

MRS. ROSEN: Oh, come, come, on certain occasions we must take certain chances.

[*A beat and* BOOMER *sits and plays her melody.* MRS. ROSEN *listens, with cup and saucer.* BOOMER *stops.*]

BOOMER: I can't get past that place.

MRS. ROSEN: Very nice to that point. Pleasingly unfamiliar. So, don't give up.

BOOMER: Yeah, sure, you know, but I'm stuck.

MRS. ROSEN: Yeah, sure, you know, but nevertheless, don't give up.

BOOMER: Yeah, but-

BECKA: The great thing is, even in my headphones, I can still hear you playing that same thing over and over again. I can't help wondering if it's occurred to you to play something new just as a favor to other people in the house to whom that piece of music is extremely familiar?

[MRS. ROSEN *focuses on* BECKA *and–though we can't hear it–her earphones suddenly go up ferociously in volume, forcing her to rip them off her head.*]

IRENE: What's the matter?

BECKA: Someone just turned the volume up on my headphones and about short-circuited my brain.

IRENE: "Someone"? Someone who?

[DEAN WALLER, *38, in sweats, fresh from a run, has come in the back door, through the kitchen and into the living room.* BECKA *quickly disappears back into her headphones.*]

DEAN: Hey ho, hey ho, hey ho!

BOOMER: Hi, Daddy!

DEAN: Boomer! [DEAN *sweeps* BOOMER *into his arms. Carrying her, he moves to* BECKA, *lifts one side of her headphones away from an ear.*] Hello, Rebecca.

IRENE: You came.

DEAN: I came? Is that really pretty shocking?

IRENE: I didn't mean it to come out like that.

DEAN: Then I wonder why it did.

IRENE: Why don't we sit down for fifty minutes and analyze it.

DEAN: That would be terrific but I'm here to meet these very thoughtful teenagers.

IRENE: They're expected momentarily.

DEAN: [*Turning to* BOOMER.] Are you okay, pup?

BOOMER: I guess, maybe, yeah. After I beat up the rented Santa Claus, I ran to your office. I told Hilda I had to see you, but she said, "He's with a little girl right now who has a terrible problem, sweetie." And I said, "But I'm a little girl also and I have a terrible problem too!" And she said, "Well then, we'll try to work you in."

DEAN: I'm sorry sweetheart. She told me you'd come and I called here but nobody answered.

BOOMER: You did?…Oh– okay.

DEAN: Everybody finds out eventually that there's no Santa Claus. But the pain passes, I promise, and as we grow older, we replace fantasies like Santa with realities which are just as wonderful. Just as wonderful.

BOOMER: Thank you, daddy.

DEAN: You're welcome.

IRENE: Thank you, daddy. [*A beat.*]

DEAN: I don't mean to criticize…

IRENE. But…? [DEAN *looks at* BECKA. *To* IRENE.]

DEAN: I get the feeling you're not reinforcing Becka the way I suggested.

IRENE: You get the feeling I'm not reinforcing Becka the way you suggested. I'm trying, Doctor. What about you? What are you doing in that direction other than making pronouncements?

DEAN: Let's not do this.

IRENE: Let's not.

DEAN: I should talk to Becka.

IRENE: I'd leave it. I'm on the case.

DEAN: I think it's important that she know where both of us stand on the matter.

IRENE: I'm sure she knows exactly where we both stand on the matter, which probably had a good deal to do with why she handled the matter as she did in the first place.

DEAN: You're saying she was striking out at us and not performing the computer age act of charity she claims?

IRENE: Is that a real question, Dean, to be answered by a human being?

DEAN: [*To* BOOMER.] You'll be fine.

BOOMER: Promise? [*Silence. Waiting for the Hackers. But then–two professionals now.*]

IRENE: I'm referring a child I saw this morning to you for counseling.

DEAN: What seems to be the problem?

IRENE: Solid average range IQ, but reading and spelling problems which are manifesting themselves in various forms of anti-social behavior.

DEAN: I'll take care of it. Appreciate the referral.

IRENE: Hey, you're great with other people's children.

DEAN: You're saying I'm not?

IRENE: I'm saying you are.

DEAN: It sounds like you're saying I am, but you mean I'm not.

IRENE: I'm saying exactly what I mean–you are extraordinary with other people's children.

DEAN: Thank you.

BOOMER: Daddy, are you going to come for Christmas dinner?

[DEAN *and.* IRENE *look at each other.*]

DEAN: Well, I don't know that we would all be comfortable. Whudduyou think?

BOOMER: I'll be comfortable.

IRENE: Of course we should all have dinner together.

DEAN: I'm not so sure. Why don't we think about it. We have time.

IRENE: Good. You consult your people, we'll consult ours. [*A beat.* DEAN *approaches* BECKA.]

DEAN: Becka; would you like to tell me what happened, sweetheart?

BECKA: Uh-uh.

DEAN: Then let me put it another way: What happened, Rebecca?

BECKA: Do you have another...you know. Do you have a...

BOOMER: ...a girlfriend yet?

DEAN: No, I don't have a girlfriend.

BECKA: We don't believe you.

BOOMER: I do, I believe him.

DEAN: Becka, you know Mommy and I didn't separate because either of us—

[BECKA *locks herself into her headphones.*]

DEAN: [*Cont'd.*] Thanks for your time, Beck. Anytime I can be of assistance, don't hesitate. [DEAN *turns away, finds himself looking at a stranger.*]

MRS. ROSEN: Hello, how are you?

DEAN: Fine, I'm fine, thank you. [*A beat; to* IRENE.] Who is this?

IRENE: This is Mrs. Rosen. She's going to stay with us through Christmas.

DEAN: Stay with you through Christmas?

IRENE: That's right.

DEAN: I see. [*A beat.*] You look familiar to me.

MRS. ROSEN: I wonder why.

[*The doorbell rings.*]

IRENE: Let me handle this, okay?

DEAN: Why'd you ask me to come out if you're going to handle it?

IRENE: I asked you to come out to lend moral support, Dean.

DEAN: [*A beat.*] I can do that.

[*Lights cross fade to living room—several minutes later.*]

SCENE 5

RON. ALVIN LEE, SARAH, *and* MANTHING *seated on the couch.* IRENE *with* BOOMER *on her lap.* BECKA *somewhat isolated.* DEAN *against the fireplace.* MRS. ROSEN *listening from the semi-privacy of the foyer.* RON *plays absently with a pocket-size battery game.*

RON: I don't wanna be impolite, Mrs. Waller, but really: I mean, Santa Claus! Kids are older today than when you were a child.

IRENE: I think that's all the more reason to hang on to some fantasies. I know adulthood looks attractive from where you are but, believe me, it's vastly overrated. Don't rush it. It'll be here soon enough.

RON: Yeah, okay, we understand the thrust of what you're saying, Mrs. Waller, we do. But how are we supposed to ignore the facts?

IRENE: Facts?

RON: Yeah. I mean, once I learned that one plus one is two in my Computers for Pre-Schoolers class when I was three, how was I supposed to buy into something like Santa Claus anymore?

MANTHING: Yeah! Can't buy into that Mrs. Waller. Imposeeb! [*Impossible.*]

RON: I'm sorry, Mrs. Waller, but it's pretty tough to kid yourself about facts. Right, pals and buddies?

SARAH: Absolutely, Ronnie.

MANTHING: That's exactly the thing about facts, Ronnie—they're facts.

RON: Alvin Lee?

ALVIN LEE: Facts are facts, Mrs. Waller, ma'am.

RON: Right, Beck?

BECKA: [*Torn*] Yeah, I guess.

IRENE: Rebecca, however, Ron, *didn't* take Computers for pre-natal infants. No, she didn't become an all-knowing cynic until the ripe old age of twelve. [*She has to take another very deep breath.* DEAN *steps in.*]

DEAN: May I? Can I see your game there, Ron? [RON *hands him the computer game.*] So. Facts are facts. In which case, if I were to drop this, whudduya figure it'd do?

RON: I figure it'd fall and break. So I really hope you're not planning to do that, Dr. Waller.

DEAN: My own opinion is that you don't know, that none of us knows, it'll fall.

RON: Pardon me, Dr. Waller, but I'm pretty sure it's gonna fall. See, things ya drop *always* fall. There's this deal called gravity!

[BECKA'S *eyes are drawn toward* MRS. ROSEN *who's just barely visible in the foyer.* DEAN *holds the battery game up.*]

DEAN: *So far* things you drop always fall. That doesn't mean, however, things you drop always *will* fall. Despite the deal called gravity. If I drop this, it just might, this very next time, not fall but rise. It could. Theoretically, it's possible.

ALVIN LEE: I think I see what you mean, Dr. Waller, that's real—

[RON *fires a look at* ALVIN LEE *that shuts him up in mid-sentence.*]

DEAN: And by the same sort of reasoning, you see, there could be a Santa Claus. I would think three young people like you, vitally interested in scientific possibility, would relate to that sort of logic. Whudduya say?

ALVIN LEE: Whudduyou think Ronny? I mean, I could sorta maybe see-

RON: Ya wanna bag it, Alvin Lee—completely and until further notice.

MANTHING: Sack and bag it, Al!

ALVIN LEE: Sure, Ronny.

RON: Appreciate it. No offense, Dr. Waller, but that kinda quasi-spiritual, speculative logic, as you call it, doesn't even *register* on my Maybe Meter. You, Beck?

[BECKA *is torn, caught up in the distant* MRS. ROSEN *and the confusion of what's happening.*]

BECKA: Doesn't register.

IRENE: Well, I say there *is* a Santa Claus! And I say it's logical and I say it's a fact! Now does anyone have anything to say to that? Ron?

RON: Gee, I'm afraid I don't know *what* to say to that, Mrs. Waller.

IRENE: Rebecca—care to comment?

RON: If driven to the wall for a response, however, Mrs. Waller, what I'd say is this: *Prove it!*

IRENE: Thank you, I will! Tomorrow, Christmas Eve, I'm going to produce the gentleman. Santa Claus, the one and only, right here, and I want you three in attendance. At eight o'clock. Sharp!

RON: Eight's good for me. Alvin Lee?

ALVIN LEE: I'll ask Mom. [*He gets a withering look from* RON.] Sure.

SARAH: Eight's perfect for me, Ronnie.

MANTHING: I love eight, Ronnie.

RON: We can make that, Mrs. Waller. Eight. We'll be here. Open-minded.

IRENE: Good. Now, g'bye. See your friends to the door, Rebecca.

[BECKA *shows* RON, SARAH, *and* MANTHING *to the door. Ever the gentleman,* ALVIN LEE *shakes with* IRENE.]

ALVIN LEE: Thank you for inviting me, ma'am.

RON: [*For everyone.*] Ya know, Beck, if there is a Santa Claus, you gotta figure that he has a computer, right? Why don't *you* tap into El Tubbo's computer—tell him there's big trouble down here and he better fly through the sky in his sleigh pulled by his reindeer to the rescue.

[RON *thinks this is pretty amusing.* BECKA *tries to laugh along, but this has become much uglier than she ever anticipated. The hackers pass* MRS. ROSEN. ALVIN LEE *catches up. He offers is hand to* MRS. ROSEN.]

ALVIN LEE: Good night, Rebecca. Good night, ma'am.

MRS. ROSEN: Good night, young man.

[MRS. ROSEN *takes* LEE'S *hand, shakes it. He's eye to eye with her a moment. Then.*]

BECKA: G'night.

RON: Dork!

MANTHING: Dweeb!

ALVIN LEE: [*To* RON.] What's with you?

[*Outside on the porch, as* RON *passes under the edge of the house, a load of snow plops down on his head.* RON *clears his face, looks up.*]

MRS. ROSEN: Well, you certainly seem correct about the forces of gravity, Ronald. Things do, indeed, seem to fall down.

[RON *goes off, followed by his disciples. Leaving* BECKA *and* MRS. ROSEN— *eye to eye.*]

MRS. ROSEN: [*Cont'd.*] Having second thoughts about the favor you did your sister?

BECKA: [Short beat.] Not really.

[*She walks past* MRS. ROSEN *into the house, but seems to get a sharp kick in the rear end as she passes. She looks around angrily, only to find* MRS. ROSEN *standing innocently in the doorway, waving after the departing boys. Meanwhile, in the living room,* DEAN *and* IRENE.]

IRENE: I know you were trying to help...

DEAN: But...

IRENE: Weighted objects that go up instead of down?

DEAN: Santa Claus? Here? Tomorrow night at eight o'clock?

[*And then, instead of picking on each other, they unite against* RON.]

DEAN AND IRENE: Quasi-spiritual, speculative logic...? [IRENE *and* DEAN *glance at* BECKA *as she enters.*]

IRENE: If this all happened, Beck, because you were trying to impress the very impressive Ronald Cavendish, I'd suggest you learn to pick men who are a little less mechanical and a little more human.

BECKA: Like you did?

IRENE: Don't you dare compare that pompous horse's hind end to your father! Your father is an enormously caring, gentle, funny, sweet man who's...who's simply forgotten how to be less mechanical and more human. [*A beat...and* IRENE *starts angrily for the kitchen, then comes right back.*] If you're fortunate enough to win a stunning young man like that, Rebecca, you can look forward to a life of impersonating a brainless, witless, gullible toad like your friend Sarah, simpering and giggling and nodding benignly as your arrogant mate dictates your life to you. [*She starts for the kitchen, comes right back.*] And that doesn't happen to be your father, either. He's always encouraged me to stand up for my rights against him. Which I have done. And will continue to do.

[*She stares at* DEAN, *he at her, and this time she exits quickly to the kitchen.* BECKA *looks at her father a moment, then tells her sister.*]

BECKA: I need to use my computer.

[BOOMER *moves from the computer to the couch.*]

DEAN: I'd like a word with you first. [*To* MRS. ROSEN.] Would you excuse us, please?

MRS. ROSEN: Excuse you from what, dear? I'm afraid you'll have to list all of your deficiencies for me before I can determine whether—Oh, I see, absent myself from you; yes, of course. Language can be so mystifying.

DEAN: Where do I know you from?

MRS. ROSEN: Beats the heck outta me. Where do you think you know me from?

DEAN: I'm sure it's impossible. You would have been a much older person by now.

MRS. ROSEN: Got not a clue what you're going on about, amigo. I'll just step outside.

[*She steps onto the porch, but turns her attention back to the house and dur-*

ing the following move off the porch into the shadows. DEAN *pats the couch and he and* BECKA *sit side by side,* BOOMER *on the other side of them.*]

DEAN: Why do you think you did what you did to your sister today?

BECKA: I told Mom; she can tell you.

DEAN: Mom told me what you said. I'd like to cut out the middle man and hear it directly from you. Is it possible that it really was just to impress this boy?

BECKA: I don't have to impress Ronald Cavendish—what do I care what he...[*A beat: she'd love to ask have her father's help in righting this situation, but...*] Look, I'm too tired to talk about this now.

DEAN: I don't find that a satisfactory answer, sweetheart.

BECKA: I bet it'd be satisfactory for some kid who came to see you as a patient,

DEAN: Never. I'd torment the poor kid until I got the answer I wanted. C'mon, smile, that was kinda funny and unmechanical, I thought. Wasn't it?

BECKA: Funny, Dad.

[*He smiles;* BECKA *doesn't, though she might like to just a little bit.*].

DEAN: You know, I remembered something tonight that I'd forgotten— or something maybe I haven't wanted to remember since my own childhood. Wanna know what it is?

BECKA: No thank you. May I be excused, please?

DEAN: [*Ironically.*] Sure. And don't dwell on this whole matter.

[BECKA *goes to the computer alcove, puts on her headphones.* IRENE *enters from the kitchen.*]

IRENE: So, baby, tomorrow night, the real Santa will be here—

DEAN: [*Simultaneously.*] Did you understand what I was trying to—

IRENE AND DEAN: Why don't we talk at once? I thought we were.

IRENE AND DEAN: After you.

IRENE: So, baby, tomorrow night the real Santa will be here.

BOOMER: How can the real Santa Claus be at our house when there isn't a real Santa Claus? He can't. Cuz somebody who there isn't one of can't be anywhere at eight-o'clock. [*As it dawns on her.*] And that means there's no Tooth Fairy and probably no Easter bunny and it probably means there's no God...! It means there's just Moms and

Dads. Moms and Dads give you Christmas presents and give you money when your teeth fall out and bring you Easter eggs, and who made the world, how did we get here? Oh, Mommy and Daddy, I'm scared!

[*Both parents start for her but* BOOMER *runs upstairs. During the following, we'll see* BOOMER *come out of the window upstairs, onto the widow's walk and then onto the roof*]

DEAN: Am I nuts or were we a lot younger when we were her age?

IRENE: You're not nuts. Misguided maybe.

DEAN: I'm getting a lot of compliments tonight–feels good.

IRENE: I'm sorry, I think I meant that to be amusing. Will you play Santa Claus tomorrow night?

DEAN: She'll know me in a second.

IRENE: I think her desire to believe is still greater than her desire not to.

DEAN: In case you haven't noticed, children know when adults are lying.

IRENE: Thank you for that illuminating insight, Dean. Working with children all day also, I've never noticed that phenomenon.

[BECKA *plays her computer game and wears her headphones but she's tuned to her parents.*]

DEAN: Irene, you're acting like—

IRENE. Don't, Dean. Don't define, don't analyze, don't explain me, please. Don't you see that this is where our difficulties started—

DEAN: I shouldn't say anything to you, but it's all right for you to define me and analyze me and to tell me where our difficulties began.

IRENE: You started dissecting *everything*—the kids, me, steamed vegetables —turning everything into...into a statistic.

DEAN: And you don't?

IRENE: You're supposed to understand and sympathize with the problems of others, especially children, supposed to deal with their pains and feelings and fantasies. Grow down, Deanie, even adults are allowed to hang on to a bit of the child in them, aren't they, even grown-ups approaching mid-life?

DEAN: Certainly a full agenda of accusations there, Irene. I don't think I want to respond at this time, I might say something I regret.

IRENE: In other words, you might say something spontaneous.

DEAN: And to you, spontaneity is running around like a headless chicken.

IRENE: I'll handle the Santa Claus problem tomorrow night, don't concern yourself about it.

DEAN: Then I think I'll go.

[DEAN *exits the house angrily.* IRENE *exits just as angrily to the kitchen.*]

BECKA: Jerks! Jerks! Jerks! Jerks! Jerks! Jerks! Jerks! Jerks!

[*On the roof,* BOOMER *watches her father go...and begins stomping the roof angrily. Suddenly she slips down the hard, slick, steep roof, clinging for dear life.* MRS. ROSEN *watches dispassionately from below.* BOOMER *cries out weakly, not nearly loud enough to be heard.*]

BOOMER: Daddy...! Mommy..! [MRS. ROSEN *looks in the direction where* DEAN *disappeared. She barely lifts a finger in that direction. Then toward the house. Suddenly* DEAN *runs back on stage and* IRENE *bolts out of the house, followed by* BECKA.] Mommy...! Daddy...!

[*Parents and sister arrive, peering up at* BOOMER *clinging to the edge of the roof.*]

DEAN: All right, sweetheart, all right, here I come!

IRENE: Hang on, baby, I'm coming! [*Dean quickly climbs the tree. Can't reach her. Can't quite get from the tree to the widow's walk. Swings down.*]

DEAN: Don't panic, sweetheart, Mommy and Daddy will get you down! [*To Irene.*] I could climb out the widow's walk, try to—

IRENE: No, no, the roof's too slippery! Becka!

DEAN: Right!

BECKA: Lift me!

DEAN AND IRENE: Right!

[*Without further discussion,* DEAN *and* IRENE *form a platform with their interlocked hands for* BECKA *to climb onto.* BECKA *reaches as high as she can but can't reach her sister.*]

BECKA: Can't reach!

BOOMER: I'm slipping!

BECKA, IRENE AND DEAN: Nooo!

IRENE: Don't slip, don't slip...

DEAN:....you're not slipping!

BOOMER: I'm slipping!

DEAN: ...no, you're not!

[BOOMER *suddenly slips another foot or so, hangs perilously over the edge of the house.*]

DEAN: [*Cont'd.*] Gotta lift Becka a little higher!

IRENE: Little higher!

[*The parents strain with all their strength to lift* BECKA *high enough to reach her sister.*]

BECKA: Just a tiny bit...[*But they just can't quite get her there.*]

IRENE: I can't lift any...I'm losing my grip!

DEAN: Get on my shoulders, Beck!

[BECKA *slides onto her father's shoulders and frantically looks around for something to grab onto or climb onto. There's nothing! But now* MRS. ROSEN *raises her hands slowly upward...and as she lifts her hands,* DEAN, IRENE, BECKA *also rise, just high enough so that* BECKA *can reach her sister and* BOOMER *can lock her arms around her sister's neck and let loose of the roof and come safely down into her reaching mother's arms.* MRS. ROSEN *moves back several steps.* DEAN *lifts* BECKA *off his shoulders and he and* IRENE *and* BOOMER *fall into a heap, laughing, crying, holding* BOOMER *fiercely.* BECKA *is separated from the three of them, feeling guilty and hurt. She turns to* MRS. ROSEN. MRS. ROSEN *reaches for* BECKA's *face.* BECKA *pulls back.* MRS. ROSEN *insists and moves* BECKA's *mussed hair out of her face. Her bracelets jangle melodiously.* MRS. ROSEN *glances past* BECKA *at us.*]

MRS. ROSEN: Yet, Christmas still approaches us at the speed of time. [*She makes that sound to imitate the speed and is illuminated by light.*] F. sted mon canta. And such a long way still to go. [*Hands raised in supplication toward us, the lights fade black around her.*]

SCENE 6

In the living room, BOOMER *is wrapped in a blanket on the couch, holding a stuffed animal, her parents around her.*

 BECKA *sits on the stairs, in her sleeping tee-shirt, an old softball shirt of* DEAN's, *listening.*

 MRS. ROSEN *is at the breakfast counter, also listening.*

BOOMER: How did you know I needed help?

DEAN: I didn't. I just suddenly felt I had to come back to apologize to Mommy and I saw you.

IRENE: You were coming back to apologize?

DEAN: Don't hold it against me.

IRENE: That's why I was on my way outside. I wanted to try to catch you to say I was sorry.

[*These admissions, though, seem to make them uncomfortable, so they have to make light.*]

IRENE AND DEAN: Naaaa!

BOOMER: Oh, Mommy and Daddy, I wish Santa could be real and come here and make Becka and those kids shut up.

[IRENE *and* DEAN *put their arms around* BOOMER *and come face to face around the little girl's body.*]

IRENE: You never know what might happen, baby.

BOOMER: Can I fall asleep down here?

IRENE: Sure. [DEAN *and* IRENE *get up.*]

DEAN: Good night, sweetheart. [IRENE *and* DEAN *pass* BECKA.] Goodnight, Rebecca.

BECKA: Night.

[*Her parents go out the front door.* BECKA *peeks through the window in the computer alcove.*]

IRENE: Let's not kid ourselves that because we had a moment of conciliation our problems are over.

DEAN: No, let's not do that. [*A beat.*] Well. I should be getting home, or to my apartment, or to whatever it's fair to the place where I have most of my clothes now and where I sleep. Good night.

IRENE: Good night.

[BECKA *watches her parents, locked eye to eye. Then* DEAN *heads off-stage.* IRENE *watches him disappear.* BECKA *goes into the kitchen, passing* MRS. ROSEN *at the breakfast counter, smiling her smile.*]

BECKA: How come you smile like you know something nobody else does?

MRS. ROSEN: Perhaps because I do. So, you don't figure if there's a Santa Claus he has a computer?

[BECKA *returns with a box of cookies.*]

BECKA:. Sure, *if* there was a Santa Claus, which there isn't, he'd have a computer. Everybody has a computer.

[IRENE *enters, starts making a shopping list for Christmas dinner.*]

IRENE: Whenever you'd like to go to sleep, I'll show you to your room and the bath.

MRS. ROSEN: Oh, I am too old to bother with sleeping and bathing. If I begin to smell, just tell me and I'll spritz myself with perfume.

IRENE: [*To* BECKA.] Can we talk?

BECKA: Judgmental or non-judgmental?

IRENE: [*To* BECKA.] I need to know what Santa's supposed to bring Boomer, so I can decide whether to get it or not.

BECKA: She wants about fifty things.

IRENE: What does she want the most?

[BECKA *shrugs moodily.*]

MRS. ROSEN: One of those electronic do-dads on which a talented person can compose music.

IRENE: Just a little synthesizer, ya mean? Too expensive this Christmas.

MRS. ROSEN: Not to Santa Claus.

IRENE: Right.

BECKA: [*Looking at list.*] We're not having turkey and goose Christmas dinner?

IRENE: There's only the three of us—and Mrs. Rosen—and our budget's a little thin, so we're having chicken.

BECKA: So, tell your husband to give you some more.

IRENE: "My husband" and I have an agreement about money, so I'm sorry but I'm not about to—

BECKA: Excellent! Merry Christmas and pass the cranberry sauce and chicken.

IRENE: *Stop this!*

BECKA: *I don't have to if I don't want to!*

[BECKA *and her mother eye to eye a moment.*]

IRENE: Would you excuse us a moment, Mrs. Rosen?

MRS. ROSEN: Again? Of course. [MRS. ROSEN *goes into the living room. Listens.*]

IRENE: We're in a very scary period, baby, as a family, as individuals. I feel like we're, all of us, losing things–feelings and beliefs and each other.

And I pretend I do but I really don't know what to do about it. Know what I mean?

[BECKA *shakes her head no.*]

I think you do. When Daddy first moved out, you propped me up. Now you don't even talk to me.

BECKA: Yeah, well, then I thought you really were living your life the best you could. Now...[*A beat.*]

IRENE: I miss you, Rebecca.

[*A beat and* BECKA *goes into the living room. The lights are dim, the Christmas tree lights throwing eerie colors.* MRS. ROSEN *steps out of the shadows, startling* BECKA.]

MRS. ROSEN: Wanna play a game?

[*The Christmas lights make* MRS. ROSEN'*s face look ethereal.* BECKA *shakes her head, moves quickly to the computer alcove.* BOOMER *sleeps on the couch.*]

MRS. ROSEN: [*Cont'd.*] Come on—little game of chance. What have you got to lose?

[BECKA *looks at* MRS. ROSEN. *The challenge in her eyes goes deep.* BECKA *flips her computer on. Then flips on the computer lamp, again throwing eerie light on the two of them.*]

MRS. ROSEN: [*Cont'd.*] Prove to me there's no Santa Claus by proving to me that he *doesn't* have a computer.

BECKA: I got better things to do than that.

MRS. ROSEN: Gotta become monotonous playing it safe. No risk. Come on. Prove to me there's no Santa Claus. Betcha can't. Betcha you're not good enough on the computer. Betcha ten silver dollars against ten cents.

BECKA: Where you gonna get ten silver dollars?

MRS. ROSEN: Show me your dime, I'll show you my silver dollars.

[BECKA *pulls a dime out of her computer table, holds it out to* MRS. ROSEN. MRS. ROSEN *put it into her hand, closes the hand, then opens it. The dime's gone. She reaches for* BECKA'*s nose and begins to "milk it." Silver dollars start to fall from* BECKA'*s nose into Mrs Rosen's hand. She sets the stack on the table, reproduces the dime, sets it next to the silver dollars.*]

BECKA: Elementary school magic.

[MRS. ROSEN *waits. And finally, accepting that she's in the midst of some wondrous, mysterious adventure,* BECKA *focuses on the task of proving there's no* SANTA CLAUS.] All right, lady, you got a bet.

MRS. ROSEN: Excellent! But these machines are such a mystery to me. Tell me, if I am not too stupid, what you're going to do to disprove the existence of Santa Claus.

BECKA: Try to open his window.

MRS. ROSEN: Open his window?

BECKA: Access his computer.

MRS. ROSEN: Ah–like open a window and look into his world?

BECKA: You got it.

MRS. ROSEN: What are you going to do first?

BECKA: Tell you to leave me alone so I can get this over with.

MRS. ROSEN: Of course. [*She starts away.*]

BECKA: Hey.

[MRS. ROSEN *stops, the flickering tree lights illuminating her face in an otherworldly way.*]

BECKA: [*Cont'd.*] How come I think I know you?

MRS. ROSEN: Perhaps we have met in another place and time. Or perhaps in one another's dreams.

[BECKA *snorts, dismissing such talk, but her eyes linger on* MRS. ROSEN *a moment, then she pounds the keys. Her modem clacks away. At the breakfast counter* IRENE *stares, munching a carrot, trying to control the desire to sob, to scream. She whacks the carrot against the counter, against her head, throws it down, grabs the box of cookies* BECKA *brought out, grabs several and stuffs them furiously in her mouth. Then, senses someone behind her. Turns. Startled to find* MRS. ROSEN *taking in her behavior,* IRENE *tries to keep the mouthful of cookie contained.*]

IRENE: [*Mouth full.*] Cookie?

MRS. ROSEN: No thank you.

[IRENE *is stuck with the cookies in her mouth.*]

MRS. ROSEN: [*Cont'd.*] Give!

[IRENE *turns to find* MRS. ROSEN'*s hand extended to her mouth with a handkerchief. Does she want* IRENE *to spit the cookies into the handkerchief?*]

MRS. ROSEN: [*Cont'd.*] Spit.

[IRENE *does*. MRS. ROSEN *flicks a crumb from* IRENE's *mouth, discards the wad of cookie in the handkerchief.*]

IRENE: Thank you—I'm trying to lose weight.

MRS. ROSEN: Why try? Why not just do it?

IRENE: Do you treat everyone like they aren't terribly bright or over the age of ten?

MRS. ROSEN: Well, you know, actually, yes, I think I do. [*A beat.*] I would like to contribute something to the Christmas dinner. [*By the look of her it seems highly unlikely she can afford to contribute.*]

IRENE: Absolutely not, you're a guest in our house. Things will work out just fine—I'll take a little from here, put it there. Maybe if I...

IRENE AND MRS. ROSEN: ...really stuff that chicken. [MRS. ROSEN *and* IRENE *connect a beat, smile at each other.*]

MRS. ROSEN: It's occurred to me a time or two that maybe we should never get involved with other people. Never care. And, of course, eat whatever we want.

IRENE: Sounds wonderful. A life of aloneness, cynicism, and gluttony. Mm-yum-yum! [*She picks up her carrot. Snaps off a bite.*] There's something very peculiar about you.

MRS. ROSEN: No—really? In what way?

IRENE: I feel that I know you—or that you know me. Or something.

MRS. ROSEN: Hmph. Ever been to New Guinea?

[*Embarrassed now to seem so vulnerable,* IRENE *ducks her head to her shopping list.*]

IRENE: No.

MRS. ROSEN: Des Moines?

IRENE: I didn't mean we knew each other in literal terms.

MRS. ROSEN: Ah—silly me. I can be so literal sometimes. You're talking quasi-spiritual and speculative.

[MRS. ROSEN *quickly, easily kisses* IRENE *on the forehead. Startled,* IRENE *pulls back.*]

IRENE: Don't do that—why did you do that?

MRS. ROSEN: Well, I don't know. I don't know what came over me.

IRENE: Look, I'm not ten years old. I'm sorry I said anything. I assure you

I don't need your whatever you think you're offering. I'm sure you understand.

MRS. ROSEN: Perfectly. Thank you for clarifying what was previously a very murky matter. Why don't I leave you to figure everything out all by yourself.

[IRENE *chomps aggressively down on her carrot, lowers her head to the shopping list, touches at her leaking eyes.* MRS. ROSEN *goes back into the living room. In the computer alcove,* BECKA *punches in a command. The screen flashes, illuminating her face weirdly. She smiles smugly.* MRS. ROSEN *touches* BECKA *gently, startling her.*]

MRS. ROSEN: [*Cont'd.*] So, what stunning lack of proof so far?

BECKA: There's no North Pole in telephone information.

MRS. ROSEN: Mm-hmm.

BECKA: There's no North Pole listed on any bulletin board I'm tied into.

MRS. ROSEN: Mm-hmm.

BECKA: No Santa Claus listed in Alaska.

MRS. ROSEN: Perhaps we should exclude other names by which he might be listed somewhere.

BECKA: Already tried all the other names.

MRS. ROSEN: Of course. Like what?

[BECKA *punches in a command. The list comes up on screen.*]

MRS. ROSEN: [*Cont'd.*] Santa Claus. S. Claus. St. Nicholas. St. Nick. Nick Claus. Ho-Ho Claus. Ha-*Ha* Claus. Hmm. Didn't know any other names for Santa Claus?

BECKA: If I did, I woulda tried 'em, don'cha figure?

MRS. ROSEN: Undoubtedly. Nevertheless, in the spirit of thoroughness, we must exclude all names now, mustn't we? We need another source of information besides your obviously copious knowledge of the subject.

[BECKA *eyeballs her, then snaps a book into* MRS. ROSEN'S *hands.*]

MRS. ROSEN: [*Cont'd.*] Accessible Computer Information Numbers. Ah yes, excellent. What should we look under?

BECKA: Liburies.

MRS. ROSEN: A Libury's a good idea. Except it's library, isn't it—spelled l-i-b-r-a-r-y.

BECKA: I always say libury.

MRS. ROSEN: Which still, amazingly enough, doesn't make it right. [*Without a glance at the index.*] Page 62. Though I must confess I like libury. We bury our lies there and seek the truth. Is that what you had in mind?

BECKA: Nope, sure wasn't.

MRS. ROSEN: I didn't think so. [*She sticks a finger in the book: Page 62.*] Ah, here we are: a library information number. Available until ten o'clock at night. Well, we'll have to continue in the morning, won't we?

BECKA: Why don't you just admit I'm gonna win, gimme the ten silver dollars, and forget it.

MRS. ROSEN: You want to do that? Take them, we'll forget the bet.

[*A beat and* BECKA *snaps the machine off and starts away.* MRS. ROSEN *stops her with a touch.*]

MRS. ROSEN: [*Cont'd.*] Nersay fest nersan.

BECKA: What language is that?

MRS. ROSEN: Mine.

BECKA: What's that mean—what you said?

MRS. ROSEN: It means: Learn what must be learned. Arap key kon. While there is time.

BECKA: Time for—

[MRS. ROSEN *puts a finger to* BECKA's *lips, silencing her.*]

MRS. ROSEN: Sshh. Sometimes don't talk. Sometimes, only listen. And look for signs. And think. It gives your vocal chords a rest, to say nothing of the ears of those near and dear. Sleep, dream, awaken.

[MRS. ROSEN *moves her hand to* BECKA's *cheek, rivets* BECKA *with her eyes a moment, then lets her go.* BECKA *heads upstairs, leaving* MRS. ROSEN *looking after her.* MRS. ROSEN *stands in the eerie reflection of the lights from the tiny Christmas tree, staring up toward the girls' room.* IRENE *comes from the kitchen.* MRS. ROSEN *steps back into the shadows.* IRENE *turns off the Christmas tree lights, starts to awaken* BOOMER, *then covers her carefully and leaves her sleeping on the couch. She goes upstairs. When* IRENE *has passed,* MRS. ROSEN *steps out of the shadows. She speaks to us.*]

MRS. ROSEN: [*Cont'd.*] Estupee, estupai, estupan. There was hope, there is hope, there will always be hope. During the short recess we are about to take in this human drama, let us all repeat that to ourselves.

Perhaps there will be some force in our united wish that these human beings will improve. Estupee, estupai, estupan. [*She looks at the Christmas tree. The lights flicker to life and, in fact, begin to twinkle, to change colors, becoming solid, varied, a different solid color.* MRS. ROSEN *stands in front of the little tree, wiggling her fingers at the tree, seeming to make the lights become a rainbow of sparkling colors.* MRS. ROSEN *goes to the computer, stands in front of it and holds her hands out to it as if beckoning it to some conspiracy.*] Ohrem. Ohrem mansu. Sensi! [*The unspoken translation: Talk. Talk to me. Please!*] *And now, without her touching the machinery, the printer begins to print and the screen throws beams of multicolored light around her. Lightning fills the windows. Thunder rolls and claps. A howling wind blows, sending* MRS. ROSEN'*s hair out in ribbons behind her.*] Elvo! Sutam elvo! Domito, elvo! [*The unspoken translation: Love! Real love! Come now, love!*] *The beams of light envelope her and then the stage becomes black. Except for a light on* BOOMER, *who sits up, staring at all of this in amazement. Her hand comes to her mouth and then we fade to black.*]

[*Intermission*]

ACT TWO

SCENE 1

MRS. ROSEN, *dressed in a beautiful 40s ensemble, stands outside, holding a full grocery bag in hand.*

MRS. ROSEN: You're back, I'm back, the sun is up, the final day in our drama begins. Once again: estupee, estupai, estupan.

[*She walks into the foyer...as* BECKA *comes downstairs into the living room, heading for the kitchen.* BECKA *stops. What she sees is a huge Christmas tree which, overnight, has replaced the tiny one.*]

MRS. ROSEN: [*Cont'd.*] Good morning, Rebecca.

[*Startled,* BECKA *turns.* MRS. ROSEN *heads for the kitchen.* BECKA *follows.*]

MRS. ROSEN: [*Cont'd.*] Shouldn't you be at your computer, contacting the "libury'?"

BECKA: Coupla minutes. Where did this tree come from?

MRS. ROSEN: Oh, that little one just grew up during the night. It's the water, I think.

BECKA: I buy that.

[MRS. ROSEN *sets the bags down on the breakfast counter. During the following,* MRS. ROSEN *unloads the bag. The bag seems bottomless—the amount of food that emerges is quite extraordinary. Occupied with getting her juice and talking to and wondering about* MRS. ROSEN, BECKA *doesn't notice the incredible mountain of food for a while.*]

BECKA: [*Cont'd.*] You did the tree.

MRS. ROSEN: "Did the tree"?

BECKA: Made it grow...I

MRS. ROSEN: Make a tree grow? I'm afraid not. The most I've ever done in that area is grow an ugly little thing on my nose here once that I had surgically removed.

[BECKA *doesn't crack a smile.*]

MRS. ROSEN: [*Cont'd.*] Rebecca, don't you ever laugh and act silly?

BECKA: Laugh—sure. Act silly—what for?

MRS. ROSEN: Do you know how to stop being such a somber, sober, serious young lady?

BECKA: I'm not a somber, sober, serious young lady.

MRS. ROSEN: —She said somberly, soberly, and seriously. Listen to me: You're a sensitive, intelligent, perfectly terrific young lady—whudduya wanna be such a pain in the behind for?

BECKA: I'm also not a sensitive, intelligent and perfectly terrific young-lady either.

MRS. ROSEN: Excuse me, my error—how would you define yourself?.

BECKA: I'm a somber, sober, serious, humorless four-eyed dork—that what you wanna hear? I'm a stupid, insensitive, bookworm of a nerd! How's that?

MRS. ROSEN: Rebecca Waller, sit down! Right here!

BECKA: Who're you telling to sit down?

MRS. ROSEN: [*Ever so politely.*] I don't know—who do you think I'm telling to sit down?

[*A momentary standoff...then* BECKA *sits.*]

MRS. ROSEN: [*Cont'd.*] Look at me while I address you.

[*A beat.* BECKA *does.*]

MRS. ROSEN: [*Cont'd.*] Now, listen to me, while there is time...

BECKA: You keep saying that! I hate it when people keep saying the same thing over and over. Time for what?

MRS. ROSEN: Time for what needs to happen to happen.

BECKA: What needs to happen?

MRS. ROSEN: What needs to happen is what needs to happen. When it happens, you will know.

BECKA: How come you know what needs to happen?

MRS. ROSEN: How come? Because I do. Not everything is something children need to know just because they do not like not knowing. But here is something you can know. So have the sense to listen. When we are in pain, we often do mean things to each other. Even sisters, even fathers and mothers, husbands and wives who share a home, sometimes hurt each other deeply. But we have to know when to stop blaming each other and even when to stop blaming ourselves. To be a living human person is to feel hurt...and not prayers or wishes, not gifts of toys or money, or any other thing but the love of other living human persons can make the hurt go away. Consider what I have said. Listen with this...[*She touches* BECKA'*s head.*]...while you listen with this. [*And now she touches* BECKA'*s heart. And* BECKA *looks her in the eyes —something has penetrated...but then breaks away and storms out of the kitchen and to the computer alcove. She and her mother come face to face momentarily.*]

IRENE AND BECKA: Morning. [BECKA *ducks her head, sits with determination at the computer.* IRENE *continues toward the kitchen, sees the tree, stops, then continues on to the breakfast counter...where she finds an incredible amount of food.*]

IRENE: Where did all this food come from?

MRS. ROSEN: Oh, I just picked up a few things. [MRS. ROSEN *pulls out a goose, which she hands to* IRENE.]

IRENE: Where did you get all this?

MRS. ROSEN: Oh, at the...[MRS. ROSEN *points vaguely.*]

IRENE: How did you get there and back?

MRS. ROSEN: It really wasn't that difficult.

IRENE: You transported all these groceries and that tree out there?

MRS. ROSEN: Oh no, that tree is your old one. It grew overnight. It's the water.

[MRS. ROSEN *pulls out a very long French bread, which she hands to* IRENE, *who is staring most peculiarly at her.*]

MRS. ROSEN: [*Cont'd.*] Please, let us be more selective about what we dwell on and what we simply accept. What is here is here; I went, I came back; there was a small tree, now there's a big tree. Accept! Things are waiting to be lovingly chopped and minced and parboiled and baked in preparation for tomorrow's Christmas dinner.

[BOOMER *comes downstairs. She stares at the Christmas tree...then goes into the computer alcove.*]

BOOMER: I hate you and I'm not talking to you, but can I tell you something?

BECKA: Uh-uh.

BOOMER: It's really important.

BECKA: *This* is more important than anything you have to tell me.

[BECKA *remains fixed on the computer.* BOOMER *doesn't move, so* BECKA *looks at her.*]

BECKA: [*Cont'd.*] What?

BOOMER: Last night, when I was sleeping on the couch...[*Faced with actually telling someone what she thinks she saw last night,* BOOMER *punts.*]. Skip it.

[BOOMER *goes to the breakfast counter where* MRS. ROSEN *is sipping coffee.* IRENE *is writing out a list of things to do today.*]

MRS. ROSEN: Good morning, dear.

IRENE: Ready to go, baby?

[BOOMER *nods, but her attention's on* MRS. ROSEN.]

IRENE: [*Cont'd.*] What's the matter?

[BOOMER *shakes her head.*]

IRENE: [*Cont'd.*] All right, we're off to the mall to buy something to give Daddy tomorrow. Let me get my coat and we'll roll out. [IRENE *goes to the foyer for* BOOMER'*s jacket and her own coat and purse, leaving* MRS. ROSEN *and* BOOMER *locked eye to eye.*]

BOOMER: Last night, I think I had a dream.

MRS. ROSEN: Oh?

BOOMER: I dreamed you made that little Christmas tree change into that new big one by magic.

MRS. ROSEN: Magic—my my.

BOOMER: Are you a magic person?

[*Before* BOOMER *can get a definitive answer to that one...*IRENE *returns with her coat on and purse over her shoulder. She holds* BOOMER*'s jacket open for her to put on.*]

IRENE: Come on, baby, let's go.

BOOMER: Daddy's not gonna dress up as Santa and try to trick me tonight, is he, Mommy?

IRENE: Certainly not.

BOOMER: Okay, good, because that would really steam me. [BOOMER *eyes* MRS. ROSEN *as she exits through the kitchen with her mother.*]

BECKA: [*Calling.*] Mrs. Rosen!

[MRS. ROSEN *goes to the computer alcove.* BECKA *indicates the screen.* MRS. ROSEN *looks over her shoulder.*]

MRS. ROSEN: Ah: "Other Names for Santa Claus. Mr. Chub, Capt. White Whiskers, Fatty. Sweetcheeks"—Oh, I like that!–"Kriss Kringle, Ole Sled Head..." [*A beat.*] Hmm. Kriss Kringle. Heard that one before?

BECKA: Sure, I guess, yeah, when I was a kid.

MRS. ROSEN: Yes, a Dutch name. The Dutch come from the Netherlands. Which is very near Sweden and Finland. Which are very near the North Pole. And do you know what Kriss Kringle means in English?

BECKA: Large obese individual?

MRS. ROSEN: Christ child. Isn't that curious? [*A beat.*] While you prove that none of these people can be located, I'll just amuse myself. Call me as the evidence continues to mount hopelessly against me.

[BECKA *turns back to her machine...and* MRS. ROSEN *steps back as lights cross fade to...*]

SCENE 2

That night. The living room. IRENE *and* MRS. ROSEN *decorating the tree.* BECKA *at the computer.* BOOMER *sits at the piano and plays her melody, playing only the right hand, her stuffed animal in her left hand, held close.*

MRS. ROSEN: Boomer, did you play the song you wrote for your mother and sister and your friends?

BOOMER: What song I wrote?

IRENE: Did you finish your song?

BOOMER: Uh-uh.

MRS. ROSEN: But I heard you play it.

BOOMER: When?

MRS. ROSEN: Why, after I gave you my poem.

BOOMER: What poem?

MRS. ROSEN: Oh you! I thought it was only elderly dodos like me who are so forgetful. [*To* IRENE *and* BECKA.] It just so happens I wrote a Christmas poem, of all things, and Boomer said she'd write music to go with it. But now I see she's just a teensy eensy weensy bit shy about singing it.

[*Fascinated,* BOOMER *stares at* MRS. ROSEN...*who magically produces a small sheet of paper which becomes larger as she unfolds it. It has words and music written on it.*]

MRS. ROSEN: [*Cont'd.*] Here it is, you little silly, you!

[*Ever more fascinated,* BOOMER *looks at the sheet of paper.*]

BOOMER: It's my writing.

IRENE: If you wrote it, whose writing would it be?

BOOMER: Mine.

IRENE: My thinking exactly.

MRS. ROSEN: Gather round, everybody.

[IRENE *and* BECKA *come close.*]

MRS. ROSEN: [*Cont'd.*] Feel like. being silly, Rebecca?

BECKA: [*A beat.*] Yeah, .sure, I could be silly.

MRS. ROSEN: You and your mother and I will sing the do-wahs and shoo-bie-doops.

IRENE: [*To* BOOMER.] Go on, baby, it's almost eight o'clock. [MRS. ROSEN *pulls an old pocket watch out, glances at it.*]

MRS. ROSEN: We have exactly the right amount of time.

[*On the roof, we see a figure who appears to be* SANTA CLAUS. *He almost falls down the chimney, trying to situate himself for his descent.*]

DEAN/SANTA: Whoooooooaaaa!

[*We expect the song to be good. It's not—it's terrible.* BOOMER's *ballad melody has been given a raucous rap rhythm.* BOOMER *plays and* MRS. ROSEN *sings and dances the rap, backed up by* BECKA *and* IRENE, *who dance and do all the appropriate rap sounds effects.*]

MRS. ROSEN Two, three, four..."Hey, hey, hey/What's the matter with mankind?/Has he got all his brains in his behind?/Is he such a schmoc that he don't reason/That.bein' mean to other people/Ain't the way to show the spirit of the season./Mankind, mankind,/Get it straight, get it right/Or eat liver and onions all of Christmas night!"

[BOOMER *stops playing, leaps away from the piano as if she'd been bitten.*]

BOOMER: Yuck! What a stupid song! Ick! I didn't write this! That's the worst song I ever heard in my life!

BECKA: No, no it's not! It's funny!

BOOMER: Funny?

BECKA: Yeah! And it's supposed to be, isn't it, Mrs. Rosen? It's supposed to be a funny song.

MRS. ROSEN: Yes. Yes, it's supposed to be funny, Rebecca.

BECKA: I knew it! Mommy, Mom, Irene, see, isn't that incredible, I knew it was supposed to be funny!

[IRENE *doesn't quite know what to make of* BECKA's *enormous pleasure. But she smiles and nods and the two come very close to touching.*]

IRENE: Oh yes, sweetheart, and it's so good to see you—

[*But now the doorbell rings.*]

IRENE: [*Cont'd.*] Uh oh, all right, places, everyone.

[IRENE *goes to the front door, leaving* BOOMER *and* BECKA *alone with* MRS. ROSEN. *She smiles at them...and the girls sober up...their eyes boring into her.*]

BECKA AND BOOMER: [*Simultaneously.*] Who are you?

[MRS. ROSEN *touches their cheeks.*]

MRS. ROSEN: Perhaps you will be able to answer that for yourselves. Soon. Let's see.

[IRENE *opens the door to* RON, ALVIN LEE, MANTHING, *and* SARAH.]

RON: Good evening, Mrs. Waller. We're here as requested to see the real Santa Claus. Is the real Santa Claus here yet?

IRENE: Expected momentarily—come in, come in.

ALVIN LEE: [*Shaking hands.*] Good evening, ma'am.

IRENE: Hello, Alvin Lee. In here, everyone.

[IRENE *leads the way into the living room.* ALVIN LEE *wants* BECKA *to acknowledge him; he kind of leans her way and tips his cowboy hat.*]

ALVIN LEE: Evening, Rebecca.

[BECKA, *confused, distracted, nods.*]

IRENE: Please, sit anywhere with a good view of the fire-place.

[RON, SARAH, MANTHING *and* ALVIN LEE *move to the couch.*]

IRENE: [*Cont'd.*] Is it eight o'clock yet?

RON: Seventy-fifty-nine and fifty-six seconds, Greenwich mean time. Fifty-seven, fifty-eight, fifty-nine...

[BOOMER *looks at* BECKA,. *who looks at* RON, *who winks at* BECKA, *who doesn't wink back. On the roof,* SANTA *gets ready to disappear down the abyss of the chimney.*]

DEAN/SANTA: Ho-ho-ho!

IRENE: Well now, what was that?

[BOOMER *leaps to the fireplace, peers up it.* ALVIN LEE *can't help himself and he does the same.*]

DEAN/SANTA: Where's that good little Boomer Waller? I want to talk to her. Ho-ho-ho!

BOOMER: I see him, I see him!

IRENE: Boomer, it's Santa!

ALVIN LEE: It is Santa! .

IRENE: Santa's come to see you, baby.

BOOMER: Becka, it's Santa!

DEAN/SANTA: Here comes Santa down the chimney! [DEAN/SANTA *starts down the chimney.*]

BOOMER AND ALVIN LEE: [*Reporting to the others.*] He's coming down the chimney!

DEAN/SANTA: *Oh boy, here I come. Ho-ho...*[*Silence. A beat.*]

RON: Gee, I wonder what happened to the other "ho"?

[BOOMER *and* ALVIN LEE *look up the chimney.*].

BOOMER AND ALVIN LEE: He's stuck!

DEAN/SANTA: Ho-ho-ho! Boy, SANTA must have gained some weight since last year or this chimney shrank. Ho-ho...[*First a lone boot drops to the hearth...then* DEAN/SANTA *crashes onto the hearth, practically landing in the laps of* BOOMER *and* ALVIN LEE, *his beard hanging off his ear.*]

DEAN: Well, hello, everyone. Meeerrrry Christmas.

[BOOMER *peers at him a moment, then strips the beard off*]

BOOMER: Did Mommy rent you for the evening, Daddy?

DEAN: No, no, I did this free of charge.

RON: Gee, I'm surprised he fell; I kinda figured he'd rise. Huh, pals?

SRARH: I certainly anticipated that he would rise, Ronnie.

MANTHING: I figured he'd rise way up!

IRENE: I'm sorry, we were just trying to...

BOOMER: Help.

DEAN....help. Yeah.

[RON *is trying to keep from dissolving in hysterics.*]

BECKA: It's not funny, Ronald!

[RON *turns to look at* BECKA.]

BECKA: [*Cont'd.*] My father crashes down a stupid chimney and you laugh because now my little sister knows for sure there's no Santa Claus! Don't you know,...don't you know it's Christmas?

[IRENE *starts instinctively for her child...but* DEAN *puts a hand on her arm and stops her.* IRENE *reaches for the hand that touches her and clutches it.*]

BECKA: [*Cont'd.*] I mean, Christmas is supposed to be about a...a...a spirit! It's supposed to be about...about caring, about...love...[*Lost, reeling in pain.*]...and I don't know why I did what I did to my sister or how to bring my family back together again...[*A beat.*]...and I'm just so ashamed.

[BECKA *backs away, turns, and exits the house through the front door. This time it's* DEAN *who starts instinctively for the door...and* IRENE *who stops him. A beat.*]

IRENE: Well, kids, thank you for coming. Good night. And Merry Christmas.

RON: And a very Merry Christmas to you, too, Mrs. Waller.

[RON *exits, followed by* MANTHING *and* SARAH.]

ALVIN LEE: 'Scuse me, Miz Waller, ma'am. I never meant to ruin

Christmas for your little gal, ma'am. I just sorta went along like a... like a coward 'cause I wanted these guys here to tell me I'm okay or somethin', I guess; but, I'm real awful sorry, ma'am.

[*He holds out his hand for a shake.* IRENE *takes the hand.*]

IRENE: Thank you, Alvin Lee. But you could have asked me and I would have been happy to tell you you're more than okay.

ALVIN LEE: Really?

IRENE: Really.

ALVIN LEE:. Oh. Well, thank you, ma'am. [ALVIN LEE *tips his hat to* BOOMER, *shakes with* DEAN.] Merry Christmas, Dr. Waller. [*Tips his hat to* MRS. ROSEN.] Evenin'.

[ALVIN LEE *exits.* BECKA *is in the shadows of the tree.* RON *shoves* ALVIN LEE *in the chest.*]

RON: You made a big mistake, *Al*vin. You're out, your persona au gratin around me!

MANTHING: You're au gratin, Al!

[RON *starts away but* ALVIN LEE *suddenly grabs his wrist, spins* RON, *and has him in a behind-the-back armlock, bending him over in pain.*]

ALVIN LEE: I didn't make a mistake. You made the mistake. You stink! You're a mean boy and that's no good. Now, get outta here. [ALVIN LEE *shoves* RON *along.*] Go on, git!

[RON *heads off, followed by* SARAH *and* MANTHING. ALVIN LEE *finds himself face to face with* BECKA. *In the living room,* IRENE, DEAN, BOOMER *watch through a window.* MRS. ROSEN *behind them.*]

ALVIN LEE: [*Cont'd.*] That was beautiful what you said in there, Rebecca.

BECKA: Thank you. I like what you just said. [*A beat—eyes deflecting hither and yon.*]

ALVIN LEE: Well, g'night. Rebecca. [*He offers his hand.*]

BECKA: G'night, Alvin Lee.

[*Their hands meet in a handshake that's really more, that's really right there on the edge of hand-holding.*]

IRENE: [*In the living room.*] Well, whudduya say we finish decorating the tree and make some cocoa with diet marshmallows...

[*She's looking at* DEAN *in his suit and can't help herself. She starts to laugh. She clamps her hand across her mouth. Hypersensitive,* DEAN *reacts.*]

DEAN: May I suggest that the next time you plan something like this you at least check the circumference of the flue.

IRENE: [*Biting her lip.*] Me?

[IRENE *bursts out laughing.* BOOMER *misreads it.*]

BOOMER: You think it's funny that Daddy crashed down the chimney and made a fool of himself?.

IRENE: [*Howling.*] Oh, no, baby.

BOOMER: Then how come you're laughing like that?

IRENE: Because it's been so long since I saw Daddy look so wonderfully, properly, lovably ridiculous.

[DEAN *looks at himself...and he begins to laugh too,* BOOMER *starts to laugh.* BECKA *walks in the door, smiling. Looks at these three people, laughing hysterically.*]

IRENE: [*Cont'd.*] You're right. I should have checked the circumference of the flue. I'm sorry.

DEAN: Na, I'm sorry. I stuffed the suit too full of pillows. I suppose I thought there was an inverse relationship between guilt and girth.

BOOMER: What's that mean?

IRENE: I have no idea.

DEAN: Well, it means I—

IRENE: And let's not analyze it.

DEAN: Let's not.

[*She smiles her affection on* DEAN...*who sees* BECKA. *The laughter dies away.*]

DEAN: [*Cont'd.*] You all right, sweetheart?

[BECKA *nods.* BOOMER *moves toward her.*]

BOOMER: Thanks for sticking up for me.

[BECKA *nods.*]

BOOMER: [*Cont'd.*] If you know there's no Santa, I can too, 'cuz I wanna grow up to be just like you. I love you.

[BOOMER *hugs* BECKA. *A beat...and* BECKA *returns the embrace ferociously.* MRS. ROSEN *drifts past* DEAN, *singing quietly.*]

MRS. ROSEN: "What's the matter with mankind? Does he have all his brains in his behind?"

DEAN: I keep thinking I know you.

MRS. ROSEN: Very odd.

BOOMER: So, now could you and Daddy make up, Mommy? [*A beat. During the following,* MRS. ROSEN. *slips away.*] I don't wanna be a whud-duya call it—a tastistic from a broken home.

IRENE: Statistic.

BOOMER: Yeah. I want us to not get divorced and not stop loving each other.

DEAN: Nobody stopped loving anybody. I think Mommy and I were paying so much attention to people *outside* our house that we were kind of ignoring the people inside our house.

BOOMER: Do you agree, Mommy?

IRENE: I gotta admit that makes a lotta sense to me.

DEAN: We hope you'll both give us a chance to earn your forgiveness.

BOOMER: I will, Daddy, I'll let you earn my forgiveness. Will you, Becka? [*Everyone looks at* BECKA. *A beat.* BECKA *studies her father and then her mother a moment, as if investigating with her eyes their very souls.*]

BECKA: I'll give it a shot. [*A beat.*] Dad, last night you said you remembered something from when you were a little kid and I wouldn't listen.

DEAN: Yes.

BECKA: What did you remember?

DEAN: I remembered that little scientific-brained Dean Waller ruined Christmas when he was eight for his little brother and sister. And there was some distant relative or friend of the family...I can't quite remember who she was exactly—but she tried to make me see the error of what I'd done, but I was too smart and, in our family, for as long as we were all together, Christmas was never...was never what you said it should be. And I realize that even as a grown-up, I've stopped believing in...well, in certain kinds of dreams; and that's not good.

[BECKA *and* BOOMER *look at each other.*]

BOOMER: What'd the strange lady look like?

DEAN: Who? Oh. Well, I don't remember exactly, but she sort of looked like...

BECKA AND BOOMER: Mrs. Rosen?

DEAN: Well, sort of, yeah. But she must've been at least as old as Mrs. Rosen way back in the dark ages of my youth. She'd have to be close to eighty years old now.

[BECKA *and* BOOMER *just look at each other as we cross fade to...*]

SCENE 3

Moonlight outside. The snow falls harder now.
The house is dark but for the warm glow of the blinking Christmas tree lights. Suddenly lightning flashes and there's a sharp clap of thunder as a glorious light floods through the windows into the house. And now BECKA *comes quickly down the stairs into the foyer. She looks into the living room for* MRS. ROSEN. *Doesn't see her. She runs into the kitchen. No* MRS. ROSEN *there. She runs back into the living room to find* MRS. ROSEN *standing there.*

MRS. ROSEN: Looking for me, Rebecca?

BECKA: [*Whispering.*] Mrs. Rosen, Mrs. Rosen, c'mere! [BECKA *runs to the computer alcove, flips on her computer.* MRS. ROSEN *follows.*]

MRS. ROSEN: What are you doing? I thought Boomer decided it was all right that there is no Santa Claus. Forget this business with the machine. You win the twenty dollars.

BECKA: No—I had a dream.

MRS. ROSEN: I see. And what happened in your dream?

BECKA: You came to me. You said call Kriss Kringle, he has something to tell me.

MRS. ROSEN: Hmph.

BECKA: But I woke up before you could tell me his area code and phone number. What's his area code and phone number? [BECKA *throws the switch on the modem.*]

MRS. ROSEN: I am sure I do not know. What are you doing?

BECKA: I switched my modem to 1200-baud and now using full—

MRS. ROSEN: —Using full duplex and mark parity, you're going to write an application program with a special algorithm to search for the correct byte sequence.

BECKA: I thought you didn't know anything about computers.

MRS. ROSEN: Believe me, I am only guessing. That process could take you all night. Even if there were a Santa Claus and you did get in touch with him, tomorrow morning would be too late. Maybe you should take one really good guess. What if his area code had something to do with him or with Christmas?

BECKA: Yeah...like what?

MRS. ROSEN: Well, let's see—what month is this?

BECKA: December!

MRS. ROSEN: Just as I suspected. What number month of the year is it?

BECKA: Twelve!

MRS. ROSEN: Number twelve. And what day is Christmas?

BECKA: Twenty-fifth.

MRS. ROSEN: Hmm. So what would that be? Twelve, twenty-five.

BECKA: 1-2-2-5.

MRS. ROSEN: Did you know you have to dial one first to call long distance. So, let's try 1, then area Code 2-2-5 and then the regular information sequence, 5-5-5, 1-2-1-2.

[BECKA *punches it in. The modem clacks away. The machine flickers sharply, buzzes.* BECKA *looks at the screen, then at* MRS. ROSEN *in wonder.*]

BECKA: "North Pole. Directory of phone numbers!"

MRS. ROSEN: My my my. Can you make the machine show you the names of everyone who has a telephone there?

[BECKA *punches in a command. The machine flickers sharply, buzzes.*]

MRS. ROSEN: [*Cont'd.*] One name! What does that say? I do not have my glasses!

BECKA: "Kringle, Kriss!" Kriss Kringle!

MRS. ROSEN: Quickly, try the number—maybe he hasn't loaded his sleigh and flown off into the sky yet.

[BECKA *punches in the number. The modern clacks away. We hear a number ringing. It rings once, twice, a third time.*]

BECKA: We're too late.

[*And then instead of a fourth ring, the printer starts to print, the wind howls, the light goes crazy.*]

MRS. ROSEN: What does it say?

BECKA: It's some funny language.

MRS. ROSEN: [*Reading.*] "Salla, Rebecca. Desto terrado nela echonio."

BECKA: What does that mean?

MRS. ROSEN: Well, I would only be guessing, of course, but I believe that means: Greetings, Rebecca, I had begun to fear I could not wait for you."

[BECKA *leaps at* MRS. ROSEN, *dances them up and down.*]

BECKA: We did it! We did it! We did it!

MRS. ROSEN: Quickly, yell for your sister.

BECKA: But I'll wake everybody else up.

MRS. ROSEN: Believe me, you will only wake the proper person.

[BECKA *bolts for the stairs and yells.*]

BECKA: Yo, Boomer! [BECKA'*s voice echoes into the distance:* "*Yo,* BOOMER! *Yo,* BOOMER! *Yo,* BOOMER!" *After a moment,* BOOMER *stands at the top of the stairs, holding her stuffed animal. The light in the stairwell is wonderful. As* BOOMER *descends, it's like walking through an illuminated tunnel. In the foyer,* BECKA *meets* BOOMER *as she comes out of the tunnel and leads her into the living room. She watches* MRS. ROSEN *gesture to several areas and the lights change; then she gestures at the Christmas tree and it glows ever more wonderfully.*]

BOOMER: So you are a magic person. What are you doing?

MRS. ROSEN: We are waiting.

BOOMER: What for?

MRS. ROSEN: For someone to arrive.

BOOMER: In the middle of the night—who?

MRS. ROSEN: My son.

[BOOMER *notices* BECKA *at the window.*]

BOOMER: How come you're lookin' at the sky? How's he gettin' here— private jet?

BECKA: Sleigh.

BOOMER: Oh sure. And pulled by eight tiny reindeer, right?

BECKA: Yep.

BOOMER: Are you crazy, that would make her son...

BECKA: Yep.

[BOOMER *is suddenly fully awake. She looks at* MRS. ROSEN, *reads the truth on her face and charges across the room and joins* BECKA *at the window. The sky is clear and full of stars.*]

BOOMER: What happened to the snow?

MRS. ROSEN: It'll begin again soon.

BOOMER: There're no clouds. Look at all the stars. [*To* MRS. ROSEN.] Did you do that?

MRS. ROSEN: It's really not that big a deal. Making a really good grilled cheese sandwich is much harder.

[*Now an eerie sound comes from distant space and there's a strange light that shoots across the sky.*]

MRS. ROSEN: [*Cont'd.*] Outside!

BECKA: Outside!

BOOMER: Outside!

[*They go outside. From the porch they watch the light streak down as it comes around the house. The girls run around the side of the house. The light streaks by again.*]

MRS. ROSEN: Inside!

BECKA: Inside!

BOOMER: Inside!

[*The girls run back in, followed by* MRS. ROSEN.]

MRS. ROSEN: Chimney!

BOOMER: Chimney!

BECKA: Chimney!

[*They run to the chimney…and we watch* SANTA CLAUS *appear in the hearth. For a moment, all we can see are his legs, boots, and the bottom of his glorious coat. The girls stare a moment…until* BOOMER *tip-toes to the fireplace, peers up and…*SANTA *peeks out at her and then emerges fully into the room. The girls jump back.*]

SANTA: Hi, Ma.

MRS. ROSEN: Hello, lumpkin. [MRS. ROSEN *gives* SANTA *a hug and a peck and pinch on the cheek. Turns to the girls.*] What are you doing back there? Come meet my baby. That's Rebecca and that's Boomer, Santa.

SANTA: Come and let me see you. [*The girls creep forward.* BOOMER *touches* SANTA*'s coat, his arm, his shoulder with a tentative, forefinger; then she* *takes* SANTA's *nose between her thumb and forefinger and gives it a reassuring squeeze.* SANTA *takes her nose and gives it a little squeeze.*]

BOOMER: How come you didn't say ho-ho-ho?

SANTA: I've had a bit of a sore throat, so I'm only saying that on my exits.

BOOMER: Oooh.

BECKA: How come you speak English?

SANTA: Oh, I speak whatever language, am whatever color, of whatever faith as the children I come to visit.

BOOMER: When you laugh, does your tummy really shake like a bowl full of jelly?

SANTA: Certainly not! I've been dieting for a hundred and forty-seven years.

BOOMER: You must not be sticking to it, boy.

SANTA: I confess to a certain weakness where sweets are concerned. My mother insists children would like me just as well if I were slim and trim, but I don't know. What do you think?

BOOMER: My mom's on a diet—she could teach you about five thousand ways to make cauliflower. I think you should definitely work on a good bod for next year!

SANTA: Cauliflower...?

BOOMER: Not just, cauliflower.

SANTA: All right—done—I will, I will work on a good bod for next year!

BOOMER: You know what I always wanted to know: Do your reindeer ever go poop on people's roofs?

SANTA: You know, I thought I'd been asked every question there was to ask.

BOOMER: Uh-oh, was that a bad question?

SANTA: To the contrary, a most interesting question.

BOOMER: Oh, good, I was worried there for a second. So what's the answer?

SANTA: Well, no, no they don't ever go poop on people's roofs.

BOOMER: Boy; that's a relief.

SANTA: Yes, yes, it is.

BECKA: Are you Santa Claus or are you Kriss Kringle or St. Nicholas...?

SANTA: The spirits of many people live in me. Mohammed and Moses, Buddha and Confucius and Vishnu and Jesus of Nazareth. And fine people like Mahatma Gandhi and Albert Schweitzer and Mother Teresa and Martin Luther King. And many, many people whose names you've never heard.

BECKA: Why haven't we heard their names?

SANTA: Ah, because they do the fine things that they do, not to be known by name, but simply for the good of other living human persons.

BECKA: But what if you want to be really, really big time, major famous?

SANTA: How many people have to consider you a really, really big time, major excellent human person in order for you to consider yourself famous, Rebecca? Millions? Twelve thousand two hundred and sixteen? Or just one human person who believes passionately that you are a fine and important human person?

BOOMER: Are you the Tooth Fairy and the Easter Bunny?

SANTA: In a sense, yes.

BOOMER: Boy, you must have lotsa outfits.

BECKA: You're all those people, too?

SANTA: No. But what they are makes me what I am. You notice anything similar about all those people—the ones whose names you know?

BOOMER: They all have beards!

BECKA: The Tooth Fairy?

BOOMER: Oh yeah. Uhm, lemme think.

BECKA: They all love us.

SANTA: Yes, that's right.

BOOMER: Oh yeah.

BECKA: And they all dream of a better world.

SANTA: Indeed they do.

BECKA: So people who care the most about other people live in you.

SANTA: Something very much like that, Rebecca.

BECKA: People who love other people no matter what.

SANTA: No matter what.

BECKA: People who...who believe that...who believe no matter what color we are or what language we speak, we're all a family.

SANTA: Yes. [*They are still and close and connected.*] Well, I have other stops to make and the night is passing. I really must go.

MRS. ROSEN: Take your medicine.

SANTA: I will, Mother, I will,

MRS. ROSEN: And I want you to remember what you promised Boomer about working on a good bod.

SANTA: Yes, yes, that too.

[*They kiss cheeks and* SANTA *heads for the fireplace.*]

BOOMER: Didn't you bring us any presents?

SANTA: Sleep. See what the morning brings. [*He fixes on* BECKA.] Well done, Rebecca J. Waller. I take part of you with me, to be part of me, from this moment on, always. [*He kisses* BECKA's *forehead and turns to* BOOMER.] Merry Christmas. [*He takes her nose between his thumb and forefinger again and squeezes as he whispers.*] Ho-ho-ho.

[*The girls touch him lingeringly...and then he steps into the fireplace — lightning and thunder, the lights dim—and a magical light shoots up and out of the chimney and he's gone.*]

BOOMER: We're awake, right?

BECKA: [*To* MRS. ROSEN.] Are we?

MRS. ROSEN: We are awake...or perhaps, at last, all dreaming each other's dream.

BECKA: I want you to have this.

[*She takes a bracelet from her arm and slips it onto* MRS. ROSEN's *arm, and perhaps we understand where all of* MRS. ROSEN's *jewelry comes from.*]

MRS. ROSEN: Thank you.

BOOMER: I want you to have this. [*She gives* MRS. ROSEN *her stuffed animal.*]

MRS. ROSEN: And thank you. [MRS. ROSEN *moves the girls toward the stairs and up toward the bedrooms.*] And now I must go to bed. I haven't slept since the night before Chanukah began—so many families to visit — and I have to be in Kenya tomorrow. [MRS. ROSEN *guides the girls onward.*]

BECKA: Will you go back to live with Santa at the North Pole?

MRS. ROSEN: When there is time, yes.

BOOMER: How come the North Pole?

BECKA: Yeah, how come you didn't settle in Hawaii or Bermuda or some-where?

MRS. ROSEN: At the North Pole there is no traffic, no smog, plenty of fresh fish. And to tell you the truth, we got a very, very good deal there on some real estate.

[*They disappear up the steps as....below, an* ELF *peaks around the edge of the fireplace. Then several other* ELVES *appear. They fill the Christmas tree area with gifts, some wrapped, some open. On the breakfast counter, they put out some food and a floral arrangement and then have to hurry to disappear as the lights cross fade to...*]

SCENE 4

Christmas morning. BOOMER *and* BECKA *hurry down the stairs, amazed.*

BOOMER: Mommy! Daddy!

BECKA: Mom! Dad!

[BOOMER *runs to her synthesizer; there she finds a piece of sheet music; she begins to play it; it's the complete version of her song.* BECKA. *begins to open a gift.* IRENE *and* DEAN *come downstairs and stare in awe.*]

DEAN: [*Aside to* IRENE.] How'd you do it?

[*She looks at him.*]

DEAN: [*Cont'd.*] Don't look at me.

[*They eyeball each other, each sure the other has accomplished this wonder.*]

IRENE AND DEAN: Coffee. [*They move to the breakfast counter,* DEAN *in the lead.*]

DEAN: Eye!

[IRENE *moves through the gifts and to the counter. Her confusion mirrors his, but then...she heads back into the living room on her way toward the stairs.*]

IRENE: I think I just figured out who did this.

BECKA AND BOOMER: Who?

IRENE: [*Calling.*] Mrs. Rosen.[*No answer.*] Have you guys seen Mrs. Rosen yet this morning?

[BECKA *runs part way upstairs.*]

BECKA: Whudduya mean? She can't be gone. Mrs. Rosen?...Mrs. Rosen
—don't be gone!

DEAN: All right, just a minute, let's not get upset until we know—

BECKA: She wouldn't leave without saying good-bye.

BOOMER: Maybe she's still asleep.

BECKA: Yeah!

BOOMER: Yeah!

BECKA: She wanted to get some sleep because she has to be in Kenya today.

DEAN: Kenya?

IRENE: Today?

BOOMER AND BECKA: Never mind.

BECKA: I'll go see if she's asleep.

[BECKA *runs upstairs.* BOOMER *continues to play.*]

IRENE: Boomer, when did you finish your song?

BOOMER: I don't know. I mean, I didn't. I mean it was just sitting here
with my synthesizer, my song, so I must have written it, except how
could I, so I didn't. Never mind.

[IRENE *looks at the sheet music.*]

IRENE: It's in your writing, but you don't know when you finished it. It
has words, too.

BOOMER: I know. It's a big mystery, boy. I guess I finished it sometime
and I forgot to remember that I did it. Or something.

IRENE: Are you all right, Boom?

BOOMER: Never better.

[BECKA *comes downstairs.*]

BECKA: She's gone.

[BOOMER *stops playing. A beat. And now* BECKA's *printer begins printing
on its own. Everyone turns to it.*]

IRENE: Excuse me, Becka, but how is that doing that?

[BECKA *runs to the machine. The others follow.*]

DEAN: What is it, sweetheart?

BECKA: A note. From Mrs. Rosen.

IRENE: A note from Mrs. Rosen?

[IRENE *and* DEAN *look at each other. This gets curiouser and curiouser.*]

DEAN: What's it say?

[BECKA *has read it. She presses her head to her mother's shoulder, passes her the note.*]

IRENE: It says: "I am never further from you than your dreams. I am always with you. Mrs. R."

[*Now, outside we see yet another* SANTA CLAUS *approach the house. Though extremely well-intentioned,* ALVIN LEE's *outfit is obviously homemade.*]

ALVIN LEE: Ho-ho-ho! Where's that good little Boomer Waller?

[BOOMER *runs to the window, followed by* IRENE, DEAN, *and* BECKA.]

ALVIN LEE: [*Cont'd.*] Santa Claus wants to see that good little girl!

[*The Wallers are stacked in the window.*]

DEAN: It's Santa Claus, baby! [*Then testing the theory hopefully.*] Isn't it? Is that Santa, sweetheart?

[BOOMER *waves at* ALVIN LEE *and holds up a finger.*]

BOOMER: Just a minute, Santa!

[ALVIN LEE *waves.* BOOMER *huddles the family.*]

BOOMER: [*Cont'd.*] Mommy, Daddy, I know who it is. It's Alvin Lee. But let's make him feel good and I'll pretend I think he's really Santa.

IRENE: Oh, that's very nice of you. We'll all pretend.

DEAN: Let's go outside and invite him in.

BECKA: Invite him in? We're in our jammies!

IRENE: Personally, I think we look stunning.

[BECKA *buys it and heads for the door, opens it.*]

BECKA: Here she comes, Santa!

[BOOMER, *followed by* BECKA, *comes out the door. Hand in hand, they approach* ALVIN LEE.]

BOOMER: Santa! Thanks for coming to my house, Santa! This is the nicest thing that ever happened to me in my whole, entire life! You—coming to see me—in person!

ALVIN LEE: Ho-ho-ho! Merry Christmas, Ma'am! Meeerrrrry Christmas!

DEAN: Come on in for some hot chocolate, Santa! Come on!

[DEAN *and* IRENE *usher* ALVIN LEE *into the house.* BECKA *and* BOOMER *linger outside. They look up as the lights start to close in around them.*]

BECKA: Mrs. Rosen, wherever you are, know that you are loved.

BOOMER: Merry Christmas, Mrs Rosen.

[*The two sisters stare heavenward...and a single gentle light bathes their smiling faces. And then we fade to black.*]

CURTAIN

TINY TIM IS DEAD

by Barbara Lebow

CHARACTERS:

VERNA, in her 30's, seven months pregnant. She is part street survivor, part little girl, part protective mother. All parts are, in turn, given equal expression. She swings suddenly from trust to paranoia; fears others' anger.

BOY, between 5 and 8 years old, thin, mute, acutely observant. He is VERNA's shadow, at the same time is protective of her.

CHARLIE, around 30, somewhat melancholy; a gentle man. He is a blue collar worker down on his luck. He is escaping a happier past and is, at the same time, weighted down by the loss of it.

OTIS POPE, about 50, an observer, a cynic; angry, with one disabled arm. He keeps a stack of newspapers and books, frequently reading and annotating them. He uses argument, anger, sarcasm, and his intellect to keep others at a distance. He is amused by his own sense of humor and is his own best audience.

AZALEE HODGE, around 40, her hope not quite gone. She has clearly known better days, is determined to climb back up. Her feelings for the others make it difficult for her to leave them.

FILOMENO CORDERO, late 20's, a recent arrival; optimist. He feels he has escaped from someplace so frightening that the U.S. is his safe haven and will provide. At times unable to communicate clearly in English, he identifies with BOY.

They are all street people, scrounging, occasionally staying in shelters. All except FILO have slept on this street before.

Place: A dead-end city street.

Time: The present.

Act I — December 24, evening.

Act II — The following morning.

NOTE :

The characters of **POPE**, **AZALEE**, and **BOY** are African-American; **VERNA** and **CHARLIE** are Caucasian; **FILO** is Hispanic.

ACT I

Lights rise on a dead-end street in a forgotten part of town. It is littered with McDonald's containers, a few cans and bottles, some large cardboard boxes [Sears Kenmore Refrigerator and Sony TV, big enough to sleep in], and assorted trash. Echoing the shape of a living room are a van-seat "sofa," a broken down chair, some crates, blankets, a mattress with a pile of books and newspapers near it. There's a trash bag half-filled with cans and bottles. Overhead is a shape that indicates a viaduct or overpass, from which a single caged light hangs. Some of the scene is obscured by shadow. Prominent, however, is a battered trash can with glowing embers in it. From time to time throughout the play people will warm themselves by it. Wisps of near and distant city sounds; sirens, laughter, traffic, are heard as background throughout the play.

VERNA: [*offstage, playfully,*] All-ee, all-ee in free! Ten, nine, eight, seven, six—

[VERNA, *seven months pregnant, hurries in, out of breath, as she continues counting. She pushes a rusted shopping cart. She is wearing layers of ill-fitting, unmatched clothing, including black Mary Jane shoes and crumpled anklets. Her hair is disheveled. She has a fresh bruise on her face. A bulging plastic bag hangs from her wrist. The cart is filled with the rest of her possessions, including several broken baby dolls, one sitting prominently on top.*]

VERNA: [*Cont'd.*] —five, four, three—

[*She hides the cart at the edge of the shadows, and quickly looks to see if she's been followed.*]

VERNA: [*Cont'd.*] —two, one!

[*She ducks behind a box, waits a moment, then pops up, calling off.*]

VERNA: [*Cont'd.*] You can't catch me!

[*She giggles, ducks back down again, waits, slowly peers out, shouts in a very different voice.*]

VERNA: [*Cont'd.*] You sons of bitches! I'm smarter than you! You sons of bitches!

[*She ducks once more, waits, looks out, is satisfied. She goes nearer to the cart, speaks reassuringly.*]

VERNA: [*Cont'd.*] You see, baby, we're going to be all right. They'll never catch us, put us in that shelter, take the key and lock us up, lock us up. No, sir! They want to take you away from me, but don't you worry, they will not.. The shelter police. They stand on street ringing bell, dressed up like Santa. They watch me. They wave. Lead us right into the shelter if we're fool enough to follow, to fall into their trap. But we're too smart for them.

[*She pulls the cart into the light.*]

VERNA: [*Cont'd.*] The coast is clear. Still, best to lie low a few minutes more, just in case.

[*She begins to rummage in the bag she was carrying, removing odd bits of Christmas scraps, scavenged from downtown trash cans, adorning herself a bit, mimicking holiday voices.*]

VERNA: [*Cont'd.*] "Soon we will mingle once more with the carefree holiday throng." "Merry Christmas", kiss, kiss. "Thank you, darling", kiss, kiss. "Same to you", kiss, kiss.

[*She tosses the fragments aside as unsatisfactory.* BOY, *who has been hidden amidst the things in the cart, starts to get up, visible for the first time.*]

VERNA: [*Cont'd.*] Careful, Boy! You'll topple over.

[*He starts to scrunch down again.*]

VERNA: [*Cont'd.*] You can come out. Just rest you, rest you. Plenty of time to dance after supper. I've been looking for your present, but I haven't found it yet.

[BOY *sits on top of the things in the cart.* VERNA *continues to reject everything she pulls from the bag. She finds and reads a party napkin.*]

VERNA: [*Cont'd.*] "Bradley, Ridley, and Hadley, Inc. Merry Christmas."

[*She tosses it, continues pulling out party remnants, sadly rejecting them.*]

VERNA: [*Cont'd.*] Left us their echoes, that's all. Not enough here to feed a goat. Wait! What's this?

[*She pulls out an almost perfect piece of wrapping paper, hiding it from* BOY.]

VERNA: [*Cont'd.*] Don't you look, no, no. There just might be something for your stocking in the morning. [*Continuing the search.*] And you'll come down the stairs and try to guess what's in all the boxes under the tree, but I won't tell you, no, no. The lights will be blinking, but you can't touch them 'cause you might get a shock. And you have to wear your pajamas and a bathrobe and see how many cookies Santa ate last night. [*Disposing of the rest of the bag and its contents.*] Somebody sucked out the good parts before us. Never you mind, there's something in store.

[CHARLIE *slides out from one of the boxes. He is happy, seems to have a slight buzz on, as if he's had a few beers. Occasionally he sniffles or wipes his nose.* VERNA *is happy to see him.*]

CHARLIE: Hi, Verna.. You sure come runnin' in like a storm. Hurricane Verna. I figured I'd better make myself scarce till the all clear.

VERNA: The shelter police are after us again.

CHARLIE: The Shelter Police. Sounds like a TV show. [*Playing cop, interacting with* BOY.] Da daa— "The Shelter Police." [*To* VERNA.] I told you, there ain't no such thing.

VERNA: They got dressed up in a Santa suit this time. They're after us, Charlie.

CHARLIE: No, they ain't.

VERNA: They want to put us in jail throw away the key, tie my arms in a knot so I can't move, can't touch, can't hold my baby.

CHARLIE: No, they don't. [*Firmly.*] Anyway, the shelter ain't no jail and you and the kid would be better off there.

VERNA: They'll try to take him away from me.

CHARLIE: They don't want to hurt you, Verna. They only want to see that both of you are—

VERNA: [*Suddenly frightened.*] You sound like a pod. A pod. Like they took you over. You look like Charlie, but really you're one of them. [*Covering her eyes.*] If I look at you, your eyes will be empty!

CHARLIE: Hey, Verna— [*Imitating an alien.*] Look. It's the shelter pod. [*Moving towards her.*] "The Pod Squad" [*Laughing, tickling her like a kid.*] It's really me. Honest.

[BOY *smiles at* CHARLIE'S *antics.* VERNA *slowly turns and looks in* CHARLIE'S *eyes. She laughs.* CHARLIE *sees her bruise for the first time, touches it gently.*]

CHARLIE: [*Cont'd.*] Hey, what happened now, Verna?

[VERNA *winces, touches her cheek, discovering the bruise.*]

CHARLIE: [*Cont'd.*] Someone pick on you? You get in another fight?

[*Still feeling her cheek,* VERNA *turns slightly away, her eyes wide open, blank. She stands, unmoving.* CHARLIE *shrugs, pulls something from his pocket.*]

CHARLIE: [*Cont'd.*] Got you a turkey sandwich or two. Stuffing don't travel too good.

[*He holds out some sandwiches wrapped in sodden paper. The reality of the sandwiches pulls* VERNA *back.*]

VERNA: See, Boy? Presents already.

CHARLIE: Went to two church dinners to get 'em. A good night for it. A beautiful night. Warm. No white Christmas this year. Which is definitely a plus. For us.

VERNA: A night for more Boy presents, don't you think, Charlie?

CHARLIE: [*A parent with a surprise.*] I don't know.

VERNA: Yes, you do. Keeping a secret to make a surprise, aren't you?

CHARLIE: [*With a secret smile.*] Maybe.

VERNA: He needs something nice. He needs crinkly paper to open up and smile at him. [*Suddenly wary.*] Otis Pope with you?

CHARLIE: [*Looking all about, even up his sleeves.*] No. Still at Christmas dinner someplace, I guess. Got the fire going and went off again.

VERNA: I don't want Otis Pope.

CHARLIE: He's OK.

VERNA: He yells at me. He doesn't like me. He yells at me.

CHARLIE: You shouldn't take it personal, Verna. He yells at everybody.

VERNA: [*Giving sandwiches to* BOY.] You open, Boy. You eat.

[*He opens a sandwich, starts eating.*]

CHARLIE: Too bad you're scared of the shelter. I know they got room for you two.

VERNA: You say something? I didn't hear it.

CHARLIE: Got a lighted tree and everything. Red and green and silver sparkling. Presents for the kids.

VERNA: We're having our own Christmas tree. Right, Boy?

[BOY *nods, offers* VERNA *the remainder of a sandwich.*]

VERNA: [*Cont'd.*] No. You finish it up. Christmas dinner. Look at me. Fat belly. Need a diet, I do, I do. Tomorrow, plenty for all. Turkey and cranberry sauce. Chestnut stuffing and giblet gravy. The crispy skin picked right off the roasting pan. Mmm, mmm! I'll be all filled up. Tonight, you eat.

[BOY *indicates he's full.*]

VERNA: [*Cont'd.*] So save for later. Put it in the bank. Draw interest. In an hour or two— [*Zapping sandwich like a magician.*] —candied yams on the side.

CHARLIE: Like to see that— if it was true.

VERNA: Could be true.

CHARLIE: Never.

VERNA:

How do you know? [*She sticks out her tongue at him.*]

CHARLIE: [*Exasperated.*] Maybe you're right, Verna. I give up.

[VERNA *helps* BOY *out of the cart as* OTIS POPE *lopes in. He carries some scraps of wood and cardboard, some of which he adds to the fire. He lays the rest nearby, will continue to add it from time to time.*]

POPE: Give up what? Didn't know you had something to give up.

VERNA: [*Nervously.*] Joyeux Noel, Pope.

POPE: What's she sayin' now?

VERNA: Merry Christmas, Pope.

POPE: Yeah, great.

[BOY *runs over as if to greet* POPE *before* VERNA *can stop him.* POPE *sees* BOY *looking up at him.*]

POPE: [*Cont'd.*] What you want, kid? Stay over there with your mama.

VERNA: He just wants to be a friend, so don't get mad, OK?

POPE: I don't need no friend. 'Specially no snot nose kid.

VERNA: Come on, Boy. He's closed the door.

[BOY *does not move.*]

POPE: Why you talk like that? "Closed the door." Why you can't talk normal? No wonder this kid ain't never gonna say nuthin'.

[BOY *begins to tug at* POPE'S *jacket.*]

CHARLIE: He wants you to say somethin' back to Verna. You know, from when she said Joy-ux Noel.

POPE: [*Pushing* BOY *off.*] I told you get away from me!

[BOY *will not leave.*]

VERNA: Don't be mad, daddy! Don't hurt him!

POPE: I ain't your daddy, Verna! Told you that a hundred times. [*Turning his growing anger on* BOY.] What you doin' in my face? You better get out my way, boy! Get back to your crazy mama and quit lookin' at me! Get, I said! [*Chasing* BOY.] Get!

[BOY *runs back to* VERNA, *who quietly berates him, giving him a whack on the backside.* BOY *sits, curled up, chastened. All this as* CHARLIE *tries to divert* POPE.]

CHARLIE: You hungry, Pope?

POPE: Since when that your business?

CHARLIE: I mean, you have a Christmas dinner?

POPE: Your brain turned to oatmeal, Charlie? All this Christmas shit.

[CHARLIE *starts to pull something out from his jacket and show it to* POPE, *hiding it from* VERNA.]

CHARLIE: I got some presents.

POPE: What you got is their Christmas guilt. [*He laughs.*] Temperature drop a little, you get their cold weather guilt, too.

CHARLIE: Thought you might of went to a church or someplace yourself.

POPE: Let someone clean his conscience on me?

[CHARLIE *shrugs, puts the present away.*]

POPE: [*Cont'd.*] Let some church hand out someone's leftovers to me? With gravy on it? Man gives me something, he's gonna look me in the eye, direct. He's gonna see who he gives it to.

[POPE *takes a deck of cards from a pocket, tosses it down on a crate next to* CHARLIE. *He shuffles and deals the cards with his good hand. He automatically begins playing cards with* CHARLIE, *who is so slow and involved with gazing at the cards, that* POPE *sometimes throws a card for him.* VERNA *and* BOY *are at the boxes.*]

VERNA: [*To* BOY.] Where you like better to sleep? Sony TV, all night there'll be lots of pictures. In color. Sears Kenmore Refrigerator, we'll dream ice cream and day old meat loaf and fruit salad with coconut on top.

[BOY *cannot decide.*]

VERNA: [*Cont'd.*] How about we both go in Sears Kenmore and snuggle up?

[*She begins to arrange the box with bedding from the cart.*]

POPE: Shit, Verna! The boy needs him a decent bed!

[VERNA *whimpers and covers her head as if ducking a blow.*]

POPE: [*Cont'd.*] Not some damn box already been used by some fuckin' wino! He ain't no doll what belong in a box! He's a damn kid, Verna!

[*During* POPE'S *tirade,* AZALEE HODGE *enters, ragged, plain, not very clean, and with aching feet.*]

AZALEE: [*Over* POPE.] Now, now. Now, now. Don't you pay him no mind, Verna. He's just shootin' off, like always.

[AZALEE *goes right to* VERNA, *to comfort her.* VERNA *calms and softly begins humming "God Rest Ye Merry Gentlemen" while she sets up.* POPE *pointedly does not react to* AZALEE'S *entrance, keeping busy with the card game.*]

CHARLIE: Azalee? Thought I said goodbye to you.

AZALEE: Sure did.

CHARLIE: Thought you was goin' into the shelter.

AZALEE: I am. Got me a place waitin'. Come to say goodbye again since I found out you all ain't gonna see me no more. Something big gonna happen to me tonight.

POPE: [*Not looking up.*] 'Bout as big as what happened to Verna. How many babies you drop already, Verna?

AZALEE: You lay off her, Pope. She don't know no better, same as a innocent child. [*To* VERNA.] How you doin', honey?

[POPE *keeps playing cards with* CHARLIE, *reacting with growing disgust at what follows.*]

VERNA: [*Singing, oblivious to* ALL.] ..."Remember Christ the saviour was born on Christmas day—"

AZALEE: [*Cutting her off.*] That's nice, sugar. Brought you something from the grab bag at the shelter.

[*She takes two small packages from an overstuffed purse.*]

AZALEE: [*Cont'd.*] And one for your boy.

[VERNA *is terrified of the gifts, does not want to touch them.*]

VERNA: No! It's a trick!

[*She looks beyond* AZALEE, *as if expecting someone to be following.* AZALEE *presses the gifts on* VERNA *and* BOY.]

AZALEE: Don't you worry none. I told the shelter folk it was for my nephew and they didn't ask no questions... [*Encouraging* VERNA.] Go on. Open 'em up now. I got to be goin' back in a little while.

[*BOY looks at* VERNA. *She nods her approval. They both open the gifts carefully, being sure not to tear the paper.* VERNA *takes out a pair of warm mittens.* BOY *finds a decorated muffler.* VERNA *wraps it around his neck, puts on the mittens.*]

VERNA: See, this is just what we need. And it's on the way to something better. A big pile of presents under the tree. And something beautiful from me. Something you'll keep forever. [*Reciting a thank you note.*] Dear Azalee Hodge, Thank you for the lovely—

[*She takes off the mittens and gives them to* BOY.]

VERNA: [*Cont'd.*] —ensemble.

[*She looks at* AZALEE; *a question.*]

AZALEE: That's fine, sugar. I understand.

VERNA: [*Continuing the note*] My boy and I thank you for your kind thoughts on this holy day. We hope to return the favor soon. Sincerely yours, Verna.

AZALEE: That's real sweet, hon. Don't you worry 'bout returnin' no favor. It wasn't no favor.

[BOY *begins walking about, trying out his gift, parading proudly, picking things up with the mittens on. While he is busy,* VERNA *speaks quietly to* AZALEE.]

VERNA: I'm worried, Azalee. I told him there'd be something from me, too, but the cupboard's bare. There's nothing. And he's so jumping up and down! He thinks there's going to be a big present this year. What if there isn't? I promised him, but it was a lie. It's bad to tell a lie. Especially to Boy.

AZALEE: You wasn't lyin', sugar. You was only hopin'.

[*Worried but hopeful,* VERNA *looks at* BOY.]

VERNA: Last year I found an airplane with one wing perfect. We said it was made special, just to fly in circles.

AZALEE: You never know.

[*She goes to* BOY.]

AZALEE: [*Cont'd.*] You'll see, sonny, your mama's tellin' the truth. Any time now something even better be showing up for you, like a shiny red fire engine. That's what happens on Christmas.

VERNA: [*Alarmed.*] But, Azalee—

POPE: Christmas is bullshit.

[VERNA *clamps her hands over* BOY'S *ears.*]

POPE: [*Cont'd.*] [*To* AZALEE.] And you ought to know better, encouragin' someone like her! What she doin' with that kid anyways? Crazy white woman got him near as bad as she is!

[VERNA *begins scrubbing* BOY'S *face with an old kerchief.*]

AZALEE: Can it, Pope! Boy can hear good as you and me. Just because he don't say nothin' don't mean he can't hear you talkin' nasty 'bout Christmas and mean about Verna.

POPE: Don't tell me 'bout that boy. She raisin' him up to be crazy like her. And a dummy to boot!

AZALEE: You gettin' meaner every day! And got no sense. I used to think—

POPE: [*Over* AZALEE, *not listening to* her.] Don't even have no name yet. Whoever heard of that? Boy his size.

VERNA: He does have a name. He does.

POPE: He have a name? What is it?

VERNA: He hasn't told me yet. When he's ready, he's going to tell me.

[BOY *looks up and touches* VERNA'S *face.*]

CHARLIE: I try to explain. She could take him to the clinic, free. They might fix him up there. Make him so he could talk and everything. Or see he learns to talk with his hands. I could take him for you, Verna, if you don't want to. It's only—

VERNA: [*Getting up, pacing.*] No. No. No, no, no, no, no, no, no!

AZALEE: It's all right, honey. He don't mean nothing.

POPE: [*Throwing down his hand of cards.*] What's the use?

[VERNA *continues her "No" lament loudly.*]

CHARLIE: I don't mean nothin', Verna. I ain't gonna touch the kid.

[*He makes a peace sign, leans back into the card game.* VERNA *is now rocking with her chant.*]

POPE: Holy shit! Make her shut up, will you?

[AZALEE *goes to* VERNA, *holds her, shouts over the noise.*]

AZALEE: It's all right, Verna! He ain't comin' near you!

[VERNA *stops suddenly. She looks up at* AZALEE.]

AZALEE: [*Cont'd.*] Now, you listen and I'll tell you what's happenin' to me later on.

POPE: She gonna make it with Rudolph the Red Nose!

[CHARLIE, *not wanting to laugh at* AZALEE's *expense, is a semi-apprecia- tive audience.* POPE *picks up his cards and starts playing again.* AZALEE *ignores his remark, holds* VERNA's *face between her hands.*]

VERNA: What is it, Azalee?

POPE: The "Rent a Homeless" done rented her out to some charity ball.

AZALEE: [*Focusing on* VERNA.] I'm gonna tell you somethin' nice.

POPE: She goin' on TV. Gonna be on the nightly news.

AZALEE: I'm gonna be part of something special, something wonderful, Verna. Can you hear me?

[VERNA *nods.*]

AZALEE: [*Cont'd.*] I'm gonna be part of the Christmas Eve Cinderella Night of Beauty!

VERNA: Cinderella Night of beauty...

AZALEE: They gonna do what they call a "holiday make-over". Gonna make me back to how I used to be. Or better. So take one last look, boys. Gonna be a new Azalee tomorrow!

POPE: Hallelujah!

AZALEE: You don't bother me, Otis Pope! I gotta be back there by eight- thirty and I mean they're gonna do it all! Hair and clothes and make- up. They had the beauty college students to volunteer. And they're startin' with a bubble bath! The first shift be goin' in soon. For fif- teen minutes each. My turn come at the end. A fifteen-minute bub- ble bath!

POPE: What you gonna do when you beautiful from "Cinderella Night of Beauty", then? Seem to me you need a week of beauty, at least. Maybe a month.

AZALEE: Not see you again, is one thing. Be clean and decent and get a interview to lead me back to a real job is another thing.

[*A full, Mantovani style, orchestrated version of "Oh, Little Town of Bethlehem" begins faintly in the distance.*]

POPE: Maybe you almost be good enough for the U.S. Army.

AZALEE: I don't belong out on the street.

POPE: No. You better than the rest of us.

VERNA: Congratulations, Azalee.

AZALEE: Thank you, honey.

VERNA: Merry Christmas, Azalee.

[VERNA *and* AZALEE *embrace. The music surges as it comes closer; a sentimental background.*]

POPE: Oh, Christ!

AZALEE: [*To* VERNA.] Thank you, sugar. Same to you.

CHARLIE: [*Looking to the heavens.*] Where's it comin' from?

[*The music grows even louder and then drags and goes flat like a warped record or stretched cassette tape. In answer to* CHARLIE'S *question,* FILOMENO CORDERO *enters. He almost dances in, very lively, very out of sync with the music, as if he is trying to lift it up. He is highly energetic and quite cheerful. He carries a small tape player close to his ear. He waves at* CHARLIE.]

FILO: Feliz Navidad, Charlie! This place easy to find, jus' like you say!

[CHARLIE *greets him.* ALL *watch this apparition approach* POPE.]

POPE: [*Loud and emphatic.*] Turn that damn thing off!

FILO: You don't like it? [*He giggles.*]

POPE: I wouldn't like it even if it was in tune! Turn it off!

[FILO *obliges.*]

POPE: [*Cont'd.*] Who's this nut, anyway?

CHARLIE: I know him. He just come up from down south a few days ago, lookin' for work. Right, Filo?

[FILO *nods.*]

CHARLIE: [*Cont'd.*] I met him over at the church dinner and we got to talkin'. He don't know hardly no one here.

[POPE *just stares at* FILO.]

CHARLIE: [*Cont'd.*] Hey, it's Christmas, Pope.

FILO: [*Moving to shake* POPE'S *hand.*] Filomeno Cordero. Call me Filo.

POPE: [*Offering no hand in return.*] Say what?

CHARLIE: He's OK.

POPE: [*To* FILO.] You keep away from me! I ain't touchin' him. No tellin' what he's got.

[FILO *turns and smiles at* BOY, *who is watching him carefully. He rubs* BOY'S *head affectionately.*]

VERNA: He likes children.

FILO: [*To* BOY.] Hello, niño.

AZALEE: [*To* FILO, *explaining.*] He don't talk.

[FILO *crouches, facing* BOY, *and does an exaggerated version of his greeting, mouthing his words silently to* BOY. *As the* OTHERS *speak, he traces figures in the air.* BOY *mirrors him.*]

VERNA: He likes children.

POPE: Why you tell this clown to come here?

AZALEE: It's a free country. He can tell anyone he got a mind to.

CHARLIE: He's new. Don't know no one.

POPE: He ain't in this world. He's trippin', man. A crackhead. In the stratosphere, like all your friends.

CHARLIE: This is Pope, Filo.

POPE: Otis Pope.

AZALEE: He always try to insist on that Otis, but mostly they call him Pope. Call me Azalee. This is Verna and her boy.

VERNA: What world are you from, Mr. ...Mr. ...

FILO: Filo.

VERNA: Mr. Filo. What world?

FILO: World where is warm and the sun shine every day. World of el ocano azul ...the ocean blue.

VERNA: [*Entranced.*] The ocean blue...

AZALEE: Why you come here then?

[*Pause.* FILO *takes in the whole scene, like a child at a circus.*]

FILO: Opportunity!

[*Pause.*]

FILO: [*Cont'd.*] One day I gonna have a lot of money, buy everybody a house. Whatever you want.

VERNA: You hear that, Boy? A house!

POPE: Man be crazy.

FILO: [*A helpful announcement, directed toward* CHARLIE.] Needle man on next corner.

POPE: Who? Your friend don't talk right, Charlie.

FILO: Needle man. Man with needles. [Acting it out, on CHARLIE.] New, like from el hospital.

CHARLIE: Came by here an hour ago. Not many customers today.

POPE: Everybody inside, gettin' high on turkey.

FILO: He givin' out needles like Santa Cloth.

VERNA: Santa Claus.

FILO: Like Santa... Clauzzz, ask everyone be good, say he come tomorrow same as always, even on Christmas.

POPE: Man be crazy. Ask for trouble.

FILO: [Laughing.] He don't care. He have a mission. [To POPE.] You have a mission, man?

POPE: Make you shut up, my mission.

CHARLIE: [To POPE.] Needle man's just tryin' to help people. [To himself.] If it ain't too late.

FILO: [To POPE.] Yeah. He tryin' to help.

POPE: Damn fool think he stop AIDS by hisself. He get arrested, so what? One more nut case.

FILO: You ready to go, Charlie?

CHARLIE: Nah. These are my amigos here. Stick around a while. You're just in time to see Azalee before her turnover.

VERNA: [Quickly.] Turn around.

AZALEE: [Quickly] Make-over! Take a good look at the "before," Filo. You might never get to see the "after."

POPE: Azalee entering the Miss America Show tomorrow. [Sings] "There she goes, Miss America..." Gonna win a lot of useless prizes.

FILO: [A boast.] Filomeno Cordero already win the jackpot today!

[He takes things out from under his jacket, up his sleeves, under his belt, wherever he's been hiding them, as he speaks, laughing, giggling, enjoying himself immensely as he displays each item, first doing an improvised spiel, in Spanish, on each. VERNA applauds, squeals excited responses. BOY echoes her movements silently. POPE glowers.]

FILO: [Cont'd.] [Two cans of soup] From the Klingman Road Baptis' Church. [A red tie] Church of the Holy Redemption. [A shirt on its cardboard, in cellophane] Tabernacle de los Twelve Disciples. [A pair of Jockey shorts, shown first as Santa's beard] La Iglesia de la Seora

Doa Maria. [Already opened pack of cassettes] And this— esta msica celestial— "Holiday Favorites From Around the World"— this from Temple Emanu-El!

AZALEE: For a newcomer you sure get around.

FILO: One place lead to another. You got a lot of presents in this city.

CHARLIE: Looks like you took 'em all, man.

FILO: For to share. Whoever wants. You want something?

VERNA: Do you have a shiny red fire engine, just right for a little boy?

FILO: [Sadly.] No. [Bringing the soup cans to VERNA] But your boy is lucky. In my country I never get no present. In my country a kid like him be living in the sewer or shot dead by police, same like a rat or a dog or some kind of—

AZALEE: [Jumping in to change the subject] I'd like to hear more of that music. You got some that ain't flat?

FILO: Estan extendidos todos— The tapes all stretched out. But you try it.

[FILO gives the soup cans to VERNA.]

FILO: [Cont'd.] You get two good meals outa this. How you like it?

VERNA: [To BOY.] Now you choose. Which one you want for breakfast? Split Pea with Ham. Homemade Chicken with Noodles. Aren't they pretty?

FILO: It say you don't put no water in.

[BOY chooses one. AZALEE and CHARLIE select a tape and put it on. VERNA speaks as the intro plays. It drags and changes volume.]

VERNA: All right. We sleep with this one tucked under so it's nice and warm when we wake up.

[She gives can to BOY, who takes it into the box-shelter, where he stays for a while. She takes the other can to AZALEE, who is happily anticipating the music.]

VERNA: [Cont'd.] Merry Christmas, Azalee.

[AZALEE takes the can as a warped Bing Crosby begins to sing "White Christmas."]

AZALEE: Oh, man! I love me some Bing!

[ALL, except POPE, listen, trying to pretend the music isn't flat. After a while, AZALEE gives the soup back to VERNA.]

AZALEE: You keep this, honey. I won't be needin' it.

[VERNA *presses it on her.*]

VERNA: A present is love, Azalee. That you can look at and hold in your hand.

AZALEE: Well sure then, fine. If it makes you happy.

VERNA: Thank you for the present, Filo.

[*She and the* OTHERS *listen to the awful music with differing reactions.*]

POPE: Turn that shit off!

AZALEE: No! I'm enjoying it!

FILO: [*After a while, offering some of his gifts.*] You want something, Pope? Charlie?

POPE: Somebody try to buy you off and you fall for it, man. This stuff all a payoff to they peace of mind. And then they still gonna write it up off they income tax.

FILO: I only want to give you something. But you want to be *canalla*, is OK with me. I keep it to trade, man.

CHARLIE: Don't mind him, Filo. Pope staked out this spot and preaches at whoever comes by. That's the way he is. He can't help it.

AZALEE: [*To* CHARLIE.] What you talkin' 'bout, "can't help it"? You think you know Otis Pope? He's a changed man from how he used—

POPE: You leave off of that, Azalee! You rememberin' a dead man.

CHARLIE: [*To* POPE.] All I meant was that the stuff is nice.

AZALEE: Sure is. And from nice folk, too, tryin' to change things.

POPE: What these "nice folk" do for you in January? In September? Look around you, Az. Nothin's gonna change for us. This your past, present, and future.

FILO: People jus' bein' generous, man.

CHARLIE: And whoever give it don't even know who we are.

POPE: I know who they be, man.

[*He goes to player, turns it off and removes the cassette. He holds it up to* FILO.]

POPE: [*Cont'd.*] This famous rich white man singin', "May your days be merry and bright"— This the man what beat up on his children, I read it in the paper. Two of his kids kill theirself. Merry and bright, all right!

[*He destroys the cassette.*]

AZALEE: You ought to be ashamed!

POPE: [*To* AZALEE, *his anger building.*] You the one ought to be ashamed, joinin' in, takin' all their stuff. Anyway, I got it all wrote down. [*Showing his notebook.*] What they give; what they take away. Fuckin' heaven at election and give you hell the rest of the year! Includin' Christmas, Easter, and the Fourth of July!

[VERNA *crouches at the opening of the box, protecting herself and* BOY *from* POPE'S *anger.*]

CHARLIE: Maybe it don't matter, long as they give somethin', sometime. [*Reaching into his jacket.*] You didn't even see what I got.

POPE: You want to hear what I got, Charlie?

FILO: [*Defending* CHARLIE.] He don't want to hear.

POPE: Nine dollars from the plasma center. You know what they sell it for to some hospital? Some hospital what smooth out white ladies' wrinkles on they Night of Beauty? Over one hundred dollars, man! My blood!

VERNA: Too loud, too loud! Be nice, daddy. Please be nice.

AZALEE: Your preachin' be scarin' Verna and the boy, Pope.

POPE: [*Noticing them.*] Damn right!

[*He goes to* VERNA, *leans over her, shouting.*]

POPE: [*Cont'd.*] You hidin' like a ostrich, Verna! You better be scared 'cause you can't hide in this world, neither of you! Bloodsuckers gonna get you both!

[POPE, *disgusted, turns away, sticking a cigarette in his mouth.*]

CHARLIE: Thought you quit smoking, Pope.

POPE: Day your blood clean enough to sell, you talk to me 'bout quittin' something!

[CHARLIE *turns away.* POPE *strides off angrily.* VERNA *sits, rocking a doll.* AZALEE *helps* BOY *out of the box. He sits next to* VERNA.]

FILO: He happy bein' mad. He like tellin' everybody what to do.

CHARLIE: Maybe he got a right. It's his corner.

[FILO *goes to see if he can salvage his tape.* AZALEE *collects more things from her box.* CHARLIE *tries to change the mood.*]

CHARLIE: [*Cont'd.*] Hey! Look at what I got. A fruitcake...

AZALEE: [*Waving it off.*] No, thanks!

[VERNA *is suddenly delighted with the cake offered by* CHARLIE. *She takes it; a treasure.* CHARLIE *holds up a small book with a worn leather cover.*]

CHARLIE: ...And a book. A Christmas book. I read it before and I seen it on TV. The same story.

AZALEE: [*Taking the book.*] Let me see that. [*Leafing through it.*] Yep. Used to watch this same as I watched "The Wizard of Oz." This the one with Scrooge.

VERNA: [*Laughing.*] Ebenezer Scrooge! Bah, humbug!

[*She repeats this several times while* AZALEE *examines the book.*]

AZALEE: Seem to have some pages missin', but there's a bunch of nice pictures.

VERNA: God bless us, everyone!

AZALEE: See. She know the story, too. Missin' pages don't matter none.

CHARLIE: Everyone knows this book. Same as the Bible. I used to read it to my own.

[*Pause.*]

AZALEE: Who to, Charlie?

CHARLIE: [*Lowering his voice.*] Nothin'.... To somebody.

FILO: Never heard of it, man. Let me see.

[*He takes the book reverently.*]

FILO: [*Cont'd.*] Parece muy importante.

[*He turns some pages.*]

FILO: [*Cont'd.*] It sure look cold in this book. Like now.

AZALEE: You call this cold? This just a bit chilly.

FILO: Chili? Chili es muy caliente. This weather muy frio para m. ...You know, where I come from we never have this story.

CHARLIE: Every kid in America knows it. Or saw it on TV. Right?

AZALEE: Till it comin' out my ears.

VERNA: [*Very upset about* BOY.] He didn't see it.

AZALEE: Why sure he did.

VERNA: [*Near tears.*] Never.

FILO: [Waving to BOY.] Amigo! Just like me.

VERNA: No. He's not like you. He's an all American boy.

CHARLIE: How about I give him the book, Verna?

VERNA: [*Beaming.*] Thank you, Charlie.

CHARLIE: I could even read it to him.

AZALEE: It ain't as good as the show on TV.

VERNA: The show...like on TV. I wish he could see it like everyone else.

AZALEE: Well, he can't, sugar. There ain't no TV out here.

CHARLIE: They got a good TV at the shelter, Verna.

VERNA: No, no, no! We don't need their TV. We don't need any TV at all. We could do it. [*Putting pieces together, remembering.*] We could give him that book in a show, couldn't we, Azalee?   Charlie? No one thinks we can do it, but then opening night comes and it's a real show with costumes...and special effects! [*Quickly leading* BOY *to a crate near trash can.*] You'll sit here and watch. [*Relieved and happy.*] It's the big present I promised you. I'm gonna be Tiny Tim!

FILO: What's that? A tinny tin.

VERNA: [*Running on.*] He's so good, everyone loves him.   He's Bob Cratchit's baby— a tiny, little boy. He's lame. [*Seeing* FILO'S *confusion,* she *demonstrates.*] He walks like this and then they see in the future that he dies, but it's only a dream and we're all happy, happy, happy! (*Back to* BOY.) Wait! You need a ticket! [*Giving the fruitcake to* BOY.] You give the cake to Charlie. It's your ticket, your donation, to get in. It's for poor people. He's the usher.

[*She rummages in the cart, comes up with an old flashlight. It works! She gives it to* CHARLIE, *who just stands there.*]

VERNA: [*Cont'd.*] This is his best present ever!

[*The* OTHERS *don't move. They simply look at her.*]

AZALEE: It's better on the TV.

VERNA: [*Instantaneously frightened.*] No, it isn't! We can do it here. We don't have to see it any place else!

CHARLIE: The kids at the shelter get to watch it on TV. He could see the real show at the shelter and—

VERNA: [*Distressed, cutting him off.*] They'll steal him, snatch him away! Make me sign the paper and say goodbye.... [*Trying to explain.*] A baby comes wrapped in blood, like a present. Every time I find him I wash him clean and they tell me write name on paper and I never see him again. Only this one no crying comes out so they don't take him yet. Don't let them take him, Charlie. He is mine. He is for me. But he has got no present for Christmas. I could not find it. This story is his present.

CHARLIE: You have to show him to somebody. So he can be counted. Like the boy in the book. Like Tiny Tim. He had a happy ending 'cause somebody with money counted him and helped him out. Someday you have to show him.

VERNA: No. Not till he's old enough to take care of himself. Please, please, Charlie! Let's tell Boy the story.

CHARLIE: Verna, we can't.

VERNA: [*Frantically, desperately.*] We have to! Azalee, tell him! We have to!

AZALEE: [*Aware of* VERNA'S *condition.*] Hold it, Charlie. Maybe we can.

FILO: Sound better an' better to me. [*To* VERNA.] You be the Virgen Maria.

VERNA: The what?

FILO: The Vir-gen Mary. You a natural, man. That light there the star in the east. I'm gonna be a wise man and Charlie—

AZALEE: That's the wrong story. Go check it out. We're gonna do the show for the boy, just like Verna wants.

VERNA: All ready, Boy! You're getting your present now!

[*As the scene continues,* VERNA *arranges the crates for an audience near the trash can. She and* BOY *sit, waiting.*]

AZALEE: I'll stay on till my turn at Night of Beauty. We'll tell him a nice story.

POPE: [*Entering from the shadows, swigging from a small bottle.*] This story 'bout exploitation.

FILO: You political, man?

CHARLIE: Yeah, Pope's political, all right. Ain't gave up on changin' the world. He's good at makin' speeches.

AZALEE: He's runnin' for mayor next week.

FILO: Maybe he have a bomb. [*To* POPE, *laughing.*] You have a bomb? You want to blow somethin' up?

POPE: [*Drinking more.*] Yeah. The plasma center. The labor pool. The chamber of commerce. You.

CHARLIE: [*Getting the book.*] It's just a story, Pope. For kids.

POPE: You all gonna tell it wrong. You gonna make a fairytale out of it and keep that no-name kid stupid!

[*He turns away from the* OTHERS, *disgusted, and sits at a distance from them, continuing to drink.*]

VERNA: [*Trying to hurry past* POPE'S *interruption.*] Start reading, Charlie!

[AZALEE *and* FILO *sit on the crates* VERNA *arranged.* CHARLIE *stands in front of them with the book.*]

CHARLIE: [*Reading.*] "A Christmas Carol by Charles Dickens."

[ALL *except* POPE *applaud as* CHARLIE *turns to the first page.*]

CHARLIE: [*Cont'd.*] "Marley was dead, to begin with".

FILO: That's the ghos' in the picture. He look fantstico! That's goin' to be my part. Marley's Ghos', man. You tell me when is my turn.

POPE: Scrooge the only true part in it. [*With admiration.*] He's one mean bastard!

CHARLIE: But he got changed in the end.

POPE: Makes no difference what it say in that book you got. What happens the next day after that story over? After everyone goes home happy? I'll tell you how it really comes out. Soon as you close the cover, he's back to hisself again, telling everybody go to hell. And that cripple kid the one he drops first.

CHARLIE: Look, Pope, just let me get started, OK? Then we'll see how it comes out. I used to read it to my own kids...

[AZALEE *alone notices this information.*]

POPE: [*Not caring.*] Go ahead.

CHARLIE: [*Finding the place.*] "Scrooge! a squeezing, wrenching, grasping, scraping, clutching—"

FILO: Wait! I don't understand nothin' here. What's "esquenching," "escrutching"—

CHARLIE: Sorry. Means he's like this.

[*He stands, tries to be Scrooge.*]

CHARLIE: [*Cont'd.*] Bah, humbug! I hate Christmas! I'm gonna keep all my money to myself!

POPE: [*Clucking to himself.*] Look at that...look at that. [*Pushing* CHARLIE *aside.*] You think you Scrooge? I worked for the man half my life! He's tight with a dollar and free with takin' advantage. He thinks he knows more than the workin' man. He imagines what's good for—

CHARLIE: OK, OK. I get the idea. [*Starts acting again.*] He was so damn mean, he froze from the inside out. His voice was like snow bein' shoveled off a sidewalk...

[*He makes a harsh, scraping voice, waving his finger, getting into it.*]

POPE: Cut the shit, Charlie! You look like Bugs Bunny!

CHARLIE: You know somethin' 'bout tellin' a story to a kid?

POPE: Least I know Scrooge. Seen him just today.

[*He pushes* CHARLIE *aside again and moves to the* OTHERS.]

POPE: [*Cont'd.*] [*To* FILO.] You hungry? Tough shit! [*Puts hand in his pocket. To* VERNA.] Want a quarter?

[*She reaches out, he turns away, covers his eyes.*]

POPE: [*Cont'd.*] Can't see you! [*To* AZALEE.] Need a doctor? Can't help you? [*To* BOY.] Worryin' on your family? Ain't my problem— I ain't got no family! [*Laughs, takes a swig.*] Only one I think about is me!

CHARLIE: Damn if that ain't just like Scrooge!

[*He leads the* OTHERS *in applauding, encouraging* POPE. ALL *are enjoying.*]

POPE: Shut up, Charlie. Keep tellin' the story. You wasting time.

CHARLIE: OK, OK. He... his... his hair was all frosty—

FILO: [*Laughing.*] He sound like somethin' good to eat!

POPE: [*Turning on him, Scrooge-like.*] Nothin' good 'bout me, man. You see my hair, man? White, like a crust of ice. I freeze it from the inside, man. I'm a walkin' Frigidaire!

FILO: What's that?

CHARLIE: A refrigerator. An icebox. You know. It keeps the food cold.

FILO: [*To* POPE.] You un frigorfico!

POPE: A freakin' what, you call me?

FILO: Fri-go-rfico.

POPE: You call me that again, I'll freag your rifico!

CHARLIE: [*Breaking in.*] Once upon a time, on Christmas Eve, old Scrooge sat in his office, countin' up his profits. [*Paying little attention to the book.*] It was freezin' out; colder than here. The door was open so he could keep an eye on the guy who worked for him. It was Bob Cratchit—

[*He takes a little bow, indicating he's taking on this role. The* OTHERS *applaud.*]

CHARLIE: —who was writing down stuff about accounts.

[POPE *evaluates* CHARLIE.]

POPE: You black, Charlie.

CHARLIE: What?

POPE: Bob Cratchit black in this story.

CHARLIE: But I don't know how to—

POPE: Don't matter what you don't know how to. [*Bitterly.*] This the United States of America. Bob Cratchit black.

CHARLIE: OK. I'm black.

[*He shrugs, sets the flashlight between his knees, and attempts to warm his hands over it. He makes a feeble and short-lived effort at "being black."*]

POPE: What you doin' now, fool?

CHARLIE: Tryin' to warm my hands over this here—

[*He glances at the others, indicating his clever improvisation.*]

CHARLIE: [*Cont'd.*] —candle, sir. Merry Christmas, sir.

POPE: You costin' me money, fool! There's fifty men be fightin' for your job.

FILO: [*Rising.*] You 'spose' to say, "Bah, hamburger!"

[ALL *except* POPE *laugh.* FILO, *not understanding why, nevertheless joins in.*]

POPE:[*To* FILO.] What you laughin' at? Can't even talk English. Piss off!

[FILO *laughs harder.* POPE *lunges at him.*]

FILO: No hay razn para—

POPE: I said, piss off! I ain't givin' no jobs to no filthy foreigners.

[FILO *laughs and runs out of harm's way.*]

POPE: [*Cont'd.*] [*To* CHARLIE, *moving him around*) And don't you stand there like you on vacation. Go get me some cigarettes. You got to finish those books. But first, these shoes here be needin' a shine.

CHARLIE: Yes, sir, Mr. Scrooge.

[CHARLIE *begins shining* POPE'S *shoes. During the ensuing argument,* FILO *goes to* CHARLIE, *asks him something, takes red tie off.*]

AZALEE: [*Rising, explaining to* BOY.] They supposed to collect for the Salvation Army shelter or something now and Scrooge says Marley's dead and—

POPE: Nobody needs to collect when they already got welfare and food stamps.

AZALEE: But that's what it says in the story!

POPE: Scrooge pays taxes to support all those bleedin' heart, Liberal programs.

AZALEE: Maybe so, but—

POPE: But, nothing. Butt out, is what! They's already enough shelters in this damn city!

AZALEE: All overloaded! They's too many still out here!

POPE: You tellin' me they can't live without no Cinderella Night of Beauty Christmas Holiday makeover?

AZALEE: That's only—

POPE: We takin' back all that welfare, anyhow. Too many children?— Put 'em in a orphanage! All them homeless messin' up the streets— throw 'em in jail! Or let 'em get AIDS and get rid of them and they kind for good.

[*Abruptly,* CHARLIE *turns away, self-absorbed for a moment.*]

AZALEE: I can't tell are you playin' or not, Otis.

POPE: You want that boy to have a story? Well, this is IT.

[CHARLIE *quickly continues the narration to distract* POPE *and* AZALEE.]

CHARLIE: Scrooge says it's time to close up. [*Now directing the story to* BOY.] So Cratchit runs home, real happy, and Scrooge has to feel his way in the dark—

[POPE *makes a half-hearted effort to "feel" his way to another area as* CHARLIE *continues.*]

CHARLIE: [*Cont'd.*] —to his lonely, stinkin' apartment, which he could of afforded a much better one if he wasn't so tight. [*Tickled.*] He puts on some kind of nightdress—

POPE: [*Glaring at* CHARLIE.] Say what?

CHARLIE: —and a funny little hat they wore back then.

[POPE *takes another drink from his bottle.*]

CHARLIE: [*Cont'd.*] Suddenly, all hell breaks loose. First there's ghosts.

[*He signals to the* WOMEN, *who provide sound effects directed to* BOY.]

CHARLIE: [*Cont'd.*] Bells begin to ring. Then all at once, they stop.

[*They stop.* CHARLIE *appreciates their performance.*]

CHARLIE: [*Cont'd.*] [*To the* WOMEN.] Very nice! ...[*To* BOY.] Then there is a great, awful moaning noise—

[*He signals to the shadows.* FILO *wails.*]

CHARLIE: [*Cont'd.*] —and the sound of chains dragging on the floor. Scrooge flips out.

POPE: [*Hamming it up.*] There's somethin' scary out there. It's comin' right into my door!

[VERNA *and* AZALEE *increase their noisemaking.* POPE *takes a few steps back, staring with terror at something he seems to see before him. He shivers.*]

POPE: [*Cont'd.*] I know him... It's Marley's ghost!

[*There is a quick beat of silence wherein* POPE *is frozen and* ALL *wait expectantly.* CHARLIE *hits the button and the beat of reggae music issues strongly from the tape player.* FILO *emerges from the dark, moving rhythmically. The sunglasses are over his eyes. He's got an old mop-head, vaguely resembling dreadlocks, tied onto his head with the red tie. The* OTHERS *are shocked into immobility as he starts to sing in attempted imitation of Bob Marley.*]

FILO: [*Singing.*]

EBENEZER! EBENEZER!
    SCROOGE! EBENEZER SCROOGE!
    SCROOGE! EBENEZER SCROOGE!
    LA GENTE SLEEP IN BOXES AND EAT OUT OF THE GARBAGE—

POPE: [*Outraged.*] What you think you're doin'?

[*The accompaniment continues playing under what follows.*]

FILO: Marley's ghos', man.

POPE: Wrong Marley, fool! This supposed to be Scrooge's partner who comes back to haunt him.

FILO: Both Marleys is dead, ain't they? So why it matters which one I be?

THE OTHERS: Go on, Filo. You're right. It don't matter. Go ahead, Filo.

POPE: You expect me to be scared of this? [*To* BOY.] You believe anyone be scared of this fool, Boy?

[BOY *smiles, shakes his head.*]

POPE: [*Cont'd.*] Even the dummy smilin'. You ain't scarin' no one, Marley.

[FILO *starts singing again, trying to squeeze his words into the rhythm.* AZALEE *picks up on his movement, follows him.* VERNA, BOY, *and* CHAR-LIE *watch, enjoying.*]

FILO: LA GENTE SLEEP IN BOXES AND EAT OUT OF THE GARBAGE,
BUT YOU MALO, MALO, MALO!
IF YOU GOT SOMETHING,
YOU 'SPOSE TO SHARE IT WITH EVERYONE ELSE.

POPE: Not with you, man!

[AZALEE *improvises,* VERNA *and* CHARLIE *copy her as an uneven* CHO-RUS, *physically getting more into it.*]

CHORUS: YOU GOT TO
TAKE IT, TAKE IT, TAKE IT,
SOON AS YOU
MAKE IT, MAKE IT, MAKE IT;
AND THEN YOU
SHAKE IT, SHAKE IT, SHAKE IT –
YOU GONNA SPREAD IT ALL AROUND.

POPE: This is pitiful.

[FILO *shrieks, then sings again, directly at* POPE. *By now the* OTHERS *support and copy his moves.*]

FILO: YOU MALO COMO EL DIABLO—
[*Enjoying.*] That means you a devil—

POPE: You watch who you callin' a devil!

FILO: CANALLA, CANALLA, CANALLA!

[POPE *glowers.* FILO *continues singing.*]

FILO: [*Cont'd.*] EBENEZER! EBENEZER!
YOU NEVER GONNA REST IN PEACE,
'CAUSE SOON— [*Victorious at the near rhyme.*]
'CAUSE SOON YOU'RE GONNA BE DECEASED.

CHORUS OH, YES, YOU'RE GONNA BE DECEASED!

[CHARLIE *takes some firewood and taps the trash can lightly with it, a drummer. The* OTHERS, *including* BOY, *dance in spontaneous combinations.*]

FILO: [*Sings.*] YOU GOT TO—

CHORUS: TAKE IT, TAKE IT, TAKE IT!

FILO: SOON AS YOU—

CHORUS: MAKE IT, MAKE IT, MAKE IT!

FILO: AND THEN YOU—

CHORUS: SHAKE IT, SHAKE IT, SHAKE IT—

FILO: AND CHORUS YOU GONNA SPREAD IT ALL AROUND!
YOU GONNA SPREAD IT ALL AROUND!
YOU GONNA SPREAD IT ALL AROUND!

[*Gradually the* CHORUS *fades, as does their laughter.*]

POPE: You ain't right for the part— whatever you name is.

FILO: I'm tryin', man.

POPE: You ain't nothin' but a damn foreigner.

FILO: OK. OK. I do just what Charlie tell me. [*Checking with* CHARLIE, *he wails dramatically.*] Escchame! Listen to me! Ebenezer Scrooge, you got a chance to— [*He begins laughing.*] —a chance to—

[*He laughs harder, falls to the floor.*]

POPE: [*Disgusted.*] What's he doin' now?

CHARLIE: He tells him about the strange, spooky spirits.

VERNA: [To BOY.] This is the good part.

FILO: [*It's hard to pronounce.*] The strange, spooky spirits!

[FILO, *trying to speak, only laughs more at his own attempts, until he is a mass of uncontrolled laughter, repeating his attempts at "strange, spooky spirits."*]

POPE: Shit. Looks like your friend gone and fucked up the story. You better take him out of here, Charlie.

CHARLIE: He'll be okay. Let's finish the story for the kid.

POPE: For him? He just sits like a owl with his big eyes and don't no one know what he's thinkin'. You all want to fill up his mind with lies. And ain't none of you got no idea about the real truth.

AZALEE: Your idea of real ain't real. Your truth only gonna turn him angry, like you.

CHARLIE: Just let me read him the story.

[*While they go on,* VERNA *grabs the flashlight, ducks out of sight for a moment.*]

POPE: Your brain been washed, Azalee. Used to be you could think.

AZALEE: Used to be you could—

[*Before* AZALEE *can finish,* VERNA *emerges with her unbuttoned sweater pulled up over her head, aiming the flashlight in front of her, speaking with dramatic fervor*].

VERNA: I am the Ghost of Christmas Past!

POPE: Look like a nut case to me.

AZALEE: [*A warning.*] Otis Pope!

VERNA: I am the Ghost of Christmas Past.

POPE: Go away, Verna. I ain't playin' this game no more. I'm finished.

VERNA: [*Taking his arm.*] Rise and come with me! We're gonna fly!

POPE: You're flyin' already, Verna! Leave me alone.

VERNA: [*Waving her arm.*] Now we're flying and flying till we come to the past and— [*Aiming flashlight at* POPE'S *face.*] —one little boy is left alone.

POPE: [*Overly loud and clear*] I said I'm finished. Why don't you all fly off and play someplace else? [*He is suddenly amused.*] You be the head of the formation, Verna. Don't bump into no pigeons now!

[*He turns away, laughing.* VERNA *tags him.*]

VERNA: You're it!

[*She and the others quickly run and hide.*]

POPE: And stay there!

[FILO *giggles and runs past* POPE *while* AZALEE *runs the other way.* ALL *hide.*]

POPE: [*Cont'd.*] This ain't no game!

[*No one is visible. Only a few giggles are heard.*]

POPE: [*Cont'd.*] I ain't playin' along!

[*Silence. Stillness. He turns about.*]

POPE: [*Cont'd.*] Never come back be fine with me.

[*A long silence,* POPE *alone. He reaches for his bottle.*]

AZALEE'S VOICE: [*Ghostly.*] You like being alone, Otis Pope?

POPE: Like it fine.

FILO'S VOICE: [*Imitating* AZALEE'S *tone.*] You the one mad at everything, why you don't go someplace else, Otis Pope?

POPE: This my place, damn it! My corner, my city, my country! I fought for this country. You just a foreigner spongin' off it!

FILO: [*Standing, visible; not playing any more.*] You got it easy. I almos' drown in a stinkin' boat for to come to this country.

POPE: My great granddaddy done that, fool! [*Moving toward* FILO'S *voice.*] I bet you ain't even legal. Immigration be interested in you.

CHARLIE: [*Standing, visible.*] I never knew you was in the army, Pope.

POPE: We ain't talkin' 'bout the army. We talkin' 'bout this greaseball here.

CHARLIE: That ain't right, Pope. We're just playin'.

POPE: You come over here, tell me to my face what ain't right, see what happens, Charlie.

VERNA: [*Coming out.*] He doesn't like being alone.

[POPE *takes a long drink, puts the bottle down.*]

AZALEE: [*Coming out.*] He don't want to play none. It ain't no use. Look like our show is over. Anyway, time for me to get back to the shelter.

[*She begins collecting her things.*]

VERNA: Not yet, Azalee. Please, Otis Pope.

[CHARLIE, *followed by* FILO, *moves closer to* POPE.]

CHARLIE: Come on, Pope. For the kid. Azalee could stay a while if you'd only—

POPE: You deaf, too, Charlie? I said no!

AZALEE: They's a lot to get ready. Got to try on some new clothes. Got to make a list of all the jobs I ever had and write them out clear. They call that a resum. Got to—

POPE: [*Getting up.*] Resum! Since when minimum wage need a resum?

[*He begins closing in on* AZALEE.]

POPE: [*Cont'd.*] When you gonna stop lettin' them pull the wool over your eyes? You already been thrown in the garbage. You disposable, like all the rest.

[CHARLIE *moves over to distract him.*]

CHARLIE: So, Pope! What part of the army was you in? You must've been a captain or something, right?

AZALEE: He don't like to—

FILO: [*Saluting.*] El capitn Papa. Un soldado valiente.

[FILO *pretends he's shooting at* POPE.]

CHARLIE: I always thought your arm got hurt in a fight or somethin'. You know, punchin' somebody out.

AZALEE: [*A warning.*] He don't like to talk about it.

[FILO *shoots again, takes the bottle and drinks as* CHARLIE *speaks.*]

CHARLIE: I mean, where was you? In 'Nam? I never been in the service myself, but I—

[POPE'S *good arm swings out suddenly, knocking the bottle from* FILO'S *mouth.*]

POPE: I told you keep your filthy hands off! Now you gone and put your damn mouth on that bottle!

FILO: Hey! What you doin', man?

POPE: [*Pushing* FILO *down, shaking him roughly.*] No tellin' what kind of disease you got!

FILO: You loco! Everyone comin' down, man. [*Shouting.*] You all crazy!

[POPE *has* FILO *pinned to the ground, continues shaking him.*]

AZALEE: Stop it, Otis! Stop it!

[POPE *pushes the* OTHERS *away.*]

VERNA: [*Ducking.*] No! Don't hit me! Don't hit me!

[FILO *starts cursing* POPE *in Spanish, trying to get up.* POPE *holds him down.* VERNA *quickly throws things from the shelter-box back into the cart.*]

VERNA: [*Cont'd.*] We've got to get out of here, Boy.

[*She begins crying like a child, terrified of the violence, pushing the cart past the box where* BOY *remains.* POPE *enjoys his power over* FILO. FILO'S *swearing grows more intense.*]

VERNA: [*Cont'd.*] Please, don't hurt us! Please, please don't hurt us!

[A sudden change, as in the opening.]

VERNA: *[Cont'd.]* God damn son of a bitch!

[Then, whimpering again, she stumbles, trying to get away. CHARLIE comes to help her. She screams, afraid of him, grows more hysterical. CHARLIE backs off. VERNA'S cries overtake POPE and FILO, who fall silent and watch her. AZALEE approaches, then holds and comforts her. ALL are very still, almost frozen. POPE turns away from the group. CHARLIE reaches into the box, helping BOY come out.]

CHARLIE: *[Softly.]* It's okay, Boy. The Ghost of Christmas Past still has a few more things to show old Scrooge. Right?

[BOY leaves CHARLIE and goes to VERNA. Gradually, she calms. ALL are silent, not looking at each other. CHARLIE helps FILO up. AZALEE begins gathering her things again. CHARLIE makes an effort to be cheerful.]

CHARLIE: *[Cont'd.]* Hey! How about we do a happy part? I'm gonna be old Fezziwig.

VERNA: *[From far away.]* Fezzy... wig.

CHARLIE: *[To POPE, hopefully.]* Yo! Ebenezer Scrooge! Get your ass over here!

[POPE does not move or respond in any way.]

CHARLIE: *[Cont'd.]* What the hell!

[He quickly grabs a tape and sticks it in the player. It's an old-fashioned polka.]

CHARLIE: *[Cont'd.]* Let's just have the party! Everyone, we're having a party!

[He intercepts AZALEE, who is on her way off, takes her hand, leading her back in. FILO and VERNA relax a bit.]

FILO and VERNA: *[Softly.]* Let's have a party! Come on! A party! (etc.)

[CHARLIE starts dancing a bit formally with AZALEE, then encourages FILO and VERNA. As they twirl briefly, BOY goes over to POPE, who remains standing by himself. VERNA, a bit dizzy, sits. FILO keeps dancing smoothly by himself. BOY faces POPE. POPE ignores him. After a while, POPE suddenly, fiercely, jerks a limb, as if to frighten BOY. BOY, however, mirrors the move. AZALEE notices and signals FILO and CHARLIE to watch as POPE and BOY continue to stare at each other and do this intermittent jerking, POPE somehow pulled into the game. Suddenly he notices the OTHERS watching, angrily pushes BOY aside, and cuts off the music. FILO grabs the tape player.]

FILO: Hey! That's my musica, man! Mine!

POPE: Get out of here, you crackhead!

[FILO *glares at* POPE, *cursing him in Spanish. He runs off with the tape player.* AZALEE *helps* CHARLIE, *who has weakened, sit down. He closes his eyes.* VERNA *leads* BOY *towards the boxes.*]

VERNA: It's time for bed, Boy. Time you went to sleep. Tomorrow's Christmas and we have to get up early. We'll get our blanket and go to sleep now.

[*She puts* BOY *into box then pulls the wagon near, talking to herself, as* AZALEE *goes over to* POPE, *who's writing in a notebook in his corner.*]

VERNA: [*Cont'd.*] [*To* BOY *in box.*] Don't worry, everything's fine. Everything's fine.

[VERNA *follows* BOY *into box.* CHARLIE *is unmoving, asleep.* AZALEE *approaches* POPE.]

AZALEE: I saw you playin' with the boy, Otis. Can't decide if you've turned all bad or not.

POPE: [*Indicating* CHARLIE.] Put your baby to sleep?

AZALEE: He's just comin' down, is all.

POPE: You jealous of Verna. Want your own little boy to take care of.

AZALEE: Charlie's got a good heart. Maybe you're the one jealous.

POPE: You livin' in the past. They's no feelin's in me.

AZALEE: We used to have us a good time.

POPE: What you tryin' now?

AZALEE: It just hurts me for you to be so hard. The harder you is, the more sweet goodness just shines out of that boy, like he was tryin' to make up for you. That's pullin' me away down low. He looks at you the same way I used to.

[POPE *turns away from her, continues not to look at her.*]

AZALEE: [*Cont'd.*] You was a hero. Back from the war, hurt, and out marchin' for other folks' rights.

POPE: You see what good it done. Things even worse now.

AZALEE: "My sweet girl", you used to call me. "My sweet girl."

POPE: Why you can't let go of history, Az?

AZALEE: I never thought we'd meet up again, especially out here. You're the last person ought to be on the street.

POPE: Me? You the one with all the fancy business school trainin'. You the one come from a good family. Where's that high falutin' family of yours now?

AZALEE: They got no idea where I am, so leave them out of it, Otis. I'll get back to them when I'm on my feet again.

POPE: They know you was locked up for drugs? They visit they little darlin' in the rehab?

AZALEE: All that was a slip I ain't gonna make again. It's you I want to know about now. You don't even have to worry 'bout no job. You collectin' disability, ain't you?

POPE: Never say that word to me. I work for what I get.

AZALEE: What you got is too much pride and a shell thick as that wall there. How many cans you got to pick up? How many days you got to be turned down at the labor pool before you—

POPE: This is war, Az. You don't take from the enemy.

AZALEE: What war? Your war is long over.

POPE: [*The street.*] This war. This war ain't over. We just like POW's— gotta break out before they finish us off. You dreamin' it's over, but you gonna be woke up hard.

AZALEE: You got turned all around, Otis. I can't trust you no more.

POPE: Trust? That's one thing you can do, Az. I never lie to no one.

AZALEE: I ain't so sure.

POPE: Ain't I always told you the truth?

AZALEE: Yes. You tell the truth.

POPE: What you want to know then?

AZALEE: [*Hesitating, then deciding to take the chance.*] I don't know why I bother, but... if we was off the street and you was clean and slick and proud as ever you used to be—

POPE: [*Gently as he slowly faces* AZALEE.] Go on.

AZALEE: You think you might—

POPE: Yes?

AZALEE: You think we might—

POPE: What?

AZALEE: Well...

[*Pause.*]

AZALEE: [*Cont'd.*] [*Almost a whisper.*] You think we could ever be together again, Otis?

POPE: [*After a moment.*] Sure. [*He pauses.*] Soon as that Night of Beauty change street trash like you into the queen of England! [*He laughs.*]

AZALEE: [*A cry of pain.*] Otis!

POPE: [*Continuing to consider more queens, alternately laughing to himself.*] The queen of Sheba... Queen of Baltimore... Queen of Timbuktu!

AZALEE: [*Over* POPE'S *laughter.*] Don't nothin' matter to you but your own mean self, Otis Pope! You ain't human no more! You ain't human!

[*She backs away from* POPE *as* VERNA *emerges and* CHARLIE *awakens. He reaches for her hand, holds it. She gets herself under control.*]

AZALEE: [*Cont'd.*] It's OK, Charlie. Verna. I'm OK. [*Deadly quiet, to* POPE.] You the only one makes me feel like street trash, but them days is over.

POPE: [*Shrugging.*] I told you how things was with me now.

AZALEE: [*Getting her shopping bags.*] I feel bad to walk out on your boy's present, Verna, but I can't stay no longer.

VERNA: He's sound asleep. We can give him the rest of it tomorrow morning. Mommy always says, "We'll see tomorrow". Daddy says, "Ask me tomorrow". [*Touching a tear on* AZALEE'S *face.*] Tomorrow, Azalee.

AZALEE: I don't think so, Verna. You find someone else to do my part. I got to hurry anyhow or I'll be late. But you give that boy a big hug for me.

VERNA: [*Embracing* AZALEE.] Merry Christmas, Azalee.

AZALEE: And to you, sugar. [*Then kissing* CHARLIE'S *forehead.*] Charlie.

[VERNA *disappears into the box.* AZALEE *picks up her things, looks at* POPE, *and exits.* FILO *steps from the shadows.*]

FILO: [*Near tears.*] What you do to her, Pope? You think is fun you hurt a woman? You same like la polica derechista! They take your mother, your sister— so you never see them no more.

[POPE *ignores him. Suddenly,* FILO *lunges, brandishing the tape player as a weapon.*]

FILO: [*Cont'd.*] I'm gonna kill you, Pope! I smash your fuckin' mouth! I break your face up, Pope!

POPE: You nothin' but a little cockroach. [*Laughing.*] You want to be squashed for real?

[FILO *is about to strike when* CHARLIE *grabs him from behind. They struggle. The party music gets switched on and blares from the player.* CHARLIE'S *arms are around* FILO.]

CHARLIE: Go on now, Filo. You go on and get what you need before you get hurt.

FILO: I got friends. They're gonna get you, Pope!

POPE: I'm shittin' my pants! [*He chuckles some more.*]

CHARLIE: Gimme the box, man. Gimme the box.

[*He takes the tape player, and turns it off, still holding* FILO, *who continues to struggle ineffectively.*]

CHARLIE: Come back later. When you're feelin' better.

[*He opens his arms.* FILO *runs off like a bird released from an encircling hand.* POPE *glares at* CHARLIE.]

CHARLIE: [*Cont'd.*] He don't mean nothin'. He ain't got no friends. His own people kicked him out.

POPE: Why you pick someone like that?

CHARLIE: The guy's all alone.

POPE: He's stupid and dangerous, Charlie. Comin' way down. [*Throws a couple of* FILO'S *things after him.*] Hey, Filo! You forgot your presents!

[VERNA *comes out from the box, signalling quiet. She has added some nighttime bits of clothing; a quilted bed jacket, fluffy slippers, a few hair curlers placed haphazardly.*]

VERNA: Shhh. The children are asleep.

CHARLIE: That's good, Verna.

[VERNA *sees a Big Mac container, scurries after it. She takes something wrapped in newspaper from a pocket, puts it in the Big Mac holder, wraps it all in the piece of Christmas paper she secreted earlier, winding it with ribbon as she speaks.*]

VERNA: Something crinkly for tomorrow. After the story. Tomorrow comes Tiny Tim. He's going to like that part. He's going to like that part the best, clap his hands... Goodnight, Charlie. Otis Pope. Merry Christmas.

CHARLIE: Merry Christmas, Verna.

[*She tiptoes back to the box, carefully hides the present, and settles in, disappearing from view.* CHARLIE *begins weeping.*]

POPE: Now what? You worryin' on that virus again? You probably OK, thanks to needle man.

CHARLIE: [*Not hearing.*] Verna's kid— what chance he got? What kind of chance he got for anything?

POPE: We can't hardly talk when you like this.

CHARLIE: It's all messed up. The story... Everything's messed up for Verna and the kid. Peace on earth. My god!

POPE: Don't do him no good to get the wrong idea of the world from a story. People killin', blowin' each other up. Right here, too.

[POPE *is very subdued, struggling against his pain.*]

POPE: [*Cont'd.*] Strong young men, like he could be some day. Killin' each other like bugs. Peace on earth be a lie.

CHARLIE: I know.

POPE: Anyhow, you worried 'bout a little kid might not even be hers.

CHARLIE: Even if he ain't, he is.

[*Pause.*]

POPE: How long you been 'round here now, Charlie?

CHARLIE: Few months.

POPE: Verna been 'round time enough to have three, four kids. She liable to run off and forget she even have a child. Once left one this big [*Very small.*] hid in a little shoe box or somethin' in the park. Left it all day. Come back lookin' for her doll, she say. "Somebody done took my doll baby," she say, when she find it gone.

CHARLIE: Damn! Something awful happen to it?

POPE: [*Shrugging.*] Didn't die, if that's what you mean. City [county] took it for safe keepin'. Gave it away like the others, I suppose. Same as a dog in the pound. These babies keep comin' and you worried 'bout spoilin' this one's story. Story? Story ain't nothin' real, man.

[*No reaction from* CHARLIE.]

POPE: [*Cont'd.*] Hey, man, you asleep?

[*Indeed,* CHARLIE *has nodded off.* VERNA *slides her head out of the box.*]

VERNA: We want to dream a lighted tree.

POPE: Yeah, sure.

VERNA: Make the music again, Charlie.

POPE: That damn music is—

CHARLIE: [*Barely opening his eyes, but cutting* POPE *off.*] Sure, Verna.

[VERNA *goes back into the box.* CHARLIE *pulls himself up, moves towards his own sleeping box. He manages to put a distorted version of "Silent Night" into the tape player. The music begins as* POPE *goes to warm himself by the fire.* CHARLIE *stops before entering his shelter.*]

CHARLIE: [*Cont'd.*] Pope... Leave somethin' alive, Pope. OK?

[*Pause.* POPE *does not turn around.*]

POPE: Go to sleep, Charlie. Go to sleep.

[CHARLIE *slides into his box. Disgusted with the music,* POPE *goes over and turns it off. He looks at the boxes where the* OTHERS *are sleeping, then adds some scraps to the trash can. He stands at the fire as lights fade to black.*]

END OF ACT I

ACT II

[In the blackout an explosion of laughter and Latin music is heard. Lights rise. It is the next morning. The stage remains the same, but a bit brighter. BOY *and* FILO *are dancing to the current cassette.* FILO *is wearing a ladies' hat and something tied around him as a skirt.* VERNA *is enjoying this immensely. Even* POPE *is amused.* CHARLIE, *weak, as though he has the flu, is holding the book again. He stops the cassette.* BOY *goes to sit next to* VERNA *where he picks up and holds the wrapped Big Mac box.]*

CHARLIE: Now, you got to talk, Filo. Like a girl. Like Azalee, if she was here.

FILO: *[In falsetto.]* Like this, man? Now I Scrooge' girlfriend?

CHARLIE: I suppose. You was his girlfriend. Now you're married to me.

FILO: Oooh, ain't you lucky, man!

CHARLIE: Let's just finish this up. I ain't feelin' too hot.

FILO: Let's go!

CHARLIE: *[With little energy.]* Belle, I saw an old friend of yours today.

FILO: *[In falsetto, flirtatious.]* Who was it, man?

CHARLIE: Guess.

FILO: Was we once kind of... you know... ?

[FILO wiggles his hips, then laughs again. CHARLIE *is less involved, distracted by physical discomfort.* VERNA *places* BOY'S *gift under one of the crates for safe-keeping. Only* POPE *is laughing.]*

FILO: *[Cont'd.]* Hey, Pope! I make you laugh, no?

POPE: You hilarious in drag, man.

[Pause. In the silence, FILO *looks around, then down at his costume, growing uncomfortable.]*

FILO: Maybe we not 'spose to laugh at this story. Maybe is un sacrilego, no?

POPE: What you say?

FILO: Sa-cri-lego.

POPE: *[Amused.]* Sacrilege? Not exactly.

CHARLIE: This ain't church, Filo. It's just a story.

POPE: That's all they got in church— stories. Bullshit.

FILO: You better watch out, man. You don't know who's watching. Like God.

VERNA: God is every place. Even in the bathroom.

FILO: They seen him walkin' around, man.

VERNA: He might come around that corner any minute.

POPE: Who you talkin' 'bout now? The needle man?

FILO: Jess. Jesus. He been seen in Carolina.

POPE: [*Giving up.*] Aw, hell! You promised he'd be a good boy today, Charlie.

CHARLIE: He's cool, man. North or South Carolina, Filo?

FILO: Carolina. Where I was before. They say they seen him. He rise up from the dead. They talk about it on the radio. And at the mission. Everyone all excited. "He comin' back!", they say, "He comin' back! Right here in Carolina!"

POPE: That ain't Jesus, dummy! They talkin' 'bout Elvis! He be seen more than Jesus nowadays. People lightin' candles, makin' pilgrimage to his house. Elvis a new religion, man. Soon they be givin' presents on his birthday, sing the hymn of the blue suede shoes. Amen!

CHARLIE: Maybe someone just oughta read the story to the kid. We can't do it right without Azalee.

POPE: Filo's prettier than Azalee!

CHARLIE: I gotta get to work soon.

POPE: Ain't no labor pool today.

[*All* VERNA'S *words are directed to* CHARLIE *as a plea to keep going.*]

VERNA: Keep telling it, Charlie! Next comes the Ghost of the Present. Scrooge says, "I wonder—"

CHARLIE: I got other things to do. Gotta meet someone.

FILO: Me, too.

POPE: Ain't nobody 'round yet on Christmas mornin'. You suppose' to plan ahead.

CHARLIE: I just ain't feelin' too good.

VERNA: [*More urgently.*] —Then Scrooge says, "I wonder what will happen next", and the Ghost of Christmas Past disappears.

POPE: [*To* CHARLIE.] And you ain't got no cash. So what you gonna do?

[CHARLIE *moves aside, slightly bent over, holding his stomach.*]

FILO: [*To* CHARLIE.] People wakin' up all over town. Is gettin' late, man.

CHARLIE: Yeah. It's gettin' late, Verna. I gotta see some people.

VERNA: [*Frantically.*] Ebenezer Scrooge! Ebenezer Scrooge! I am the Ghost of the Present! Look upon me! [*Turning to* CHARLIE.] Please, Charlie! Please!

[CHARLIE *looks at* BOY, *then checks the book, forcing himself to keep telling the story.*]

CHARLIE: He saw this big guy and a lot of food... Turkeys, poultry, meat... them— whaddaya call 'em— minch pies... [*The food descriptions are making him even queasier.*] Apples, and, uh, citrus— oranges, grapefruits and such. And people was sellin' things.

VERNA: [*As if hawking.*] Grapefruits! Get your big, fat grapefruits!

FILO: Two for seventy centavos.

[THEY *play to* BOY. CHARLIE *is weak;* POPE, *unexpressive.*]

VERNA: Oranges! Fresh Florida oranges!

FILO: Four dollars a pound.

VERNA: Raisins and chocolate candy! Brush after eating!

FILO: I give you a special deal, man—

AZALEE: [*As she enters.*] How about some of these?

VERNA: Pardon?

[*The action stops.* ALL *watch as a transformed* AZALEE *enters carrying a small bag of apples. She is clean and neatly dressed, although her clothing is second-hand. She would not attract attention on the street, but easily fits in with a crowd of lunchtime office workers. She clearly feels good and speaks in a carefully-modulated voice.*]

AZALEE: [*Giving the bag to* VERNA.] I can only stay for a moment, but I have some shiny red apples for you and your boy.

[*Pause.*]

VERNA: Azalee! It's you. Ms. Azalee Hodge!

AZALEE: [*The old AZ.*] It's me, all right!

VERNA: [*Dancing about.*] Azalee is Cinderella! Azalee is Cinderella!

[AZALEE *turns about and poses happily, like a model.* ALL, *except* POPE, *gape.*]

VERNA: [*Cont'd.*] Did you come in a royal carriage?

AZALEE: A white stretch limo. My chauffeur's awaitin'.

POPE: You interruptin' the story.

FILO: You be one pretty lady, Azalee. You like to come dancin' with me?

[*He does a wicked few steps, laughs.* AZALEE *plays her lady's role.*]

AZALEE: I respectfully decline your offer. But thank you just the same.

[*Only* POPE *pays no attention.* VERNA *gets* BOY. AZALEE *approaches them.* VERNA *and* BOY *touch* AZALEE'S *face, hair, coat.*]

VERNA: She's real. She touches real. Our fingers don't go through her.

[*As* AZALEE *continues, her attention turning to* ALL, VERNA *takes an apple, starts it with a small bite, and gives it to* BOY. *She saves the others.*]

AZALEE: I'm real, all right. Real as I used to be. Livin' out here's what's not real. When it happened to me, that wasn't real. Now I'm back in step.

CHARLIE: You're lookin' good, Az.

AZALEE: Thank you, Charlie.

CHARLIE: You really got a chauffeur?

AZALEE: Might as well have. I feel like a million dollars.

CHARLIE: That Night of Beauty worked good.

AZALEE: You could do it, too. You quit lookin' like a homeless, get cleaned up and smellin' good, first thing you know you're walkin' straight, like you know where you're goin'. Next thing, folks just start treatin' you different. Even at the shelter. Hey, what's the matter?

FILO: [*Laughing.*] He cold, man. He shakin'.

AZALEE: Why don't you get you some methadone, Charlie?

FILO: No, lady. He no wantin' methadone. He waitin' for the real thing.

CHARLIE: I gotta go now. We stopped anyway.

VERNA: We're almost at Tiny Tim.

FILO: Charlie in a bad way, man. We got to go.

AZALEE: [*To* CHARLIE.] You stay around. Be a few hours till you can do business. Why don't you finish the story like Verna wants? It'll help keep your mind off how you're feeling.

VERNA: Azalee came back so Boy could have the whole story. Now you've got to stay, Charlie. You, too, Filo. When it's over, Boy gets to open up his stocking stuffer! Thank you, Azalee. Now we're at the Cratchit's house. Azalee, you be—

AZALEE: [*Trying to leave, to* VERNA.] No, sugar, I can't. You see, they had all that fruit at the shelter and I only came back to—

POPE: My Fair Lady come back to show off. She ain't gonna hang around with us none. She gonna strut uptown, turn this way and that. She come to say goodbye is what. Thinks she never gonna see us again. Ain't that the truth, Ms. Hodge?

[*Pause.*]

AZALEE: I come to pick up the story. Finish what I start, in spite of you, Otis Pope. Nothin' you do bother me now. Tomorrow I got interviews.

[FILO *whistles and laughs.*]

POPE: You watch out if it rains. You melt like a ice cream cone. You turn back into a pumpkin.

AZALEE:

[*Ignoring* him.] What part we up to?

VERNA: Tiny Tim, Tiny Tim, Tiny Tim! [*To* AZALEE.] You're his pretty mama.

AZALEE: Who his daddy?

FILO: Filomeno Cordero apply for the job.

VERNA: [*To* AZALEE.] Charlie.

AZALEE: Well, that's all right, then.

[CHARLIE *pulls* AZALEE *aside as the* OTHERS *build a table from crates and a board.*]

CHARLIE: Maybe you can help me out, Az, now that you're well-fixed.

AZALEE: Ain't nothin' more in my purse than there was last night. You in trouble. I can see that.

POPE: Bob Cratchit got the shakes.

CHARLIE: But, Az—

FILO: What happen next?

[AZALEE *rubs* CHARLIE'S *hands between hers.*]

AZALEE: You soon be warmin' up in this little house we got.

[SHE *turns and sees the finished "table."*]

AZALEE: [*Cont'd.*] We is at the house of the Cratchits.

[VERNA *takes* CHARLIE'S *hand, pulling him off with her.*]

VERNA: Come on, father, we'll be late for Christmas dinner.

AZALEE: Hang on, Charlie. Little bit longer only. No one ready to help you yet.

POPE: Bob Cratchit gonna be sick all over that cute little house.

AZALEE: Don't pay him no mind. Scrooge the jealous type.

POPE: You say. Scrooge about to depart this story.

AZALEE: We'll finish it the right way, then. Without you.

POPE: That's fine.

FILO: Yeah. The right way, pretty lady.

[POPE *starts walking off.* BOY *follows him, grabs his sleeve and pulls him back.* POPE *shakes* HIM *off, but stays.*]

AZALEE: [*To* BOY.] Where's my children? And where's my husband, Bob, and our poor little Tiny Tim? [*Beckoning to* BOY.] I need me some children first, to be waitin' with me.

[*She looks at* BOY. *He gives a questioning look to* POPE.]

POPE: [*To* BOY.] Don't look at me. You do what you want. Don't matter none to me.

[AZALEE *reaches out to* BOY, *hugs him as she pulls him over.* POPE *exits.*]

AZALEE: That's right. Your name's Peter.

FILO: [*To* AZALEE.] Here your other boy, mama. What my name is?

AZALEE: [*Holding him off.*] You called Willie.

FILO: Willie. [*Closing in on* AZALEE.] What's cookin', mama?

AZALEE: [*Pushing him away.*] Christmas dinner. And nothing else! Now let's set up the table since your daddy and Tiny Tim be comin' home any minute.

[BOY *and* FILO *help* AZALEE *"set" the table, covering it with newspaper, as* VERNA *enters using an inverted sponge mop for a crutch. She is dragging* CHARLIE *by the hand.*]

VERNA: Wasn't the snow beautiful today, father? And you carried me on your shoulders and...

FILO: [*Waving.*] Papa! Papa!

[VERNA *finds herself in the midst of the scene. She looks about.*]

VERNA: God bless us, everyone!

[CHARLIE, *in great discomfort, shivering, looks up at* AZALEE.]

CHARLIE: Az!

AZALEE: [*Very aware of his condition.*] You boys take your brother to see all that good cookin'.

[FILO *and* VERNA *move away with* BOY, *leaving* AZALEE *and* CHARLIE.]

FILO: We gettin' a great big fat bird, could be un papagayo.

VERNA: It's a goose.

FILO: An' maybe some yuca y pescado y frijoles, arroz con pollo con pepitas muy calientes! Papas, maiz...

AZALEE: [*With compassion.*] What is it, Charlie?

[CHARLIE *becomes even sicker as he speaks, a major effort.*]

CHARLIE: [*Close to tears, shaking his head.*] Man... if... if Tiny Tim did die! ... Hopeless... Christmas... my kids... couldn't send them nothing... an insult to my own kids! ... Specially with what I used to do for them... It ain't my fault if the fuckin' plant got shut down... Things happen when you can't work no more

AZALEE: I understand, Charlie.

CHARLIE: So many babies with nothin' to eat...

[*He weeps silently. Pause.* AZALEE *goes to him and kneels next to him.* POPE *returns quietly, observing.*]

AZALEE: [*Gently.*] Listen here. You Bob Cratchit now. He's a man what's full of hope, no matter how bad things get.

POPE: [*With bitterness.*] He what's known as a casualty of war.

[AZALEE *lifts* CHARLIE'S *face, looks in his eyes.*]

AZALEE: You understand? Only gonna get better from here on. Here come Tiny Tim and his brothers now. Don't let 'em see you bein' so low.

[CHARLIE *tries to pull himself together and* VERNA, BOY, *and* FILO *begin running and limping around.*]

FILO: We want food! We want food!

[VERNA *joins in.* ALL *except* POPE *sit around the "table."* VERNA *and* FILO *are still chanting.* BOY *copies* FILO'S *actions, continues to do so.* AZALEE *carefully serves and divides* CHARLIE'S *fruitcake with an old knife from* VERNA'S *cart.*]

VERNA: What a beautiful goose! [*An aside to* BOY.] It's really very little, but we think it's big.

AZALEE: [*Slapping* FILO'S *hand.*] You keep your hands out them potatoes!

[FILO *starts licking his fingers. He gets very involved in this activity, continuing for a long while under what follows, dipping into imaginary food and licking it off.*]

VERNA: The gravy is thick and smells good all over the house.

AZALEE: The butter's meltin' out of the cornbread right onto the tablecloth.

CHARLIE: There's bowls of stuffing with nuts...

AZALEE: Sweet potato casserole covered with wavy white marshmallows, a little bit brown on the top.

VERNA: Cranberry sauce with chunks of orange.

CHARLIE: Milk for the kids.

VERNA: Now daddy says grace.

[AZALEE *gets a blanket and puts it around* CHARLIE, *who is shivering.* POPE *observes from his corner.* FILO *crosses himself and plays along.*]

CHARLIE: [*Softly, mostly to himself.*] You gotta give up something to get something... If I ain't got no money, I can still figure a way to get my kids anything they need... I can do it... One way or the other.

[*He looks at the* OTHERS, *his teeth chattering.*]

CHARLIE: [*Cont'd.*] I'd do it.

AZALEE: 'Course you would.

VERNA: It's all right, father.

CHARLIE: I wouldn't be like— what's his name—?

POPE: Bob Cratchit.

CHARLIE: Like him. I wouldn't sit back and wait on other dudes.

POPE: Good for Bob Cratchit.

CHARLIE: I can do it... [*Making a determined decision.*] ...without no methadone!

[*After a moment,* ALL *look at* AZALEE.]

AZALEE: Dig in, boys.

[*She sits and watches them eat the fruitcake, stretching it. They are gulp-*

ing and talking at once. CHARLIE *sits very still, clutching the blanket around himself.*]

VERNA: I want the drumstick!

FILO: This taste like dried up fish! [*He laughs.*]

VERNA: Peter wants more potatoes!

FILO: Taste like mashed up plañtanos, not cooked enough. [*He laughs.*]

AZALEE: Pass the apple pie!

FILO: Da me el arroz con pollo, man! [*He laughs a lot.*]

AZALEE: Shhh!

[AZALEE *stops the action, sees the image.*]

AZALEE: [*Cont'd.*] Pie la mode with fudge vanilla ice cream.

[*She takes a small taste of the cake, imagining.* BOY, VERNA, *and* FILO *repeat her action together, as if in ritual, finishing the cake.*]

VERNA: God bless us, everyone!

AZALEE: That was one fine meal. The best Christmas dinner we ever had.

[*Pause.* AZALEE *gets up to leave. She looks around uncomfortably, begins walking away.* VERNA *follows her.*]

VERNA: Now we sit by the fire and tell beautiful stories.

AZALEE: I got to get back to the shelter before they give my place to somebody else.

VERNA: Don't leave us alone, mother.

AZALEE: [*Strongly conflicted.*] Tiny Tim got to finish the story. I stayed too long already.

POPE: You leavin' your poor little children, mama? How they gonna manage without you?

AZALEE: [*With unconvincing cheeriness.*] You all take care, now. You gonna be fine and dandy.

[*She starts off.*]

POPE: Tiny Tim gonna die.

VERNA: [*To* BOY.] No, he isn't. Not really.

AZALEE: [*Stopping her exit.*] What you up to, Pope?

POPE: You leavin', so you got nothin' to say on the matter.

AZALEE: [*Forcefully.*] Why don't you just let these folk finish the story like they want? They ain't got nothin' else.

VERNA: Mr. Scrooge will save me in the end!

CHARLIE: [*Suddenly very focused.*] His father's gonna save him.

POPE: You all crazy. Least a hundred more like him be out on the street since they house got tore down to build a new stadium. Football more important than babies... Ain't nothin' gonna help a kid like him.

AZALEE: You're wrong. There's lots of things.

FILO: Yeah. You sell him to a rich familia.

CHARLIE: His father gets a good job—

VERNA: [*Rising.*] He goes on TV!

FILO: He be famous, man!

POPE: Maybe you got somethin', Verna. You makin' sense for a change. Maybe TV could do it... What disease the kid got?

FILO: [*Sitting up.*] He got somethin' bad. [*Thinks for a moment, then pleased with himself.*] Yeah, he interminably ill, man!

VERNA: My little leg, you see. And now I've got something worse.

[*She limps forward, coughing pathetically.* POPE *jumps up and takes center stage. He uses a stick for a microphone.*]

POPE: Ladies and gentlemen, welcome to the Tiny Tim Telethon!

[*At this, while* POPE *continues,* VERNA *goes excitedly to consult with* AZALEE, *further holding her there.*]

POPE: [*Cont'd.*] We got stars, stars, stars! We gonna be up all night here, get circles under our eyes, undo our ties, show you how much we care. First, before our great lineup of entertainment, here's the poster boy hisself— Tiny Tim!

[FILO, *copied by* BOY, *applauds and whistles.* CHARLIE *sits aside, weak and ill, trying to participate.* VERNA *leaves* AZALEE, *goes over to* POPE, *smiles at the world.*]

POPE: [*Cont'd.*] Look at this boy, ladies and gentlemen! Born with an incurable case of Poverty! Your nickels and dimes and dollars will go to important research to find a cure for this dreaded disease. So call now. Our lines is open!

[VERNA *looks at* AZALEE *for encouragement. This time* AZ *reluctantly applauds with the* OTHERS.]

POPE: [*Cont'd.*] You somethin' else, kid! I ask you, ladies and gentlemen, you ever seen such a case?

[*Applause.* AZALEE *is more enthusiastic for* VERNA, *who is pleased with her own impersonation.*]

POPE: [*Cont'd.*] Tell me, son. How long you been poor?

VERNA: I am rich in spirit.

POPE: Rich in spirit. You hear that, folks? He's really stupid!

[*Applause.*]

POPE: [*Cont'd.*] [*To* VERNA.] What would you have liked to be if you was goin' to grow up, Tiny?

VERNA: Last Christmas vacation I went with mom and dad and Sean to St. Augustine, Florida.

POPE: What you talkin' about?

VERNA: We drove in the family car and spent the night in a motel on the way.

POPE: That's real nice, but—

AZALEE: Let her tell it—

VERNA: We went to an old, old cemetery. [*In her mother's voice.*] "Stay together, children". [*herself.*] Sean and I held hands and looked at all the dead people underground and we stretched out on the ground to see how big they were. Then we found two little tombstones, side by side, and they were teeny tiny and we knew we could never fit in there because there were babies under there that died in seventeen eighty-four and seventeen eighty-five. Sean read it to me. "Sarah, our beloved daughter". Sarah died when she was one year old. The other one said "Helen". She had only numbers, no words. She died when she was three months old. Sean figured it out. And the sorrow reaches all the way to today. Sorrow hangs in the air when children die. I can touch it. Like a rope. Long ropes of sorrow... as long as time.

[*Pause.* AZALEE *comes to* VERNA, *reassuring her.*]

POPE: [*Gently.*] Why that's fine. That's fine, Tiny Tim.

[VERNA, *becoming Tiny Tim again, limps off to the side.* ALL *remain silent for a moment.* POPE *changes the mood.*]

POPE: [*Cont'd.*] This kind of thing makes a telethon. You send in that money now. Time for the show, ladies and gentlemen. Who we got first?

[POPE *holds the stick out to* AZALEE, *who declines, but* FILO *strides center.*]

FILO: Ladies and gentlemen! Da, da, de, daaa! Filomeno Cordero! [*Another fanfare.*]

POPE: All right, but get it over fast. You got one minute. The clock is runnin'. [*Stick as pendulum.*] Tick tock, tick tock, tick—

[FILO *grabs a blanket, using it as a cape.*]

FILO: Filomeno the Great! [*Fanfare.*] He can do anything! He does for Tiny Tim his wonderful dance. [*As he dances, describing his steps.*] He dances like this. He dances like that. And then something con mucho magico... Filomeno Cordero disappear his foot!

[*He raises one foot behind the blanket, continues to dance on the other*].

FILO: [*Cont'd.*] And he still dancing, ladies and gentlemen, he still dancing!

[*He hops back near one of the boxes.*]

FILO: [*Cont'd.*] Now, everybody, Filomeno the Great, Filomeno Cordero, firs' he disappear his foot, now he disappear hisself!

[*He raises the blanket. When it falls, he has vanished into the box. There is a beat of silence.* VERNA *is amazed.*]

POPE: Now that's good. I like that! I hope he disappear hisself for good!

[FILO *comes out of the box to take a bow.* ALL *applaud.*]

FILO: Thank you. Thank you.

[VERNA *steps forward, leaving the crutch behind.*]

VERNA: And now Verna will perform her famous ballet dance.

[*As* VERNA *gets into position, her arms overhead—*]

POPE: Tick tock, tick tock—

[VERNA *does an awkward free form dance, using her arms a lot.* FILO *hums a waltz-like accompaniment. After a while, he joins the dance.* POPE *reminds him.*]

POPE: [*Cont'd.*] Tick tock, tick tock—

[FILO *whirls* VERNA *faster and faster until she protests. He won't stop.* VERNA *screams.* BOY *and* AZALEE *get up.* POPE *seizes* FILO, *pulls him away from* VERNA *and throws him aside.* VERNA *sits, breathless, holding her belly, tended to by* AZALEE *and* BOY. FILO *suddenly grabs the knife from the "table," brandishes it at* POPE. CHARLIE *stands, weak, but ready.* POPE *raises the stick, ready to strike.*]

FILO: You get away from me!

[*He seems about to spring, then smiles brightly, laughs, lowers the knife.*]

FILO: [*Cont'd.*] She gonna be OK. I'm only playin', man.

VERNA: [*Dizzy, smiling.*] It's a merry, merry, merry-go-round!

FILO: You see, man? I know what I doin'. Now she higher than before. Hey! Qu pasa? What you lookin' at now?

POPE: Go on. Get out of here.

FILO: I don't mean nothing bad. I do something real good for her.

[*Pause as* POPE *looks at him.* FILO *is genuinely contrite.*]

CHARLIE: It's over, Pope.

FILO: I don't want to hurt no one.

POPE: Give me that knife. I'll hold on to it.

FILO: [*Giving* POPE *the knife.*] Sure. You take it.

[CHARLIE *sits down, away from the* OTHERS.]

POPE: You got anything else on you?

FILO: Nothing, man. I'm clean, man.

POPE: Tell her you're sorry or whatever, then get on out.

FILO: [*To* VERNA.] I got an idea. Better than anything you seen yet.

[VERNA, *still weak, leaning back in her seat, is slowly captivated by* FILO'S *performance.* AZALEE *and* BOY *remain wary.*]

FILO: [*Cont'd.*] I show you the real TV. You win all the prizes, get el niño whatever he need.

[*He looks at* POPE, *who continues to watch him carefully.* FILO *speaks gently, directly to* VERNA, *continuing to use the blanket.*]

FILO: [*Cont'd.*] I am the quiz show, very, very rich. I think of somethin', you guess what it is. I make— [*He hides behind the blanket, buzzes, then pops out again.*] —mean no, you wrong, man. [*He hides, chimes, pops out.*] —mean yes, you got it, win mucho dinero. Now— you tell me. I'm thinking... of un animal.

VERNA: [*Translating to* BOY.] An animal.

FILO: Now you guess it.

VERNA: Does it have four legs?

[FILO *buzzes.*]

AZALEE: [*To* VERNA, *eager for* FILO *to finish.*] That means it's a human being, sugar. You hurry and guess it now.

VERNA: [*To* FILO.] Is it? A human being?

[FILO *chimes.*]

VERNA: [*Cont'd.*] A lady?

[FILO *buzzes, laughs.*]

VERNA: [*Cont'd.*] [*Still weak, but pleased with herself.*] It's a man!

[FILO *chimes.*]

CHARLIE: Ask if he's famous.

AZALEE: Sure. Someone big, like the president.

VERNA: Someone who takes care of everyone, especially little children.

[FILO *buzzes and laughs.*]

FILO: He don't like children at all!

AZALEE: Only one person that could be. Otis Pope!

[FILO *chimes.*]

VERNA:: You mean Scrooge.

AZALEE: Same thing!

[FILO *chimes some more.*]

FILO: [*Showing his head above the blanket.*] One million dollar for Tiny Tim!

[FILO *chimes and buzzes alternately, moving about, very hyper. He falls to the ground hooting and moving under the blanket like a tiger in a sack. He is at the edge of the shadowed area, completely covered by the blanket. His activity suddenly stops.* BOY *goes over to observe the phenomenon closely.* VERNA *signals to* AZALEE, *who follows him, then steers him away.*]

AZALEE: Looks like that crack done let go of him. He ain't gonna bother no one for a time.

[*She seats* BOY *at the ersatz table, near the now shivering* CHARLIE. VERNA *pulls herself up slowly with the crutch, leans on it. She walks with more difficulty, in real pain. She limps into the shadows and disappears, unnoticed by the* OTHERS. AZALEE *sits next to* CHARLIE, *comforting him.*]

POPE: [*Disgusted with* FILO.] Soon as he wakes up, he's gone for good. [*Looking from* CHARLIE *to* AZALEE *to* BOY.] While you all havin' fun, time been runnin' out on Tiny Tim. You all playin' games while time runnin' out on everything, on all the things that need fixin'. [*Slowly and deliberately.*] Jobless, tick-tock; homeless, tick-tock; white against black, tick-tock; soldiers shootin', tick-tock; gangs shootin', tick-tock; filthy air, tick; HIV, tock; hungry kids, tick; old folks, tock; family, Charlie; god, Filo; self-respect, Az; dreams, Verna; life, Boy! Tick-tock, tick-tock, tick-tock, BOOM!

[*He pauses, smiles. Then speaks again as if to TV audience.*]

POPE: [*Cont'd.*] In the meantime, folks, you can make out a check to the Tiny Tim Telethon and—

[POPE *moves over to* CHARLIE *and stands there.* CHARLIE *moans softly.*]

POPE: [*Cont'd.*] Ladies and gentlemen, I believe Tiny Tim's father got somethin' to say.

[*He holds the "microphone" down for* CHARLIE.]

AZALEE: [*Trying to stop him.*] He's sick, Pope.

CHARLIE: ... Don't want any money.

POPE: It ain't for you, it's for research.

CHARLIE: All I want is a decent job so my kids will have——

POPE: A job! This man wants a job, folks! Well, we ain't got no offers for you as yet, Cratchit, but that don't matter 'cause we're gonna help. Wait till you hear!

AZALEE: Pope!

POPE: You goin' to Disneyland, Bob Cratchit! You and the whole family. Four days, best hotels, the works.

[CHARLIE *does not hear him; is confused and ill.*]

AZALEE: [RISING.] You got to stop this!

POPE: Wait. Wait a minute, folks. I'm gettin' a signal,... Ladies and gentlemen, I have a announcement to make. I just been gave the news that Tiny Tim— Tiny Tim is dead!

[BOY, *frightened, clutches* AZALEE.]

AZALEE: You got no heart left, Otis Pope! It's one thing for you to take out your misery on me, but this sorry child ain't here for you to hurt! [*She turns to* BOY.] Don't you worry, Boy. It's part of the story. Your mama fine and dandy, hidin' right back there. Tiny Tim only be dead for now. You wait and see. It's gonna be all right soon. I'll go get your mama.

POPE: Yeah. Go get him his crazy mama he so worried over. [*To* BOY.] You little, but you already a fool.

AZALEE: [*To* BOY.] Look here, baby. The telethon's all finished. Your mama gonna tell you the future part, about Tiny Tim.

[AZALEE *starts to move toward the shadows to get* VERNA.]

POPE: [*To* AZALEE.] Anyway, soon as they find out Tiny Tim dead, everyone be wantin' their money back!

AZALEE: [*To* BOY.] Don't pay him no mind. Folks ain't so stingy.

[*She continues toward the shadows.*]

AZALEE: [*Cont'd.*] Tiny Tim! Verna! Come on, honey! I got to be goin'!

[AZALEE *disappears into the shadows.* CHARLIE *stumbles part of the way after her, collapses onto the van seat.* POPE *moves purposefully to put some of his belongings into the duffel bag.*]

POPE: I might be goin' first! This old place 'bout used itself up.

[BOY *goes to feel the cloth over* FILO. *He throws it aside. There's nothing beneath it but* FILO'S *sunglasses. He looks at the glasses, his fear building. He starts to run after* AZALEE, *but she intercepts him, returning cheerfully.*]

AZALEE: She's sound asleep. Takin' a little nap. Can you read to him some, Charlie?

[CHARLIE *turns away.* AZALEE *gets the book.*]

AZALEE: [*Cont'd.*] You want to hear more of the story, don't you, Boy?

[BOY *nods.*]

AZALEE: [*Cont'd.*] See, Charlie? You got to read to him.

[CHARLIE *wearily takes the book from* AZALEE *as she seats* BOY *next to him.* CHARLIE *reads softly and slowly, with effort, while* AZALEE *speaks to* POPE.]

CHARLIE: [*Under* POPE *and* AZALEE.] "The phantom slowly, gravely, silently, approached. When it came near him, Scrooge bent down upon his knee, for in the very air through which this spirit moved it seemed to scatter gloom and mystery. It was shrouded in a deep black garment, which concealed its head, its face, its form, and left nothing of it visible save one outstretched hand..."

AZALEE: [*Over* CHARLIE, *to* POPE.] She's gone. That old stick she use for a crutch gone, too. And Filo ain't nowhere in sight.

POPE: Good!

AZALEE: You don't think that crazy man done somethin'—

POPE: Maybe she just gone off to drop her baby.

AZALEE: She ain't no animal! What if he—

POPE: Or she run away and forgot who she were again. She'll be back sooner or later.

AZALEE: She was lookin' ghostly white.

[BOY *suddenly leaves* CHARLIE *and goes toward the sleeping box.*]

AZALEE: [*Cont'd.*] I don't know what we're gonna do with that boy.

[AZALEE *hurries over to stop* BOY.]

AZALEE: [*Cont'd.*] She's not in there, sugar. But she'll be back soon. Tiny Tim gonna come back soon.

[*She brings him back towards* CHARLIE.]

AZALEE: [*Cont'd.*] Charlie's gonna finish the story for you.

CHARLIE: [*Near collapse.*] I can't!

[AZALEE *moves away with* BOY. *He pulls at her arm. She bends to him. He shows her* FILO'S *sunglasses, waving them in an urgent question.*]

POPE: Why don't he say what he want 'stead of wavin' his arm like some stupid bird?

AZALEE: He worryin' on Filo [*To* BOY.] That Filo is gone. Don't you worry 'bout him. Don't you worry 'bout Otis Pope, neither. You got nothin' to worry about. We gonna do more of the show in a minute.

[*There is a sudden moan from* CHARLIE.]

AZALEE: [*Cont'd.*] I'm with you, Charlie.

[*She goes over to him.*]

POPE: [*With sarcasm.*] Sure. They're gonna do the show and Charlie's gonna be the future ghost.

[POPE *looks at the trembling* CHARLIE, *who is doubled over, covered with the blanket.*]

POPE: [*Cont'd.*] This gettin' worse. He got it bad.

[*While* POPE *and* AZALEE *are distracted by* CHARLIE, BOY *sneaks back to the shadows.*]

AZALEE: You got to go someplace, Charlie. It's the only way. I know. I been there.

[CHARLIE *moans something. Only one word comes out of the sound.*]

CHARLIE: Alone!

POPE: He's scared they gonna find something in his blood.

AZALEE: [*Touching* CHARLIE, *trying to comfort him.*] You don't have to go through it like this. Your blood's gonna be fine.

POPE: He likes to suffer.

AZALEE: You could go to emergency.

POPE: They keep him waitin' fifteen hours over there.

AZALEE: I can take you someplace, Charlie. There's people to help out.

POPE: He's makin' a new resolution. Those has got to be done the hard way.

AZALEE: [*To* POPE.] You don't know nothin' 'bout it!

[*She notices* BOY *beginning to pull out the boxes and run around frantically, looking in corners and under things.*]

AZALEE: [*Cont'd.*] Now see what he done got into lookin' for Verna!

POPE   You the one started it, not tellin' him she's gone.

AZALEE: Seem she'd be back in a minute. She never leaves him alone. He's gonna hurt hisself.

POPE: You better stop him.

AZALEE: You stop him. I got Charlie.

POPE: What I know 'bout kids?

AZALEE: You was one, wasn't you? Just 'cause I'm a woman, you think—

[BOY *knocks something over, wildly.* POPE *grabs him. Under this, a distant siren comes closer, then stops.*]

POPE: What you think you doin', boy?

[BOY *is squirming and struggling to break free.* AZALEE *begins helping* CHARLIE *off.*]

POPE: [*Cont'd.*] Wait a minute!

AZALEE: Charlie's my baby now.

POPE: He's a damn junkie!

AZALEE: Not now, he ain't!

POPE: You gonna come back for this boy?

AZALEE: [*On the way out.*] You drop him off at the juvenile if she don't show up.

POPE: You take him with you now!

[AZALEE *exits with* CHARLIE. POPE *shouts after them.*]

POPE: [*Cont'd.*] He ain't my responsibility!

AZALEE: [*Offstage.*] Ain't no one else!

[BOY *gives a hard kick.*]

POPE: Ow! Damn it! You gonna stop this, boy, or am I gonna haul you like a sack o' beans right over to juvenile?

[BOY *quiets.* POPE *speaks to him throughout the scene as if to an adult, an adversary.*]

POPE: [*Cont'd.*] [*Continuing the threat.*] Yeah. That juvenile's a awful place. I stayed there more'n once myself.

[BOY *looks up at him.*]

POPE: [*Cont'd.*] If I let you go, you gonna stay put?

[BOY *doesn't move.*]

POPE: [*Cont'd.*] All right, then.

[POPE *puts him down. Immediately,* BOY *starts to run off.*]

POPE: [*Cont'd.*] [*Quickly.*] You run off, you never see your mama again.

[*The ploy works.* BOY *stops abruptly.*]

POPE: [*Cont'd.*] How you think she'll find you, not sure where you is?

[BOY *looks at* POPE *for a long time, not ready to obey. The contest escalates.*]

POPE. [*Cont'd.*] You sit quiet over there... [*Grudgingly.*] —and I'll finish the story.

[BOY *retrieves the Big Mac gift from beneath the crate where* VERNA *placed it, takes his position at the table again, the present beside him.*]

POPE: [*Cont'd.*] Yeah, you go on and open that now.

[BOY *puts gift on table, crosses his arms, waits.* POPE *continues to pack up his things. He is irritated, trapped.*]

POPE: [*Cont'd.*] [*Resentful.*] OK. You waitin' for the story to be over first, like she say.

[BOY *continues to wait.*]

POPE: [*Cont'd.*] You listen and I'll show you just how stupid it is, then I got to be on my way, too.

[BOY *looks at him, deliberately uncrosses his arms.* POPE, *caught in his own power game, is forced to go on, humiliated, even more resentful.*

POPE: [*Cont'd.*] [*Sarcastically belittling the story.*] After the scary future Ghost go away, Scrooge suddenly get saved and says how sorry he be and promise always to be good and give presents. He lift Tiny Tim up on his back. Then they is a beautiful snow storm.

[*He tosses some shreds of paper trash into the air over his head, waits as they waft down.*]

POPE: [*Cont'd.*] The end! [*Going to collect his sleeping mat and duffel bag.*] Now, boy, you know that ain't real. No one here gonna give away his money. No one 'round here gonna take care of you— or me. Now, you remember that. That's gonna help you a lot in this life.

[*It is growing darker, as if from snow clouds.* POPE *continues on his way off, turning to* BOY.]

POPE: [*Cont'd.*] [*Tough and bitter.*] Christmas only an excuse to hope for something, to make a promise. But all days is the same. And every day break the promise of the day what come before.

[*He begins walking off, then stops and searches his pockets. He finds a candy bar, returns, and gives it to* BOY *in an offhand manner, a final gesture by the winner.*]

POPE: [*Cont'd.*] [*Matter of fact, no hard feelings.*] If you get hungry 'fore anyone come, this'll do you fine. Nothin' here for me no more. It's all used up. Now I'm on my way. You ain't my responsibility. Your mama in the hospital or somethin', it ain't my fault. 'Least I'm not turnin' you over to no juvenile place. She don't find you, someone else come along. That's how it be.

[*He starts to walk off, stops.*]

POPE: [*Cont'd.*] I got to be movin' on. [*Pause.*] Look, boy, someone come along soon. First thing you need is find you a proper name. Bill, maybe. Nah. Joe. Joseph. How 'bout that? [*Pause.*] Kareem——that's a good one——What you think of Kareem? [*Pause.*] Or Curtis. Nah. Nelson. Now, that's a real good one...

[BOY *turns away from him.* POPE *hesitates, then exits quickly.* BOY *sits waiting. The light fades more.* BOY *remains still, holding the gift, watching the exit. Finally, he gets up and looks down the alley way. He returns to the table, picking up one of* VERNA'S *dolls on the way. He sets it down on a crate next to him, then slowly begins to open the Big Mac present.*]

[*A siren starting nearby grows and fades away.* BOY *stops opening the present and listens. As the siren fades, he returns to the gift. Very carefully, he extracts a perfect, round, golden Christmas tree ornament. He holds it up*

*and turns it around. He strokes it. He holds it against his cheek, not mov-
ing. It grows even darker.*]

[*Still holding the ornament,* BOY *sits listening, waiting, as the lights slowly
fade to black.*]

END OF PLAY

Afternotes:

CHARLIE's addiction to heroin should not be obvious to the
audience at first, but reveal itself slowly as his need grows in Act II. He
seems quite normal in behavior until then, somewhat expansive, showing only the "slight buzz," drowsiness, and occasional sniffles which are
also attributable to many other conditions. It is important that he not be
the stereotypical crazed addict so often seen on TV and film.

Similarly, FILO's crack addiction, while revealed earlier, should
follow the course from high to paranoid violence with the understanding that he has just taken a hit at the start of each act. His basic decency
and optimistic good humor must be evident before the effect of the
drug changes him drastically.

THE MATCH GIRL'S GIFT: A CHRISTMAS STORY

by Laurie Brooks Gollobin

"Listen! This is the beginning.
And when we get to the end,
we shall know more than we do now."
— Hans Christian Andersen

CHARACTERS

LIZZIE: Ten years old, ragged clothing, rags tied around her feet
for shoes, apron and shawl.

PITCH: Ten years old, a chimney sweep. His clothes and skin are
layered with soot from the chimneys.

GRAN: Irish accent. Dressed all in white, a ghostlike figure.

KATHERINE: A lady in her late twenties. Henry's mother.

EDWARD: A gentleman, Henry's father. Well dressed, mannered,
businesslike.

HENRY: Ten years old, impulsive, energetic.

SETTING

*New York City, in a fashionable neighborhood. The play takes place in the
street outside a brownstone and its interior. Christmas Eve, the turn of the
century, 1898.*

[*Street lights. Music (carollers). Early evening. Christmas Eve. Snow covers one of New York's most fashionable streets. Sounds of jingle bells, laughing voices, noisemakers. At center is the facade of an elegant town house.
Near the grand house kneels the match girl,* LIZZIE. *She is dressed in rags,
with a threadbare shawl wrapped around her shoulders. Her feet are bare,
with rags tied around them against the cold of winter. In her soiled apron
she carries bundles of stick matches. Near her is a model house made entirely from matches and other found objects. It is a replica of the elegant
town house. Lovingly, she puts a few matches in place.*]
[*Song: "Now the Wintertime is Nigh." Music and Lyrics by Steve Wheaton*]

CAROLERS: Now the wintertime is nigh,
Frosty cheek, sparkling eye,
Everywhere the welcome cry
A Merry, Merry Christmas.
Hear the city clamor well,

Bustling crowd, pealing bell,
Sing we all a glad Noel,
A Merry, Merry Christmas.

LIZZIE: [*Sings*] La, la, la, la, la, la, la, hm-m-m, hm-m-m,
A house is really just a place, just a place, ordinary space,
It's not the answer to my ev'ry prayer,

   [*Song: "Just Four Walls." Music by Steve Wheaton, Lyrics by Laurie Brooks Gollobin and, Steve Wheaton.*]

LIZZIE: [*Sings*] It's just four walls,
Just four walls
Windows and doors and clean swept floors,
For sleeping tight on a snowy night,
A house is the place to be.
It's just four walls,
Just four walls,
And though I'll never see
What living there might be
But tell the truth, I'll tell the truth
It would be all the world to me.

   [*The clock strikes the hour seven o'clock. Offstage voices, laughing at some private amusement of the season. LIZZIE hastily wraps the house up in a bundle of rags and hides it out of sight. Enter HENRY, followed by KATHER-INE and EDWARD, dressed in their holiday clothes.*]

KATHERINE: Slow down, Henry. I'm quite out of breath trying to keep pace with you.

HENRY: It's Christmas Eve, Mother! I want to open my presents.

KATHERINE: Not until midnight, dear. That's when Santa Claus comes.

HENRY: I'm too old for Santa Claus, Mother.

KATHERINE: Too old for Santa Claus? Well then, perhaps you're too old for presents, too?

HENRY: Of course not. No one's too old for presents. Did you get me the toy soldiers I wanted, Mother?

EDWARD: Henry! One would think all you care about is what you'll receive. Christmas is more than that.

KATHERINE: Look at this lovely night. The snow so white and pure. Look, there's a falling star. Make a wish.

HENRY: I wish I'd get the toy soldiers for Christmas.

EDWARD: Fol-de-rol. Wishing has its place, I suppose, but better to keep your mind on practicalities in this world.

KATHERINE: Yes, but it is a lovely night for wishing.

[EDWARD *turns to the grand house.*]

EDWARD: It is a grand house, isn't it, Mother?

KATHERINE: Of course, dear. It's the finest house in New York, built by the finest architect.

EDWARD: Oh, you flatter me, Mother.

KATHERINE: Not at all. No one could have done better.

[LIZZIE *sneezes.*]

HENRY: There's someone in the alley.

[EDWARD *brandishes his walking stick.*]

EDWARD: You there. Come out! [*Pause.*] Come out, I say!

[LIZZIE *comes slowly forward.*]

EDWARD: Well, well, what have we here? Whatever are you doing in this neighborhood?

[*Lizzie hesitates, backs up.*]

EDWARD: Speak up, child.

KATHERINE: She's ill. Poor little thing.

EDWARD: What do you have in that bundle? You haven't stolen it, have you?

KATHERINE: Oh, I'm sure that can't be.

HENRY: Let me see. Can I have it?

EDWARD: Certainly not !

KATHERINE: Probably everything she owns is wrapped up in that parcel.

EDWARD: Go on home now. You don't belong in this district.

[LIZZIE *steps back, falls, her matches and bundle sprawling onto the street.*]

KATHERINE: Oh, dear.

HENRY: Why, they're bundles of matches.

EDWARD: A street seller. I might have known.

KATHERINE: I'm afraid so, dear.

[HENRY *picks up matches.*]

HENRY: [*Making a face.*] They're all wet.

[LIZZIE *is frozen to the spot, staring at Henry.*]

HENRY: Are you hurt?

[LIZZIE *is transfixed.*]

HENRY: I said, are you hurt?

EDWARD: You there, girl, my son is speaking to you.

KATHERINE: Probably not quite right in the head, poor thing. Best to leave her alone.

[LIZZIE *tries to speak, cannot.*]

EDWARD: Yes, time to be going inside.

LIZZIE: [*To* HENRY] Please, sir, buy my matches, poor little girl.

KATHERINE: Oh, she does speak!

EDWARD: Matches, indeed! Go home directly, and tell your wicked parents to lay off the drink and keep you home where you belong. You must be half frozen with cold.

KATHERINE: It is growing colder, I believe.

EDWARD: It's the damp, I fear. We should go in before we all freeze.

[*The family turns and heads for the door of the house.*]

HENRY: I feel like putting my feet right inside the fireplace and my hands, too.

EDWARD: Will there be room for two of us in there, do you think?

KATHERINE: Haven't you forgotten someone?

EDWARD: Who?

KATHERINE: Why me, of course! I shall need warming up, too.

[EDWARD *and* KATHERINE *move to the house.* HENRY *lingers for a last backward glance at* LIZZIE.]

HENRY: Mother, she hasn't any shoes on.

KATHERINE: Best not to think of it, dear. There are hundreds like her in the city.

EDWARD: Henry, come inside now.

[EDWARD *enters the house.*]

KATHERINE: Time to light the lamps or Santa Claus will never find us.

HENRY: Oh, Mother, you're silly.

[*The family enters the house and the door closes. Lights go on in the house, one by one.*]

LIZZIE: Merry Christmas!

[LIZZIE *gazes in the window of the grand house. Enter* PITCH, *the chimney sweep, carrying his brushes and scraper. He wears a coat and cap caked with soot and grime, as are his face and hands. He wears shoes that are too large for his feet and worn through in several places. There are large holes in the knees of his trousers.*]

PITCH: Lizzie !

LIZZIE: Ssshh'h. They just now gone in.

PITCH: Careful. If they catch you gawkin' in the windows you'll spend Christmas Eve in jail.

LIZZIE: Pitch, look. She's takin' off her fur muff and hat. Don't they look soft?

PITCH: Soft as the hands of them that don't know a day's work.

LIZZIE: They're gentlemen. They have servants that do the work for 'em.

PITCH: Why should they work when they got us to do it?

LIZZIE: Isn't he the handsomest boy you've ever seen? Like a prince.

[LIZZIE *retrieves her model house and unwraps it.*]

PITCH: He's not a prince. He's just rich.

[LIZZIE *works on the house.*]

PITCH: Have you finished it?

LIZZIE: Almost.

PITCH: It's a wonder, the way you fitted them matches together and all.

LIZZIE: Took me forever and a day to hide 'em so they wouldn't notice.

PITCH: It looks just like the grand house. As good as those dollhouses in the shops. We could sell it for pocketfuls of cash.

LIZZIE: God's eyeballs, Pitch. I'd never sell it.

PITCH: We could have meat pies tonight and hot soup. A Christmas Eve feast.

LIZZIE: No. Besides, I'm still working on it.

PITCH: Is that why you're still here? Everyone's else's gone home.

LIZZIE: I ain't goin' home.

PITCH: You'll freeze.

LIZZIE: I'd rather freeze than get my skin flailed off. I ain't sold no matches today.

PITCH: Best not to go home at all than go home without a penny.

LIZZIE: I ain't going home ever again. I'd rather die than go home.

PITCH: Wish I ain't gone home tonight.

LIZZIE: Oh, Pitch.

    [*She looks at the raw flesh at his knees.*]

LIZZIE: They're bleedin' bad.

PITCH: Dickie rubbed in the salt brine. Says we got to toughen 'em up for climbin' the chimneys.

LIZZIE: That Dickie's a mean one.

PITCH: He was starin' at me the whole time he was rubbin', waitin' for me to cry.

LIZZIE: He could wait all day and all night, too.

PITCH: I ain't never cried in all my life and never will. He called me a crybaby, anyway. Said he'd sell me to the rat catcher!

LIZZIE: He'll do no such thing.

PITCH: I'm braver than Dickie. He cries in his sleep. [*Conspiratorially*] He's scared of the dark.

LIZZIE: You're not scared of the dark.

PITCH: I ain't scared of nothin'.

LIZZIE: Nothin'?

PITCH: Nothin' in this wide world.

    [PITCH *tries not to smile and almost succeeds.*]

LIZZIE: Pitch . . . remember what Gran said about the truth?

PITCH: [*Reciting from memory*] Telling the truth is best. It's easiest to remember.

LIZZIE: Pitch. You've got on your lying smile.

PITCH: I do not.

LIZZIE: You always smile when you don't tell the truth. You can't fool me.

PITCH: Well, I ain't scared of almost nothin'.

LIZZIE: You're the bravest climbing boy in all New York.

PITCH: Well, climbin' boys got to be brave. That's the truth.

LIZZIE: And match girls, too.

PITCH: Here. I brung you a bit of bread.

LIZZIE: I can't take your bread. You're hungry.

PITCH: No, I'm not. A nice lady give me supper for sweeping her chimneys. Sat me right down at the dining room table, fine as can be.

[PITCH *is smiling his lying smile.*]

LIZZIE: Pitch . . . .

PITCH: What?

LIZZIE: You're smiling again. Tell the truth.

PITCH: No.

LIZZIE: Tell.

PITCH: I ain't had nothin' to eat since yesterday.

LIZZIE: You have the bread.

PITCH: No, I brung it for you.

LIZZIE: But you're hungry and I'm not.

PITCH: Now who's lyin'?

LIZZIE: I ain't lyin'.

PITCH: I'll lay the table. Then you'll eat.

[PITCH *takes an old rag out of his pocket and, with a grand gesture, spreads it on the ground. He reaches in his pocket for the bread. It has completely dissolved into crumbs that fall onto the snow.*]

PITCH: Crushed.

LIZZIE: Scramblin' up the chimneys.

PITCH: Well then. We'll eat the crumbles.

LIZZIE: You eat them. Don't let them go to waste.

[PITCH *eats the crumbs. The following lines are a litany the children have repeated many times before.*]

PITCH: Tell me about grandmas, Lizzie.

LIZZIE: A grandma is someone who loves you.

PITCH: My Grandma would bring me sweets.

LIZZIE: She wouldn't have sweets. But, oh, the stories she'd tell. She'd hold you close and tell your favorite stories over and over again. Even stories about us. Those are the best stories. Because we're in them.

PITCH: I wish I had a grandma, Lizzie.

LIZZIE: If you did, you'd keep her close to you. Never let her out of your sight.

PITCH: Never let her out of my sight.

LIZZIE: Or they'll take her away and you'll never see her again.

PITCH: If they try to take my Grandma away, I'll bash 'em, that's what.

LIZZIE: So cold. I'm so cold.

[PITCH *takes off his coat and puts it around* LIZZIE'S *shoulders.*]

PITCH: Will you be my grandma, Lizzie?

LIZZIE: Oh, Pitch, I can't be your grandma. I ain't gonna get big. I'll die before I get big.

PITCH: Lizzie! Don't say that.

LIZZIE: It's true. I know that now.

PITCH: I'll make you a home with a warm fire. Then you'll get well.

LIZZIE: I ain't gonna get well. And when I die, you must be your own brave self. I ain't afraid.

PITCH: Remember what Gran said? What you taught me? Never give up. I'm growin' every day, Lizzie. Soon I'll be too big to climb the chimneys and Dickie'll never see me again.

[*He takes his brush and sweeps the snow aside.*]

PITCH: I'll be a crossing sweeper on Fifth Avenue. [*He pretends.*] Here, Miss, step light, there's a bit of wet there. Wouldn't want you to fall down and soil that fine gown. All the ladies and gentlemen will love me. I'll be a wondrous crossing sweeper. Now you try, Lizzie.

LIZZIE: I'm done with dreaming. It ain't done no good.

PITCH: But it was you taught me how, Lizzie.

LIZZIE: I don't care. I'm too tired. And Gran's dead.

[LIZZIE *takes off* PITCH'S *coat and throws it at him.*]

PITCH: [*Fighting tears, he makes a fist.*] If you won't dream, I swear I'll let you have it.

LIZZIE: Go ahead.

[PITCH *hesitates.*]

LIZZIE: Go on, I said. Hit me.

PITCH: [*He struggles with himself.*] I can't.

LIZZIE: Suit yourself.

PITCH: Please, Lizzie. If you won't dream, then I can't.

LIZZIE: You have to dream. To help you see your future.

PITCH: Not without you. I won't get big if you don't. I'll lie right down to sleep in the snow and never wake up. And I'm not smiling.

LIZZIE: Pitch, what's to be done with you?

[PITCH *puts his coat back around* LIZZIE'S *shoulders.*]

PITCH: Do my favorite dream, Lizzie.

LIZZIE: You're the stubbornest boy in the whole world.

PITCH: Do the dream, Lizzie.

LIZZIE: [*Sighs.*] When we get big we'll live in the grand house . . . with a warm fire, good food and a dry place to sleep. We'll have a home.

PITCH: I'll chop the wood and lay the fire.

LIZZIE: Then we'll help those who need it. Good, clean work for every-one, food and shelter. Tuck the little ones in at night and never, never send their grandmas away.

PITCH: Then you'll be my grandma, Lizzie.

[PITCH *snuggles close to her. The sound of a piano comes from the grand house and* KATHERINE'S *lovely voice singing. During the song,* LIZZIE *takes off* PITCH'S *coat and covers him with it.*]

[*Song: "Now The Wintertime Is Nigh," music and lyrics by Steve Wheaton.*]

KATHERINE: Now The Wintertime is nigh,
  Frosty Cheek, sparkling eye,
  Everywhere the welcome cry,
A merry, merry Christmas.
Hear the city clamor well,
Bustling crowd, pealing bell,
Sing we all a glad noel,
A Merry, Merry Christmas.

[PITCH *is fast asleep.* LIZZIE *starts to doze and* GRAN *descends from the night sky.* *NOTE: *If theatre is not equipped with fly space then* GRAN *can appear from the wings.* GRAN *is dressed from head to toe in flowing white rags: dress, shoes and shawl. Her hands are covered with white gloves* *and her hair is a wild white halo about her head. She speaks with an Irish accent.*]

GRAN: What are you doin' child! Wake Up! Wake up!

LIZZIE: Gran! Is that you? Am I dead?

GRAN: Get up, Lizzie. Get up with you now.

LIZZIE: Oh, Grandma, every night I prayed you'd come. Will you take me with you?

GRAN: No, child. I will not take you away from this world before you have found your place in it.

LIZZIE: I hate this world. I want to be with you.

GRAN: And wouldn't I give all the gold in Dublin to have you near me. But listen, Dearheart. It is time for you to have a different kind of dream. Strong dreams. Dreams of the future. Wakin' dreams that show you what might be.

LIZZIE: Gran, I . . .

GRAN: Dreams, Dearheart! What have I taught you?

[LIZZIE *hangs her head.*]

GRAN: What's this now? Surely you haven't forgotten how to dream!

LIZZIE: The dreams didn't come true, Gran.

GRAN: As bad as that, is it?

LIZZIE: Don't scold me, Gran.

GRAN: Look at me, child. Even though your dreams haven't come true, that doesn't mean they never will. Now. I've brought you a Christmas gift.

LIZZIE: A gift! For me?

GRAN: A gift of wakin' dreams. Listen well, and I will tell you a story. Once there was a little girl who thought she would die before she grew up. And it is true that she was in grave danger. She was hungry and cold and not a soul in this world cared for her. She had even given up dreamin' for somethin' better. And that, dearheart, was the most dangerous thing of all, for without our dreams, we are without hope. Then one Christmas Eve the little girl had three wakin' dreams that took her to the place she most wanted to go.

LIZZIE: She went into the grand house.

GRAN: That she did. That is what she dreamed of.

LIZZIE: But what happened, Gran?

GRAN: The ending of the story is for you to decide. That is my gift. Three times you will go into the grand house. You need only light a match.

LIZZIE: But I'm not allowed to light the matches, no matter what. They will beat me.

GRAN: Fools! What do they know of dreams? They've long ago given up their dreamin'. Listen to me, Dearheart. There isn't much time. Take my gift. Light a match.

[LIZZIE *reaches into her pocket for the matches, takes out a match, then hesitates.*]

LIZZIE: I cannot go into the grand house. I am . . . a match girl.

GRAN: Aye, and so much more.

[GRAN *produces a small mirror.*]

GRAN: [*cont'd*] Look into the glass. What do you see there?

LIZZIE: Dirty face, tangled hair, dress all in . . . tatters.

[LIZZIE *holds up the folds of the dress that fall ragged from her fingers.*]

GRAN: True enough. But what have I taught you lies beneath?

LIZZIE: A heart that can give . . .

[LIZZIE *looks in the mirror. Then shrugs.*]

LIZZIE: A match girl.

GRAN: You must look deeper than your eyes can see.

LIZZIE: I don't understand.

GRAN: Some beauty cannot be seen with your eyes. It lies within. Use the dreams, Dearheart. Light the match.

[LIZZIE *hesitates.*]

GRAN: Hurry. There's not much time now! Light the match!

[*Music.* LIZZIE *strikes the match. As it blazes to life, a light appears that symbolizes the match burning throughout the fantasy. A bell tolls the hour, eight o'clock. The house opens to reveal the grand house, dominated by a warm, glowing fireplace.* GRAN *walks* LIZZIE *into the room. She lifts an ornate Victorian dress from a coat stand and helps* LIZZIE *put it on over her rags.* LIZZIE *steps into a waiting pair of party slippers.* GRAN *lifts* LIZZIE'S *hair and pins it back with a huge bow.*]

GRAN: Remember: A heart that can give.

[*Music.* GRAN *fades, then exits. We see the transformation in* LIZZIE *through her posture, her breathing, her attitude and her speech.* LIZZIE *warms herself in the glow of the fireplace, then begins to cautiously examine her surroundings. Enter* HENRY *carrying rolled up papers under his arm.* HENRY *watches* LIZZIE *look around.* LIZZIE *does not see him. She finds an ornate music box and opens it. Christmas music tumbles out.*]

HENRY: That's mine.

[LIZZIE *jumps in surprise.*]

HENRY: Put it down. Didn't anyone ever tell you not to take things that don't belong to you?

LIZZIE: But I wasn't going to take it.

HENRY: Then what were you doing with it?

LIZZIE: Looking at it.

HENRY: Why are you staring at me? It's rude to stare.

LIZZIE: You're so . . . handsome.

HENRY: Staring is still rude.

LIZZIE: I'll try not to stare.

HENRY: See that you do. And all these things are mine so see that you don't take any of them.

LIZZIE: All these things?

HENRY: Everything.

LIZZIE: That's a lot of things.

HENRY: Yes. So you'd best be careful what you touch. Most of the things in the house are mine.

[HENRY *is trying not to smile.*]

LIZZIE: I'll try.

[HENRY *puts down the papers and removes from a hiding place a dish filled with bonbons.* LIZZIE *stares at* HENRY. HENRY *leisurely eats the candies.* LIZZIE *moves closer to him. Stares. Moves directly behind him. Stares.* HENRY *turns. They are face to face. She sniffs the candy.*]

LIZZIE: Are those chocolate?

HENRY: This one is chocolate. [*He pops it in his mouth.*] These green ones are peppermint. Some are marzipan.

[LIZZIE *stares as* HENRY *eats another candy.*]

HENRY: I'm not supposed to eat sweets. Mother says they're bad for my constitution.

LIZZIE: What's constitution?

HENRY: Your health, silly. Everyone knows that. You won't tattle to Mother and Father, will you?

LIZZIE: Tattle?

HENRY: You know, tell about the sweets.

LIZZIE: You mean snitch? I'd never do that. Only troublemakers do that.

HENRY: You have dirty ears. Don't you wash them?

LIZZIE: I wash them. I just forgot today.

HENRY: Well, it looks as if you could grow potatoes in there.

[HENRY *eats another candy.*]

HENRY: I have my bath every Saturday night without fail.

LIZZIE: [*Gathering her courage.*] May I have a sweet?

HENRY: These are mine.

LIZZIE: Yes, but there are so many. I only want one.

HENRY: You should get your own.

LIZZIE: Don't you know how to share?

HENRY: Of course. But why should I?

LIZZIE: Because it's fair. Gran says sharing's a gift to yourself.

HENRY: How can giving something be getting something? That's nonsense.

[*Approaching voices.*]

HENRY: Quick! Hide this.

[LIZZIE *hides the candy dish. Enter* KATHERINE *and* EDWARD.]

KATHERINE: Ah, there she is, our own dear Cousin Elizabeth. Welcome. Welcome.

[KATHERINE *embraces* LIZZIE.]

EDWARD: Let me look at you, child.

KATHERINE: I believe she looks like Alice, don't you think so, dear?

EDWARD: I believe she favors my side of the family, Mother.

KATHERINE: How was your journey? Are you tired?

EDWARD: Such a long coach ride. You must be exhausted.

KATHERINE: A rest would definitely be appropriate.

LIZZIE: Oh no, I'm not tired at all.

EDWARD: It'll be a long time until midnight. We wouldn't want you to fall asleep at table, would we, Dear?

KATHERINE: Certainly not.

LIZZIE: Oh, no, I won't, thank you, your Lordship.

EDWARD: [*Laughing*] Your Lordship? My goodness! I don't require that title. I am only a hardworking architect. You may call me Uncle.

LIZZIE: Yes, Sir, Uncle.

EDWARD: What a charming child.

KATHERINE: We're so delighted you're here, aren't we, Henry?

HENRY: I don't know yet.

KATHERINE: Henry!

HENRY: Well, we hardly know one another.

KATHERINE: You'll soon be the best of friends. Henry spends entirely too much time alone, I fear.

EDWARD: Better to spend time alone productively than run with those rowdy hooligans in the street.

[HENRY *fetches the rolled up papers.*]

HENRY: Father, will you look at my drawings? I've finished a new one.

EDWARD: Perhaps later, Henry.

[HENRY *unrolls the papers for his father to see.*]

HENRY: Please, Father. I do want to show them to you. I've drawn a country house with gardens and a footbridge and shrubbery shaped like exotic animals. See? There's a rhinocerous and this one's a zebra. I know you can't tell it's a zebra. It looks more like an ordinary horse, but when I plant the honeysuckle in between, it'll . . .

EDWARD: Henry, stop prattling. What did I tell you about that? A gentleman does not prattle. He thinks before he speaks.

[HENRY *thinks.*]

HENRY: Will you look at my drawings?

EDWARD: No. Not now.

[HENRY *sadly rolls up the sheets of paper.*]

KATHERINE: Perhaps you could take a quick look, dear. He's worked so hard on them.

EDWARD: Being an architect is more than a few marks with charcoal on paper, Mother. It takes study, patience and perseverence. Not to mention the proper attitude.

KATHERINE: Of course, dear.

EDWARD: Henry must learn proper behavior first. And so far he's made a rather poor showing of it.

KATHERINE: Yes, dear.

EDWARD: Henry, why don't you put your energy into making your cousin feel welcome.

KATHERINE: And Elizabeth will be like a dear sister to you, won't you, Elizabeth?

LIZZIE: Yes, Ma'am. Thank you, Ma'am.

EDWARD: Well, that's decided.

KATHERINE: Very well. Can we begin the Christmas Eve festivities?

EDWARD: Carry on, Mother.

KATHERINE: Well, perhaps we could have a game.

EDWARD: We could play at cards.

HENRY: Cards are boring. Let's play Blind Man's Bluff!

EDWARD: Much too boisterous. Something is liable to be broken.

HENRY: We could move the breakables out of the way.

EDWARD: A place for everything and everything in its place.

HENRY: Let's pretend. We can do a play.

EDWARD: Henry, you are incorrigible. You know how I feel about play-acting.

HENRY: But, Father, even the finest families do play-acting. We could do Three Fingered Jack, the Terror of Jamaica! I can be Jack!

[HENRY *leaps onto the furniture and slashes the air with his imaginary rapier.*]

KATHERINE: Henry, not on the furniture!

EDWARD: Henry, get down from there at once. It is inappropriate for a young gentleman to play at Three Fingered Jack.

HENRY: How about The Red Rover?

EDWARD: Henry, pretending is frivolous. I simply cannot encourage that behavior.

HENRY: But, Father, I . . .

KATHERINE: Perhaps just this once. It's Christmas Eve.

EDWARD: Fol-de-rol.

HENRY: It's not fol-de-rol, Father.

KATHERINE: Don't argue with your father, Henry.

HENRY: I never have any fun.

EDWARD: Fun is not important, Henry. Improving yourself is important.

[*There is an awkward pause while everyone takes this in.*]

KATHERINE: Why don't you give us a riddle, Dear.

EDWARD: What, me?

KATHERINE: Don' t be modest. You're best at riddles.

EDWARD: You flatter me, Mother.

KATHERINE: Not at all, Father.

EDWARD: Well, I did hear a new one yesterday.

KATHERINE: Do let's hear it.

HENRY: I hate riddles.

EDWARD: [*Clearing his throat. Grandly.*]
In spring I look gay decked in comely array,
In summer more clothing I wear,
As colder it grows I throw off my clothes,
And in winter quite naked appear.

[HENRY *and* LIZZIE *giggle at the thought of Father naked.*]

EDWARD: What's so funny?

HENRY: Nothing, Father.

EDWARD: Well, can you guess the answer?

KATHERINE: Let me see. In spring I look gay decked in comely array . . .

HENRY: In summer more clothing I wear . . .

EDWARD: As colder it grows I throw off my clothes . . .

[*The children giggle.*]

HENRY: And in winter quite naked appear.

EDWARD: Well, can you guess?

KATHERINE: I haven't a clue.

HENRY: I know . . . I know . . .

EDWARD: What is your answer, Henry?

HENRY: I can't quite think of it.

EDWARD: Well, don't say you know the answer if you don't.

HENRY: I know the answer. I do.

LIZZIE: A tree. That's the answer. A tree changes with the seasons.

EDWARD: Good guess, Cousin Elizabeth.

HENRY: That's not the answer.

EDWARD: That's quite the correct answer.

HENRY: I knew it, too.

KATHERINE: Henry.

HENRY: Well, I did. I was only being polite to Cousin Elizabeth. I wanted her to have a turn.

[HENRY *has a lying smile he cannot hide.*]

EDWARD: Henry, that is a prevarication. It's simply not true.

HENRY: Yes, it is.

EDWARD: Don't be impertinent. I'm trying to teach you something about playing fair.

KATHERINE: It's Christmas Eve, Father.

EDWARD: That's no excuse for inappropriate behavior.

KATHERINE: Perhaps we could overlook inappropriate behavior, just this once.

EDWARD: Why, Mother, that would be condoning it! He must be punished.

KATHERINE: But surely not tonight.

EDWARD: Don't contradict me, Mother. Henry, you will stand facing the wall until you are ready to improve your behavior. Is that understood? I said . . . is that understood?

[HENRY *does not reply.*]

EDWARD: Do I need to get my switch?

HENRY: No.

EDWARD: No, what?

HENRY: No, sir.

EDWARD: Good. Then you may begin.

[HENRY *turns to the wall.*]

EDWARD: You must learn to behave in order to a be a gentleman, Henry. Just like I did. Gentlemen do not cheat. Come along, Mother. Let's see how cook is progressing with tea. All this clamor has made me hungry.

KATHERINE: I'm feeling a bit faint actually.

EDWARD: Take my arm, Mother.

HENRY: Father?

EDWARD: What is it, Henry?

HENRY: I'm ready to improve my behavior now.

EDWARD: Not yet, Henry. You must think on it.

[HENRY *angrily turns back toward the wall.*]

EDWARD: Come along, Mother. Cousin Elizabeth?

LIZZIE: May I stay here with Henry?

EDWARD: You may stay with Henry, but do not talk to him until he is purged of his inappropriate behavior. Mother?

[KATHERINE *and* EDWARD *exit.* LIZZIE *stares at* HENRY, *sits in a chair, swings her legs. Then her arms.*]

LIZZIE: How long will it take you to be   [*She thinks.*] . . . purged?

HENRY: Go away. I hate you.

LIZZIE: I haven't done anything wrong, have I?

HENRY: You're here, aren't you?

LIZZIE: I'm glad I'm here. I'm sorry you hate me.

HENRY: If they catch you talking, it'll be the worse for me.

LIZZIE: Worse for you? If I'm talking how can that be your fault?

HENRY: Because everything's my fault.

[HENRY *turns back to the wall. Then turns again to* LIZZIE.]

HENRY: Don't you want to know why?

LIZZIE: Why?

HENRY: Because I can't stand still, I don't care for lessons, I'm impertinent, I cheat at games, and I prattle.

LIZZIE: What's prattle?

HENRY: That's when you speak when you have nothing important to say.

LIZZIE: How do you know if what you're saying is important?

HENRY: That's the problem. I can never tell what's important and what's not. Are you well-behaved?

LIZZIE: I don't know.

HENRY: Well, either you are or you aren't.

LIZZIE: What is well-behaved?

HENRY: Are you bad or are you good?

LIZZIE: Oh, I'm bad, but I try to be good.

HENRY: Father is always angry with me. He says I'm incorrigible.

LIZZIE: In . . . what?

HENRY: Incorrigible.

LIZZIE: What does that mean?

HENRY: It means I never learn. I hate books. I hate lessons. I hate reciting. I love drawing. I love sweets and I love play-acting. Especially Three-fingered Jack, the Terror of Jamaica!

[HENRY *grabs a stick of wood from the woodbox and brandishes it about like a sword.*]

HENRY: Stand back, you cutthroats, or I'll do you in.

LIZZIE: Who, me?

HENRY: Yes, you. This is the last time you'll ever sail the high seas again.

LIZZIE: I . . . I . . .

HENRY: Get a sword.

LIZZIE: What?

HENRY: Get a sword. Defend yourself!

LIZZIE: Oh!

[*She gets a piece of wood for a sword. They play at sword fighting.*]

HENRY: Take that . . . and that . . . and that.

LIZZIE: I'm not afraid of you, you scoundrel! Take that . . . and that . . .

HENRY: And that . . . and that . . . and that . . .

[HENRY *manages to lose his balance and knock over some small furnishings. The children tumble head over heels. There is much loud noise.* ED-WARD *and* KATHERINE *enter.*]

EDWARD: Children! What's going on in here?

KATHERINE: What are you doing on the furniture?

EDWARD: I was going over some papers in my study and was regaled with such a racket I couldn't tell up from down.

KATHERINE: It sounded like herd of wild antelopes.

[LIZZIE *and* HENRY *look at one another. Then at* KATHERINE *and* ED-WARD *and back at each other. They begin to giggle.*]

EDWARD: Henry, you have some explaining to do.

HENRY: It wasn't my fault.

[HENRY *has on his lying smile.*]

EDWARD: Surely lying isn't the way to improve your behavior.

KATHERINE: I'm sure there must be some good explanation.

EDWARD: Don't bother, Mother, he simply cannot learn how to behave.

HENRY: I was trying.

EDWARD: Incorrigible, that's what you are. A son of mine who cannot behave. It's unthinkable.

LIZZIE: It was my fault.

HENRY: What?

EDWARD: Whatever do you mean?

LIZZIE: My fault, Uncle, sir.

EDWARD: Explain yourself, Cousin Elizabeth.

LIZZIE: I was bored because Henry was staring at the wall, trying so hard to purge himself, so I started talking.

HENRY: [*Surprised*] That's true.

EDWARD: Hold your tongue, Henry. You mean you were the instigator?

LIZZIE: Yes, sir. I was the . . . whatever you said.

EDWARD: The instigator. The one who started it.

LIZZIE: Yes, Uncle, sir. Best to tell the truth. It's easiest to remember.

EDWARD: [*Laughing*] I don't believe I've ever heard it put quite that way before.

LIZZIE: That's what Gran says.

EDWARD: Well, she is quite correct. Thank you for telling the truth. How refreshing.

KATHERINE: Yes, that's lively.

EDWARD: However, I cannot ignore the matter. You will both stand facing the wall.

HENRY: But she was the instigator.

EDWARD: A gentleman accepts responsibility. You may begin your punishment.

LIZZIE: May I stand near the fire? It's so warm.

EDWARD: Well, yes, I suppose. But no talking. If there are any more shenanigans, there will be no Christmas this year.

LIZZIE: Yes, Uncle, sir.

EDWARD: And just to make sure, we'll stay here until tea is served. You may begin to purge yourselves.

[HENRY *and* LIZZIE *stand facing the fireplace upstage within reach of each other.*]

EDWARD: [*Offering his arm to* KATHERINE.] Mother, you should sit down.

KATHERINE: I am feeling a bit tired.

EDWARD: As am I.

[KATHERINE *takes his arm affectionately.* LIZZIE *watches the two grown-ups.*]

EDWARD: [*Sighs*] Katherine, I believe it is harder to be a father than it is to design the finest house in New York.

KATHERINE: Just do the best you can, Father.

EDWARD: Oh, I am. But what if my best isn't good enough? What if he turns out to be a ragamuffin . . . or a hooligan . . . or worse?

KATHERINE: Try not to worry too much, father. These things take time. I'm sure he'll make a success of it.

[EDWARD *covers* KATHERINE *with a nearby shawl. She closes her eyes and sighs.*]

EDWARD: Yes, but I have such high hopes for him. A man of real vision can shake the world. Look at Vanderbilt. Look at Carnegie.

KATHERINE: Yes, dear. You're a fine model for him.

EDWARD: Oh, dear Lord. What if he turns out to be like me?

[*As the clock strikes the hour, nine o'clock,* HENRY *reaches out and takes* LIZZIE'S *hand. The match sputters and goes out. The family fades.*]

LIGHTS SHIFT.

LIZZIE: Wait! Not yet. Gran!

[LIZZIE'S *dress falls to the ground and she is again in rags.*]

LIZZIE: Oh, Gran! Is it over so soon?

PITCH: Lizzie, are you there?

LIZZIE: I think so.

PITCH: You gave me a fright! I woke up and you'd . . . gone off. Where did you go?

LIZZIE: Oh, Pitch. I've had the most wonderful waking dream. I've been in the grand house.

PITCH: And I'm the Queen of Sheba!

LIZZIE: I know it's unbelievable, but it's true. It's warm inside and Henry has sweets and everything's so clean it shines.

PITCH: Who's Henry?

LIZZIE: The prince.

PITCH: Oh, him.

LIZZIE: But it's strange. I thought with all those riches they'd be happy.

PITCH: I'd be happy if I was rich.

LIZZIE: Henry isn't happy. He can't stand still, he doesn't care for lessons, he's impertinent, he prattles, and he cheats.

PITCH: Sounds like a fine fellow.

LIZZIE: Wait. Gran gave me three waking dreams and I've only had one. I'm going back.

PITCH: God's eyeballs, Lizzie! You've gone stark, raving mad.

LIZZIE: Oh, I know you don't believe me, but you will. I'll make you believe me. You'll see.

PITCH: Don't go, Lizzie.

LIZZIE: I'll be back.

PITCH: What if you don't come back.

LIZZIE: Here.

[LIZZIE *gives* PITCH *her model house.*]

LIZZIE: I wouldn't leave my house, would I? You watch it for me until I'm back.

PITCH: Lizzie? Can I go with you?

LIZZIE: I don't know.

PITCH: Can we try?

LIZZIE: Take my arm.

[PITCH *takes* LIZZIE'S *arm.* LIZZIE *takes a match out of her pocket, and strikes it. The light symbolizing the burning match comes to life. All else fades.*]

PITCH: Lizzie, where are you? Where did you go?

[PITCH *exits.*] *LIGHTS SHIFT.*

[*The family is seen in the nursery again, gathered around a tea table in front of the fireplace. They come to life as* LIZZIE *walks into the scene, looking around for* PITCH.]

KATHERINE: Tea time, Cousin Elizabeth.

LIZZIE: It didn't work.

KATHERINE: What didn't work, dear?

LIZZIE: Oh. I don't think I'm purged yet.

EDWARD: That's quite all right, Cousin Elizabeth. These things take time.

[HENRY *takes a cake from the table and pops it into his mouth whole.*]

KATHERINE: Henry! Wait until we're all seated and served, please.

[LIZZIE *is overwhelmed by the lavish amount and design of the food.*]

EDWARD: Cousin Elizabeth, you'll sit here.

[EDWARD *pulls out a chair for* LIZZIE. *She hesitates.* HENRY *pinches her. She sits.*]

KATHERINE: Henry here.

[HENRY *sits.* KATHERINE *pours the tea.*]

KATHERINE: Cousin Elizabeth, do you care for cream with your tea?

LIZZIE: Oh, yes, please.

[KATHERINE *passes* LIZZIE *the cream pitcher. Instead of pouring some in her tea,* LIZZIE *drinks directly from the pitcher.* HENRY *stops her, frowns, takes the pitcher, and pours cream in his tea to show* LIZZIE. LIZZIE *repeats the gesture in her own tea.*]

HENRY: Mother, may I sit next to my dear cousin?

KATHERINE: Why, of course.

[HENRY *moves next to* LIZZIE *and puts her napkin in her lap.* LIZZIE *watches* HENRY *sip his tea.* LIZZIE *sips her tea. Too loudly.* KATHERINE *and* EDWARD *stare at her.*]

HENRY: Have one of these cakes, Cousin Elizabeth. They're lemon.

[LIZZIE *takes one. Then another. She is reaching for another when* HENRY *pulls the tray out of reach.*]

EDWARD: You must be hungry from your long trip, Cousin Elizabeth.

LIZZIE: [*With a full mouth.*] It's so good.

KATHERINE: There's no hurry, dear, it won't run away.

[HENRY *laughs too loudly.*]

HENRY: That's funny. Food running away.

EDWARD: Henry . . .

[*They are all staring at* LIZZIE *who is devouring everything in sight.*]

EDWARD: Ahem. Mother, you're not eating. Aren't you hungry?

KATHERINE: Ah... no, Father. I seem to have lost my appetite. You're not eating either.

EDWARD: Yes, I am. No, I'm not. It seems Cousin Elizabeth is eating enough for all of us.

HENRY: I'm hungry.

[HENRY *begins to eat with more gusto. His parents look at him disapporvilngly.*]

EDWARD: Henry, you must set an example for Cousin Elizabeth.

HENRY: [*with his mouth full.*] Yes, sir.

EDWARD: Henry, don't talk with your mouth full. Chew, swallow, then speak.

[HENRY *takes little, tiny bites to show* LIZZIE. LIZZIE *imitates him.*]

KATHERINE: I'll ask cook for more sandwiches.

LIZZIE: There are more?

KATHERINE: Of course.

[KATHERINE *gets up. Her napkin falls on the floor.*]

LIZZIE: You dropped your rag.

KATHERINE: My what, dear?

LIZZIE: Your rag. You dropped it.

[LIZZIE *picks up the napkin and hands it to* KATHERINE.]

KATHERINE: [*Taken aback.*] My rag. How thoughtful. Thank you.

LIZZIE: May I keep mine?

[*She ties it around her head like a scarf.*]

LIZZIE: This will keep my ears warm.

HENRY: [*Tying his napkin around his head, too.*] You're so funny, Cousin Elizabeth. Isn't she funny, Mother?

KATHERINE: Well, I . . .

HENRY: You're a caution, Cousin Elizabeth. A caution!

EDWARD: You're both very silly.

HENRY: That's because it's Christmas!

[LIZZIE *ties the napkin around her neck and tucks it fetchingly in her bodice.*]

LIZZIE: It could also keep my neck warm.

KATHERINE: [*Forgetting herself.*] That is quite nice. I suppose one could use one's napkin as something else.

EDWARD: Nonsense. A napkin is a napkin.

HENRY: Look at mine.

[HENRY *has fashioned his napkin into a cravat.* KATHERINE *puts her napkin on her head. The children laugh.*]

EDWARD: Really, Mother. Will we need to work on your behavior, too?

KATHERINE: Certainly not, dear.

EDWARD: Henry, stop this frivolous behavior at once.

HENRY: That's not fair. You didn't correct Cousin Elizabeth. She was the instigator.

EDWARD: I'll have a bit more tea, Mother.

[KATHERINE *pours tea for* EDWARD.]

HENRY: What about Cousin Elizabeth?

KATHERINE: Why, of course, would you care for more tea, Cousin Elizabeth?

LIZZIE: Yes, please.

HENRY: Mother, may I be excused for a minute?

KATHERINE: Of course, dear.

[HENRY *gets the rolled up drawings and brings them to the table.*]

EDWARD: Henry, we're at tea.

HENRY: I wanted to ask you about connecting these trellises in the garden.

EDWARD: Henry, not now.

[HENRY *unrolls the papers out on the table.*]

HENRY: Please, Father, it'll only take a moment.

EDWARD: Henry, what are you doing? Be careful. Henry!

[HENRY *manages to spill tea all over the papers and his father.*]

EDWARD: Now see what you've done!

HENRY: I didn't mean to. It was an accident.

EDWARD: You never take responsibility for anything, do you, Henry?

[LIZZIE *gets up and begins wiping the papers clean with her napkin.*]

KATHERINE: I'm beginning to feel a bit faint.

HENRY: I just wanted to show you my drawings.

EDWARD: Well, they're ruined now.

[EDWARD *takes the drawings and throws them into the fireplace.*]

HENRY: Father, no!

[HENRY *rushes over to the fireplace and reaches in for the papers.*]

KATHERINE: Henry!

EDWARD: Henry, be careful of the fire!

[*There is a scuffle at the fireplace.*]

EDWARD: You must never do such a dangerous thing again. Never!

[EDWARD *hugs* HENRY *furiously.*]

EDWARD: My God! You might have caught on fire!

KATHERINE: Thank Heaven you're both quite safe.

[HENRY *surveys the rescued papers.*]

HENRY: How could you do that? How could you?

EDWARD: Impertinence! Henry, if you say another word I'm going to get my switch.

HENRY: I hate you. I'll hate you forever.

[EDWARD *lifts his arm to strike* HENRY. KATHERINE *faints.*]

EDWARD: Mother! Henry, get the smelling salts.

[HENRY *gets the smelling salts and hands them to his father.*]

EDWARD: You should be ashamed of yourself. Upsetting your mother like this.

[EDWARD *passes the smelling salts under* KATHERINE'S *nose.*]

EDWARD: Mother, are you there?

KATHERINE: I think so, dear.

HENRY: It was my fault.

EDWARD: Are you recovered, Mother?

KATHERINE: Yes, if the room would only stop spinning.

HENRY: It was my fault.

EDWARD: Just rest, Mother. You'll be right as rain in a moment.

KATHERINE: Is Henry hurt? He put his arm in the fire.

HENRY: I'm fine, Mother.

EDWARD: [*A gesture quiets Henry.*] I'm going to take your Mother into her bedroom so she can lie down. She's had quite enough for one day and so have I.

HENRY: I'm sorry, Father.

EDWARD: [*As if he hasn't heard.*] Come along, Mother. You need to rest.

KATHERINE: Perhaps that would be best.

[EDWARD *begins to exit with* KATHERINE *leaning on him for support.*]

HENRY: I didn't mean to cause trouble, Father.

EDWARD: Frankly, I'm not in the mood to hear your excuses. Christmas is spoiled for all of us.

[*Exit* KATHERINE *and* EDWARD, HENRY *sniffles.*]

LIZZIE: You're not going to cry, are you? None of us cry. If we start to cry we might not ever be able to stop.

HENRY: Oh, Cousin Elizabeth, I'm incorrigible.

LIZZIE: Henry, you were good.

HENRY: I'm never good.

LIZZIE: You told the truth!

HENRY: He didn't even hear me. He doesn't care, anyway. Why doesn't he yell at you? He never blames you.

LIZZIE: He doesn't love me. He loves you.

HENRY: Do you really think so?

LIZZIE: Plain as the nose on your face.

HENRY: If only I could believe that.

[HENRY *gets the partly burned drawings to show* LIZZIE.]

HENRY: Will you look at my drawings?

LIZZIE: Let me see. Oh, Henry, these are very good.

HENRY: They're ruined now.

LIZZIE: You can still see the lines.

HENRY: Someday I'll build this cottage and live there. See the gardens?

LIZZIE: It's the most beautiful cottage I've ever seen. As beautiful as this house

HENRY: Do you really think so? I wish my father thought so. But he's always so angry.

LIZZIE: He won't be angry forever.

HENRY: You don't know my father.

LIZZIE: Gran says never give up. When things go wrong, think what you can do to make them right.

HENRY: Nothing can make this right.

LIZZIE: Maybe we can find a way. Close your eyes.

HENRY: What for?

LIZZIE: We'll play a game.

HENRY: I don't feel like playing a game.

LIZZIE: This is a game that can help. It's a pretending game.

HENRY: Father says pretending is silly.

LIZZIE: Anyone who can play at Three-Fingered Jack knows pretending isn't silly. It's how you see what might be. Try it.

[HENRY *dutifully closes his eyes.*]

LIZZIE: Now dream.

HENRY: But I'm not sleeping.

LIZZIE: That doesn't matter. You just imagine. Let your mind go anywhere it wants to go. Then see what happens.

HENRY: Oh.

LIZZIE: What happened?

HENRY: I saw myself in front of a giant Christmas tree.

LIZZIE: That's it. Close your eyes and play again.

[HENRY *closes his eyes, then smiles hugely.*]

LIZZIE: What?

HENRY: Father's there, too. He's happy.

LIZZIE: What are you doing?

HENRY: He's so proud of me. He wants to look at my drawings.

LIZZIE: What else?

HENRY: He's saying [*Imitates Father's voice.*] "This is extraordinary work, son. You'll be a fine architect and a gentleman."

LIZZIE: That can happen.

HENRY: No, it can't. I can't even convince him to look at my drawings.

LIZZIE: Let's try the game together. One more time.

[*Both children close their eyes and concentrate.*]

HENRY: I see the Christmas tree.

LIZZIE: Me, too. It's all lit up with candles.

HENRY: I see Father's face.

LIZZIE: I see it, too.

HENRY: He's opening a gift. It's from me!

LIZZIE: What is it?

HENRY: I don't know. I don't have a gift for him. I wouldn't know what to give him. What could I give him that he would like?

[*There is a pause as* LIZZIE *opens her eyes and smiles a bittersweet smile. She hugs* HENRY *fiercely.*]

HENRY: What was that for?

LIZZIE: Can I have a sweet now, Henry?

HENRY: How can you think of sweets at a time like this?

LIZZIE: Please, Henry.

HENRY: Oh, I suppose so. But we have to play the game again. I don't have the answer yet.

[LIZZIE *takes a candy and eats it.*]

LIZZIE: I want to remember the taste of this forever.

HENRY: There are plenty more.

LIZZIE: Not for me. Henry, write a card for your Father.

HENRY: But I have no gift.

LIZZIE: Do it for me. Just in case. Please.

HENRY: Very well.

LIZZIE: Write that you love him.

[*As* HENRY *gets the card, the clock begins striking eleven o'clock.*]

LIGHTS SHIFT

[LIZZIE *goes to* PITCH, *still asleep. She covers him with his coat.* GRAN *appears.*]

GRAN: Once there was a little girl who thought she would die before she grew up. And it is true that she was in grave danger.

LIZZIE AND GRAN: She was hungry and cold and had no one in the world to take care of her. She had even given up daring to dream of something better. And that was the most dangerous thing of all, for without dreams, we are without hope. Then one Christmas Eve the little girl had three waking dreams that took her to the place she most wanted to go.

LIZZIE: I'm sorry, Pitch. I know I said I'd leave this with you but I'm afraid I've found a better use for it. Henry needs this more than we do. I know the ending to the story.

[LIZZIE *gets the bundle containing her model house. The light signifying the match sputters and goes out.* LIZZIE *strikes the final match to enter the third fantasy. The light glows again, signifying the match. There is a lovely Christmas tree.* LIZZIE *enters the grand house. She looks around to be sure no one is there, then takes a shawl from the furniture and wraps the model house in it. She attaches the card from* HENRY. *She places the package under the Christmas tree.* HENRY *and* KATHERINE *enter.* KATHERINE *is carrying a tray of cakes.*]

KATHERINE: There. Don't you feel better? Sometimes a Christmas treat and a hug can make all the world brighter. Would you care for a cake, Cousin Elizabeth?

LIZZIE: Oh, yes, thank you.

[LIZZIE *takes just one cake.*]

KATHERINE: Cheer up, Henry. I'll say my gift to your father is from both of us.

HENRY: But I want to give him a gift just from me and now there's no time to get one.

[*The clock strikes twelve.*]

KATHERINE: Twelve o' clock. Merry Christmas, Dears.

HENRY: I don't feel very merry.

KATHERINE: There's a special gift for you under the tree.

HENRY: I don't care. I only want Father not to be angry with me.

KATHERINE: Let's not speak of that. Let's speak of cheerful things.

HENRY: Won't he even come down to open gifts?

KATHERINE: I don't know, dear.

[KATHERINE *hands a wrapped package to* HENRY.]

KATHERINE: Open your gift, dear.

HENRY: [*Listlessly*] Thank you, mother.

KATHERINE: Go on, read the card.

HENRY: To Henry, Merry Christmas. Love, Mother and Father.

[HENRY *opens the gift. It is the toy soldiers he wanted.*]

HENRY: Toy soldiers! Thank you, Mother.

[HENRY *kisses his mother, but puts the toy soldiers aside.*]

KATHERINE: And there is a gift for you, too, Cousin Elizabeth.

LIZZIE: A gift for me?

KATHERINE: Read the card first.

[LIZZIE *gives the card to* HENRY.]

LIZZIE: You read it, Henry.

HENRY: To our dear Cousin Elizabeth. A part of us forever.

LIZZIE: Oh, thank you, this is the best gift I could have imagined!

KATHERINE: Perhaps you'd best wait until you've opened it to declare that.

[LIZZIE *opens the package.*]

LIZZIE: Oooooooh.

[*She takes out of the box a locket and chain. She is speechless.*]

KATHERINE: Do you like it? See? It has a tiny photograph of us all inside the locket.

LIZZIE: It's all the world to me. Thank you, Auntie, thank you.

[KATHERINE *embraces* LIZZIE. LIZZIE *will not let her go.*]

KATHERINE: There. You're holding me so tight I feel faint.

[EDWARD *enters and clears his throat, making a hrumphing noise.*]

EDWARD: Good Evening. Thought I'd join the festivities.

KATHERINE: Yes, of course. Do come in. You're just in time to open my gift. And it's from Henry, too.

[KATHERINE *gives* EDWARD *a package.*]

EDWARD: How thoughtful, Mother. And you must open mine.

[EDWARD *gives her a small box.*]

KATHERINE: I do hope you'll like it.

[EDWARD *and* KATHERINE *open their packages.*]

EDWARD: Oh, my dear Katherine. A new set of drafting tools. These are very fine indeed. I shall endeavor to put them to good use.

KATHERINE: What a lovely pair of ear bobs. They're pearl, aren't they?

EDWARD: Indeed. From the deepest oceans.

[EDWARD *and* KATHERINE *embrace. There is a silence.*]

EDWARD: Henry . . .

HENRY: Yes, father?

EDWARD: [*Hesitates*] Merry Christmas.

HENRY: Merry Christmas to you, too, father.

LIZZIE: Wait. There's another gift under the tree.

KATHERINE: Oh, my, we wouldn't want to overlook someone, would we?

EDWARD: Who is it for?

LIZZIE: It's for you, Uncle, Sir.

LIZZIE: Read the card first.

[EDWARD *looks at the card, then at* HENRY.]

KATHERINE:: Let me see, Father. "To my dear Father, Love, Henry."

HENRY: It's from me?

KATHERINE: That's what it says.

[LIZZIE *kicks him.*]

HENRY: It's from me.

KATHERINE: Open it, dear.

[EDWARD *opens the shawl to reveal the model house.*]

EDWARD: Why, it's a model of our house.

LIZZIE: No mistaking it.

[HENRY *and* LIZZIE *exchange a look.*]

EDWARD: I've never seen anything quite like it. It's entirely made of matches. Why, Henry, this is amazing work, an architect' s delight.

[HENRY *is silent.*]

EDWARD: Henry, I'm truly touched. Why, it means more to me than . . . well, I can hardly say. Thank you.

HENRY: You're welcome.

EDWARD: This supporting structure is so innovative. Wherever did you get the idea?

HENRY: [*Pause*] I didn't.

EDWARD: Now don't be modest. We have lots to talk about. Look at these remarkable patterns.

HENRY: Father, I . . . I . . .

EDWARD: Out with it, Henry. You're babbling.

KATHERINE: What's the matter, Henry?

LIZZIE: I think he's overwhelmed.

HENRY: I didn't make the model house.

EDWARD: Of course you did, Henry. Don't be silly.

HENRY: I didn't, Father. I wish I had, but I didn't.

EDWARD: Well . . . then who made it?

HENRY: It was Cousin Elizabeth.

EDWARD: Cousin Elizabeth?

KATHERINE: How remarkable.

HENRY: She used matches and stones all glued together with mud.

EDWARD: Mud?

LIZZIE: Henry. You told the truth.

HENRY: [*Glumly*] It's easiest to remember.

LIZZIE: Oh, Henry, I'm so proud of you.

HENRY: Thank you for trying to help me, Cousin Elizabeth.

EDWARD: I don't understand.

LIZZIE: I only wanted you to be proud of Henry, Uncle, Sir.

KATHERINE: Well, I'm proud of you both. I'm so pleased you told the truth, Henry.

HENRY: A gentleman always tells the truth.

EDWARD: That was quite the correct thing.

HENRY: Thank you, Father.

EDWARD: You have behaved like a gentleman, Henry.

HENRY: Will you look at my drawings now?

EDWARD: [*Laughing*] You never give up, do you, Henry?

HENRY: No sir.

EDWARD: Well, I suppose tenacity can be a good quality. Very well. I'll take a look at your work.

[KATHERINE *and* LIZZIE *hug as* HENRY *gets the drawings and lays them out for his father to see.*]

EDWARD: Now, let me see. [*He looks.*] Henry, these show potential. What in the world is this?

HENRY: Trellises, father, but I'm not sure how to connect them. They form the border for the garden path but I don't know how to . . . oh, I'm prattling. I'm sorry, Father.

EDWARD: Henry. There is a difference between prattling and asking for help. Now. Are all these trellises?

HENRY: Here. And here.

EDWARD: What a distinctive design. Tell me how you want them connected and I'll see what I can do to help. Mother, bring Henry my new drafting tools. He'll be needing them.

HENRY: And so will Cousin Elizabeth.

EDWARD: Indeed, Henry. So will Cousin Elizabeth.

[*The light begins to flicker and goes out. The family freezes and fades.*]

LIGHTS SHIFT.

LIZZIE: Not yet. Please. Come back.

[LIZZIE, *dressed in her rags, strikes a match to try to bring the fantasy back. It burns, then goes out. She strikes another match and another and another. Then she throws them down on the ground and collapses in the snow.*]

LIZZIE: I hate this world. I hate it.

[GRAN *appears.*]

LIZZIE: Gran!

[GRAN *takes* LIZZIE *in her arms.*]

LIZZIE: I made them happy, Gran. All of them. [*Pause.*] Do you have any more waking dreams?

GRAN: No, Dearheart. You must make your own dreams now.

LIZZIE: I'm too tired, Gran. Too cold. I just want to sleep.

GRAN: Quickly, look once more in the glass.

[LIZZIE *hesitantly looks in the glass that Gran has produced.]*

LIZZIE: Just a match girl, Gran.

GRAN: And so much more.

[GRAN *lifts the locket at* LIZZIE'S *neck and opens it for her to look.*]

GRAN: Look in the locket. What do they see?

[LIZZIE *is too overcome with emotion to speak.*]

GRAN: A heart that can give.

LIZZIE: Oh, Gran. Thank you.

GRAN: I have done what I can. The ending of the story is up to you.

LIZZIE: Gran, don't leave me. Keep me with you always.

GRAN: If that is your wish.

[GRAN *takes* LIZZIE *in her arms and holds her.*]

GRAN: Look, there's a falling star. When a star falls a child is going up to heaven.

[*Music.* GRAN *and* LIZZIE *begin to ascend upwards.*]

LIZZIE: No more cold. No more hunger.

GRAN: No more dreams.

[PITCH *enters.*]

PITCH: Lizzie! Don't go. Please stay.

[LIZZIE *looks to* GRAN.]

GRAN: You must choose.

PITCH: Never give up, Lizzie. Remember our dream. When we get big we'll live in the grand house with a warm fire, good food and a dry place to sleep. We'll have a home.

[PITCH *is beginning to cry.*]

LIZZIE: Don't, Pitch.

PITCH: We'll help those in need. Good, clean work for everyone, food and shelter.

LIZZIE: You musn't cry.

PITCH: Tuck the little ones in at night and never, ever send their grand-mas away.

LIZZIE: If you start to cry you might never be able to stop.

PITCH: What if I am crying? What if I cry forever? Don't leave, Lizzie. If you die my favorite dream will never come true.

[LIZZIE *looks to her Grandma.*]

GRAN: It is your choice.

[LIZZIE *kisses her Grandma.*]

LIZZIE: Will you come back for me someday, Gran?

GRAN: Yes, dearheart. Someday we will be together. Remember your worth. A heart that can give.

LIZZIE: I love you, Gran. I love you.

[LIZZIE *slides out of* GRAN'S *arms and onto the ground.* GRAN *watches in the shadows.* PITCH *catches* LIZZIE *as she falls in the snow.*]

PITCH: Lizzie! Lizzie! Don't die! Please don't die!

[PITCH *tries to shake her awake, but she does not respond.*]

PITCH: Lizzie! Lizzie!

[PITCH *lifts her up and carries her to the grand house. He lays her on the doorstep and knocks loudly on the door. Then he hides out of sight. The door opens and* KATHERINE, EDWARD *and* HENRY *are there in their night-clothes.*]

EDWARD: There's no one here. Who would knock on our door at this hour?

HENRY: Look.

KATHERINE: It's a little girl.

EDWARD: It's that street seller. The match girl.

[HENRY *bends down and touches* LIZZIE.]

HENRY: She's cold.

EDWARD: Don't touch her, Henry.

HENRY: We must take her in.

EDWARD: What? We'll do no such thing. This is not an orphanage.

KATHERINE: Henry, that's a nice thought, but we don't even know her.

HENRY: That doesn't matter.

KATHERINE: But, Henry . . .

HENRY: Mother, sharing is a gift to yourself. It's Christmas Eve.

EDWARD: Fol-de-rol. Close the door. The police will deal with this matter.

HENRY: But Father, a gentleman always takes responsibility.

EDWARD: Impertinence, Henry!

KATHERINE: But isn't that what you've been trying to teach him, dear? Responsibility?

EDWARD: Why, yes, you're right, Mother, but I'm not quite sure that . . .

[HENRY *sees the locket around her neck and opens it.*]

HENRY: Look. There's a picture. Why, these people look like us.

[KATHERINE *looks.*]

KATHERINE: How remarkable!

HENRY: Help me bring her inside.

EDWARD: Henry, I hardly think . . . well, I'll ring for the Constable. Perhaps something can be done for her. Come in and close the door.

HENRY: No, Father, I won't.

EDWARD: Impertinence! How dare you!

HENRY: I won't close the door and leave her there.

EDWARD: Henry, you will do as I tell you!

HENRY: I won't! No matter what!

KATHERINE: [*Taking a huge, deep breath, firmly.*] Stop this!

[EDWARD *looks at* KATHERINE, *shocked at her outburst.*]

EDWARD: Mother, calm yourself. You'll have a fainting spell.

KATHERINE: [*Thinks. Surprised.*] I feel quite fine, thank you, dear.

EDWARD: But, Mother . . .

KATHERINE: Father, listen to Henry.

EDWARD: Why, Mother, of course, if you say so.

HENRY: I want to help her.

EDWARD: But this is madness.

KATHERINE: No, dear, it is entirely the sanest thing we have ever done.
Henry, help me lift her inside.

EDWARD: No! No, Mother. Henry and I will carry her.

HENRY: Thank you, Father.

EDWARD: You're quite welcome, Son.

KATHERINE: I'll ring for the doctor.

[EDWARD *and* HENRY *lift* LIZZIE *into the house and cover her with a
warm shawl while* PITCH *watches from his hiding place. The grand house
fades to a soft glow. Only* PITCH *is in the light.*]

PITCH: Merry Christmas, Lizzie.

[PITCH *takes out his brushes and sweeps the sidewalk.*]

PITCH: Never give up, that's what I say. I'm growin' every day. Soon I'll
be too big to climb the chimneys and Dickie'll never see me no more.

[*He wipes the tears from his eyes and sweeps the snow aside.*]

PITCH: I'll be a crossing sweeper. [*He pretends.*] Here, Miss, step light,
there's a bit of wet there. Wouldn't want you to fall down and soil that
fine gown. All the Ladies and Gentlemen will love me. I'll be a wondrous crossing sweeper. Someday.

[*Music. Lights fade to spot on* PITCH, *then blackout.*]

THE END

A PARTRIDGE IN A PEAR TREE

by Lowell Swortzell

CAST

THE STORYTELLER (a member of the Chorus)

THE WIDOW

TIB, her daughter

SIMON, the birdseller

THE MAYOR

AN OLD MAN

TOWNSPEOPLE (the Chorus)

TIME AND PLACE

Long ago in medieval Europe, on the outskirts of a small town, at Christmastime.

SETTING

A bare stage and three benches are the only requirements of the play. Because the gifts of the twelve days of Christmas are depicted in pantomime, all properties should be imaginary.

SCENE: *A bare Stage, except for three benches, Center, Left and Right.*

AT RISE: THE STORYTELLER *is discovered as he comes forward to greet the audience. As* THE STORYTELLER *describes the town, he points to specific locations.*

STORYTELLER: [*Bows.*] Imagine you see a country road just outside a village in Europe hundreds of years ago. It is a happy town, especially at this time of year, for everyone is busy preparing himself for the winter holidays. [*Several* TOWNSPEOPLE *hurry along the road, meeting and greeting one another.*] Here in the middle of the road lives the Mayor. A crowd always gathers about him because he is the most important man in the town. His word is law. [THE MAYOR, *surrounded by* TOWNS-PEOPLE, *takes his place at the bench, Center.* STORYTELLER *crosses Left.*] Over here lives a young birdseller who works hard all year long in order to give his relatives splendid gifts at Christmas. [SIMON *enters and takes his place, at the Left bench.*] Simon is said to be the best seller of birds in all of Europe. Even so, he hates to part with them because birds are his fondest friends. [*In pantomime,* SIMON *feeds the imaginary birds in his house.* STORYTELLER *crosses Right.*] And over here lives the

Widow and her daughter, Tib. [*They take their places.*] When she has her mind set on something, as she does now, the Widow is a difficult woman. Just listen. [STORYTELLER *retires to the side of the Stage.*]

WIDOW: [*To* TIB.] Tib, your stitching, let me see your stitching.

TIB: [*Handing her the imaginary dress.*] Exactly as you taught me, is it not, Mother?

WIDOW: [*Examining it closely.*] Perfect. What a wonderful wife you will make.

TIB: [*With a sign that indicates she had heard this many times before.*] Yes, Mother.

WIDOW: And why shouldn't you? You can sew as well as I. You can cook as well as I. You can keep house as well as I. The perfect daughter of a perfect mother must have a perfect husband.

TIB: Yes, Mother. But everyone turns from me.

WIDOW: What about the birdseller down the road? He's honest. I think he would make a good husband.

TIB: He turns away, too.

WIDOW: Then you must trick him.

TIB: But he is a kind man.

WIDOW: If you follow my advice, the birdseller will be your husband on Twelfth Night.

TIB: How can that be when Christmas is already here?

WIDOW: An old legend makes it possible, one that says if a lady accepts the gifts of a gentleman on each of the twelve days of Christmas, the gentleman must marry her.

TIB: But, Mother, no one will give me a gift even on one day of Christmas.

WIDOW: The birdseller will.

TIB: No, he will bow, close his door, and say I am bold. Mother, I wish I were not bold.

WIDOW: Come here and I will tell you what to do. [*The* WIDOW *whispers in her ear.*]

SIMON: [*Running outside his house, as if he were chasing a bird.*] Come back. [*He watches the imaginary bird fly into an imaginary tree.*) Oh, dear, now I'll never catch you. Not in the top of that tree. [*Jumping up he tries to reach the bird.*]

TIB: [*Breaking away from her* MOTHER'*s whisperings.*] I'm too bashful, Mother. I can't do that.

WIDOW: Of course you can. Mine is the perfect scheme of a perfect schemer.

TIB: But *I* am not perfect.

WIDOW: Nonsense! Now go, and don't be timid. Be like your mother. [*She pushes* TIB *down the road toward* SIMON.]

SIMON: [*He is preoccupied looking up into the imaginary tree and does not see* TIB *approaching.*] Even though you've flown into the tree, you don't have to eat the fruit. Do you hear?

TIB: [*Coming up behind him and addressing him in a sweet voice.*] What's the matter, Simon?

SIMON: My partridge is high in the tree, and won't come down. [*He jumps again.*]

TIB: Forget him and talk to me.

SIMON: How, when I am about to lose a precious bird, can you be so bold?

TIB: Simon, I don't know what else to be! [*Then in a voice that imitates the* WIDOW, *she shouts*] Very well, you *shall* lose it.

SIMON: Lose what?

TIB: Your partridge and your pear tree. I am taking them home with me. [*Bending over, and in pantomime, she rips the tree from the ground, and carries it toward her house.*]

SIMON: [*Calling after her, as he watches in amazement.*] I've always said you'd be a nice girl if you weren't bold. But I had no idea you were *this* bold!

TIB: [*Struggling to her front door, she calls:*] Mother, come see what I have.

WIDOW: [*In pantomime, she opens the door and comes out to greet* TIB.] What a large gift! Mayor, friends, come see what Simon has given my daughter. [*The* MAYOR *and the* TOWNSPEOPLE *gather around quickly.* SIMON *stands nearby.*]

MAYOR: What is it?

TIB: [*Sings as she holds up the imaginary tree:*]
On the first day of Christmas

My true love gave to me

A partridge in a pear tree.

[EVERYONE *exclaims on the beauty of the gift.*]

WIDOW: Isn't Simon thoughtful to think of my daughter, Tib?

SIMON: I am too polite to tell you what I think of your daughter, Tib.

WIDOW: A sweet young man, isn't he, Mayor?

MAYOR: What has happened to you, Simon?

SIMON: Tib came and took my part— [*He is interrupted before he can complete the word "partridge."*]

WIDOW: Took his "heart." Did you hear that, everyone?

TOWNSPEOPLE: We heard.

OLD MAN: Poor boy.

SIMON: [*Disgusted.*] Oh, very well. Let her have the partridge in the pear tree, if it brings her any happiness. I must be off to market. Good day. [*He goes inside his house.*]

TOWNSPEOPLE: Good day, Simon. [*They go off in various directions, some following the* MAYOR *into his house.*]

WIDOW: [*To* TIB.] Tib, I will plant the tree. [*She finds it very heavy when she attempts to pick it up.*] Next time take something lighter, please, Tib.

TIB: Yes, Mother.

WIDOW: And remember to follow my instructions. [*Huffing and puffing from the strain of the tree, she exits.*]

SIMON: [*Comes out of his house, carrying an imaginary cage.*] With these birds I will buy a new tree and a new partridge, and all will be well again.

TIB: Simon, may I walk with you to market?

SIMON: After what you did yesterday, I don't want to walk or talk with you again.

TIB: [*At first very sweetly.*] Unfortunately, I can't help myself, Simon. [*Then, remembering her instructions.*] Except to your birds. I'll be happy to take them. Thank you. [*She grabs the cage and runs.*]

SIMON: [*Surprised.*] My cage of birds! Give it back, Tib. [*Shouting.*] Help! Help!

[*Soon the* WIDOW, *the* MAYOR *and* TOWNSPEOPLE *surround* SIMON *and* TIB.]

MAYOR: What's the cause of this disturbance?

SIMON: My birds. Do you see them? [*Pointing to the cage* TIB *holds.*]

MAYOR: Of course, I see them. But they seem to belong to Tib.

SIMON: They were mine a moment ago..

MAYOR: Tib, explain this.

TIB: [*Holds up the cage and sings:*]
On the second day of Christmas

My true love gave to me

Two turtle doves and

A partridge in a pear tree.

WIDOW: Turtle doves! A romantic gift, wouldn't you say, Mayor?

MAYOR: Especially to your daughter. Simon, explain yourself.

SIMON: Tib took my dove— [*Again, he is interrupted by the* WIDOW.]

WIDOW: Took his love, did you hear that, everyone?

TOWNSPEOPLE: Yes, we heard.

OLD MAN: Poor boy!

SIMON: [*Disgusted.*] What's the use? I cannot argue with you. Besides, I must get to market. Good day. [*He returns to his house.*]

MAYOR: Good day, Simon. [*He returns to his house, followed by* TOWNSPEO-PLE.]

WIDOW: [*To* TIB *as they return to their house.*] I can manage birds better than trees. For tomorrow, you must listen carefully…[*She leads* TIB *off, whispering in her ear.*]

SIMON: [*Coming out of his house.*] These hens will bring a better price than the doves. And if the doves make her happy, perhaps Tib will leave me alone.

TIB: [*Calling from Offstage.*] Simon! Simon! [*She runs to him.*] I want to thank you for yesterday's gift.

SIMON: Stay well away, that will be thanks enough.

TIB: [*Sweetly.*] I wish you didn't mean that.

SIMON: But you take my birds.

TIB: [*Becoming bold.*] It seems I have no choice but to take your birds. So…Thank you! [*She snatches the birds and runs.* SIMON *follows her and bumps directly into the* WIDOW *as she enters.*]

WIDOW: Another gift? Simon, this is getting serious.

SIMON: Yes, it is, for soon I'll have no birds.

WIDOW: [*In a loud voice.*] The Mayor will want to see this.

MAYOR: [*Coming out of his house.*] What?

WIDOW: Mayor, it's happened again.

MAYOR: What?

TIB: [*Sings:*]
On the third day of Christmas

My true love gave to me

Three French hens,

Two turtle doves, and

A partridge in a pear tree.

WIDOW: How did Simon know that Tib has always wanted French hens?

SIMON: [*To himself.*] Whatever I say will make me look foolish. Therefore, I'll keep quiet.

WIDOW: So lovesick he can't talk. See him, everyone.

TOWNSPEOPLE: We see him.

OLD MAN: Poor boy.

SIMON: I must get to market while I still have something left to sell. Good day. [*He goes into his house as the* TOWNSPEOPLE *disperse.*]

WIDOW: *To* TIB *as they return homeward.*] I wish he had something besides birds. Hens are noisy. Help me quiet these cacklers. [*They go off as* SIMON *comes out of his house.*]

SIMON: [*Holding up another imaginary cage.*] My best birds. I hate to sell them. Still I must, and all will be well again.

TIB: [*Offstage.*] Simon, guess who's here.

SIMON: [*Clutching the cage.*] I'm ready for you this time, Tib. You won't get these birds.

TIB: [*Crossing to* SIMON.] Mother's tired of birds. They squawk all the time.

SIMON: Not when they are happy.

TIB: [*Sweetly at first, then boldly.*] Simon, I wish I didn't have to make you and your birds unhappy, but I do. [*She grabs the cage, only to find that* SIMON *comes with it. He lunges forward as she pulls.*]

SIMON: I'm tied to the cage. You can't get away this time.

TIB: [*Calling off.*] Mother, your plan isn't working.

WIDOW: [*Entering.*] Nonsense! [*Noticing the cage.*] Not more birds! Simon, young men give young ladies gifts other than birds, you should remember that.

SIMON: I have not given this young lady these birds, and I can prove it. [*Calls to the* MAYOR.] Mayor, please come here.

MAYOR: Yes, Simon, coming. [*He comes out of his house, followed by the* TOWNSPEOPLE.] Good day, Widow. What, has Tib received another gift?

WIDOW: Not only that, but see what comes with it. He loves Tib so much he has wrapped himself up in the present.

TOWNSPEOPLE: We see.

OLD MAN: Poor boy!

MAYOR: Untie yourself, Simon. You cannot include yourself in the package. The birds are enough.

WIDOW: What has he given you now, Tib?

TIB: [*Sings, as she unwinds the rope from* SIMON.]
On the fourth day of Christmas

My true love gave to me

Four collie birds,

Three French hens,

Two turtle doves, and

A partridge in a pear tree.

WIDOW: [*In an artificial voice.*] How nice! Four more birds!

MAYOR: Simon, your generosity to Tib can mean only one thing. Are you certain you know what you are doing?

SIMON: I know what I'm doing. I'm going away to visit my cousins. Just as fast as I can. Good day. [*He exits into his house as the* OTHERS *go off, save for* TIB *and the* WIDOW.]

WIDOW: Birds are such a bother! What are we going to do with these?

TIB: I don't know. This is your scheme, Mother.

WIDOW: Yes, and I must think of something to stop him from going away. [*They go off as* SIMON *comes out of his house.*]

SIMON: A day away in the country will do me good. My five cousins will cheer me up, and I can deliver my presents to them. I can hardly wait to see them.

TIB: [*Offstage.*] Simon! Where are you going?

SIMON: I won't answer.

TIB: [*Enters and sees* SIMON.] Can it be? Simon without birds?

SIMON: I am going away to forget my misfortunes.

TIB: [*Observing him.*] What is that you carry in your coat pocket, Simon?

SIMON: A gift.

TIB: Let me see. [*She sticks her hand in his pocket and pulls out the gift. She exclaims:*] Real gold! Simon, you shouldn't be so extravagant.

SIMON: And you shouldn't be so bold. Give me those rings.

WIDOW: [*Offstage.*] Did I hear correctly? [*She enters.*] Did you say rings?

SIMON: For my cousins.

WIDOW: Such an appropriate gift. [*Calling:*] Mayor, everyone, hurry here. Instead of birds, he has given Tib golden rings.

MAYOR: [*Entering from his house.*] Simon, are you certain you mean these rings for—

SIMON: Yes, they are a gift, one for each [*But before he can say "cousin," he is interrupted.*]

WIDOW: One for each finger. How lucky she is. Most brides receive only one ring, but Tib gets a handful. [*Quickly, and in pantomime, she places the rings on* TIB's *fingers, then holds up her hand.*] Isn't that a dazzling sight, everyone?

TOWNSPEOPLE: [*Exclaiming.*] Congratulations, Simon. Congratulations, Tib.

OLD MAN: Poor boy.

MAYOR: His head is turned, surely. Tib, how do you feel about this?

TIB: [*Sings:*]
On the fifth day of Christmas
My true love gave to me
Five golden rings,
Four collie birds,
Three French hens,
Two turtle doves, and
A partridge in a pear tree.

MAYOR: Well, Simon, what have you to say for yourself?

SIMON: I've been a fool, but now I see what's going on here. [*To* TIB *and her* MOTHER.] Tomorrow, I will have a surprise or two awaiting you.

WIDOW: Already thinking of surprises for Tib. How sweet!

SIMON: And some for you, too, Widow!

WIDOW: For me? How considerate! [*As he escorts her off.*] Mayor, young men in love are amusing, aren't they? [*The road is empty except for* SI-MON.]

SIMON: Five days it took me to realize that I am being tricked. But now it is my turn to play this game.

TIB: [*Entering.*] Simon, another day, another gift. What have you today?

SIMON: A lovely present. Six geese a-laying, and a-screaming, and a-squawking. The loudest, noisiest, meanest geese in the country.

TIB: [*Truly surprised.*] Oh, no! I hate to but I have no choice. I accept. [*She turns and calls out in a voice of alarm.*] MOTHER! [*The* WIDOW *appears instantly.*]

SIMON: [*Pointing to the geese.*] For you.

WIDOW: Simon, I hate birds.

SIMON: [*Ordering her.*] Take them away.

WIDOW: Yes, Simon. [*She hurries off with the birds.*]

TIB: And what have you today?

SIMON: Another lovely present. Seven swans a-swimming. Seven great big swans, with seven great big beaks, and fourteen great big dirty feet.

TIB: Dirty feet?

SIMON: DIRTY FEET.

TIB: I accept. [*Calling desperately.*] MOTHER! MOTHER!

WIDOW: [*Enters and sees the birds.*] Simon, please, we live in a birdhouse as it is.

SIMON: Take them away,

WIDOW: Yes, Simon. [*As she goes off.*] I thought a partridge, two doves, three hens, four collie birds, and six geese were bad enough, but did you ever try to carry seven swans a-swimming! [*Balancing them, she exits.*]

TIB: What have you today?

SIMON: Eight maids a-milking. And all you must do is feed them, house them, care for them and keep them happy. A generous gift, you'll agree?

TIB: A terrible gift. But I accept. Mother! MOTHER!

WIDOW: [*Enters.*] Eight maids a-milking. Well, at least they can walk home. Come on, girls. [*In pantomime, she leads them off.*]

TIB: And today, Simon?

SIMON: Nine pipers piping. They should be pleasant to have playing around the house.

TIB: Where will we put them?

SIMON: Does that mean you don't want them?

TIB: If you give them to me, I accept.

SIMON: They are yours.

TIB: [*Distressed.*] Mother! MOTHER!

WIDOW: [*Enters, and stares at the nine pipers.*] We're running out of food, Simon.

SIMON: But, Widow, what are nine mouths more?

WIDOW: Come, pipers, when you're not playing, you can help in the kitchen. [*She exits.*]

TIB: And for the tenth day, Simon? Something special?

SIMON: What's louder than nine pipers piping? Ten drummers drumming, that's what. And they are yours.

TIB: [*Holding her hands over her ears.*] With cotton in my ears, I accept.

SIMON: And for the eleventh day, I give you eleven lords a-leaping.

TIB: Perhaps another bird, Simon? They're easier to feed, and not nearly as noisy.

SIMON: [*Shaking his head negatively.*] Eleven lords a-leaping or nothing.

TIB: I accept.

SIMON: They're yours. And for the twelfth day, twelve ladies dancing.

TIB: Twelve ladies dancing!

SIMON: Just what you've always wanted, I know.

TIB: I accept. MOTHER! MOTHER! Help! Help!

WIDOW: [*Entering.*] What is it now?

TIB: Ten drummers, eleven lords, and twelve ladies.

WIDOW: In my small house? Oh, well, I'm so tired now, thirty-three more won't make any difference.

SIMON: Take them away.

WIDOW: But just a moment. I've been too busy to notice. This is the twelfth day of Christmas. [*Calling Off-stage:*] Mayor, everyone, come here.

MAYOR: [*Stepping forth from his house.*] You called?

WIDOW: Not I but true love calls, Mayor, to perform the ceremony of matrimony. My daughter has accepted the twelve gifts of the bird-seller, Simon. And you know what that means.

MAYOR: I know.

TOWNSPEOPLE: We know.

WIDOW: They are to be married at once.

OLD MAN: POOR BOY!

MAYOR: Tib, what are Simon's gifts?

TIB: [*Sings:*]
On the twelfth day of Christmas

My true love gave to me

Twelve ladies dancing,

Eleven lords a-leaping,

Ten drummers drumming,

Nine pipers piping,

Eight maids a-milking,

Seven swans a-swimming,

Six geese a-laying,

Five golden rings,

Four collie birds,

Three French hens,

Two turtle doves, and

A partridge in a pear tree.

MAYOR: You know what the legend says, Simon, so I pronounce you...

SIMON: One moment, Mayor, before you pronounce us man and wife.

Legend also says that on the twelfth day of Christmas birds and animals possess the power of speech.

WIDOW: I forgot that.

SIMON: So I thought. Mayor, ask my friends, the birds, if they were given or taken.

MAYOR: Very well. [*He goes inside the* WIDOW'*s house, and speaks to the imaginary birds.*] Birds, be quiet. This is important. Tell me did Simon give you as gifts?

VOICES: [*From Offstage.*] No.

MAYOR: Then Simon was tricked?

VOICES: [*From Offstage.*] Yes.

MAYOR: [*Coming outside.*] This changes everything, Widow.

WIDOW: Please, Simon, marry her anyway.

SIMON: Perhaps when she acts like a lady, someone will marry her.

TIB: [*Bursting into tears.*] I am so embarrassed, for I see how bold I've been, but now no one will believe me when I say I'm sorry.

WIDOW: Don't be. If you didn't get a husband, at least you got a poultry farm.

TIB: Of course, we will give back Simon's birds.

WIDOW: Nonsense, they are yours and you will feed and care for them.

TIB: Simon, I am sorry, deeply. [*She bursts into tears and runs inside her house.*]

WIDOW: [*Calling after her.*] Stop your crying. I will think of another trick to get you a husband. And I won't be outsmarted next time. [*She exits.*]

MAYOR: Simon was tricked, there's no doubt about it.

SIMON: Don't feel sorry for me. Tib has suffered more than anyone.

TOWNSPEOPLE: We know.

OLD MAN: Poor girl.

[SIMON, THE MAYOR, *and* TOWNSPEOPLE *go off in various directions, leaving only* TIB, *who sits in her house and cries.*]

STORYTELLER: [*Stepping from the side of the Stage.*] And Tib was a poor girl, indeed. She continued to cry during the entire month of January, through February, March, April, May, June, and on into summer, then through all of October and November, and harder than ever as each day of December passed.

TIB: [*Rubbing her eyes.*] Birds, don't you cry, too. [*She bends down to the imaginary birds.*] I wish I could make you happy.

STORYTELLER: Then an idea hit her. And she stopped crying.

TIB: Perhaps I can. [*Coming out of the house, she digs up the pear tree, and carries it to the door of* SIMON'S *house.*]

STORYTELLER: And down the road she carried the heavy gift. She knocked at Simon's door and ran away. [*She does this in pantomime.*]

SIMON: [*Enters and opens door.*] Who's there? [*Surprised and pleased.*] Just look, my pear tree, still with a partridge in it. [*Singing, he plants the tree in its original position:*]

On the first day of Christmas

My true love gave to me

A partridge in a pear tree.

What a lovely gift! [*He goes inside.*]

[*Running to* SIMON's *door,* TIB *returns the turtle doves, knocks, and leaves.*]

SIMON: I thought I heard something. [*He opens the door and discovers the gift.*] My friends! [*Singing, he picks up the birds and takes them inside:*]

On the second day of Christmas

My true love gave to me

Two turtle doves and

A partridge in a pear tree.

[*He is no sooner inside than* TIB *scampers to his door, places the French hens, knocks, and runs.*]

SIMON: Coming. Coming. [*Opens the door.*] Who knocks? How nice to see you. Your old nest awaits you. [*Picking them up, he sings:*]

On the third day of Christmas

My true love gave to me

Three French hens,

Two turtle doves, and

A partridge in a pear tree.

[*As he takes them inside,* TIB *places the next gift, knocks, and hurries away.*]

SIMON: Just a moment. [*Opens the door.*] My favorite collie birds! How I've missed you. [*He strokes them and sings:*]

On the fourth day of Christmas

My true love gave to me

Four collie birds,

Three French hens,

Two turtle doves, and

A partridge in a pear tree.

[*After he escorts them inside,* TIB *reappears, leaves several gifts, knocks, and runs away.*]

SIMON: What is it now? [*He opens the door, looks, and picks up the gifts.*] Five golden rings! My cousins will be pleased. And here, my geese home again. And look, still a-laying. [*He holds up an imaginary egg.*] And my swans, with clean feet, too. How happy I am to see you...So happy, in fact, I haven't stopped to think how any of you got here. No, it couldn't be Tib; she would knock down the door and throw you at me. Yet, it must be Tib. I will find out. [SIMON *goes inside and comes out the back of the house.* TIB *enters with additional gifts, places them, knocks on the door, and turns to run away, but squarely faces* SIMON.] You knocked?

TIB: I thought you were inside.

SIMON: What did you wish?

TIB: Oh, nothing in particular, Simon.

SIMON: Did you come to take something?

TIB: No, Simon.

SIMON: To leave something?

TIB: I didn't want to take them. I don't want to keep them. These belong to you. [*She points to the doorstep.*]

SIMON: Thank you for restoring my birds and rings and things.

TIB: I am sorry to have caused you so much sorrow.

SIMON: And I am sorry to have caused you so much sorrow.

TIB: It wasn't your fault.

SIMON: And it wasn't yours, entirely.

TIB: Now I must go. [*She bows.*] Merry Christmas, Simon.

SIMON: What's happened to you, Tib? You're a different person, so quiet, so timid, so thoughtful.

TIB: I've always wanted to be this way.

SIMON: I said once that you'd be a nice girl if you weren't so bold, and I was right.

TIB: Thank you, Simon. Merry Christmas. [*She starts to leave.*]

SIMON: Merry Christmas, Tib. [*As she is going.*] But wait. I won't let you go.

TIB: I must.

SIMON: Stop in the name of the law.

TIB: You can't hold me here.

SIMON: Oh, yes, I can. Just you wait and see. [*Shouting:*] Mayor, Townspeople, come here.

MAYOR: [*Appearing at once.*] You called, good Simon?

SIMON: Yes. I want you to pronounce us man and wife.

TIB: Simon!

MAYOR: Simon, she's tricked you again!

SIMON: No, I speak for myself. And you cannot refuse.

MAYOR: And why can't I?

SIMON: Because of a certain legend that says if a lady gives a gentleman gifts on the twelve days of Christmas, and he accepts them, they must be married. It's the law, remember, Mayor?

MAYOR: What has she given you?

SIMON: [*Singing:*]
On the twelfth day of Christmas

My true love gave to me

Twelve ladies dancing,

Eleven lords a-leaping,

Ten drummers drumming,

Nine pipers piping,

Eight maids a-milking,

Seven swans a-swimming,

Six geese a-laying,

Five golden rings,

Four collie birds,

Three French hens,

Two turtle doves, and

A partridge in a pear tree.

MAYOR: Tib, did you give Simon these things?

TIB: They belonged to him in the first place.

SIMON: There's nothing in the legend about that. A gift's a gift.

MAYOR: And a legend is a legend. I hereby pronounce you man and wife.

TOWNSPEOPLE: Congratulations!

WIDOW: [*Entering.*] What's going on here?.

MAYOR: You've missed the wedding.

WIDOW: Whose wedding?

MAYOR: Tib and Simon.

WIDOW: Tib and Simon! How can that be?

EVERYONE: Very simple. [*They sing:*]

On the twelfth day of Christmas

My true love gave to me

Twelve ladies dancing,

Eleven lords a-leaping,

Ten drummers drumming,

Nine pipers piping,

Eight maids a-milking.,

Seven swans a-swimming,

Six geese a-laying,

Five golden rings,

Four collie birds,

Three French hens,

Two turtle doves, and

A partridge in a pear tree.

MAYOR: Well, Widow, are you pleased?

WIDOW: A perfect daughter and a perfect son-in-law. What more can a not-so-perfect mother want?.

MAYOR: [*Sings:*] A partridge in a pear tree.

EVERYONE: [*Sings:*] And a partridge in a pear tree.

CURTAIN

A CHILD'S CHRISTMAS IN WALES
based on the story by Dylan Thomas

by Jeremy Brooks and Adrian Mitchell

CHARACTERS

DYLAN THOMAS	narrator and boy
MOTHER and FATHER	of Dylan
POSTMAN	for Cwmdonkin Drive
JIM, JACK, TOM	Dylan's friends
SMOKY	the Park Keeper
HANNAH	Father's sister, Dylan's aunt
GWYN	Dylan's uncle
NELLIE	Gwyn's wife
GLYN	Dylan's bachelor uncle
BRENDA and GLENDA	Dylan's cousins
TUDYR and BESSIE	the parents of Brenda and Glenda
ELIERI	Dylan's spinster aunt
MURGATROYD	a hotel chauffeur
FIREMEN ONE, TWO and THREE	
CONSTABLE LLOYD-JONES	
TOWN HILL BOYS and the HUNCHBACK	

TIME

The Present and the Past

PLACE

Wales/A Boy's Memory

ACT ONE

As the houselights dim, a CHOIR *of small children is heard singing the first verse of a carol.*

[*SONG: "IN THE BLEAK MIDWINTER"*]

CHOIR: IN THE BLEAK MIDWINTER
　　　FROSTY WIND MADE MOAN
　　　EARTH STOOD HARD AS IRON
　　　WATER LIKE A STONE
　　　SNOW HAD FALLEN, SNOW ON SNOW,
　　　SNOW ON SNOW
　　　IN THE BLEAK MIDWINTER
　　　LONG, LONG AGO.

[*The lights come up on a small group of figures, the* CHOIR, *huddled in overcoats, scarves and gloves.*]

BOY ONE: WHAT SHALL I GIVE HIM
　　　POOR AS I AM?

BOY TWO: IF I WERE A SHEPHERD
　　　I WOULD GIVE A LAMB.

BOY THREE: IF I WERE A RICH MAN
　　　I WOULD PLAY MY PART.

BOY FOUR: WHAT CAN I GIVE HIM?
　　　GIVE MY HEART.

[DYLAN *enters and listens.*]

CHOIR: IN THE BLEAK MIDWINTER
　　　FROSTY WIND MADE MOAN
　　　EARTH STOOD HARD AS IRON
　　　WATER LIKE A STONE
　　　SNOW HAD FALLEN, SNOW ON SNOW,
　　　SNOW ON SNOW
　　　IN THE BLEAK MIDWINTER
　　　LONG, LONG AGO.

[*The lights go down on the* CHOIR.]

DYLAN: [*alone*] One Christmas was so much like another, in those years, around the sea town corner now, and out of all sound except the distant speaking of the voices I sometimes hear a moment before sleep, that I can never remember whether it snowed for six days and six nights when I was twelve, or whether it snowed for twelve days and twelve nights when I was six. Or whether the ice broke and the skating grocer vanished like a snowman through a white trap door on that same Christmas Day that the mincepies finished Uncle Tudyr and Mother burnt the turkey and we tobogganned down the seaward hill, all the afternoon, on the best tea-tray, and Mrs. Griffiths complained, and we threw a snowball at her niece, and my hands burned so, with the heat and the cold, when I held them in front of the fire, that I cried for twenty minutes and then had some jelly. All the Christmases roll down the hill towards the two-tongued sea, like a snowball growing bigger and whiter and rounder, like a cold and headlong moon bundling down the sky that was our street. And they stop at the rim of the ice-edged fish-freezing waves, and I plunge my hands in the snow and bring out whatever I can find—holly or robins or pudding, squabbles and carols and oranges and tin whistles, and the fire in the front room, and bang go the crackers, and holy, holy, holy ring the bells, and the glass bells shaking on the tree . . . In goes my hand into that wool-white, bell-tongued ball of holidays resting on the margin of the carol-singing sea, and out comes . . . Christmas Eve and sending out messages to Father Christmas! [*The lights come up on the bed.* DYLAN *crosses to it and kneels.*] Dear old God, I'm sorry about any bad things I did today. I can't think of any, but you'll know. I hope you noticed when I dried the dishes. [*Pause.*] When you see Father Christmas coming to our house, could you tell him that I still need that red B.S.A. bicycle with a three-speed gear that I didn't get for my birthday. And a magician set that does real magic, not just tricks. [*Pause.*] And, well, I know it's difficult, but I'd be very grateful if he could let me have to, you know, frighten away the Town Hill boys, just a little, little real machine gun . . . And a big, woolly ginger dog for my very own. [*Pause.*] And bless my Mam and my Dad and Jack and Jim and Tom and Aunt Elieri. And please make this Christmas just like the last. [*He gets onto the bed. The* COMPANY *sings to the tune of* "*The Green Grass Grew All Around.*"]

[*SONG: "THE SOFT SNOW FALLS ALL AROUND"*]

COMPANY: [*off*] NOW IN THE WORLD
    THERE LAY A LAND
    THE PRETTIEST LAND
    THAT YOU EVER DID SEE.

DYLAN: [*speaking as if in his sleep*] The land of Wales . . .

COMPANY: [*off*] O THE LAND IN THE WORLD
    AND THE WORLD IN THE SKY
    AND THE SOFT SNOW FALLS ALL AROUND,
    ALL AROUND
    THE SOFT SNOW FALLS ALL AROUND.

[*The* COMPANY *enters.*]

> AND IN THAT LAND
> THERE SLEEPS A TOWN
> THE PRETTIEST TOWN
> THAT YOU EVER DID SEE.

DYLAN: [*speaking*] Swansea . . .

COMPANY: [*gathering around the bed*] O THE TOWN IN THE LAND
> AND THE LAND IN THE WORLD
> AND THE WORLD IN THE SKY
> AND THE SOFT SNOW FALLS ALL AROUND,
> ALL AROUND
> THE SOFT SNOW FALLS ALL AROUND,

> AND IN THAT TOWN
> WAS BUILT A HOUSE
> THE PRETTIEST HOUSE
> THAT YOU EVER DID SEE,

DYLAN: [*speaking*] Semi-detached . . .

COMPANY: O THE HOUSE IN THE TOWN
> AND THE TOWN IN THE LAND
> AND THE LAND IN THE WORLD
> AND THE WORLD IN THE SKY
> AND THE SOFT SNOW FALLS ALL AROUND,
> ALL AROUND
> THE SOFT SNOW FALLS ALL AROUND,

> AND IN THAT HOUSE
> THERE WAS A BED
> THE PRETTIEST BED
> THAT YOU EVER DID SEE.

> O THE BED IN THE HOUSE
> AND THE HOUSE IN THE TOWN
> AND THE TOWN IN THE LAND
> AND THE LAND IN THE WORLD
> AND THE WORLD IN THE SKY
> AND THE SOFT SNOW FALLS ALL AROUND,
> ALL AROUND
> THE SOFT SNOW FALLS ALL AROUND.

> AND IN THAT BED
> THERE WAS A BOY
> THE PRETTIEST BOY

THAT YOU EVER DID SEE.

DYLAN: [*speaking*] Tough as toffee . . .

COMPANY: O THE BOY IN THE BED
    AND THE BED IN THE HOUSE
    AND THE HOUSE IN THE TOWN
    AND THE TOWN IN THE LAND
    AND THE LAND IN THE WORLD
    AND THE WORLD IN THE SKY
    AND THE SOFT SNOW FALLS ALL AROUND,
    ALL AROUND
    THE SOFT SNOW FALLS ALL AROUND.

[*The* COMPANY *exits the stage, leaving only* MOTHER.]

MOTHER: [*softly*] And beside that boy . . . there was a Christmas stocking!

[FATHER, *dressed as* FATHER CHRISTMAS, *appears with a bulging Christmas stocking that he places at the foot of* DYLAN's *bed.* MOTHER *watches, then she and* FATHER *exit. There is silence for a moment, then an alarm clock rings.* DYLAN *wakes and examines the stocking.*]

DYLAN: And in that stocking—
  Was a teddy bear
Three inches long
And a tin policeman
From Hong Kong
And jelly babies
And a folded flag
And chocolate coins
In a little net bag
And a water pistol
With twenty-four squirts
And some Scottish soldiers
In tartan skirts
And a false moustache
And a money box
And a pair of hairy
And disgusting socks
And a diver in a bottle
A yo-yo on a string
And a tram conductor's thingummy
That goes ding-ding
And a comic annual
And some marbles, of course

And a rubber buffalo
Or maybe a horse
And a celluloid duck
That makes a mooing miaow
Like an ambitious cat
That wants to be a cow
And a packet of bullseyes
To keep your heart warm
And a small glass globe
With a soapy snowstorm
But it wouldn't be a stocking
And there wouldn't be snow
If there wasn't a tangerine
In the stocking's toe.

DYLAN: [*singing*] AND THE STOCKING BY THE BOY
   AND THE BOY IN THE BED
   AND THE BED IN THE ROOM
   AND THE ROOM IN THE HOUSE
   AND THE HOUSE IN THE STREET
   AND THE STREET IN THE TOWN
   AND THE TOWN IN THE LAND
   AND THE LAND IN THE WORLD
   AND THE WORLD IN THE SKY
   AND THE SOFT SNOW FALLS ALL AROUND,
   ALL AROUND
   THE SOFT SNOW FALLS ALL AROUND.

COMPANY: [*off*] AND THE SOFT SNOW FALLS ALL AROUND,
   ALL AROUND
   THE SOFT SNOW FALLS ALL AROUND.

MOTHER: [*off*] Dylan! Up you get! Breakfast's ready . . . Christmas breakfast!

DYLAN: [*calling off*] Coming, Mam!

[*The lights come up on the kitchen.* FATHER *is seated at the table.* MOTHER *hovers over a frying pan on the stove.* DYLAN *enters the scene.*]

DYLAN: Merry Christmas, Mam.

MOTHER: Merry Christmas, Dylan. [DYLAN *sits at the table. She serves him from the frying pan.*]

DYLAN: Merry Christmas, Dad.

FATHER: Merry Christmas, Dylan.

DYLAN: Why do we always have laverbread and cockles for Christmas breakfast, Mam?

MOTHER: Because that's what we always have for Christmas breakfast.

DYLAN: Funny sort of breakfast.

FATHER: Very nourishing. Keep you going till dinner, but leaves room for turkey and all the trimmings. When I was a boy, we always had laverbread and cockles . . .

MOTHER: So did we. And later on, Welshcakes and Cawl . . .

DYLAN: I wouldn't mind some Welshcakes!

MOTHER: You'll get some for your tea.

FATHER: When I was a boy . . . [MOTHER *bustles from the room.*]

DYLAN: Did it snow?

FATHER: Years and years ago, when I was a boy, when there were wolves in Wales, and birds the color of red flannel petticoats whisked past the harp-shaped hills, when we sang and wallowed all night and day in caves that smelt like Sunday afternoons in damp front farmhouse parlors, and we chased the English and the bears with the jawbones of deacons . . . before the motor car . . . before the wheel . . . when we rode the daft and happy hills bareback, it snowed and it snowed and it snowed.

DYLAN: Were there postmen then, too?

FATHER: Of course there were postmen, with sprinkling eyes and wind-cherried noses, on spread, frozen feet they crunched up to the doors and mittened on them manfully with blue knuckles. They stood on the white welcome mat in the little drifted porches and huffed and puffed, making ghosts with their breath, and jogged from foot to foot like small boys wanting to go out.

DYLAN: Did they bring parcels?

FATHER: All you think of is parcels. The cold postman, with a rose in his buttonnose after his Christmas drink, tingled down the tea-tray-slithered run of the chilly glinting hill, honking and roaring as he went, wagging his bag like a frozen camel's hump, skidding on his ice-bound boots like a man on a fishmonger's slab. Oh, did we have postmen, Dylan! Did we have postmen!

[*From offstage, there is a tremendous roaring and honking from the* POSTMAN. MOTHER *bustles on.*]

MOTHER: That'll be Dai, the Post, now.

[*Rat-a-tat-tat offstage. As* FATHER *gets out a bottle and pours a drink,* DYLAN *runs off. The* POSTMAN, *with a bulging sack over his shoulder, reels drunkenly in, followed by* DYLAN.]

POSTMAN: Number five, Cwmdonkin Drive . . . Dai Post, frozen to death, doing his duty.

DYLAN: Got anything for us?

POSTMAN: I might have, I might have, boy. Hold on while I hold on. Let us never forget . . .

DYLAN: What?

POSTMAN: The trials and tribulations of a postman's life.

MOTHER: Ah, no, I'm sure!

POSTMAN: Sure you are sure. Imagine! Up at the crack, shaved and tooth-brushed, bacon-and-egged, then out into the crispy streets to crunch the snow with parcels for other people . . .

DYLAN: No parcels for you?

POSTMAN: I'm not saying, but there might be one for you. [*He delves into his bag and reads from a package.*] Master Dylan Thomas, number five Cwmdonkin Drive, Swansea, South Wales. Sound like you?

DYLAN: It *is* me! [*The* POSTMAN *hands the parcel to* DYLAN, *who makes to un-wrap it.* MOTHER *takes it from him and hides it away.*]

MOTHER: Not until present-giving time, you know that, don't you?

POSTMAN: People are very generous. Oh, yes. It's a well-known charact . . . charact . . .

DYLAN: . . . teristic . . .

POSTMAN: . . . of our race, isn't it? Every house I call at, top to bottom of the hill, I've only got to get one foot across the sacred threshold be-fore someone is pressing a drink into my hand. Pressing it, by damn! [*FATHER produces a full glass from behind his back and presses it into the* POSTMAN's *hand. The* POSTMAN *drinks, lurches to his feet, and sings to the tune of "Mochyn Du."*]

[***SONG:** "THE POSTMAN'S SONG"*]

POSTMAN: WHEN THE POSTMAN COMES A-CALLING
    LET THERE NOT BE ANY STALLING
    GET THE BOTTLE AND START POURING

WHEN YOU HEAR THAT POSTMAN ROARING.

HAVE IT WAITING IN THE HALL
HAVE IT WAITING IN THE HALL
HAVE THAT GLASS OF SOMETHING WAITING
WHEN THE POSTMAN COMES TO CALL.

WHEN THEY HEAR THE POSTMAN HONKIN'
EVERY HOUSE IN DRIVE CWMDONKIN
WILL BE POURING OUT A NOGGIN
FOR TO COMFORT HIS FOOTSLOGGIN'.

ALL: HAVE IT WAITING IN THE HALL
HAVE IT WAITING IN THE HALL
HAVE THAT GLASS OF SOMETHING WAITING
WHEN THE POSTMAN COMES TO CALL.

POSTMAN: DAI POST IS FAIRLY FROZEN
BUT HIS DUTY HE HAS CHOSEN
SO ON THIS CHRISTMAS MORNING
YOU MUST HEED HIS FRIENDLY WARNING.

ALL: HAVE IT WAITING IN THE HALL
HAVE IT WAITING IN THE HALL
HAVE THAT GLASS OF SOMETHING WAITING
WHEN THE POSTMAN COMES TO CALL.

[MOTHER *deftly guides the* POSTMAN *off.*]

DYLAN: [*laughing*] He's funny. Well, he's funny at Christmas.

FATHER: There's many a man and woman funny at Christmas would make your hair fall out with gloom any other day of the year.

DYLAN: Why is that, Dad?

FATHER: One of the mysteries of life, bach. But my theory is that the singing of songs and the speaking of verse, which is what we do at Christmas, is the only fit way for humans to communicate with each other. And at Christmas everyone gets a look-in . . . even Dai Post and your Uncle Tudyr.

[MOTHER *enters with a platter on which rests an enormous uncooked turkey.*]

MOTHER: Not a word against Tudyr, Dad. Not on Christmas Day. [FATHER *catches her around the waist and holds her.*]

FATHER: Nor on any other, cariad. I am the soul of charity. Now just look at the size of that bird, boy. More like a dragon than a turkey, that is.

MOTHER: It's got to feed a hundred uncles and a thousand aunts.

FATHER: D'ye have to start cooking it already, fach?

MOTHER: Yes. I don't trust this new oven. Gas is funny stuff. Ah right for lighting, but for cooking, well, I dunno.

DYLAN: Can I go out now, Mam?

MOTHER: Yes, run along. But don't be late for your aunts and uncles and present-giving time or we'll give all your presents to the poor children of Town Hill. [*She sounds quite serious and it gives* DYLAN *pause for a second. Then he remembers and grins.*]

DYLAN: You say that every year! [*He grabs a coat, scarf and cap. The lights go down on the kitchen.* MOTHER *and* FATHER *exit in the darkness. A spot follows* DYLAN *as he moves slowly across the stage.*] On Christmas mornings, with dog-disturbing whistle and sugar-fags, I would scour the swatched town for news of the little world, and find always a dead bird by the white Post Office or by the deserted swings; perhaps a robin, all but one of his fires out. Men and women wading and scooping back from chapel, with taproom noses and wind-bussed cheeks, all albinos, huddled their stiff, black, jarring feathers against the irreligious snow. Mistletoe hung from the gas brackets in all the front parlors; there was sherry and walnuts and bottled beer and crackers by the dessert spoons; and cats in their furabouts watched the fires; and the high-heaped fire spat, all ready for the chestnuts and the mulling pokers. Not many these mornings trod the piling streets as we went squeaking through the white world on the track of the big killer cats that lurked in the snow . . .

[JIM, JACK *and* TOM *enter, moving as if wearing snow shoes.* DYLAN *joins them.*]

DYLAN: We must be patient, men. Then cool and callous in the kill.

JIM: [*shivering*] Cool won't be much problem.

JACK: Better arm ourselves. They may be upon us any moment.

DYLAN: [*gathering snowballs and looking around*] I see nothing. Only the blinding glare . . .

JIM: Of my mam's front garden. [JACK, TOM *and* DYLAN *snarl at him, then ignore him.*]

DYLAN: [*to* TOM] You see any trace of them, mun?

TOM: Aye, captain. I followed the spore of two of the critturs.

DYLAN: Describe their tracks.

JIM: Ah, come on, Dylan, you know what cats' footprints are like. Look. [*He points to the ground.* JACK, TOM *and* DYLAN *snarl again. He keeps undercutting their game.* JACK *weighs a snowball in his hand, considering* JIM *as a possible target.*]

JACK: The snows have curdled that man's brain.

TOM: Right! These are the tracks of no mere cat . . .

DYLAN: No! They are the footprints of the dreaded and terrible-whiskered sabre-clawed arctic tiger!

JACK: What! The beast that slew our trusty team of huskies. Aaaaarah!

JIM: Oh, come on, there's not much point hanging around to snowball the cats when the cats are all in by the fire because they've got more sense. [JACK, TOM *and* DYLAN *groan, disgusted with* JIM.]

JACK: [*shouting suddenly*] There it is! The terrible beast itself!

DYLAN AND TOM: Where? Where?

JACK: There! [ALL *look around vaguely.* JACK *points at* JIM *when he's not looking.*] There! Kill! Kill!

JACK, DYLAN, TOM: Kill! Kill! Kill! Kill! Kill! [JACK, DYLAN *and* TOM *advance on* JIM *and snowball him into the ground.* JIM *plays dead but comes alive cheerfully enough when they pick him up and dust the snow off him.*]

TOM: Now what'll we do?

DYLAN: Let's post Mr. Daniel a snowball through his letterbox.

JIM: Let's write rude things in the snow.

DYLAN: Let's write "Mr. Daniel looks like a spaniel" all over his lawn.

TOM: No, I know. Let's go up the park and track Palefaces.

JIM, DYLAN, JACK: Yeah! Right! Let's! [JIM, JACK *and* TOM *snowshoe off.*]

DYLAN: Cwmdonkin Park was only a little park, but it held within its borders of old tall trees, notched with our names and shabby from our climbing, as many secret places, caverns andforests, prairies and deserts, as a country somewhere at the edge of the sea. And though we would explore it one day, armed and desperate, from end to end, from the robbers' den to the pirates' cabin, the highwayman's inn to the cattle ranch, from the park keeper's hut to the gents' toilet, yet still the next day it remained as unexplored as the North Pole and the South Pole. And it all belonged to us . . .

[*Lights come up on the park. A* HUNCHBACK *sits on a park bench. There is an iced-up water fountain and the corner of a bandstand.* JIM, JACK *and*

TOM *crouch behind the bench, in hiding. As* DYLAN *joins them, assorted* PALEFACES *stroll on, muffled against the cold. Among them are* UNCLE TUDYR, AUNTIE BESSIE *and their two daughters,* GLENDA *and* BRENDA, *who tease each other behind their parents' backs. The* BOYS *speak in loud whispers.*]

JIM: Keep down! Palefaces!

DYLAN: Let's lay traps for 'em! Tripwires hidden in the snow!

JIM: Too late for that. Let's see 'em safe out the park.

TOM: I'll stalk 'em while you give 'em the Hiawatha chant. Here, Dylan, lend me your water pistol. [DYLAN *hands his water pistol to* TOM *who, in a crouch, darts from cover to cover, dogging the footsteps of the strolling* PALEFACES *while* DYLAN, JACK *and* JIM *chant from their hiding place by the bandstand. The* HUNCHBACK *ignores all this and is himself ignored.*]

DYLAN, JACK, JIM: [*chanting*] Down the trails of Park Cwmdonkin
    Stalks a brave of noble bearing
    Stalks a brave called Tom the Hunter
    On his head the plumes of battle
    On his feet the beaver sandals
    In his heart the lust for slaughter
    In his hands the tools of killing
    Stalks the paleface park intruders
    Stalks them but must leave them living
    Leave them to their aimless walking
    Leave them to their boring talking
    Leave them save they turn and threaten
    Stalk them through the park.

[*On this last line,* UNCLE TUDYR, *who has paid no attention to* TOM *until this point, turns as he exits and stuns him with a ferocious scowl.* TOM *scuttles back to the* BOYS *as the* PALEFACES *exit.*]

JACK: Well done.

TOM: Nothing to it, man.

DYLAN: Aye, aye . . . Town Hill louts! Gimme the gun, Tom, I'll track 'em out the park. [*The* TOWN HILL BOYS *swagger on. They stop in a huddle to light cigarettes and snigger among themselves.* DYLAN *sticks a sugar-fag between his lips and assumes a threatening straddled crouch, both hands holding the pistol at arm's length.*]

JACK, TOM, JIM: [*chanting*] Through the dells of Park Cwmdonkin
    Tracks a brave of fearsome visage
    Tracks a brave called Dylan Hawkeye

> On his face the paint of battle
> In his eyes the glint of danger
> In his heart the lust for slaughter
> In his hands the tools of killing
> Tracks the dread Town Hill invaders
> Tracks them but must leave them living

[*The* TOWN HILL BOYS *confront* DYLAN. *He backs off slightly, but keeps them covered with the gun. one of them casually plucks-the sugar-fag from* DYLAN'*s mouth, pops it in his mouth and chomps it up. The* OTHERS *guffaw.* DYLAN *moves out of their way as they proceed off, but swivels to keep them covered.*]

> Leave them to their dirty joking
> Leave them through his heart be choking
> Leave them save they turn and threaten
> Track them through the park.

[*On the penultimate line, one of them turns suddenly with a threatening hiss that just about knocks* DYLAN *off his feet.*]

JACK: Well done, Dylan! That scared 'em!

DYLAN: Thought they were coming at me then. [*He pats his pistol.*] Trusty Betsy saw me through.

JIM: Here, gimme that gun.

DYLAN: Who you gonna track, Jim?

JIM: I'm gonna give the hunchback the fright of his life.

JACK: Watch the keeper don't get you.

JIM: You keep cave. [*Gun in hand, he starts to wriggle forward slowly on his belly, freezing whenever the* HUNCHBACK *makes the slightest movement.*]

DYLAN, JACK, TOM: [*chanting*] Down the paths of Park Cwmdonkin
> Slides a brave of noiseless movement
> Slides a brave called Jim the Silent . . .

JACK: [*urgently*] Keeper, keeper, keeper, keeper, keeper! Smoky . . .

[*The chanting stops.* JIM *scrambles back to the safety of the other* BOYS. SMOKY, *the park keeper, strolls on, his pipe billowing smoke. He wears a flat cap and a brown tweed suit with a corporation badge on the breast pocket and carries a pointed litter-stick. He ignores the* HUNCHBACK, *who ignores him.*]

SMOKY: I like to see a bit of snow. Keeps the park tidy. [*He tries the water fountain but it doesn't work.*] Iced up. Ah, well. There are always sacrifices. [*He strolls off, noticing the* BOYS *in hiding but not acknowledging their presence. The* BOYS *come downstage and squat in a line.* DYLAN *doles bullseyes from a paper bag.*]

TOM: Hey, thanks! Get any other candy in your stocking, Dylan?

DYLAN: Jelly babies and chocolate money.

TOM: Give, give.

DYLAN: Didn't bring 'em.

JIM: I got sugar-fags. Here. [*He hands the sugar cigarettes around. The* BOYS *swank around with them, imitating uncles with their cigars.*]

TOM: I got licorice allsorts. Here. [*He hands the candy around. They squabble and swap for the best ones. After a pause,* ALL *look at* JACK.]

JACK: I got sugared almonds.

JIM AND TOM: Give, give!

JACK: Didn't bring 'em.

JIM, TOM, DYLAN: Boo! Boo!

DYLAN: Show me a poor man
     He'll give you his heart.
     Show me a rich man
     He won't give you a —

JACK: All right! Ah right! I'll save you some.

DYLAN: Here! If we found that gold in Rhossili sands, what'd we buy? All the bullseyes in Swansea?

TOM: Not just bullseyes. All kind.

DYLAN: What kinds?

TOM: You start.

DYLAN: Hymn number four hundred and seventy-nine, please.

[*He runs up the steps of the bandstand, strikes a holy attitude and sings, approximately, to the tune of "Hail Thou Once Despised Jesus."*]

[**SONG**: *"CANDY SONG"*]

DYLAN: HARDBOILEDS, TOFFEE, FUDGE AND ALLSORTS
    CRUNCHIES, HUMBUGS, GLACIER MINTS
    MARZIPAN FINGERS, PLAIN CHOCS, MILK CHOCS

FRUIT-'N-NUT CHOCS AND BUTTERWELSH.

JACK: Butterscotch, twpsin!

DYLAN: Butterwelsh for the Welsh. Hymn four hundred and seventy-two, James. [JIM *takes* DYLAN's *place on the bandstand and sings, approximately, to "Rock of Ages."* DYLAN *conducts with a sugar-fag.*]

[*SONG: "CANDY SONG"*]

JIM: GUMDROPS, CLEAR GUMS, WINE GUMS, SHERBERT
  NUTTY BRICKS, JELLY BEANS AND TURKISH DE-
  LIGHT.

[JACK *takes* JIM's *place. During* JACK's *song,* TOM *does a slow, stately march, as if in solemn procession, to be in position for his turn.*]

JACK: CHOCOLATE TOFFEE, COFFEE TOFFEE
  MINT TOFFEE AND TOFFEE BRICKS
  SUGAR BEANS WITH A LICORICE HEART
  AND TWISTED BARLEYSUGAR STICKS.

TOM: CANDY FLOSS AND PALE PINK CANDY
  SWANSEA ROCK AND CANDY STICKS
  BLACK CURRANT PASTILLES . . .

ALL: BLACK CURRANT PASTILLES
  BLACK CURRANT PASTILLES
  AND LICORICE STICKS

[*Crescendo to the end.*]

  BLACK CURRANT PASTILLES AND LICORICE STICKS!

[ALL *are now crowded around or on the bandstand in attitudes of worship. They sing the following as if it is a drawn out "Amen."*]

ALL: I-I-I-I-CE CREA-EA-EAM!

DYLAN: Duw! Duw! I can't bear it! I can't bear it! Damn, we'll just have to find that gold!

SMOKY: [*as an almost unintelligible roar from offstage*] Hey-you-boys-there!

BOYS: Keeper! Keeper! Keeper!

[SMOKY *enters.* JIM, JACK *and* TOM *dart around* SMOKY *so that he whirls about trying to grab them.* DYLAN *jumps from the bandstand, lands badly and stumbles. The other* BOYS *dash off.* SMOKY *grabs* DYLAN's *collar.*]

SMOKY: What you doing on my bandstand then, boy? You know that's Council property, my bandstand, don' you? Well, then, look you over by here! See them letters? Dirty words. Carved in the paint, that is. Carved in! Your lot did that.

DYLAN: Wasn't us. The Town Hill boys . . .

SMOKY: Don't you give me no Town Hill boys. I know what I. know. And you know that climbing on the bandstand is not allowed. Park regulations, innit? .Well, now I've caught you, what am I going to do with you, you'll be asking yourself . . .

[TOM *comes swooping in and dashes up the bandstand steps. Once up, he executes a wild dance.*]

TOM: [*chanting*] Smoky, Smoky
          Can't catch me!
          Poky old Smoky
          Wee, wee, wee!

[SMOKY *drops* DYLAN *and makes a lunge for* TOM'S *dancing legs.* TOM *jumps over his head, is caught by* DYLAN, *and both scamper off shouting the "Smoky, Smoky" tease.* SMOKY *sniffs, shrugs and sings to the tune of "O Come, All Ye Faithful." The* HUNCHBACK, *who has listened to the* BOYS' *candy songs and watched their tussle with* SMOKY *quite impassively, eats his lunch as* SMOKY *sings. He lets the newspaper drift to the ground.*]

[*SONG: "PARK KEEPER'S SONG"*]

SMOKY: O KEEP OUT, YOU BAD BOYS
          SNEAKING THROUGH THE BUSHES
          O KEEP OUT, O KEEP OUT OF CWMDONKIN PARK
          KEEP YOUR BOWS AND ARROWS
          BATS AND BALL AND CAP GUNS
          O KEEP YOUR SAVAGE SHOUTING
          O KEEP YOUR SAVAGE SHOUTING
          O KEEP YOUR WILD RUNNING FROM
          CWMDONKIN PARK.

          O KEEP OUT, YOU BEGGARS
          TRAMPS AND DRUNKS AND ROBBERS
          O KEEP OUT, O KEEP OUT OF CWMDONKIN PARK
          KEEP YOUR OLD NEWSPAPERS
          CANS AND CANDY WRAPPERS
          O KEEP YOUR FILTHY LITTER

[*The* HUNCHBACK *looks up, takes offense and hunches off.*]

O KEEP YOUR FILTHY LITTER
O KEEP YOUR MESSY WAYS FROM
CWMDONKIN PARK.

O KEEP OUT, YOU LOVERS
WRESTLING IN THE BANDSTAND
O KEEP OUT, O KEEP OUT OF CWMDONKIN PARK
KEEP THE NAUGHTY THINGS YOU
WOULDN'T TELL YOUR MOTHER
O KEEP YOUR SECRET LAUGHTER

[*Two* LOVERS *appear from behind the bandstand, hurriedly arranging their dress, and slink off guiltily.*]

O KEEP YOUR SECRET LAUGHTER
O KEEP YOUR WICKED THOUGHTS FROM
CWMDONKIN PARK.

[SMOKY *picks up the* HUNCHBACK*'s litter on his spiked stick, then comes downstage to address the audience, stuffing tobacco into his pipe.*]

SMOKY: Those wild boys! Nothing's safe from 'em! Mind you, I was one myself once. The things we used to get up to in this park! A whole world of adventure it was . . . ambushes, houses in the trees, Indians in the shrubberies . . . the kids these days got no imagination, not like we did. Oh . . . and the snow we had in them days! Not like this . . . [*He kicks at the snow contemptuously.*] . . . feeble stuff! Real snow, we had. Came singing out of the sky like flocks of white angels. Oh, yes. Oh, dear, oh, dear, yes. Flocks of white angels, I tell you, pure as pure . . . [*In clouds of tobacco smoke, he ambles off, kicking at the inferior snow.*]

[DYLAN *and* TOM *run on, puffing and laughing, and collapse downstage.*]

DYLAN: Duw! Duw! Old Smoky was fit to kill me then! Fit to kill me, mun! If you hadn't leapt in, Tom . . . Well, I dunno what . . .

TOM: Hand you over to P.C. Lloyd-Jones, he would. Look here, Constable, this boy here . . .

DYLAN: Climbing my bandstand . . .

TOM: Carving his name in my trees . . .

DYLAN: Walking on my snow . . .

TOM: Breathing my air. . . [*He and* DYLAN *collapse with laughter.*]

DYLAN: Where's the others?

TOM: Scarpered. Said they'd wait for us near the haunted house.

DYLAN: Let 'em wait forever, the cowards. Hope they get eaten by ghosts. I've got to get back . . .

TOM: Yeah, Christmas dinner! And present giving and . . .

DYLAN: Aunts and uncles and . . .

TOM: Stupid cousins! [*He and* DYLAN *sing to the tune of "Ar Hyd y Nos."*]

[*SONG: "AUNTS AND UNCLES"*]

DYLAN: AUNTS AND UNCLES COME TO DINNER
 EACH YEAR THE SAME
 PUB OR CHAPEL, SAINT OR SINNER
 EACH YEAR THE SAME
 UNCLE GWYN, FAT GARAGE OWNER
 UNCLE GLYN, THE LEFT WING LONER
 UNCLE TUDYR, DREADFUL MOANER

DYLAN AND TOM: EACH YEAR THE SAME.

DYLAN: AUNTS AND UNCLES COME FOR DINNER

DYLAN AND TOM: EACH YEAR THE SAME

DYLAN: PUB OR CHAPEL, SAINT OR SINNER

DYLAN AND TOM: EACH YEAR THE SAME

DYLAN: AUNTIE HANNAH, SECRET DRINKER
 AUNTIE BESSIE, ASPIRIN SINKER
 AUNTIE NELLIE, PRIMMER AND PINKER

DYLAN AND TOM: EACH YEAR THE SAME.

TOM: STUPID COUSINS COME FOR DINNER

DYLAN AND TOM: EACH YEAR THE SAME

TOM: NEVER FATTER, NEVER THINNER

DYLAN AND TOM. EACH YEAR THE SAME
 COUSIN GLENDA, TOUGH BUT TINY
 COUSIN BRENDA, HUGE AND WHINEY

DYLAN: LONG TO CHUCK THEM IN THE BRINY

DYLAN AND TOM: EACH YEAR THE SAME.

DYLAN AND TOM: [*punching each other lightly on the shoulder as the same thought strikes each of them*] Hey! Christmas dinner! [*They run off. The lights go down on the park.*]

[*The lights come up on the dining room. The dinner table has been set. There are chairs, a decorated Christmas tree and a hallstand.* FATHER *and* MOTHER *are fussing over the table, decorations, drinks.* DYLAN *enters from the front door, hanging up his coat, cap and scarf on the hallstand.*]

FATHER: That you, Dylan? Only just in time.

DYLAN: Where's the uncles? Where's the aunts?

FATHER: Chipping their way up the glacier outside, I expect.

DYLAN: I saw Uncle Tudyr and his family in the park. And Auntie Hannah's slithering this way.

FATHER: Good old Hannah. [*He mimics her.*] "I'll take a drop of rum in my tea, because it's only once a year."

MOTHER: Now then, DJ! Not in front of the boy.

FATHER: If the boy understands, he's old enough to hear. If he doesn't understand, he's young enough to wonder. When your Auntie Hannah was a girl, Dylan, she was dandled on the knee of your great-uncle, that fine religious poet Gwilym Marlais Thomas. She's never since found a man who could measure up to him, so her heart is full of unnameable longings . . . and she puts rum in her tea.

HANNAH: [*off*] Merry Christmas!

FATHER AND MOTHER: [*calling off*] Merry Christmas, Hannah!

DYLAN: [*calling off*] Merry Christmas, Auntie Hannah!

[HANNAH *enters and hangs up her outdoor clothing.*]

HANNAH: Merry Christmas, everyone! Come here, Dylan, you cherub! [DYLAN *suffers himself to be kissed and receives a large parcel. He begins to unwrap it.* FATHER *hands* HANNAH *a drink as he does all subsequent guests. To* MOTHER.] I saw Gwyn garage and Nellie puffing up the hill.

MOTHER: Ah, dear Nellie!

HANNAH: I don't know how she puts up with him, with his great black hands and his shocking tales about the criminal underbelly of Swansea.

MOTHER: Ah, but you have to be sorry for him, too, married to Nellie, with her bossy ways.

FATHER: [*of* DYLAN's *present*] Now that's a wonder, Hannah. It's a real train, Flo. Got its own little boiler, probably, and proper rails, too.

GWYN: [*off, calling*] Merry Christmas!

NELLIE: [*calling off*] Yes, Merry Christmas, indeed!

[GWYN *and* NELLIE *enter and hand presents to* DYLAN *as they take off their coats.*]

ALL: Merry Christmas, Gwyn! Merry Christmas, Nellie.

DYLAN: Thank you, Auntie Nellie. Thank you, Uncle Gwyn. Ooooh, a real brass telescope! Ooh, thank you!

GWYN: Bought it off a one-eyed lascar in a dirty little dockside drive.

DYLAN: And a . . . Oh, it's a . . .

NELLIE: It's a wig . . . a pirate wig. I knitted it myself.

DYLAN: [*donning the wig*] Oh, thank you, Auntie Nellie. It's just what I always wanted. [*He scans the audience with his telescope, then lays it and the wig aside to return to the train set which* FATHER *is helping to assemble.* FATHER *stands.*]

FATHER: Here, Gwyn, you take charge of this number and I'll get you a ginger wine. You'll have Glyn-the-vegetables to help you any moment. [GWYN *gets down on his knees by the train set.*]

GWYN: Rugby and socialism, all Glyn thinks about.

FATHER: Got hit on the head by Tom Paine's Rights of Man when he was a baby. Never recovered.

[GLYN *enters and starts to take off his coat by the hallstand.*]

HANNAH: If he's such a revolutionary, why doesn't he spend his Christmas in Moscow? [GLYN *enters the room.*]

GLYN: Small time entrepreneur . . . greengrocer . . . in a capitalist state . . . that is, Wales. Can't afford fare to Moscow, so here I am. Merry Christmas, all!

ALL: Merry Christmas, Glyn!

GLYN: And a revolutionary New Year! Here, boy. [*He hands a parcel to* DYLAN, *who opens it and reads from the box.*]

DYLAN: "The Easi-Hobbi Game for Little Engineers." [*To* GLYN.] Thanks a lot, Uncle Glyn.

GLYN: Teach you to be your own boss . . . only thing to be under capitalism.

GWYN: Shut your political gob, Glyn, and get you down here where the work's going on. [GLYN *joins* GWYN *and* DYLAN *over the railway tracks.*]

HANNAH: Ooh, I could eat a horse. A very small one, that is. A pony, perhaps. Who else is coming this year, Flo?

MOTHER: My sister Bessie . . .

DYLAN: I like Auntie Bessie, but she's always got a headache.

MOTHER: Well, yes, bach, I know, she does take a lot of aspirins, but she doesn't really have headaches at all. She just has this terrible fear of having a headache. Even as a little girl, I remember, she was always afraid of getting something bad.

HANNAH: She had good reason. She got Tudyr Jones. Jones, Pant yr Glas, Always falling on his—

MOTHER: D.J.!

FATHER: That's what we used to sing after him at school. Dreadful little moaner.

GLYN: Your Uncle Tudyr was so glum, Dylan bach, that when he walked into a field of sheep, all the sheep left. He emptied the field the way some people can empty a room. Suddenly a terrible boredom comes over the sheep and they leave, out of a sort of animal politeness, leaving Tudyr Jones alone with his moan.

FATHER: And Flo's sister Bessie managed to catch him, the way more fortunate women catch bubonic plague.

HANNAH: No wonder she eats aspirins.

[GLENDA *and* BRENDA *enter and take off their coats by the hallstand.*]

MOTHER: [*defensively*] You are not yourself a jolly man, D.J.

FATHER: Not jolly, no. But I take a certain pleasure.

GLYN: In what, D.J.?

FATHER: In words, Glyn. In words.

GLENDA AND BRENDA: [*entering the room*] Merry Christmas, everybody! [DYLAN, *horror-struck, leaps to his feet and rushes to* MOTHER.]

DYLAN: Glenda-and-Brenda! Mam! Can I go and fetch the coal or something?

MOTHER: You stay here and greet your cousins.

DYLAN: But, Mam. [GLENDA *and* BRENDA *are upon him bearing parcels.*]

[UNCLE TUDYR *and* AUNT BESSIE *enter and remove their coats by the hallstand.*]

BRENDA: Happy Christmas, Dylan!

GLENDA: And don't try anything funny. [*She and* BRENDA *hand the presents over to* DYLAN. *He opens both packages and finds that each of them has given him a board game.*]

DYLAN: Thanks very much, Brenda-and-Glenda. I do like board games. Let's see . . . Oh, good! Snakes and Families. And Happy Ladders. How wonderful. [BRENDA *gives him a snarl and joins the* MEN *around the train set.*]

BRENDA: [*whimpering*] Don't you like them?

DYLAN: 'Course I like them. [*He places the games with his other presents under the Christmas tree.*]

BESSIE: [*entering the room with* TUDYR] Merry Christmas, everyone!

TUDYR: Nadolig Llawen.

ALL: Merry Christmas, Tudyr. Merry Christmas, Bessie!

TUDYR: A Blwyddyn Newydd Da! [*He hands a parcel to* DYLAN. *It is obviously a book.*] Seasonal greetings, young man.

DYLAN: Thank you, Uncle Tudyr. Last year, I remember, you gave me a book which told me everything about the wasp, except why.

TUDYR: This one, boy, will tell you why.

BESSIE: I've made something for you, Dylan, something to keep you warm.

DYLAN: Thank you, Auntie Bessie. [*He doesn't unwrap his gifts but puts them under the Christmas tree.*] But where's Aunt Elieri?

MOTHER: Don't worry, bach, she'll be here.

DYLAN: I love Aunt Elieri.

FATHER: Everyone loves Elieri.

MOTHER: Now, Dad!

FATHER: No, no! I wouldn't say or hear a word against her.

GWYN: To be honest with you now, I love her myself.

GLYN: I'll tell you for nothing, I'd carry that woman from here to Siberia and back on my back if I had the strength and she the whim for it.

NELLIE: Yes, there's something truly magical about her.

HANNAH: But sad with it, somehow.

DYLAN: I know why she's sad.

GLENDA: Bet you don't! Go on, tell! [DYLAN *turns his back on her, wishing he hadn't spoken.*]

[ELIERI *enters and takes her coat off by the hallstand.*]

GWYN: That's right, bach, keep it to yourself. Christmas is a time for rejoicing.

TUDYR: Very true, Gwyn, very true. Pity we haven't all got something to . . .

BESSIE: Now, Tudyr, you promised you'd be jolly.

TUDYR: [*snarling under his breath*] Jolly! [*He moves away.*]

ELIERI: [*moving downstage*] Happy Christmas, everyone.

ALL: Happy Christmas, Elieri!

ELIERI: Happy Christmas, Dylan. [DYLAN *gazes at her adoringly. She hands him a present. He unwraps it and reads from the box.*]

DYLAN: "The Hamley's Cabinet of Magic for Young Magicians." Oh, thank you, Aunt Elieri. It's just what I wanted . . . Does it do real magic? [*He opens the box, takes out a wand and looks at it doubtfully.* ELIERI *smiles at him and holds out her hand. He hands her the wand.*]

FATHER: Dylan, there's one more present.

MOTHER: From me and your dad.

FATHER: It's behind the tree.

MOTHER: I hope it's the right one. [DYLAN *dashes over and searches behind the tree. He finds his present in the wings and wheels it on—a red and wonderfully gleaming bicycle. He looks at it, speechless with joy, while* BRENDA *and* GLENDA *"ooh" and "aah." Then he props up the bike and rushes to* MOTHER *and* FATHER, *trying to hug both at once.*]

DYLAN: Mam! Dad! It's marvelous! It's wonderful! It's a B.S.A. three-speed! Oh, thank you, thank you! [*He dashes back to the bike and rides it across the forestage.*]

HANNAH: Now isn't that a wonderful contraption, Dylan?

TUDYR: But what about your train, Dylan? Shouldn't we light the boiler?

FATHER: But we haven't got any oil. [ELIERI *steps forward and raises the magic wand.*]

ELIERI: No need for that. We can do it by magic. Abracadabra! [*She waves the wand and the little train starts to go around the track. It is probably* TUDYR *who started it. There are "oohs" and "aahs" from* ALL. *She points the wand at* FATHER, *who leaps forward, transformed at once into a jolly, bonhommous man. As he starts his Christmas dinner song, to the tune of "Men of Harlech,"* ALL *gather around the dinner table.*]

[*SONG: "CHRISTMAS DINNER"*]

FATHER: CHRISTMAS DINNER! CHRISTMAS GLORY!
GRAVY FUMES ARE HOV'RING O'ER YE,
MRS. THOMAS STANDS BEFORE YE
HEAR YE NOT HER CALL?

ALL: DO I REALLY NEED TO TELL YE
THERE'LL BE SPROUTS AND THERE'LL BE JELLY
ROASTED SPUDS TO FILL YOUR BELLY
COME THEN, ONE AND ALL.

FATHER: COME AND LET ME POUR YOU
GRAVY, I IMPLORE YOU—
DYLAN, RIDE
YOUR BIKE OUTSIDE,
WE'LL SAVE SOME DINNER FOR YOU.

ALL: YOUR FOOD IS COMING ANY MINUTE
TURKEY! CHESTNUT STUFFING IN IT!
WHEN YOU GET YOUR PLATE, BEGIN IT—
EAT IT WHILE IT'S HOT.

FATHER: CHRISTMAS DINNER! TAKE YOUR PLACES
LOOSEN UP YOUR STAYS AND BRACES!
LOOK AT THOSE WIDE OPEN FACES
LONGING TO BE FED.

ALL: PARSNIP WINE—THAT TAKES SOME BEATING
DRINK IT DOWN, FOR LIFE IS FLEETING
DRINK IT DOWN, IT'S BETTER EATING
WITH A HAPPY HEAD,
BUT THE THING THAT'S NICE IS . . .
HEFTY TURKEY SLICES!

FATHER: TURKEY ROAST
MUST BE THE MOST
CHRISTMAS KIND OF—

MOTHER: [*off*] CRISIS!

[*Smoke billows from the wings.* MOTHER *staggers out of it with a black and smoking turkey one-quarter of its original size. The model train stops running and there is total silence. She puts the charred turkey down on the table, tries to say something, can't, and runs out with her apron across her face.* ALL *stare at the turkey, stunned.*]

FATHER: [*softly*] NOW SOFT SWEARING AND LOUD SIGHING,
MOTHER IN THE GARDEN CRYING,
CHRISTMAS DAY SEEMS TO BE DYING—

DYLAN: TURKEY?

FATHER: NO, THERE'S NOT.

[*There is a devastated pause.*]

DYLAN: [*looking at the wand in* ELIERI'*s hand*] Aunt Elieri . . . do something!
[ELIERI *shakes her head sadly and hands the wand to* DYLAN.]

ELIERI: I'll go and comfort your mother. [*She exits.* HANNAH *pours herself a massive drink.* BESSIE *swallows a handful of aspirin and moves toward the hallstand.*]

BESSIE: I think I'll take a little walk. My head, you know . . . [*She exits.* GLENDA *disappears in the direction of the smoke.* BRENDA *lets out a terrible howl and buries her face in her arms.*]

FATHER: Well, now, come on, it's not the end of the world.

DYLAN: [*stonily*] Yes. It is.

[GLENDA *comes racing out of the smoke, her face streaked with soot.*]

GLENDA: Uncle Dal, Uncle Dal, your house is burning down.

FATHER: God have mercy! [*He,* GWYN *and* GLYN *dash into the smoke.* TUDYR *picks up the flagon of parsnip wine and makes as if to follow them.*]

HANNAH: [*crying out*] Don't pour parsnip wine on it, Tudyr! You'll blow us all up! [TUDYR *looks at the wine, takes a swig and chokes.* NELLIE *flaps at the smoke with her shawl.*]

NELLIE: Oh, do something, Tudyr! Do something!

TUDYR: Hannah told me not to. [GLENDA *and* DYLAN *hop about at the edge of the smoke.*]

[FATHER, GLYN *and* GWYN *stagger on, wiping tears from their eyes.*]

GLYN: Can't get at it! Can't see a thing!

GWYN: Like the gates of hell in there, it is!

FATHER: Dylan! Get your coat on, run to the phone box and ring the Fire Brigade. [*He follows* DYLAN *toward the hall-stand with further instructions. There is a rat-tat-tat on the door.*]

NELLIE: Lord save us, we're all going to die!

GWYN: Belt up, Nellie.

[FIREMAN ONE *enters in a splendid gleaming helmet, with an axe.*]

FIRST FIREMAN: Happy Christmas, all! Got a bit of a fire, have we? Can we come in?

DYLAN: But I haven't phoned for you yet!

FIRST FIREMAN: Luck of the day, bach. We was just passing, with our appliance, in'it, saw the smoke. [*He shouts off.*] In here, men! Nippy does it! [*To* FATHER] Get a lot of fires at Christmas. People forget what's happening out the kitchen.

[FIREMAN TWO *runs in with a portable fire extinguisher and plunges into the smoke.* FIREMAN THREE *runs in behind him with a flattened hose.* FIREMAN ONE *grabs the nozzle from him.*]

FIRST FIREMAN: Come on, you Thomases, lend a hand now! Up and over . . . that's right . . . now round by here. [*To the* SECOND FIREMAN.] Tell us when, Peredur! [*The* FAMILY *wrestles the hose straight. He shouts to the* THIRD FIREMAN.] Let's have some pressure, then, Morgan! [*The hose fills and writhes. The* FAMILY *fights to control it. He shouts into the smoke.*] Say when, Peredur!

DYLAN: [*alarmed*] You'll flood the kitchen! What about our pudding?

BRENDA: [*snivelling*] What about the mince pies?

TUDYR: [*with relish*] Ruined already, the lot of 'em. My word on that.

FIRST FIREMAN: First things first, young man. Don't want you all fried, do we? [*He shouts off.*] Say when, Peredur! Can't see no flames. [*He is a bit disappointed.*] Not much of a fire, really.

FATHER: Big enough for us, thank you.

FIRST FIREMAN: [*calling off*] Say when, Peredur!

TUDYR: I've been dreaming of a wet Christmas.

ALL: Shut up, Tudyr!

[*The smoke starts to recede. The* SECOND FIREMAN *emerges from the smoke.*]

SECOND FIREMAN: No need for water, Jethro. The emergency is overcome, boy.

FIRST FIREMAN: [*shouting off to the* THIRD FIREMAN] Pressure off, Morgan. [*To the* SECOND FIREMAN.] Burning fat, was it? [*The swollen hose suddenly deflates. The* FAMILY *lower it to the ground.*]

SECOND FIREMAN: Same as usual. Gas oven turned too high. No damage.

Bit of a mess out there, I'm afraid. [*To* DYLAN.] Your pudding's still cooking, anyway. [GLENDA, BRENDA *and* DYLAN *cheer.*]

FATHER: Oven too high, was it?

FIRST FIREMAN: Duw! Duw! These new gas ovens, you got to be that careful! The naked flame, i'n'it? Fat spitting here, there and everywhere and once she catches, that fat . . .

[*The* THIRD FIREMAN *comes in.*]

THIRD FIREMAN: She do make a powerful lot of smoke, wuss!

[HANNAH *bustles over to the firemen.*]

HANNAH: What these heroes deserve is a drink. Parsnip wine? [*The* FIREMEN *do not react.*] Elderberry wine? [*There is still no reaction.*] Maybe an itsy-bitsy spot of rum?

FIREMEN: We wouldn't say no! [HANNAH *pours rum. The* FIREMEN *stand in line, formally, to receive their drinks.*]

[MOTHER *enters with* ELIERI. *The smoke has disappeared.*]

MOTHER: I'm so sorry. Is it all over? The pudding . . .

FATHER: Safe and steaming, cariad. [MOTHER *rushes for the kitchen.* HANNAH *raises her glass.*]

HANNAH: To our brave Fire Brigade!

GLYN: To the workers! [ALL *join the toast. As the* OTHERS *toast,* ELIERI *brings* DYLAN *downstage and whispers to him.*]

ELIERI: I knew you could do it, Dylan.

DYLAN: Do what?

ELIERI: Fetch the Fire Brigade. [*She indicates the magic wand, which* DYLAN *still holds. He looks at it with awe.*]

DYLAN: Do you think it would . . .

ELIERI: You could try. [DYLAN *moves aside and faces off-stage. He grips the wand with both hands, points the wand off and stays like this until* BESSIE'*s entrance.*]

FIRST FIREMAN: Well, friends, we must be off and about, looking for fires. Happy Christmas, all . . . and keep the gas turned low! [*There is a chorus of "Thank yous" and "Happy Christmases" as the* FIREMEN *file off, dragging the empty hose with them.* GLENDA *picks at the burned turkey.*]

BRENDA: [*tearfully*] But what about . . .

FATHER: If it costs me ten guineas, we must have another turkey.

NELLIE: It would take until midnight to cook.

GWYN: What about chickens? Chickens don't take long.

TUDYR: The shops are closed.

GLYN: My shop isn't! We could have a vegetarian Christmas. [ALL *moan*.] I've got some fine cauliflowers . . . carrots . . . turnips . . . After all, apes were vegetarians and man is descended from the apes.

FATHER: Not this branch of the family. Look at young Glenda there. We're descended from sabre-toothed tigers and we want our meat!

[MOTHER *bustles in*.]

MOTHER: [*artificially bright*] Well, it's an awful mess, but the sprouts and the spuds are alright and the pudding's cooked and I've been looking round the larder and I've found some lovely Pressed tongue . . . [ALL *groan*.] . . . and a piece of galantine . . . [ALL *groan more loudly*.] . . . and if I plumped those up with some boiled macaroni . . . [ALL *groan in agony*.] . . . well, it's better than nothing and maybe Bessie could . . . [*She looks around*.] Where is Bessie?

[BESSIE *enters*]

BESSIE: Here she is. With a surprise for you all. Come in, Mr. Murgatroyd.

[*A liveried chauffeur,* MR. MURGATROYD, *enters ceremoniously. bearing a huge silver platter with a silver domed cover. He bows to* MOTHER *and* FATHER.]

MURGATROYD: Madam. Sir. On the table?

BESSIE: If you please, Mr. Murgatroyd. [*He places the dish on the table*.]

MOTHER: But what is it?

MURGATROYD: A twenty-pound, roasted turkey, Madame.

[*He lifts the cover. There is steam, and an amazing turkey.* ALL *are stupified.* DYLAN *drops the wand to his side and stares at* ELIERI.]

TUDYR: Is there chestnut stuffing, Murgatroyd?

MURGATROYD: There is indeed, Sir. And sage and onion at the other end.

MOTHER: But . . . how?

BESSIE: I slipped down to the phone box and called the manager of the Metropole Hotel. He'd had a Christmas party cancelled at the very last minute . . .

ELIERI: The very last minute?

BESSIE: The very moment before I called . . . [ELIERI *gives* DYLAN *a significant look.*] ...and so he sent Mr. Murgatroyd in the hotel delivery . . .

GLENDA: [*looking off*] Hey, mister! Is that your Rolls Royce van?

MURGATROYD: It is the property of the Metropole Hotel, young lady. But it is in my charge. You were admiring it?

GLENDA: Yes. But it looks like it's sliding backwards down Cwmdonkin Drive. [ALL *rush to join her. They cry "Oooo-whee" as they follow the van's backward slide into a tree. There is a boomp-crash-crunch-splinter-tinkle as the van crashes.* ALL *sigh.* MR. MURGATROYD, *standing at attention with his eyes closed, keels slowly over in a faint. To save the situation,* DYLAN *begins to sing the first verse of "God Rest Ye Merry Gentlemen." The* OTHERS *join in. They lift* MURGATROYD *as they sing, dust him off, give him a quick drink and send him off. Christmas has been saved.*]

[*SONG: "GOD REST YE MERRY GENTLEMEN"*]

DYLAN WITH OTHERS: GOD REST YOU MERRY GENTLEMEN
     LET NOTHING YOU DISMAY,
     REMEMBER CHRIST OUR SAVIOUR
     WAS BORN ON CHRISTMAS DAY
     TO SAVE US ALL FROM SATAN'S POWER
     WHEN WE WERE GONE ASTRAY;
     O TIDINGS OF COMFORT AND JOY,
     COMFORT AND JOY,
     O TIDINGS OF COMFORT AND JOY.

DYLAN: NOW WHEN THE TURKEY'S BEEN DEVOURED
     THE DAY HAS JUST BEGUN
     FOR THERE'LL BE BLAZING PUDDING,
     MINCE PIES FOR EVERYONE
     AND SPOOKY TALES AND SING-SONGS, TOO
     BEFORE THE DAY IS DONE,
     O TIDINGS OF COMFORT AND JOY,
     COMFORT AND JOY,
     O TIDINGS OF COMFORT AND JOY.

ALL: NOW TO THE LORD SING PRAISES,
     ALL YOU WITHIN THIS PLACE,
     AND WITH TRUE LOVE AND BROTHERHOOD
     EACH OTHER NOW EMBRACE;

THIS HOLY TIDE OF CHRISTMAS
ALL OTHERS DOTH DEFACE;
O TIDINGS OF COMFORT AND JOY,
COMFORT AND JOY,
O TIDINGS OF COMFORT AND JOY.

[*The lights go down.*]

ACT TWO

The stage is dark. A downstage spot discovers DYLAN *and* FATHER *standing close together.*

DYLAN: What did you have for Christmas dinner when you were a boy?

FATHER: Turkey and blazing pudding.

DYLAN: Was it nice?

FATHER: It was not made on earth. [*There is a distant peal of bells.*]

DYLAN: Were there church bells, too?

FATHER: O yes, there were bells, in the bat black, snow-white belfries, tugged by bishops and storks. And they rang their tidings over the bandaged town, over the frozen foam of the powder and ice-cream hills, over the crackling sea. It seemed that all the churches boomed for joy under my window; and the weathercocks crew for Christmas on our fence. And I can still smell that blazing pudding . . .

[*The lights come up on the scene behind them.* DYLAN *draws* FATHER *upstage toward the table where the* FAMILY *is seated.* MOTHER *enters with the blazing pudding.*]

DYLAN: No, you can't. It's our blazing pudding! [*Exclamations from* ALL *at the sight of the pudding lead to the Pudding Song, sung to the tune of Llwyn On, "The Ash Grove." During the song,* MOTHER *cuts and dishes out the pudding. The dishes are handed around by* DYLAN, GLENDA *and* BRENDA.]

[**SONG:** *"OH, CHRISTMAS MEANS PUDDING"*]

ALL: OH, CHRISTMAS MEANS PUDDING
      AND PUDDING MEANS CHRISTMAS
      A PUDDING OF GLORY, WITH BRANDY ABLAZE.
      THE DARKEST OF PUDDINGS
      THE BRIGHTEST OF PUDDINGS
      A PUDDING TO LIGHT US THROUGH WINTER'S
      DARK DAYS.

MOTHER: THERE'S GOOD IN THE PUDDING,
      THERE'S APPLES AND LEMONS
      SULTANAS AND BREADCRUMBS, CHOPPED
      SUET AND RUM,
      THERE'S CANDIED PEEL, ALMONDS, EGGS,
      FLOUR, SPICE AND SUGAR,

DYLAN: THERE'S GOOD IN THE PUDDING,
      OH, PLEASE SLICE ME SOME!

[*Optional chorus. At the end of the song,* DYLAN, BRENDA *and* GLENDA *take their helpings and sit cross-legged on the floor together, beneath the Christmas tree. There is applause for* MOTHER's *performance with the pudding.*]

MOTHER: Now just you watch out for the charms, all of you.

BRENDA: What's charms?

GLYN: Little horseshoes and things, wrapped up in greaseproof. Superstitious rubbish, really. [ALL *take cautious mouthfuls of their pudding.*]

HANNAH: Very tasty, Flo.

FATHER: Tasty? Something more than that. What do you think of the pudding, Dylan?

DYLAN: It was not made on earth. [FATHER *grins and winks at him.* GLYN *extracts a small object from his mouth and unwraps it.*]

GLYN: Here, I seem to have something. Looks like a . . . a button. What's that supposed to mean?

BESSIE: Oh, dear, that means you'll be a bachelor, Glyn.

GLYN: Excellent! Marriage is a capitalist institution designed to obstruct the equal distribution of wealth.

GWYN: There's a bit more to it than that, boy. Eh, Nellie?

NELLIE: Now don't you start, Gwyn. Ooh, look, I've got one. [*She unwraps her charm.*] What a pretty little threepenny bit!

BESSIE: That means you'll be rich, Nellie.

GWYN: Can't happen too soon for me.

DYLAN: Look, Brenda's got something! What is it?

BRENDA: It's a . . . Oh, it's a thimble. What's that for?

BESSIE AND OTHERS: Old maid!

BRENDA: But I don't want to be an old maid! I want to have babies and . . . [*Her face begins to crumple.* GLENDA *snatches the thimble away from her.*]

GLENDA: Here, I'll have it. I don't want to get married.

TUDYR: Wise girl.

GLENDA: I want to be an African explorer. [DYLAN *howls with exaggerated laughter. He is silenced by a rabbit punch from* GLENDA.]

TUDYR: [*poking at his pudding*] I still got nothing.

BESSIE: Yes, you have, Tudyr, you've got something to complain about. There's lucky you are.

DYLAN: I've got one! I've got one!

ELIERI: What is it, Dylan?

DYLAN: It's . . . oh.

GLENDA: [*grabbing the charm and holding it up*] It's the donkey! Dylan's got the donkey! That's for stupid!

BRENDA AND GLENDA: [*chanting*] Dylan got the donkey! Dylan got the donkey! [DYLAN *attacks them. They fight on the floor until* BESSIE *intervenes.*]

BESSIE: Now, then, girls, stop teasing Dylan. Time to pull crackers, I think.

BRENDA AND GLENDA: Ooh, crackers! Yes, crackers! [ALL *take crackers from the table and pull them with a partner, ad libbing such things as "Go on, pull! That's it, hold on tight. Now go on, pull." The crackers go bang and burst open, scattering paper hats, riddles, whistles, noise-makers.*]

MOTHER: Let's hear the riddles.

GWYN: Hats on first, ladies and gentlemen. Hats on first. [ALL *pull on ridiculous tissue-paper hats.*] Now then, Mrs. Thomas, will you oblige us with a riddle-me-ree?

MOTHER: [*reading*] What has a bed but never sleeps? [ALL *think and mutter to each other, then shake their heads.*]

GWYN: We give up. What has a bed and never sleeps, Flo?

MOTHER: A river!

TUDYR: That's not very funny.

BESSIE: No, but it's clever, isn't it! A river-bed, you see.

BRENDA: [*reading*] When is a door not a door?

ALL: [*shouting*] When it's ajar!

GLYN: I got that one, too.

HANNAH: So did I. [ELIERI, *reading her riddle, starts to giggle.*]

GLYN: Come on then, Elieri, don't keep it to yourself.

ELIERI: Why does . . . oo! [*She giggles, then takes a breath.*] Why does . . . oo! [*She pulls herself together.*] Why does Lloyd George wear red, white and blue braces? [ELIERI's *giggles are infectious. The* OTHERS *are already laughing.*]

GLYN: Lloyd George! Damn, we've even got Welsh crackers! All right, then, why does Lloyd George wear red, white and blue braces?

ELIERI: To keep his trousers up! [ALL *but* TUDYR *fall about with laughter.*]

TUDYR: If you would all moderate your mirth a trifle, I have a riddle for you. [*He holds his hand up, waiting for silence. He doesn't read his riddle as he has made it up. As the* OTHERS *calm down.*] Thank you. Now. Why is life like a riddle? [*He looks around from face to face. There is a long silence.*]

BESSIE: Nobody knows, Tudyr. Why is life like a riddle?

TUDYR: Because it has to be given up in the end. [*There are faint groans but no laughter.*]

GWYN: I tell you, Glyn, they're not just Welsh crackers . . . they're bloody chapel crackers! [ALL *laugh. Those who have noise-makers blow on them.*]

MOTHER: I'll go and make a pot of tea. [*She exits.* GWYN *stands up and stretches.*]

GWYN: Duw, I got more wind than the month of March.

GLYN: Hang on to it, Gwyn, we don't want it. [*He stands and claps* GWYN *on the shoulder. This gives* GWYN *an idea.*]

GWYN: Tudyr, get over here. [TUDYR *comes around the table and joins* GLYN *and* GWYN.]

TUDYR: What do you want of me?

GWYN: Get the ball, Dylan. Come on, boys . . . rugby time! [*He clasps*

TUDYR *around the shoulder so that, with* GLYN, *they make the front row of a rugby serum.*] This table's the Llanelli pack. Come on! Serum down! [*The three* MEN *push against the table as if against an opposing pack.* BESSIE *and* GLENDA *tuck in behind them.*]

[DYLAN *runs off and comes back immediately with a rugby ball.*]

[ALL, *led by* FATHER, *sing the Welsh rugby song.*]

[*SONG: "SOSBAN FACH"*]

ALL: SOSBAN FACH YN BERWI AR Y TAN
SOSBAN FAWR YN BERWI AR LY LAWR
A'R GATH WEDI CRAFU JOHNNY BACH O . . .

[DYLAN *puts the ball in. It is heeled out. He grabs it and weaves about as if dodging opponents. He passes the ball to* BESSIE *across the table, runs around to receive it and is brought down, on the last line of the chorus, by a tackle from* GLENDA.]

DAI BACH'S A SOLDIER
DAI BACH'S A SOLDIER
DAI BACH'S A SOLDIER
HIS SHIRT TAIL'S HANGING OUT.

HANNAH: Come on, Brenda! [BRENDA *is reluctantly pressed into service to form a front line with* HANNAH *and* BESSIE *to go heads down against the opposing line of the* MEN. GLENDA *has the ball and pops it into the serum at an appropriate moment.*]

ALL: SOSBAN FACH YN BERWI AR Y TAN
SOSBAN FAWR YN BERWI AR LY LLAWR
A'R GATH WEDI CRAFU JOHNNY BACH O . . .

[*The ball is heeled out.* DYLAN *grabs it, makes a run and throws himself forward to score a try backstage on the words "*BACH O . . .*"*]

ALL: [*shouting*] Try! [*As the chorus begins,* DYLAN *positions himself face down on the ground with one hand on top of the ball, holding it in position for* GWYN *to convert it.* GWYN *makes to kick but* DYLAN *teases him by taking his hand away and letting the ball roll. He then positions the ball again and* GWYN *takes aim.*]

DAI BACH'S A SOLDIER
DAI BACH'S A SOLDIER
DAI BACH'S A SOLDIER

HIS SHIRT TAIL'S HANGING OUT.

[*On the last line,* GWYN *kicks the ball neatly into the wings.*]

ALL: [*shouting*] Goal!

[MOTHER *runs in. She fastens on* DYLAN *and* GWYN.]

MOTHER: Dylan! Gwyn! You'll. Smash my lovely clock, my wedding present . . . and you know what a smashed clock means, don't you?

GWYN: Somebody got to pay to mend it.

MOTHER: A broken home, that's what! Just for that, you can wash the dishes!

DYLAN: Oh, but Mam!

MOTHER: Turning my sitting room into a football pitch! No, you'll wash the dishes and that's final!

FATHER: I'll help you, Dylan. We'll have it done in no time.

[*The lights concentrate on* DYLAN.]

DYLAN: So I went off to wash the dishes, while the uncles sat in front of the fire, took off their collars, loosened all their buttons, put their large, moist hands over their watch chains, groaned a little and slept. The cat was sick in the kitchen and Auntie Bessie had to have three aspirins but Auntie Hannah, who liked port, stood in the middle of the snowbound back yard singing like a big-bosomed thrush. Later, the cousins and I blew up balloons to see how big they would blow up to; and when they burst, which they all did, the uncles jumped and rumbled. In the rich and heavy afternoon, I sat in the front room among festoons and Chinese lanterns, nibbled at dates, and tried to make a model battleship, following the Instructions for Little Engineers, and produced what might be mistaken for a sea-going trolly.

[JIM, JACK *and* TOM *appear upstage and beckon to* DYLAN.]

DYLAN: And then Jim and Jack and Tom knocked on our window to call me out into the ear-pinching air. [*To* MOTHER.] Can I go down the seashore with Jim and Jack and Tom, Mam?

MOTHER: Of course, Dylan. But only if you take your cousins.

DYLAN: But, Mam!

GLENDA: We're coming, too.

DYLAN: You can follow us, I suppose. [*He,* GLENDA *and* BRENDA *start to pull on their outdoor clothes.*]

BESSIE: [*coming up to* DYLAN *with her hands behind her back*] Oh, Dylan, you weren't going out without the present I made you? How could you? [*She unwraps a monstrous knitted object; a yellow balaclava with a purple bobble on top.*]

DYLAN: Well, it's not that cold, Auntie Bessie.

MOTHER: It's freezing. Put it on at once and say thank you.

DYLAN: [*through his teeth*] Thank you, Auntie Bessie. [*He puts on the balaclava with* BESSIE'*s fussy assistance. It is much too large for him, the bottom edge coming right down over his shoulders and the top covering his eyes so that he has to push it back in order to see.* GLENDA *sniggers behind her hand.*]

BESSIE: There! Now you'll be lovely and warm!

MOTHER: And mind you, don't get your feet wet!

DYLAN: [*snarling*] Come on then! [*He runs off, followed by* GLENDA *and* BRENDA. *The lights go down on the room and* ALL *in the scene exit in the darkness.*]

[*Lights come up on the street.* DYLAN, *followed by* GLENDA *and* BRENDA, *dragging a sledge, comes on.* JIM, JACK *and* TOM *enter after a moment and* TOM *makes an elaborate display of falling about with laughter when he sees* DYLAN'*s balaclava.*]

TOM: Dylan, have you grown even smaller or did you steal that garment from a giant? [DYLAN *launches a furious attack on* TOM. *They wrestle on the ground, cheered on by the* OTHERS. TOM *rolls clear, holding his nose.*] Dylan! You bloodied my nose! [DYLAN *whips off the balaclava and throws it to* TOM.]

DYLAN: Here, wipe it with this. [TOM *mops up and hands the balaclava back to* DYLAN, *who stuffs it in his pocket.*]

JACK: Down the sea?

DYLAN: Yes. If it's frozen over, we can walk across to Devon for a cream tea.

GLENDA: That's silly! [DYLAN *turns slowly on her. She bunches her fists defiantly.* TOM, JIM *and* JACK *watch curiously.* DYLAN *is in a spot but is saved by* BRENDA.]

BRENDA: Glenda! Glenda, push me on my sledge!

GLENDA: Why should I?

BRENDA: I gave you my thimble!

GLENDA: Pooh to that! [DYLAN *turns his back on* BRENDA *and* GLENDA. *The* BOYS *form an exclusive ring.* GLENDA *soon jostles her way into it.* BRENDA *tries to get her sledge moving.*]

DYLAN: Know what I got for Christmas? Red B.S.A. bike with three-speed gears!

JIM: You never!

JACK: Get away!

TOM: Boasting again, All you got is a yellow balaclava with a purple bobble on top.

DYLAN, Alright, smart alecs. You'll see.

JIM: You'd have brought it out if you had.

DYLAN: In this? Can hardly stand up, leave alone ride a bike. Just wait and see, that's all. [BRENDA'*s sledge makes a sudden lurch forward and she screeches.*]

BRENDA: Not so fast! Help! [*The* OTHERS *ignore her.* JIM *lifts his feet high, looking down at his footprints in the snow.*]

JIM: Look at the footprints we're leaving. Deep as wells.

DYLAN: I bet people'll think there's been hippos.

JIM: What would you do if you saw a hippo coming down Terrace Road?

DYLAN: I'd go like this . . . bang! I'd throw him over the railings and roll him down the hill and then I'd tickle him under the ear and he'd wag his tail . . . [*He demonstrates vigorously.*]

TOM: What would you do if you saw two hippos?

GLENDA: There aren't any hippos in Swansea, [*The* BOYS *turn together and stare at her. She bunches her fists and glares back fiercely. They turn their backs on her and make their exclusive ring again.*]

JACK: I don't want to boast but my father's the richest man in Swansea.

TOM: Well, my father's the richest man in Wales.

JIM: My father owns the world.

DYLAN: My grandfather . . . my grandfather used to be a guard on the railways. [*The* OTHERS *are really impressed with this. It is also a boast but, clearly, a truthful one.*]

TOM: Really and truly?

DYLAN: God's honor, bite out my tongue and spit it down the lav, my grandad was a railway guard.

BOYS: [*ad libbing*] Hey! How about that! A railway guard!

TOM: Okay, Dylan, you win. But one day we'll all be famous . . .

JIM: Famous railway guards?

DYLAN: Famous gangsters. Scarface Evans.

TOM: Babyface Dylan.

DYLAN: Well, we'd better learn to walk like gangsters, then.

JIM: How'd they walk?

DYLAN: Glancing from side to side with looks of ice. And they swagger. Swagger a bit, Jack.

JACK: Your idea, wuss. Swagger yourself.

DYLAN: Alright then, watch me, watch how I swagger. [*He tucks his elbows into his sides, points his forefingers as if they were pistols and struts about, swaying from side to side, snarling in a nasal voice from the corner of his mouth.*] You . . . dirty . . . rat. You . . . dirty . . . stinking . . .

[*A* POLICEMAN *enters and stands unnoticed.*]

DYLAN: . . . rat . . . [*One by one, the other* BOYS *and then* GLENDA *join* DYLAN *in procession. They imitate his walk and join in his chant.* BRENDA, *carrying her sledge, is about to join the tail of the procession when she comes face to face with the* POLICEMAN. *She promptly sits down on the sledge at his feet and gazes up at him innocently.*]

POLICEMAN: Hello, 'ello! What you boys up to then? [*The chanting and swaggering stops abruptly.* DYLAN, *nonplussed for a moment, has an inspiration and drags* GLENDA *toward the* POLICEMAN.]

DYLAN: Going down the seashore, officer. Taking my little cousins for a walk. [GLENDA *and* BRENDA *simper little-girlishly.*]

POLICEMAN: Oh, yes? Very proper. Very tidy. Had a good Christmas?

GLENDA AND BRENDA: Not bad.

POLICEMAN: [*regarding* GLENDA *and* BRENDA *thoughtfully*] Not bad, eh? Get any good presents?

DYLAN: I got a bicycle. Three-speed B.S.A.

POLICEMAN: Ah. Did you now? You got a license for that bike?

DYLAN: A license?

POLICEMAN: Like, if you've got a dog, you got to have a dog license. Same with a bike.

TOM: That's not true.

POLICEMAN: Did I hear you say . . .

JACK: [*quickly*] He didn't mean it, sir. It was a joke.

POLICEMAN: A joke? I see. Ha, ha, ha. Well, young man, I hope I don't catch you riding your bike without a license. Happy Christmas, all.

ALL: [*in chorus*] Merry Christmas, Constable Lloyd-Jones.

[*The* POLICEMAN *starts to move off. Before he is gone, the* BOYS *aim "machine guns" at his back. He turns and they convert their mime into nonchalant twitching and scratching. He goes off. The* BOYS *riddle him with machine gun fire.* GLENDA *uses a shot from a "pistol." The* BOYS *blow smoke from the barrels of their weapons and* GLENDA *blows smoke from her pistol.*]

DYLAN: He lived like a rat, so I shot him down like a rat.

GLENDA: Easy to be cheeky behind a bobby's back. [DYLAN *has to react to this. He approaches her belligerently. She stands her ground until they're eyeball to eyeball.*]

DYLAN: [*after a pause*] Glenda Jones. You have the face of a ferret and the heart of a black widow spider.

GLENDA: Dylan Thomas. You're all tongue and no teeth. [*She realizes that this is a bit near the knuckle. To avoid further conflict but still save face, she breaks from the confrontation with a little dance and an insulting song, sung to the tune of Good King Wenceslas.*]

[*SONG: "DYLAN THOMAS IS A FOOL"*]

GLENDA: DYLAN THOMAS IS A FOOL
  THINKS HE'S VERY CLEVER
  BUT HE'S BOTTOM OF THE SCHOOL
  GETS THE WORST MARKS EVER . . .

[*She dances off, followed by the* OTHERS, *pushing and punching each other. The lights go down on the street and concentrate on* DYLAN.]

DYLAN: And so we slipped and squabbled and crunched and punched our way down the sloping streets, down through the icicle-hung arch under the famous Mumbles Railway, the first passenger railway in the world. We climbed the humped sand dunes of the Burrows, treading on the buried snow-covered grass like ghosts on dried toast. And then we spread our wings and flew down the far side of the dunes towards the white, wide seashore.

[*The lights come up on the seashore. The* BOYS, *accompanied by* GLENDA *and* BRENDA, *"fly" in, crying "Whee-ee-ee" Their arms are extended as wings.* DYLAN *"flies" to join them downstage, staring out at the sea. There is the crying of gulls.*]

TOM: [*after a pause*] They've even frozen the sea.

JIM: Great lumps of sea.

JACK: Like there was a great big house made of ice and somebody broke it up into ice-bricks.

TOM: [*as* ALL *search the ground for flat skimming stones*] Like someone tried to make a jigsaw puzzle out of ice.

GLENDA: Like it's been hailing frozen biscuit boxes.

DYLAN: Like the river was a glacier and these are its icebergs.

[JIM *finds a skimming stone.*]

JIM: Here, I got a good stone. Flat and round. [*He crouches low and mimes skimming it over the heads of the audience.* ALL *follow it with their eyes, heads nodding at each bounce, counting.* ALL *go on searching, throwing when a good skimmer is found.*]

DYLAN: Icebergs, yeah. I'd love to see just one big iceberg.

TOM: And sail away on it with only a polar bear for company.

DYLAN: A great peaked iceberg with cliffs of white and emerald. [*He finds a good stone and throws it.*]

TOM: No. Flat on top. But nine-tenths of it hidden under water.

DYLAN: And we could dig down into the nine-tenths with ice axes and make a huge ice cavern. [JACK *throws a good stone and the* OTHERS *applaud.*]

JACK: An ice cavern hundreds of yards wide!

GLENDA: We could have a billiards table down there and play billiards with penguins' eggs. [*She throws the best skimmer yet. The* BOYS *go "Whew!" involuntarily, then turn their backs on her.* TOM *crouches down and pokes at the ground.* JACK *tastes some snow.*]

JACK: Look, I'm eating snow pie.

JIM: What's it taste like?

JACK: Like snow pie.

DYLAN: Can the fishes see it's snowing?

JIM: They think it's the sky falling down. [*Dogs bark in the distance.*]

JACK: All the old dogs have gone.

DYLAN: All those old dogs we used to know. [*A pause.*] What you doing, Tom?

TOM: Breaking the ice on this rock pool to let the shrimps breathe. [DYLAN *crouches beside him, looking closely at the ground.*]

DYLAN: It's all jewels, Tom. Look! A whole world scattered with jewels.

TOM: I got a little crab. White and greeny.

JACK: Let's have a look . . . Let's take him back, drop him down someone's neck.

TOM: Got nothing to keep him in.

DYLAN: Here . . . use this. [*He hands over his balaclava.* TOM *wraps his crab in it and then stuffs it in* DYLAN's *pocket.*]

JIM: If only we had a big catapult.

GLENDA: What for?

JIM: We could get those big chunks of ice and bombard the Town Hill boys.

JACK: Hey, yeah, wouldn't they be scared!

JIM: Great chunks of ice coming down out of the sky!

JACK: Whoo~o~osh! Hey, Mam, it's hailing bricks. [*He pretends to be scared, protecting his head with his arms. He is distracted by the sound of a train beyond the dunes.*] Hey, look! The train! [ALL *turn and look as the Mumbles train puffs along behind the dunes. It may be seen or only heard by the audience.*]

DYLAN: Hey, listen, I know what we can do with Glenda!

JACK: What's that, mun?

DYLAN: Tie her across the railway lines! Train comes along . . .

GLENDA: Stupid little twpsin!

JACK: Yeah, yeah! Tie her up, men, train's coming. Choof-choof! Choof-choof!

JIM: Head over one rail, feet over the other!

JACK: Scatter, men! Train's getting nearer! [*The* BOYS *form themselves up into a train, pistons pumping, carriages swaying, and advance on* GLENDA.]

BOYS: Choof-choof! Choof-choof! Wheehee-hee! Choof-choof! Choof-choof!

GLENDA: Stupid boys!

JACK: Train's nearly on her! Driver peers out . . .

JIM: . . . through the freezing fog. Can't see a thing!

DYLAN: When suddenly a dark figure on horseback sweeps down through the fog, a knife between his teeth! [*He breaks from the train, leaps on to* JACK's *back and becomes a mounted horseman.* JACK, *the horse, rears and whinnies.*] Slash; slash at the ropes and up she's swept across the saddle bow. The horse rears as the train thunders past, then in a single leap it clears the dunes and gallops like the wind across the sands towards the safety of Oystermouth Castle! [DYLAN *dismounts. There is a pause as the* BOYS *savor this scenario.*]

GLENDA: [*sweetly*] Thank you so much for saving my life, Dylan.

DYLAN: Wasn't me. It was the Oystermouth Ogre on that horse. [*The* BOYS *link up to become the ogre, with* DYLAN *roaring and slavering at its head.*]

JACK: So you're being eaten alive this very moment, Glenda.

GLENDA: What an exciting life I lead.

BRENDA: I've been on a train. I went to Bristol.

JIM: Did you ever come back? [BRENDA *begins to crumple.* GLENDA *launches a sudden all out attack on* JIM *with her nails, teeth, etc.* JIM *falls.* GLENDA *places a foot on him like a big game hunter with his kill. She is joined by* BRENDA. *Side by side, heads leaning together, hands demurely at prayer, they sing to the tune of "Holy, Holy, Holy."*]

[*SONG:* "BOYS, BOYS, BOYS"]

GLENDA AND BRENDA: BOYS, BOYS, BOYS,
    MAKING TOO MUCH NOISE,
    BOASTING IN THE MORNING
    AND BOASTING LATE AT NIGHT.
    BOYS, BOYS, BOYS,
    THINK THAT GIRLS ARE TOYS,
    PICKED UP WHEN THEY'RE NEEDED,
    THROWN DOWN WHEN THEY'RE NOT.
    GIRLS, GIRLS, GIRLS,
    PRECIOUS AS PEARLS,
    CLEVERER AND SMARTER
    ALWAYS END ON TOP.

[JIM *rolls clear and scampers to the safety of the* BOYS. GLENDA, *not satisfied, marches after him.*]

GLENDA: Apologize to Brenda or I'll feed your eyeballs to the seagulls.

JIM: Stupid girls . . . Duw, I'm going to crease you, Glenda.

DYLAN: Say sorry, Jim, for Pete's sake! She's dangerous!

JIM: [*muttering*] Alright. Sorry.

BRENDA: Say, I'm sorry, Brenda. Please spit in my face.

[DYLAN *gives* JIM *a push toward* BRENDA. *He stands in front of her with his eyes squeezed shut.*]

JIM: I'm sorry, Brenda. Please spit in my face. [BRENDA *hawks to summon up spittle but, gazing closely at* JIM's *face, suddenly falls in love. Unnoticed,* JACK *creeps up behind* GLENDA *with a handful of broken ice.*]

BRENDA: [*soppily*] I don't want to.

GLENDA: Oh, come on! [JACK *stuffs the ice down* GLENDA's *back.*]

JACK: Spit on yourself, Glenda! [*He dashes off, furiously pursued by* GLENDA.]

GLENDA: Jack! I'll stitch you proper! [JIM *follows them off curiously.*]

BRENDA: [*calling and trundling her sledge off after* JIM, *adoringly.*] Wait for me! [DYLAN *and* TOM, *left alone together, relax into a more natural, un-posturing manner.*]

TOM: Ice down her back! That'll teach the twpsin.

DYLAN: Once I dropped a big blob of ice cream down my Aunt Elieri's bathing dress by mistake on purpose.

TOM: You didn't. The back or the front?

DYLAN: Never you mind.

TOM: What she do then?

DYLAN: Squealed a bit and laughed a lot. And . . . Oh, it was a hot, hot, hot, hot salty day.

TOM: Funny the way in winter you can never remember what it's like in summer.

DYLAN: I can. I can remember the smells. Sea and seaweed, wet flesh, wet hair, wet bathing dresses . . .

TOM: The warm smell, like a rabbity field after rain . . .

DYLAN: The smell of sweet lemon pop and salty sun-shades and sandy toffee . . .

TOM: And hot, tossed, tumbled, dug and trodden sand . . .

DYLAN: The smell of vinegar on shelled cockles . . .

TOM: And of ships from the sun-dazed docks round the corner of the sand hills . . .

DYLAN: And the smell of the known and paddled in sea, full of drowned sailors and herrings . . .

TOM: And the coke and gunpowder smoke from the Mumbles train. [*The train crosses behind the dunes. He and* DYLAN *turn to follow it, listening to its chuffing and rattling. They turn back thoughtfully.*] Dylan . . . when you dropped the ice cream down your Aunt Elieri . . . was it strawberry or vanilla?

DYLAN: It was vanilla. But her skin was whiter.

TOM: You're soft on her, man, aren't you? [DYLAN *shrugs, admitting the charge.*] Don't blame you. But she gets very sad looking sometimes.

DYLAN: I know. She wears two poppies on Armistice Day because she lost her two brothers in the Great War. I told her once . . . when I grow up, I'll go to the war and find them for you.

TOM: [*understandingly*] Yes. I remember grownups saying an uncle never came back from the front so I went out the front garden to look for him. [*A pause.*] Just look at that sun going down.

DYLAN: Like an orange.

TOM: Like a tomato.

DYLAN: Like a goldfish bowl sitting on a sandbank. [*He and* TOM *exchange glances, grin and sing to the tune of "I Saw Three Ships Come Sailing By."*]

[*SONG: "AS I SAT ON A SANDY BANK"*]

TOM: AS I SAT ON A SANDY BANK,
    A SANDY BANK, A SANDY BANK,
    AS I SAT ON A SANDY BANK
    ON CHRISTMAS DAY IN THE MORNING.

DYLAN: I SAW THREE SHIPS COME SAILING BY,
    COME SAILING BY, COME SAILING BY,
    I SAW THREE SHIPS COME SAILING BY

ON CHRISTMAS DAY IN THE MORNING.

TOM: AND WHO SHOULD BE WITH THESE THREE SHIPS,
    WITH THESE THREE SHIPS, WITH THESE THREE
    SHIPS?

DYLAN: AND WHO SHOULD BE WITH THESE THREE SHIPS
    BUT JOSEPH AND OUR FAIR LADY.

TOM AND DYLAN: AND THEY DID CAROL AND THEY DID SING
    AND ALL THE BELLS ON EARTH DID RING
    FOR JOY THAT NOW WAS BORN OUR KING
    ON CHRISTMAS DAY IN THE MORNING.

DYLAN: [*regarding* TOM *solemnly*] I don't suppose anyone in the whole history of the world has ever had such an ugly best friend as me.

TOM: Yes, they have,

DYLAN, Who?

TOM: Me. [*He and* DYLAN *laugh.*] But I'd better vanish or I'll miss the Christmas cake.

DYLAN: Come round, after. See my bike.

TOM: 'Ello, 'ello, 'ello! You got a license for that bike, young man? [*He and* DYLAN *punch each other lightly.* TOM *runs off, The lights go down on the shore and up on* DYLAN.]

DYLAN: And then I climbed back up the desolate poor sea-facing streets where only a few children fumbled with bare red fingers in the thick, wheel-rutted snow and catcalled after me, their voices fading away, as I trudged uphill, into the cries of the dock-birds and the hooters of ships out in the white and whirling bay. And as I slap-dashed home, suddenly, out of a slow-clogged side lane came a boy the spit of myself, with a pink-tipped cigarette and the violet past of a black eye, cocky as a bullfinch, leering all to himself. I hated him on sight and sound and was about to put my dog whistle to my lips and blow him off the face of Christmas when suddenly he, with a violet wink, put his whistle to his lips and blew so . . .

[*A* BOY, *dressed almost exactly like* DYLAN, *enters. He stands in a cocky, challenging position, staring at* DYLAN, *who turns toward him as his speech ends.*]

DYLAN: . . . stridently, so high, so exquisitely loud, that gobbling faces, their cheeks bulged with cake, pressed against their tinselled windows the whole length of the white echoing street.

[*The* BOY *blows his whistle and vanishes.*]

[*As the echoes of the whistle die away, the lights come up on the Thomas living room with its occupants in a dimly lit tableau. There is a sofa and some easy chairs. The* AUNTS *and* UNCLES *sit a little awkwardly, balancing cups and saucers and plates with the crumbs of Christmas cake on them.* GLENDA *and* BRENDA *sit on the floor. There is a huge white cake with a sprig of holly on it sitting on a small table.*]

DYLAN: At tea, the recovered uncles were jolly; the iced cake loomed in the center of the table like a marbled grave, and Auntie Hannah laced her tea with rum because it was only once a year. Everyone smiled and nodded and muttered how good the cake was, though they were only eating out of politeness and picked at it crumb by crumb like starving Chinamen making a little rice go a long way. And the cups balanced on saucers, and the saucers balanced on knees, wobbled a little for lack of practice through the long year of days that were not Christmas Day. And after tea, the best was still to come . . . [*The lights begin to come up on the inside scene.*] Oh, bring out the tall tales now that we told by the fire as the gaslight bubbled like a diver. Ghosts whooed like owls in the long nights when I dared not look over my shoulder for fear of seeing what might come out of the cubbyhole under the stairs where the gas meter ticked, and I loved my fear and was safe in the thrill of it, and wanted more of it, and more. [*He moves into the scene, now fully lit, via the hallstand where he discards his outdoor clothes and hides his bloodied balaclava-with-a-crab-in-it. He enters chanting.*] Ghost stories! Ghost stories! We want ghost stories!

BRENDA: Ooh, no! Ghost stories scare me!

GLENDA: Oh, shut up, Brenda! I want ghost stories, too.

DYLAN: Whoo-oo, whoo-oo, whoo-oo, whoo-oo!

FATHER: You'll have to sing the tell-a-tale song if you want ghost stories, Dylan.

DYLAN: Oh, yes, the tell-a-tale song . . . [*There is a pause as he thinks.*] Well, I could start it, anyway.

GLENDA: Yes, go on, Dylan, you start. Well all join in.

GWYN: We're right behind you, boy. [DYLAN *sings to the tune of "O Come, O Come, Emmanuel"*]

[*SONG: "TELL-A-TALE SONG"?*]

DYLAN: O TELL A TALE OF SOMETHING TERRIBLE
AND MAKE IT REALLY HO-O-ORRIBLE
ABOUT A BOY WHO FOUND A HEAD
AND ARMIES OF THE LIVING DEAD . . .

ALL: O TELL A TALE OF SOMETHING TERRIBLE
AND MAKE IT REALLY HO-O-ORRIBLE.

[*During the following verses, ghostly mimes are practiced upon various* AUNTS *and* UNCLES, *who pretend to be terrified.*]

GLENDA: O TELL A TALE TO SET US SHIVERING
ABOUT A MERMAID'S PO-OI-OISONED RING
AND GRISLY DETAILS OF A CURSE
AND HOW THE DEVIL WOOED A NURSE . . .

ALL: O TELL A TALE OF SOMETHING TERRIBLE
AND MAKE IT REALLY HO-O-ORRIBLE.

GWYN: O TELL A TALE, A TRULY DREADFUL YARN
ABOUT A HEAP OF JELLY IN A BARN
AND BATS THAT HAVE A HUMAN BRAIN
AND SERPENTS COMING UP THE DRAIN . . .

ALL: O TELL A TALE OF SOMETHING TERRIBLE
AND MAKE IT REALLY HO-O-ORRIBLE.

FATHER: O TELL A TALE TO FEED OUR NIGHTMARES ON
OF THAT BLACK COUNTRY WHERE THE DEAD HAVE
GONE
AND BABIES BOILED UP INTO BROTH
TO FEED THE GHOST OF A HUGE MOTH . . .

ALL: O TELL A TALE OF SOMETHING TERRIBLE
AND MAKE IT REALLY HO-O-ORRIBLE.

GLYN: You're always good for a shiver, D.J. Why don't you start?

FATHER: Alright. Here's a short sharp one. You all know the Old Rectory at Rhossili. Well, I'll. tell you—and this is true—any time of the day or night, walking about the corridors of that dismal house, you can suddenly find yourself stepping into a pool of cold air. And just as you notice it, you'll hear a low voice in your ear saying, "Why don't you turn round and look at me?" And, of course, no one has ever dared to turn.

DYLAN: I would!

GLENDA: You wouldn't, Dylan. And nor would I.

BRENDA: I wouldn't even dare go in there!

ELIERI: I wouldn't either, Brenda.

MOTHER: No, nor me. Now come on, Nellie. Your turn.

NELLIE: Don't know any.

MOTHER: Tell about our Gran and the falling star.

NELLIE: But we never told anyone that!

GLENDA: Oh, come on, Aunt Nellie!

NELLIE: Oh, alright. Well, now . . . When our mother's mother was a girl, she was a housemaid to a rich family. The lady of the house worked her very hard and was always scolding her. One night our Gran was in her bed in the attic, crying her eyes out as usual, when she saw a star falling. Well, everybody knows that if you close your eyes and make a wish and the star's still falling when you open your eyes again, your wish will come true.

GLYN: Women's tales!

MOTHER: You just listen, Glyn!

NELLIE: Well, our Gran made a wish and opened her eyes and not only was the star still falling, it headed straight for her window . . . and then in it came and hovered over the foot of her bed. And she started screaming: "There's a star in my room!" Everybody rushed in but they could see nothing. Last to come in was the lady of the house. "What's all this, you little fool?" "There's a star in my room!" "Little liar!" Slap! [NELLIE slaps her own cheek hard.] And the star vanished. Our Gran left the house next morning and walked the twenty miles back to her own home. And that same morning, the lady of the house took sick. And by nightfall, she was dead.

GLENDA: Is that what your Gran had wished for?

NELLIE: Of course.

DYLAN: That's not very scary.

NELLIE: It scared our Gran all right. She was talking about it the day she died. She'd always been afraid that the lady's ghost might come and haunt her. One night she thought she saw the table moving . . . [One end of the table starts to rise and then sways to and fro.]

HANNAH: Oooh! [BRENDA screams and clutches GLENDA.]

MOTHER: Now, Gwyn . . .

GWYN: Never touched it. [The table stops swaying. ALL laugh.]

BRENDA: Are there really things like ghosts?

GLYN: Lot of superstitious nonsense.

TUDYR: I once saw the headless hound at Pen Parcau. Two o'clock in the morning. I threw a stone at it and it burst into flames.

BESSIE: Why, Tudyr, we've been married near twenty years and you never told me that!

TUDYR: You never asked me.

NELLIE: Oh, go on, Bessie . . . Tudyr just made that up this minute!

TUDYR: True as I stand here, Nellie. It's a well-known phenomenon.

FATHER: Oh, definitely, definitely! That would be one of the April Dogs. They hunt the souls of the dead through the air.

DYLAN: How can they hunt if they're headless?

FATHER: It's the heads that do the hunting. Some foolish people mistake them for curlews. [DYLAN *imitates a curlew's cry.*] That's right, similar sound. Only the April Dogs hit a lower note. [*He makes a very ghostly sound.*] It's well to know the difference.

BRENDA: Ooh, that's scary.

GLENDA: Not scary enough. Let's have a story about dragons.

DYLAN: If dragons are so scary, why does Wales have a dragon on its flag?

GLYN: To frighten the English, of course. [*He stands up on the seat of his chair.*] One day we'll let our dragons loose on 'em. Get rid of . . .

FATHER: [*as a warning*] Glyn!

GLYN: I was about to make a respectable political statement.

FATHER: There's nothing respectable about your politics, Glyn, and Christmas evening is no time for airing them. Why don't you do something useful for a change and tell us a ghost story.

GLYN: How can I? I don't believe in ghosts.

TUDYR: The man who says he doesn't believe in ghosts has no right to call himself a Welshman.

GLYN: [*shouting*] Tudyr, don't you dare . . . [FATHER *comes between* GLYN *and* TUDYR. *He puts his hand on* GLYN'*s shoulder and presses him down into his chair.*]

DYLAN: Well, now, let's see what he believes after I've told him about the soul of poor Dafydd Ellis . . .

MOTHER: Oh, no, Dylan! D.J., stop him!

FATHER: How can I stop him, fach, if he's decided?

GLENDA: Oh, come on, Dylan, tell us!

DYLAN: I was going to anyway, wasn't I? Now, before Cwmdonkin Drive was built, there was just deserted farmland here and, on the site of this very house, there was the ruins of a longhouse, one of the little one-man farms they used to have here. Dafydd Ellis was the last man to work it. He lived here alone with a few sheep and cattle. Couldn't read, of course. So the winter nights were long. One winter evening, when the wind was sighing in the shutters, Dafydd leaned forward and said to the flickering fire, "I would give my soul for someone to talk to." Over and over again, he said,"fe rown hyd yn oed fy enaid –yes, I would even give my soul." Suddenly, there . . . [GLENDA *conceals herself behind the hallstand as* DYLAN *speaks.*] . . . was an icy wind. The fire flared up, the lantern swung violently on its hook, and there was an echoing voice calling . . .

GLENDA: [*calling softly between her cupped hands*] Daf- . . . eeedd . . . Daf-eeedd . . .

DYLAN: Terrified, the old man stood and looked about him. Something seemed to touch him on the back. He turned round. Nothing there. He stumbled over to the door, but it wouldn't open. Nor would the shutters. Trembling, he sank back into his chair. And the voice whispered in his ear . . .

GLENDA: [*softly*] Daf-eeedd, give me your soul!

DYLAN: But Dafydd would not give up his soul. He made the sign of the cross, muttered the Lord's name, and died.

brenda: [*whispering*] Who was the voice?

DYLAN: It was a bad spirit who had come to claim Dafydd's soul and it couldn't escape from this place without it. The workmen who built Cwmdonkin Drive told of wheelbarrows turning over and emptying themselves, of men's caps being snatched off and whirled into the clouds, and a voice crying in the wind . . .

GLENDA AND BRENDA: Daf-eeedd, Daf-eeedd . . .

DYLAN: And even today, on dark winter nights, when there are sensitive people about, things happen here . . .

FATHER: [*whispering*] What sort of things, Dylan?

DYLAN: [*whispering*] Ah, that would be telling.

GLENDA, BRENDA, OTHERS: Daf-eeedd . . . Daf-eeedd., [*Despite brave ef-*

forts to look unconcerned, GLYN *has obviously experienced a shiver down his back.*]

MOTHER: Dylan, really! I told you not to! [DYLAN *looks triumphant.* GLYN *is a bit vexed. The other* ADULTS *exchange secret smiles.*]

GLYN: Oh, very neat, Dylan, very neat.

DYLAN: But you were scared for a moment, Uncle Glyn, weren't you?

GLYN: Scared . . .

GLENDA: Come on, Uncle Glyn, admit it!

BRENDA: Yes, Uncle Glyn, admit you were a teeny bit scared!

GLYN: Scared . . .

TUDYR AND OTHERS: Come on, Glyn! Damn, now, we saw you!

GLYN: Scared? I was bloody paralyzed! [ALL *laugh.*]

MOTHER: And now it's nearly bedtime.

DYLAN, GLENDA, BRENDA: No-o-o-o!

MOTHER: And we have to leave room for the sing-song.

GLENDA AND BRENDA: [*excitedly*] Oh, yes, the sing-song!

DYLAN: But we haven't had a story from Aunt Elieri yet.

ELIERI: Oh, I can't tell ghost stories, Dylan! Ghosts don't frighten me, they're my friends. But I will tell you a verse about a friendly ghost who is always with us at Christmas.

DYLAN, GLENDA, BRENDA: Who's that? Go on!

ELIERI: [*speaking her verse very evenly, without undue emphasis*].
 My name is Taliesin. My song is so perfect
 It will last till the world ends.
 I know well when the world ends.
 I have been there and back.
 I have been dead. I have been alive.
 I have kept festivals.
 I have been a seed of grain, which was reaped.
 I fell to the ground and was swallowed by a hen.
 I have been a hen's egg swept out to sea
 On a bed of rushes and swallowed by the red salmon.
 I have been the red salmon
 Leaping the falls at Pystyll Gwyn
 And I have kept festivals.
 I have been an otter, hunting the red salmon.

I have been a hunter, trapping the napped otter.
I have been a warrior, mocking the slow hunter
I have killed and been killed.
Forgiven and been forgiven.
Loved and been loved.
My name is Taliesin.
I am at all your festivals.

[DYLAN *gazes wide-eyed at* ELIERI. *There are quiet murmurs of appreciation from the* ADULTS. DYLAN *moves away from the* OTHERS.]

DYLAN: Come over here, Aunt Elieri.

ELIERI: Why? [*She moves toward* DYLAN, *who produces a piece of mistletoe from behind his back and holds it over her.*]

DYLAN: You're standing right under the mistletoe.

ELIERI: Oh, Dylan, you wicked boy.

TUDYR: Caught at last. By a strapping lad of . . .

GWYN: Hold off, Tudyr. [ELIERI *kisses* DYLAN. ALL *applaud.*]

GLYN: Lucky boy. Now, if I did that . . .

NELLIE: Any respectable woman would walk in the other direction.

GWYN: There speaks my respectable wife.

NELLIE: Gwyn! Really!

HANNAH: Now, then . . . Now, then! It's sing-songtime! Come on, D.J., give us Cwm Rhondda.

MOTHER: You'll get Cwm Swansea more likely. [FATHER *proceeds to sing to the tune of "Cwm Rhondda."*]

[*SONG: "SWANSEA HEROES"*]

FATHER: LET US SING OF SWANSEA HEROES
          MEN AND WOMEN MARKED FOR FAME
          IN A TOWN WHERE EVEN VILLAINS
          GET A LEGEND TO THEIR NAME
          SWANSEA HEROES, SWANSEA HEROES
          WHETHER KNOWN FOR GOOD OR ILL . . .

ALL: GOOD OR ILL.
          WHETHER KNOWN FOR GOOD OR ILL.

FATHER: HOLY JOE, THE GOSPEL PREACHER
 MADE HIS PITCH ON MUMBLES PIER,
 PROMISED HELLFIRE AND DAMNATION
 TO ALL SINNERS FAR AND NEAR.
 TERRIFIED US, TERRIFIED US,
 BUT WE LOVED TO HEAR HIM PREACH . . .

ALL: HEAR HIM PREACH.
 BUT WE LOVED TO HEAR HIM PREACH.

HANNAH: CROWDS OF FOLK CAME DOWN FROM RHONDDA
 SPECIAL TRAINS FROM CARDIFF HAIL
 ALL TO SEE THE PUBLIC HANGING
 ON THE WALLS OF SWANSEA GOAL
 ZELAPHANTA AND ALEPPE
 KILLED THEIR SHIPMATE AND MUST DIE . . .

ALL: AND MUST DIE.
 KILLED THEIR SHIPMATE AND MUST DIE.

GLYN: REMEMBERED, TOO, IS DIC PENDERYN
 MARTYR OF OUR WORKING CLASS
 HUNG BECAUSE THE MINERS' UNION
 MET AT MERTHYR, HELD THE PASS
 DIC PENDERYN, DIC PENDERYN
 IN YOUR DEATH YOU GAVE US LIFE . . .

ALL: GAVE US LIFE.
 IN YOUR DEATH YOU GAVE US LIFE.

FATHER: LAST A VERSE FOR THOMAS BOWDLER
 GAVE US SHAKESPEARE PURE AS SNOW
 TOOK ALL NAUGHTY WORDS AND THOUGHTS OUT
 LEFT IN NOTHING COARSE OR LOW
 BOWDLERIZED HIM, BOWDLERIZED HIM
 THOMAS BOWDLER CLEANSED THE BARD . . .

ALL: CLEANSED THE BARD.
 THOMAS BOWDLER CLEANSED THE BARD.
 LET US SING OF SWANSEA HEROES
 MEN AND WOMEN MARKED FOR FAME
 IN A TOWN WHERE EVEN VILLAINS
 GET A LEGEND TO THEIR NAME
 SWANSEA HEROES, SWANSEA HEROES

[JIM, JACK *and* TOM *enter without fuss.* DYLAN *wheels on his gleaming new bicycle. He shows it to the other* BOYS *and they're suitably impressed. They join in the last part of the song.*]

WHETHER KNOWN FOR GOOD OR ILL . . .
GOOD OR ILL.
WHETHER KNOWN FOR GOOD OR ILL.

[TUDYR *takes up a position downstage. He signals to* BESSIE, GLENDA *and* BRENDA *to join him. They stand together and sing "The Holly and the Ivy" as a family group.*]

[*SONG: "THE HOLLY AND THE IVY"*]

BESSIE: THE HOLLY AND THE IVY
NOW BOTH ARE FULL WELL GROWN
OF ALL THE TREES WITHIN THE WOOD
THE HOLLY BEARS THE CROWN.

FATHER, BRENDA, GLENDA: O, THE RISING OF THE SUN
THE RUNNING OF THE DEER
THE PLAYING OF THE MERRY ORGAN
SWEET SINGING IN THE CHOIR.

BESSIE: THE HOLLY BEARS A BLOSSOM
AS WHITE AS ANY FLOWER
AND MARY BORE SWEET JESUS CHRIST
TO BE OUR SWEET SAVIOUR.

FATHER, BRENDA, GLENDA: O, THE RISING OF THE SUN
AND THE RUNNING OF THE DEER
THE PLAYING OF THE MERRY ORGAN
SWEET SINGING IN THE CHOIR.

BESSIE: THE HOLLY BEARS A BERRY
AS RED AS ANY BLOOD
AND MARY BORE SWEET JESUS CHRIST
TO BE OUR SWEET SAVIOUR.

FATHER, BRENDA, GLENDA: O, THE RISING OF THE SUN
THE RUNNING OF THE DEER
THE PLAYING OF THE MERRY ORGAN
SWEET SINGING IN THE CHOIR.

[*There is a knocking offstage. The* TOWN HILL BOYS *sing "Adeste Fideles" offstage.* DYLAN *moves upstage and looks off.*]

NELLIE: Oh, listen . . . it's the carol singers!

FATHER: Ask them in, Dylan.

DYLAN: But . . . but . . . it's the Town Hill boys!

MOTHER: You know them, then. Well, ask them in.

HANNAH: Those boys are in my class. They're holy terrors.

FATHER: Well, good . . . you know them, too. Dylan, ask them in. [DYLAN
exits.]

[DYLAN *returns with the* TOWN HILL BOYS. *Nervous and awkward, they
shuffle into a formal group, clear their throats and, after an uncertain
start, sing their carol very sweetly.*]

TOWN HILL BOYS: ADESTE FIDELES,
      LETI TRIUMPHANTES,
      VENITE, VENITE IN BETHLEHEM;
      NATUM VIDETE
      REGEM ANGELORUM,
      VENITE, ADORAMUS
      VENITE, ADORAMUS
      VENITE, ADOREMUS DOMINUM.

[*The* FAMILY *applauds.* MOTHER *passes around pieces of Christmas cake
from a plate. The* TOWN HILL BOYS *make a circuit of the room amid a
chorus of "Happy Christmases," each receiving a piece of cake and, from
DYLAN, a small surplus present from the foot of the tree. He manages to
slip his unwanted balaclava to one of the* BOYS. *Just before he exits, the
BOY discovers the crab inside it. The* TOWN HILL BOYS *leave.* DYLAN
comes down and faces the FAMILY.]

DYLAN: [*calling with great pomp, like a music hall announcer*] And now . . . to
gay Paree . . . for . . . the can-can! [ALL *launch into the can-can with*
HANNAH, BESSIE *and* NELLIE *to the fore. They scandalize* TUDYR *with flying petticoats.*]

[*SONG:* "TA-RA-RA BOOM-DE-AY"]

AUNTS. TAR-RAH-RAH-BOOM-DE-AY.

ALL: TAR-RAH-RAH-BOOM-DE-AY.

TAR-RAH-RAH-BOOM-DE-AY.

TAR-RAH-RAH-BOOM-DE-AY.

TAR-RAH-RAH-BOOM-DE-AY.

[*The* AUNTS *collapse, laughing and breathless.* GWYN *gets up on a chair and hits a confident note, holding it until he has everyone's attention.*]

GWYN: Thank you.

[**SONG:** *"SHE WAS ONE OF THE EARLY BIRDS"*]

GWYN: IT WAS AT THE PANTOMIME
SWEET MABEL AND I DID MEET
SHE WAS IN THE BALLET (FRONT ROW)
AND I IN A FIVE SHILLING SEAT;
SHE WAS DRESSED LIKE A DICKEY BIRD,
BEAUTIFUL WINGS SHE HAD ON.
FIGURE DIVINE, WISHED SHE WAS MINE—
ON HER I WAS TOTALLY GONE.

GWYN: [*speaking*] All together now!

ALL: SHE WAS A DEAR LITTLE DICKEY BIRD
"TWEET, TWEET, TWEET," SHE WENT,
SWEETLY SHE SANG TO ME
TILL ALL MY MONEY WAS SPENT.
THEN SHE WENT OFF SONG,
WE PARTED ON FIGHTING TERMS,
SHE WAS ONE OF THE EARLY BIRDS
AND I WAS ONE OF THE WORMS.

GWYN: FULL OF LOVE AND POVERTY
AND ARMED WITH A CARVING KNIFE,
ONE DARK NIGHT I KNELT IN THE MUD
AND ASKED HER TO BE MY WIFE.
SOMETHING STRUCK ME BEHIND THE EAR,
SOMEONE SAID: "NOW GO AND GET
WIFE OF YOUR OWN,
LEAVE MINE ALONE!"
AND THAT WAS THE LAST TIME WE MET.

ALL: SHE WAS A DEAR LITTLE DICKEY BIRD,
"TWEET, TWEET, TWEET," SHE WENT,
SWEETLY SHE SANG TO ME
TILL ALL MY MONEY WAS SPENT.
THEN SHE WENT OFF SONG,
WE PARTED ON FIGHTING TERMS,

SHE WAS ONE OF THE EARLY BIRDS
AND IWAS ONE OF THE WORMS.

MOTHER: Alright, everyone, calm down now. Time for the last song and then it's bedtime. Come on, Elieri, let's have Calon Lan. [ALL *settle down. During the song,* GLENDA *and* BRENDA, *cuddled by* TUDYR *and* BESSIE, *fall nearly asleep.* DYLAN *sits cross-legged in the middle of the sofa.*]

[*SONG:* "*CALON LAN*"]

ELIERI: NID WY'N GOFYN BYWMD MOETHUS
AUR Y BYD NA'I BERLAU MAN
GOFYN'R WYF AM GALON HAPUS
CALON ONEST, CALON LAN.

ALL: SHINING HEART IS FULL OF GOODNESS
PURER THAN THE LILY'S WHITE
SHINING HEART IS ALWAYS SINGING,
ALL THE DAY AND ALL THE NIGHT.
DO NOT GIVE ME GOLDEN MONEY
OR THE STONES FROM DIAMOND MINES
FOR I WANT A HEART THAT'S HAPPY,
HONEST HEART, A HEART THAT SHINES.

ELIERI: CALON LAN YN LLAWN DAIONI
TECACH YW NA'R LILI DLOS
DOES OND CALON LAN ALL GANU
CANU'R DYDD A CHAU'R NOS.

ALL: JEWELS GLITTER FOR A MOMENT
THEN ARE LOST IN ENDLESS NIGHT
BUT THE PURE AND PERFECT HEART SHINES
WITH A WARM ETERNAL LIGHT.
SHINING HEART IS FULL OF GOODNESS
PURER THAN THE LILY'S WHITE
SHINING HEART IS ALWAYS SINGING
ALL THE DAY AND ALL THE NIGHT.

[ALL *begin to leave the stage in ones and twos as* DYLAN *starts to speak. When he finishes speaking, he is alone on the stage.*]

DYLAN: The air in the room was blue with cigars and silly with scent, heavy with Christmas meals and the lovely languor of satisfied dreams. The living room—the singing room—was gradually turning into a sleeping room. And so then I went to bed. Looking through my bedroom window, out into the moonlight and the unending smoke-colored snow, I could see the lights in the windows of all the other houses on our hill and hear the music rising from them up the long, steadily falling night. I turned the gas down. I got into bed. I said some words to the close and holy darkness and then I slept. [*He remains still.*]

[*SONG: "THE SOFT SNOW FALLS ALL AROUND" Reprise*]

COMPANY: [*off*] AND THE BOY IN THE BED
          AND THE BED IN THE ROOM
          AND THE ROOM IN THE HOUSE
          AND THE HOUSE IN THE TOWN
          AND THE TOWN IN THE LAND
          AND THE LAND IN THE WORLD
          AND THE WORLD IN THE SKY
          AND THE SOFT SNOW FALLS ALL AROUND,
          ALL AROUND
          THE SOFT SNOW FALLS ALL AROUND.
[*Through the reprise, the lights fade slowly to black.*]

END

A List of Books about the Traditions of Christmas

Crippen, T.C. *Christmas and Christmas Lore*. Detroit: Omnigraphics, 1961.

Hadfield, Miles and John. *The Twelve Days of Christmas*. Boston: Little, Brown and Company, 1961.

Miles, Clement A. *Christmas in Ritual and Tradition: Christian and Pagan*. London: T. Fisher Unwin, 1912. Republished by Gale Research Company, Book Tower, Detroit, 1968.

Miller, Daniel, ed. *Unwrapping Christmas*. Oxford: Clarendon Press, 1993.

Nissenbaum, Stephen. *The Battle for Christmas*. New York: Alfred A. Knopf, 1996.

Rae, Simon, ed. *The Faber Book of Christmas*. London: Faber and Faber, 1996.

Rested, Penne L. *Christmas in America: A History*. New York: Oxford University Press, 1995.

Sansom, William. *A Book of Christmas*. New York: McGraw-Hill Book Company, 1968.

Snyder, Phillip V. *The Christmas Tree Book*. New York: The Viking Press, 1976.

Waits, William B. *The Modern Christmas in America: A Cultural History of Gift Giving*. New York: New York University Press, 1993.

THEATRE FOR YOUNG AUDIENCES
AROUND THE WORLD IN 21 PLAYS
edited with introductions by
Lowell Swortzell

See the world through the ages in this international volume of classic, modern, and contemporary plays. Heading the expedition is Lowell Swortzell, whose compelling introductions propel the reader into the historical and social background of each play. Journey into myth, fantasy, and folklore, and inevitably, back home into everyday life.

Included: Jack Juggler • **MOLIÉRE** The Flying Doctor • **CARLO GOZZI** The Love of Three Oranges • Punch and Judy • **AUGUST STRINDBERG** Lucky Peter's Journey • **STANISLAW WITKIEWICZ** Childhood Plays • **GERTRUDE STEIN** Three Sisters Who Are Not Sisters • **LANGSTON HUGHES** Soul Gone Home • **WENDY KESSELMAN** Maggie Magalita • **JOANNA HALPERT KRAUS** The Ice Wolf • **PER LYSADER AND SUZANNE OSTEN** Medea's Children • **SUZAN ZEDER** Wiley and the Hairy Man • **OSSIE DAVIS** Escape to Freedom • **ISRAEL HOROVITZ** Rats • **AURAND HARRIS** The Pinballs • **DAVID HOLMAN** No Worries • **LOWELL SWORTZELL** A Visit From Saint Nicholas • **MARK MEDOFF** Big Mary • **Y YORK** Afternoon of the Elves • **LAWRENCE YEP** Dragonwings • **PETER TERSON** How to Write a Play

LOWELL SWORTZELL is Director of the Program in Educational Theatre at New York University

644 Pages
ISBN 1-55783-399-0 • $22.95 • PAPER
ISBN 1-55783-263-3 • $35.00 • CLOTH

❧APPLAUSE❧